Creating Constitutional Change

Constitutionalism and Democracy

GREGG IVERS AND KEVIN T. MCGUIRE,
EDITORS

Clashes
over Power
and Liberty
in the
Supreme
Court

Creating
Constitutional
Change

EDITED BY Gregg Ivers and Kevin T. McGuire

University of Virginia Press Charlottesville and London

University of Virginia Press
© 2004 by the Rector and Visitors of the University of Virginia
All rights reserved
Printed in the United States of America on acid-free paper
First published 2004

9 8 7 6 5 4 3 2 1

LIBRARY OF CONGRESS CATALOGING-IN-PUBLICATION DATA
Creating constitutional change : clashes over power and liberty in the
Supreme Court / edited by Gregg Ivers and Kevin T. McGuire.
     p.   cm. — (Constitutionalism and democracy)
Includes bibliographical references and index.
   ISBN 0-8139-2302-6 (cloth : alk. paper) — ISBN 0-8139-2303-4 (pbk. :
alk. paper)
   1. Constitutional law—United States—Cases. 2. Judicial
process—United States. 3. Political questions and judicial
power—United States. 4. United States. Supreme Court. I. Ivers,
Gregg. II. McGuire, Kevin T. III. Series.
   KF4549.C73 2004
   342.73—dc22
                                                2003025084

For Dorothy, a great
sister and an even
better friend.
G. I.

For my mother, Toddy,
and in memory of
her parents, Americo
and Teresa
K. T. M.

Contents

Establishment of Religion

Free Exercise of Religion

Freedom of Speech

Freedom of Association

Freedom of the Press

Search and Seizure

Evidence

Cruel and Unusual Punishment

Racial Discrimination

Gender Discrimination

Acknowledgments

Gregg Ivers first thanks Kevin McGuire, his coeditor, for his patience, smarts, persistence, and just for seeing to it that this book actually got done. If not for him, all of Ivers's wonderful half-baked ideas would still be warming in the oven. In other words, nothing would have happened. He also thanks David Kaib and Rebecca Kane, two graduate students at American University, for their research assistance and overall quality control in preparation of the essays for this book. He also thanks three American University graduates, Stacey Farber, Maura Harris, and Cori Roth, whose crack administrative skills and bottomless compassion for a scatterbrained boss gave him the time he needed to complete this project. He also adds a special thanks to Melvin Urofsky, who invited him to present an early version of his essay on Curt Flood to the Supreme Court Historical Society in October 2002, and Maeva Marcus, from whom he has learned a great deal about constitutional history, law, and politics. Finally, he thanks, as always, his lovely wife, Janet, and their wonderful—if a tad too precocious—children, Max and Claire.

Kevin McGuire expresses his gratitude to Gregg Ivers for convincing him to undertake this book and for being such a superb collaborator. He also thanks the Department of Political Science at the University of North Carolina at Chapel Hill for its consistent encouragement. Two members of his department in particular, Virginia Gray and Georg Vanberg, each offered a great deal of guidance and insight as the book took shape. In addition, he extends special thanks to Dick Holway, who was always willing to discuss the book, whether on the telephone, via e-mail, or over hotdogs during a Red Sox–Yankees game at Fenway Park. Finally, he owes a great deal to his wife, Nancy, who unfailingly allowed him to work (when he had to) and to go to the movies (when he didn't).

Both editors are enormously indebted to the good people at the University of Virginia Press. Mark Mones skillfully supervised the development of the manuscript and saw it successfully to publication. As a copy editor, Gary Kessler performed a remarkable feat: He ensured clarity, consistency, and style across the chapters, while preserving each author's distinctive voice. And Dick Holway, encouraging and patient beyond all measure, served as a first-rate editor. He was steadfastly committed to this project, and the book is surely the better for it.

Creating Constitutional Change

Introduction

GREGG IVERS AND KEVIN T. MCGUIRE

Political scientists who teach American constitutional law have known for quite some time that the development of legal doctrine is as firmly rooted in politics, institutional change, judicial personalities, social context, and organizational dynamics as it is in logic, historical precision, and formal argumentation. Until fairly recently, however, most constitutional law casebooks centering on the United States Supreme Court decisions available for undergraduate instruction were either the same ones used in law schools or slightly less complex texts explicitly modeled on the law school approach. That approach followed, for the most part, a fairly standard path. Chapters were organized by topic and featured an introductory essay describing the constitutional development of a particular area of law. A brief headnote setting out the facts of the case preceded an excerpt of the opinion—or opinions, if concurring and dissenting opinions were included—and that was generally followed by supplemental comments and questions designed to help the student pick apart the logic of the opinion. Little was offered in the way of commentary and analysis to suggest that factors other than legal doctrine affected the outcome of a particular decision. Students were encouraged to think about why one opinion might be logically inconsistent with another, or whether a particular legal theory offered as the basis for decision making was deficient or consistent with its logical premises.

So, while a student could learn a great deal about constitutional development from the vantage point of legal convention, it was entirely possible to complete a semester of constitutional law and/or civil liberties without understanding the role interest groups play in the litigation process, the political nature of judicial selection and confirmation, the strategic nature of advocacy, the policy preferences of particular justices, or the largely outcome-driven nature of constitutional theory. In short, these casebooks did not fully illuminate the complex intersection between constitutional development and the cross-cutting pressures of social, political, and economic forces.

Fortunately, political scientists and other teachers of undergraduate constitutional law courses have benefited from some refreshing changes in the design of casebooks in recent years. Brimming with research drawn from political science, sociology, and history, numerous casebooks are now available for use in undergraduate courses that treat the development of constitutional law as much more than an exercise in logic and the orderly unfolding of legal doctrine. This more interdisciplinary approach, while still fully conversant in the nuance and language of constitutional law, suggests that the justices as individuals make decisions based on personal and political preferences, and that the Court, as an institution, reacts to external pressures—some governmental and some not. Greater attention to the personal and political motives of litigants, their litigation strategies, the policy preferences of the justices, the need for the Court to assert itself and protect its authority in the separation of powers, and the effect of the Court's decisions on law and policy are more clearly attuned, we believe, to the needs and interests of undergraduate students.

In our experience as teachers of undergraduate constitutional law courses, students are more fully engaged when they can focus on the more concrete aspects of law, litigation, and constitutional development. How did a particular conflict originate? What role did interest groups play in a particular case, or series of cases, and why did that matter? What did the litigants—professionally and personally—have at stake? What was the effect of the Court's decision on politics, policy, and society? Did the Court, supposedly an institution immune to the ebb and flow of public opinion, take social and political pressure into consideration when rendering a decision or crafting the contours of an opinion? We believe that teachers and students of the judicial process, constitutional history, and American politics have much to gain in providing their students with more detailed and personal portraits of Supreme Court decisions that have left indelible marks on law and policy.

In addition to teaching courses on law, politics, and the courts, we are also authors of constitutional law and judicial politics textbooks designed for use at the undergraduate level. Here again experience has taught us that a particular book can only do so much, no matter how considerable its virtues might be. We believe that a volume emphasizing the social and political significance of—and, where appropriate, the personalities involved in—some of the most important cases decided by the Supreme Court will allow teachers and students alike to grasp their significance in a way that simply studying and analyzing opinions, or learning about legal processes and structures, devoid of the human element, cannot. Simply put, we aspire to humanize the study of constitutional politics for students and teachers alike, thereby widening the lens used to understand American constitutional development and the social, economic, and political forces at work in the law.

Organization of the Book

Our first obligation as editors is to explain why, given the literally hundreds of critical cases decided by the Supreme Court since it handed down its first decision in 1793, we chose the cases that we did. And since we exclude several cases that are perhaps among *the* most important ever decided by the Court and include many others that might not, upon first glance, seem very important at all, an explanation of our choices will help students, teachers, and other interested readers make better use of this book.

We made every effort to include at least one case touching on each major aspect of American constitutional law, balancing cases dealing with the exercise of government power against those touching on individual liberties and rights. At the same time, we also sought a contrast between landmark decisions that established enduring precedents and newer cases that either revisited major constitutional questions or addressed interesting intersections of law and contemporary public policy. The appeal of this approach is that readers can gain a sense of the historical underpinnings of constitutional law as well as their continuing relevance to the questions the justices continue to confront.

One vital area where this connection is well illustrated is the separation of powers. It is probably the key feature of the American constitution, and so the Court's cases—both past and present—dealing with the nature of legislative, executive, and judicial authority have considerable implications for the powers of the federal government.

Several chapters shed interesting light on the judiciary. Keith Whittington's essay on *Cooper v. Aaron* (1958) deals with a racial desegregation conflict in which the Court's most critical capacity—its ability to serve as the final arbiter of the meaning of the Constitution—took center stage. Some of the unique limits on judicial authority are examined in essays by Gregg Ivers and David Yalof. Ivers explores the case of *Flood v. Kuhn* (1971), a case in which the Court was unwilling to exercise its discretion and eliminate the antitrust exemption of major league baseball, while Yalof investigates whether the justices can intervene in the process of the congressional impeachment of a federal judge. The full scope of the Court's authority—and strong arguments over whether it could or should have been exercised—come together in Howard Gillman's chapter on *Bush v. Gore* (2000), the remarkable case that, in effect, decided the outcome of the presidential election between George W. Bush and Al Gore.

Just as the Court has confronted questions over the nature of judicial authority, so too has it resolved important conflicts over the power of the president. When President Harry Truman sought to take control of the nation's steel production during a time of national emergency, he found his authority tested in *Youngstown Sheet & Tube v. Sawyer* (1952), which is the subject of Maeva Marcus's essay. More recently, in *Clinton v. Jones* (1998), President Bill Clinton argued that the separation of powers rendered the chief executive immune from private lawsuits. Katy Harriger explains why the Court decided to the contrary.

Amy McKay and Michael Munger provide insight into one of the most important cases of modern constitutional law, a conflict over a mechanism of congressional oversight known as the legislative veto. Their chapter on *INS v. Chadha* (1983) explains how, in accordance with one of the most basic checks that the executive exercises over the legislature, Congress cannot enact new policy without first obtaining the president's signature. Despite this institutional limitation, Congress still exercises enormous control over even the most remote corners of American public and private life. In the case of *PGA Tour, Inc. v. Martin* (2001), the subject of Reginald Sheehan's chapter, the justices upheld the ability of Congress to use its power to regulate interstate commerce to compel professional golf to change its rules and accommodate a disabled golfer who was unable to walk the golf course.

No less important than the relationship between the federal branches, the relationship between the national and state governments has been a major preoccupation of the Supreme Court. Even in the earliest days of the republic, questions of federalism were among the most important constitutional conflicts to come before the Supreme Court. They have maintained a prominent role and have been increasingly visible on the current Court's docket. One of the more significant historical cases is *Hammer v. Dagenhart*, which is the subject of Julie Novkov's essay. In this case, some of the policies of the

Progressive Era—such as federal regulations of wages, working conditions, and child labor—came into conflict with the Supreme Court's view of whether the authority for such laws were entrusted by the Constitution to Congress or to the states. In Joseph Kobylka's essay on *Cipollone v. Liggett* (1992), a seemingly esoteric question over a concept known as federal pre-emption—in this case whether federal law regulating cigarette advertising supercedes any state laws on the same subject—had tremendous practical consequences for tobacco companies threatened with legal liability for with-holding the dangers of smoking. A more visible conflict over the relationship between the national and state governments occurred in *Printz v. United States* (1997), the subject of Nancy Maveety's essay. This case examined whether the Congress could compel state law enforcement officials to con-duct criminal background checks on gun purchasers.

Quite apart from conflicts over how the Constitution allocates power, we also sought to examine how the Constitution places explicit limits on that power. Thus, there are several chapters that address such topics as the consti-tutional guarantees relating to religion, speech, association, and the press. Two chapters examine the issue of religion under the Constitution. Kevin McGuire's essay on *Rosenberger v. University of Virginia* (1996) illustrates how the justices sought to square a public university's desire to make funds avail-able to campus organizations with a desire to avoid creating an establishment of religion by funding the activities of religious groups. Steve Brown's chap-ter examines a different question, one relating to the free exercise of religion under the First Amendment. His chapter explores the case of *Church of the Lukumi Babalu Aye v. City of Hialeah* (1993), in which a Florida community sought to ban a religious group's ritual sacrificing of small animals.

Intriguing questions of speech and association are contained in *Hill v. Colorado* (2000) and *Boys Scouts of America v. Dale* (2000). Karen O'Connor addresses how, in *Hill*, the Court sought to balance the right of abortion pro-testers to take their message directly to those seeking abortion services against the government's desire to ensure that women who might seek abortions could do so without harassment or intimidation. In their essay on *Dale*, Erin Ackerman and Joel Grossman explain how the justices weighed the right of the Boy Scouts organization to determine its own membership by excluding homosexuals against the state's interest in banning discrimination.

John Maltese's essay provides a good deal of insight into one of the most fascinating and important cases of freedom of the press, *New York Times v. United States* (1971). When the *New York Times* and the *Washington Post* be-gan publishing a top-secret document from the Defense Department, the federal government tried—unsuccessfully, it turned out—to prevent these newspapers from any further publications from the study known as the "Pentagon Papers."

Since many of the Court's most significant cases have involved the rights of the accused, we sought to include cases from various areas of criminal procedure. In his chapter on *United States v. Leon* (1984), Richard Pacelle documents the Supreme Court's relaxation of the exclusionary rule—the rule that requires that evidence illegally obtained not be permitted to be introduced in a criminal trial. Stacia Haynie's essay on *Miranda v. Arizona* (1966) analyzes what is probably the best-known decision on criminal procedure, one that requires law-enforcement officers to inform suspects of their rights when they are taken into custody. For those who are ultimately convicted of crimes, the Eighth Amendment bars cruel and unusual punishment. Although the death penalty has never been declared unconstitutional per se, the justices have from time to time limited its application. Tom Walker describes how, in a dramatic turnaround in the case of *Atkins v. Virginia* (2002), the Supreme Court reversed itself and ruled that capital punishment for the mentally retarded was unconstitutional.

Finally, issues of equality are among the most visible and debated issues of public policy, and it is no surprise that the Supreme Court would confront many of these concerns. After the Court outlawed racially segregated public schools, for example, it faced the issue of how best to provide a racially integrated education for school children. As Steven Taylor shows in his essay on *Swann v. Charlotte-Mecklenburg Board of Education* (1971), justices had to wrestle with numerous practical complexities involved in undoing the vestiges of forced segregation.

Examining one of the most salient issues of equality, Barbara Perry sheds light on the question of affirmative action in public education. Her contribution focuses on the cases of *Grutter v. Bollinger* and *Gratz v. Bollinger* (2003), which challenged the race-conscious admission policies at the University of Michigan.

Jennifer Segal Diascro examines discrimination in a different form, discrimination based on gender. In *United States v. Virginia* (1996), the Court had to confront the all-male tradition of the state-controlled Virginia Military Academy and assess whether that tradition and the type of severe training associated with it could be preserved or whether its gender-specific policy violated the guarantee of equal protection of the laws.

Although we engaged in several spirited but always good-natured conversations and e-mail exchanges in determining the cases to include in *Creating Constitutional Change*, we agreed from the very beginning that we did not want to establish a uniform template for the essays or have our contributors conform to a standard formula. Rather, we wanted these superb scholars to draw on their own expertise and imagination in deciding what element of the cases to emphasize. Some essays, as you will see, emphasize litigation dynamics, while others see internal debate among the justices on a constitutional question as a surrogate for a larger debate that society views as a cultural or social matter.

In the end, we hope this book lives up to its title by helping students and instructors better appreciate how individual litigants mix together with competing societal interests to shape American constitutional development. In one way or another, each of the cases in this volume raises an issue having a dramatic impact on law and American public policy. They are, we think, excellent and timeless examples of how social, economic, and political forces can seep into the Court's understanding of the law and create constitutional change.

Judicial Power

The Court as the Final Arbiter of the Constitution

Cooper v. Aaron (1958)

KEITH E. WHITTINGTON

> The justices of the Supreme Court provide authoritative interpretation of federal law, issuing their rulings through written opinions. But what if their opinions were just that? What if legislators and executives chose to interpret the law differently and act on their own interpretations? In 1957 the question over who has the final say regarding the meaning of the Constitution arose in Little Rock, Arkansas, when the state legislature and the governor resisted the Supreme Court's ruling outlawing racially segregated public schools. In their decision, the justices reaffirmed Chief Justice John Marshall's conviction that it is "emphatically the province and duty of the judicial department to say what the law is."

In 1954 the decades-long litigation campaign by the National Association for the Advancement of Colored People (NAACP) finally bore substantial fruit when the U.S. Supreme Court declared that racial segregation of primary and secondary public schools was unconstitutional in *Brown v. Board of Education* (1954). The NAACP had for years been chipping away at the doctrine established in *Plessy v. Ferguson* (1896) that the state governments could maintain racially separate facilities if those facilities were equal. In the 1930s and 1940s, the NAACP had demonstrated to the Court that racially segregated graduate schools and law schools could not be made equal, and the success in those cases encouraged NAACP attorneys to press ahead with broader arguments for school integration. With *Brown,* the Court followed the NAACP's lead and quit tinkering with the machinery of segregation, declaring that separate was intrinsically unequal. The following year, in *Brown II,* the Court ordered public schools to desegregate with "all deliberate speed," leaving local schools and the lower federal courts to implement that directive. The Court required a "prompt and reasonable start toward full compliance with the original *Brown* decision," but schools acting in "good faith" should be given the flexibility and time to solve the "varied local school problems" of desegregation (*Brown v. Board of Education,* 349 U.S. 294, 299, 300 [1955]).

Cooper v. Aaron (1958) arose out of the efforts to desegregate the Arkansas public schools, and it was the Supreme Court's last great school desegregation case of the 1950s. In *Cooper,* the Court reaffirmed its commitment to desegregation in the most dramatic circumstances. Perhaps most memorably, the Supreme Court used the opportunity of the *Cooper* case to revisit the foundations of the judiciary's authority within the American constitutional order and to issue the boldest pronouncement in its history on the supremacy of the Supreme Court to the other institutions of government.

The day after the first *Brown* decision, the school board for the Little Rock Independent School District in Arkansas instructed its superintendent, Virgil T. Blossom, to formulate a plan for desegregation. This initial willingness to desegregate was not surprising. Little Rock had a reputation as a fairly progressive southern town. In 1948 the law school, medical school, and graduate school of the University of Arkansas had quickly responded to Supreme Court rulings against segregation in postgraduate education by admitting black applicants without incident. The Little Rock police force was integrated, as was its public library and transportation system. The business community and the local newspaper supported integration, and blacks freely voted.

A few days before *Brown II* was issued in May of 1955, the Little Rock school board announced a program of limited, phased integration. It called for the admission of a small number of selected blacks into the prestigious but working-class Central High School in 1957, with a similar limited integration of the junior highs to follow in 1960, and elementary schools still later. Two other high schools were to remain effectively segregated.

In February 1956 the local NAACP filed a lawsuit in federal district court against various Little Rock school officials, including William Cooper, the president of the board of trustees of the school district, on behalf of the parents of thirty-three black children, including John and Thelma Aaron. The suit asked the court to block the phased integration plan as inadequate to protecting the constitutional rights recognized in *Brown*. On August 27 U.S. District Judge John Miller, an appointee of Franklin Roosevelt and formerly a prominent Arkansas politician, issued an opinion upholding the Little Rock plan. Miller emphasized that the "primary responsibility for the implementation of the constitutional principles announced [in *Brown*] is upon the school authorities" and that "it is not the duty or function of the federal courts to regulate or take over and operate the public schools" (*Aaron v. Cooper*, 143 F. Supp. 855, 864 [1956]). Since the Supreme Court had put the first responsibility for desegregation in the hands of school officials, Miller declined to intervene when the school board seemed to be acting "in good faith" and was making "a prompt and reasonable start toward full compliance with the requirements of the law" (*Aaron*, p. 866). At the school board's own suggestion, however, Judge Miller retained jurisdiction of the case to monitor the progress of the plan.

Disappointed with Judge Miller's ruling, the NAACP appealed the case to the U.S. Court of Appeals for the Eighth Circuit, which covers seven Midwestern states from Arkansas in the south to North Dakota and Minnesota in the north. Thurgood Marshall, the chief counsel of the national NAACP's Legal Defense Fund, joined the local attorneys for the oral arguments before the appellate court. In April 1957 a panel of three circuit court judges observed that "it may be that in the future, as the plan of integration begins to operate, a showing could then be made to the effect that more time was being taken than was necessary" and as a consequence the district court would then have an obligation "to see that the plan of gradual integration was accelerated at a greater rate than now proposed," but "that remains for future determination" (*Aaron v. Cooper*, 243 F. 2d 361, 363 [1957]). For the moment, the appellate court found, Little Rock was in compliance with the requirements of *Brown II*.

Meanwhile, opposition to desegregation began to build in Arkansas. Orval Faubus was a relatively liberal politician from the western Arkansas hill country. In the 1956 Democratic gubernatorial primary, Faubus denounced his strongly segregationist opponent as a "purveyor of hate," but offered voters his own pledge "to maintain segregation in a calm, orderly, thoughtful and completely legal manner" even as he characterized school desegregation as a "local problem" (Black, 1976, p. 100). Faubus won a second term handily. In the fall of 1956, however, a proposed constitutional amendment requiring state officials to oppose the *Brown* decision was approved by voters, with Little Rock voters evenly divided on the issue. In the summer of 1957, Congress approved the first federal civil rights legislation since Reconstruction, but the price of legislative victory was a weakened statute that dropped the civil rights enforcement powers that had been requested by the Department of Justice.

In August 1957 Little Rock public officials prepared to admit to Central High School the first group of nine black students who had been accepted to the school and had agreed to transfer. School attorneys had determined that the state legislature did not have the legal authority to block the plan, and Governor Faubus observed at a press conference, "Everyone knows that state laws can't supersede federal laws" (Freyer, 1984, p. 97). Faubus soon advised Superintendent Blossom that public opinion in the state had turned against immediate desegregation, however, and contacted the U.S. Justice Department to ask what the federal government planned to do to maintain public order in Little Rock but did not receive an encouraging reply. The governor then arranged for Mrs. Clyde Thomason, acting with the segregationist Mothers League of Central High School, to file suit in state court on August 27, the day of school registration, seeking an injunction blocking implementation of the phased integration plan given the threat of violence. After Faubus himself testified that violence was likely, the state court issued the injunction on August 29.

The school board immediately petitioned the federal district court to quash the state injunction. Not wanting to remain involved in the increasingly divisive issue, Judge Miller arranged for the case to be transferred to another judge. Given the retirement of one of the district court judges in Arkansas, the newly appointed Judge Ronald Davies had been temporarily transferred from North Dakota to help relieve the backlog of cases. Davies had just arrived in Little Rock when the school desegregation case was reassigned to him. On Friday, August 30, 1957, Judge Davies held that the state courts did not have the authority to interfere with the school desegregation plan already approved by, and under the continuing supervision of, the federal courts. That order was eventually upheld by the federal circuit court (*Thomason v. Cooper*, 254 F.2d 808 [1958]).

On Monday evening, Faubus sent the Arkansas National Guard to Central High School. In a televised address, the governor explained that he had mobilized the "State Militia" not to act as "segregationists or integrationists," but it will not be possible to restore or to maintain order and protect the lives and property of the citizens if forcible integration is carried out tomorrow in the schools of this community. The inevitable conclusion therefore must be that the schools in Pulaski County [where Little Rock is located], for the time being must be operated on the same basis as they have been operated in the past. (Silverman, 1959, pp. 7–8)

The school board issued a statement later that night asking "that no Negro students attempt to attend Central or any white high school until this dilemma is legally resolved" (Silverman, 1959, p. 8). Events in Little Rock quickly attracted national and international media attention. The next morning, a crowd of several hundred gathered outside Central High School in Little Rock, but no black students came to the school that day. Judge Davies ordered that desegregation proceed on schedule.

On Wednesday, September 4, the nine black students attempted to enter Central High but were turned back by the National Guard and an angry crowd. In a telegram to the president, the governor held that the key issue was not desegregation per se but the authority of a state official "to exercise his constitutional powers and discretion in maintaining peace and good order within his jurisdiction" (Silverman, 1959, p. 9). President Dwight Eisenhower responded by telegram the next day, noting his confidence that Arkansas state officials would "give full co-operation to the United States District Court" and declaring that "When I became President, I took an oath to support and defend the Constitution of the United States. The only assurance I can give you is that the federal Constitution will be upheld by me by every legal means at my command." Faubus responded somewhat equivocally, pledging by telegram that he would "co-operate in upholding the Constitution of Arkansas and the nation" (Silverman, 1959, p. 10).

On Saturday, September 7, Davies declined another school board request for delay, finding insufficient facts to support the fear of violence and observing that "there can be nothing but ultimate confusion and chaos if court decrees are flaunted, whatever the pretext" (Silverman, 1959, p. 10). On Monday Judge Davies asked the federal government formally to enter the case as an amicus curiae, or friend of the court, and to file a petition requesting an injunction against Governor Faubus and the National Guard. Upon receiving the requested petition, Davies declared the governor and the officers in command of the state National Guard to be codefendants with William Cooper and the school board in the suit initiated by the parents of John and Thelma Aaron, among others. A hearing before Judge Davies was set for September 20.

This left over a week for both sides to prepare their legal case and engage in informal negotiations. President Eisenhower explained to his attorney general that he wanted to give Faubus the opportunity for an "orderly retreat" but that the federal government could neither "compromise" nor "capitulate" on the issue of state compliance to federal court orders (Freyer, 1984, p. 105). On September 14 Faubus joined Eisenhower in Newport, Rhode Island, where the president was taking a working vacation. In a lengthy session, the president suggested that the governor change his orders to the National Guard to preserve order while allowing the black students to enter Central High. The governor indicated that a cooling-off period was needed before integration at Little Rock could peacefully begin, and the two sides reached no clear agreement. Upon his return to Little Rock, Faubus removed the troops from the school grounds but did not change their orders. The White House remained convinced that Faubus was looking for a politically acceptable way out and did not want to exacerbate the situation further by bolstering the federal presence in Arkansas.

On September 20 representatives of the governor argued to Judge Davies that the petition from the Justice Department should be dismissed. The governor contended that amicus curiae, in this case the United States, had no right to request that additional parties be added to the original suit. Moreover, the Constitution specified that only the Supreme Court could hear lawsuits between the United States and the states, and therefore the district court did not have proper jurisdiction to hear the case. Following earlier Supreme Court precedent, the argument turned in particular on whether Faubus was acting in his constitutional capacity as governor to "maintain the law and order" or whether he was merely exercising the power of the state to override the federal constitutional rights of the students. Davies rejected the state's arguments regarding his jurisdiction, whereupon Faubus's attorneys walked out of the courtroom. Davies then issued an injunction against the governor, arguing that though the governor had a "vital interest in the maintenance of law and order . . . the proper use of that power in this instance was to maintain the Federal Court in the exercise of its jurisdiction, to aid in making its process effective and not to nullify it, to remove and not to create, obstructions to the exercise by the Negro children of their rights as judicially declared" (*Aaron v. Cooper,* 156 F. Supp. 220, 226 [1957]). The district court's actions were later upheld in an appeal before the federal circuit court (*Faubus v. United States,* 254 F.2d 797 [1958]).

On Monday, September 23, the nine black students successfully entered Central High School as city police held back a large and violent crowd. By midday, school officials had decided that the situation was too dangerous to continue and sent the black students home early. The president issued a proclamation recognizing the "willful obstruction of justice" in Little Rock and commanding "all persons engaged in such obstruction of justice to cease and desist therefrom, and to disperse forthwith" (Silverman, 1959, p. 35). With unruly crowds gathering at Central High again the next morning, the president issued an executive order calling the National Guard into federal service, removing it from the governor's command. At the same time, he ordered a thousand paratroopers from the 101st Airborne Division of the U.S. Army to be sent to Little Rock from Fort Campbell, Kentucky. The soldiers were in place by that evening. As Eisenhower explained, "If you have to use force, use overwhelming force and save lives thereby," while at the same time he hoped to avoid having "brothers fighting up against brothers and families divided" (Brownell, 1993, p. 211; Richardson, 1979, p. 120). In a televised address that evening, the president observed, "Our personal opinions about the decision have no bearing on the matter of enforcement." The "responsibility and authority of the Supreme Court to interpret the Constitution are very clear," and a "foundation of our American way of life is our national respect for the law" (Eisenhower, 1958, p. 690).

On Wednesday, September 25, federal troops escorted the students into Central High and forcibly dispersed a gathered crowd. Judge Davies soon returned to his North Dakota district, but segregationist political pressures continued to grow over the course of the school year. In February the school board petitioned the district court for a postponement of the desegregation plan. Judge Harry Lemley, a Roosevelt appointee from southwestern Arkansas, was now assigned to hear the school board's motion. On June 21 Lemley granted the "tactical delay" in light of "the deep seated popular opposition in Little Rock to the principle of integration" and the consequent "adverse effect upon the educational program" that had resulted from the efforts of the previous year (*Aaron v. Cooper,* 163 F. Supp. 13, 21, 26 [1958]).

The NAACP filed immediate appeals of Judge Lemley's order with both the circuit court and the Supreme Court. The Supreme Court was unwilling to step outside of its regular procedures to take the case before the circuit court had heard the appeal but noted on June 30 that the circuit court should act quickly to allow time for a final appeal before the start of the next school year. The circuit court scheduled a special session for August 4 to hear oral arguments. Despite a NAACP letter-writing campaign to persuade the Justice Department to file an amicus brief in the circuit court, the U.S. government decided to remain on the sidelines. On July 29 Faubus won the Democratic primary for a third term as governor in a landslide.

All seven judges of the Eighth Circuit Court of Appeals heard the *Cooper* case en banc on August 4, 1958. On August 18 the circuit court accepted Judge Lemley's factual findings that the Little Rock schools had been disrupted as a result of increasing opposition to desegregation, but by a six-to-one vote, the circuit court overturned his decision to postpone integration. Although "not unmindful of the difficulties which were faced by the [school] board," the circuit court was less focused on the specific situation in Little Rock, which the school board and the district court had to manage, than on the larger policy implications of Lemley's ruling if adopted elsewhere.

> An impossible situation could well develop if the District Court's orders were affirmed. Every school district in which integration is publicly opposed by overt acts would have "justifiable excuse" to petition the courts for delay and suspension in integration programs. An affirmance of "temporary delay" in Little Rock would amount to an open invitation to elements in other districts to overtly act out public opposition through violent and unlawful means. (*Aaron v. Cooper,* 257 F.2d 33, 40 [1958])

Three days later, Chief Judge Gardner, who had filed the lone dissent in the case, granted the school board's request to stay the circuit court's decision until the Supreme Court had heard the case. The effect of the stay was to leave Lemley's original decision in place, so that Little Rock schools would open on September 2 as segregated unless the Supreme Court intervened.

At his regular press conference on August 20, President Eisenhower began by declining to comment on the Little Rock case, which was still under consideration by the courts, but noting that all Americans were obliged to comply with judicial orders regardless of the outcome and on that his "feelings are exactly as they were a year ago" (Silverman, 1959, p. 19). Later that day, Governor Faubus held a press conference of his own in which he asserted that Americans could only understand the law of the land "in terms of laws passed by their own votes at the ballot box, or in terms of laws passed by their elected representatives" (Silverman, 1959, p. 20). Faubus noted that while the people of Arkansas had made clear their continued support for segregation, Congress had declined to take any action requiring desegregation. Soon thereafter the governor called a special session of the Arkansas legislature to begin on August 26 to consider means for resisting desegregation.

The Supreme Court was out of session for the summer, but upon receiving the NAACP's appeal, Chief Justice Earl Warren announced on August 25 that the Court would meet in a special session in three days. Warren also asked the U.S. government to enter the case as amicus curiae. The NAACP had first requested that Gardner's stay be lifted, and that was the issue taken up on the 28th. The Justice Department's brief supported the substantive ruling of the circuit court and favored lifting the stay. After the hearing, the justices met in conference and found that they were in agreement that Lemley's decision had been wrong. Justice Felix Frankfurter arrived with a memorandum already written that rejected delay and the possibility that "law should bow to force" (Tushnet, 1994, p. 259). Instead of granting the NAACP's request, however, the Court ordered a full hearing on the substantive appeal of the circuit court's decision that had been filed by the school board. Justice Tom Clark of Texas nearly dissented from this decision to hold a full special session, concerned that the Court not appear to be rushing into battle against the South, but in the end he went along with his colleagues. Oral arguments on the full case were set for September 11, and the Court asked the solicitor general, a Justice Department official who represents the U.S. government at the Supreme Court, to join those oral arguments as well. In response, the school board further postponed the start of classes until September 15.

At their private conference after the oral arguments on September 11, the justices quickly agreed to uphold the circuit court's decision to overrule Judge Lemley and to vacate the stay. Warren assigned Justices Frankfurter and John Harlan to draft a brief order declaring the conclusion of the Court, which was released the next day. Warren then formally assigned Justice William Brennan to draft the full opinion for the Court, though in fact Warren had already asked Brennan even before oral arguments to begin work on such an opinion. This unusual procedure would allow Little Rock schools to open as scheduled on September 15, while still giving the justices time to prepare a complete "expression of the views supporting our judgment" (*Aaron v. Cooper*, 358 U.S. 5 [1958]).

Faubus soon responded. Drawing on new state laws passed during the special session, the governor announced a special referendum to be held on September 27 to determine whether the public high school would open on an integrated basis or be closed down and replaced with "private," segregated charter schools to be operated in the same facilities and maintained at taxpayer expense. He also ordered schools to be closed until the referendum was held. By nearly a three-to-one margin, Little Rock voters chose to close the schools.

In a brief session at noon on September 29, Chief Justice Earl Warren read aloud the opinion of the Court in *Cooper v. Aaron*. The final opinion reflected substantial negotiation among the justices. At Harlan's suggestion, each of the justices individually signed the opinion to emphasize the Court's consensus, altering the usual practice of identifying a lead author who speaks on behalf of the Court's majority. Although Frankfurter was enthusiastic about this suggestion, he also startled his colleagues by announcing that he would later release a separate opinion concurring in the judgment of the Court. For some time Frankfurter had been convinced that "the ultimate hope for the peaceful solution of the basic problem largely depends on winning the support of lawyers of the South for the overriding issue of obedience to the Court's decision," and his concurring opinion was intended to reach out to these southern moderates (Hutchinson, 1979, p. 77). Also at Harlan's suggestion, the opinion concluded by noting that the Court had unanimously approved the basic principles in *Brown* twice after having "been given the most serious consideration" and that the three new justices who had joined the Court since *Brown* stood by that decision (*Cooper v. Aaron,* 358 U.S. 1, 19 [1958]). Brennan was wary that such language would suggest that the meaning of the Constitution depended on membership of the Court, but his colleagues thought it more important to demonstrate the depth of the Court's commitment to *Brown.*

The final opinion emphasized what the Court took to be the central issue of the case, the claim that Arkansas state officials "are not bound by our holding in *Brown.*" Brennan and Justice Hugo Black had initially hoped that the *Cooper* opinion would give greater definition to *Brown II's* requirement of "all deliberate speed." Ultimately, no one was pleased with the results of this effort, and it was dropped from the final draft. By noting in the opinion that the states could not "support segregated schools through any arrangement, management, funds, or property," Brennan was able to suggest that the tactics then being implemented in Arkansas would likewise prove futile. Most of the opinion reviewed the events leading up the Supreme Court's decision, from the decision in *Brown* to the most recent decision of the Eighth Circuit. After reviewing this record, the Court accepted that the school board had acted in good faith and that conditions in Little Rock were difficult. But the key fact to the justices was that those conditions "are directly traceable to the actions of legislators and executive officials of the State of Arkansas, taken in their official capacities, which reflect their own determination to resist this Court's decision in the *Brown* case and which have brought about violent resistance to that decision in Arkansas." The actions of one set of state actors, such as the governor, could not alleviate the constitutional responsibilities of another set of state actors, such as the school board. The difficulties of law and order in Little Rock were the "product of state action," and they could "also be brought under control by state action." The Court could not allow federal constitutional commitments to be "nullified openly and directly . . . nor nullified indirectly" by state government officials (*Cooper,* pp. 15–19). Though the school board might be caught between the conflicting demands of the federal judiciary and the state government, the Court was not going to be the one to back down.

In concluding its opinion, the Court returned to the basic question, whether state officials were bound by *Brown*. This question was especially pressing in light of the strong criticisms of the substantive legal reasoning in *Brown* that had been leveled by constitutional scholars and politicians alike, raising fundamental issues regarding the obligations of government officials and citizens who are faced with a judicial decision they believe cannot be reconciled with the terms of the Constitution. Rather than offer further constitutional arguments in support of the conclusion they had reached in *Brown* to persuade critics that the Court had in fact been correct in its initial ruling, the justices instead chose to emphasize their authority to decide. In answering that question, the Court argued,

> It is necessary only to recall some basic constitutional propositions which are settled doctrine. Article VI of the Constitution makes the Constitution the "the supreme Law of the Land." In 1803, Chief Justice Marshall, speaking for a unanimous Court, referring to the Constitution as "the fundamental and paramount law of the nation," declared in the notable case of *Marbury v. Madison* . . . that "It is emphatically the province and duty of the judicial department to say what the law is." This decision declared the basic principle that the federal judiciary is supreme in the exposition of the law of the Constitution, and that principle has ever since been respected by this Court and the Country as a permanent and indispensable feature of our constitutional system. It follows that the interpretation of the Fourteenth Amendment enunciated by this Court in the *Brown* case is the supreme law of the land. . . . Every state legislator and executive and judicial officer is solemnly committed by oath taken pursuant to Art. VI, cl. 3 "to support this Constitution." . . . No state legislator or executive or judicial officer can war against the Constitution without violating his undertaking to support it. (*Cooper,* p. 18)

The substantive principles at stake in *Brown* and state obedience of them were "indispensable for the protection of the freedoms guaranteed by our fundamental charter for all of us. Our constitutional ideal of equal justice under law is thus made a living truth" (*Cooper,* p. 19).

In response to the governor's order to close the public schools, the NAACP and the Justice Department petitioned the federal district court to bar the public facilities from being transferred into private hands. Judge Lemley had retired early in September, and so the case was once again assigned to

Judge Miller, who concluded that he did not have the authority to issue such a ruling. On November 10 the circuit court prohibited the transfer and returned the case to Judge Miller with orders to integrate. In response, most of the members of the school board resigned. A new board, elected on December 6, was evenly divided between segregationists and moderates. After months of stalemate and conflict, the segregationist members narrowly lost a recall election in May 1959. On June 18 a special panel of the federal district court struck down the Arkansas school closing legislation as unconstitutional under *Cooper v. Aaron.* On August 12, 1959, the Little Rock public schools were reopened. Black students were admitted to both Hall High School and Central High School. City police forcibly broke up a large crowd that gathered outside Central High. There were no further disruptions.

In the end, *Cooper* did little to clarify the requirements of *Brown,* except to specify that public opposition and political resistance to desegregation should not be taken into consideration by lower courts in designing integration plans. The Supreme Court did not take substantial additional action on school desegregation until it required racially unitary school systems in *Green v. County School Board* in 1968 and authorized the district courts to exercise broad remedial powers to achieve racial integration, including court-ordered busing, in *Swann v. Charlotte-Mecklenburg Board of Education* in 1971. *Cooper* instead became a case about judicial authority, and on that point the justices could speak eloquently and in unison. Confident of presidential support, the Supreme Court emphasized what Eisenhower had already said: The decisions of the federal judiciary were the law of the land, and state officials were obligated to comply. For a Court that was being denounced in both the halls of Congress and the streets of the South, it was a golden opportunity for the justices to reassert themselves as, in Frankfurter's words, "the authoritative organ of what the Constitution requires" (Tushnet, 1994, p. 260). They did not hesitate to take it.

REFERENCES

Black, E. (1976). *Southern governors and civil rights: Racial segregation as a campaign issue in the second reconstruction.* Cambridge, MA: Harvard University Press.

Brownell, H., with Burke, J. P. (1993). *Advising Ike: The memoirs of Attorney General Herbert Brownell.* Lawrence, KS: University Press of Kansas.

Eisenhower, D. D. (1958). *Public papers of the presidents of the United States: Dwight D. Eisenhower, 1957.* Washington, DC: Government Printing Office.

Freyer, T. (1984). *The Little Rock crisis: A constitutional interpretation.* Westport, CT: Greenwood Press.

Hutchinson, D. J. (1979). Unanimity and desegregation: Decisionmaking in the Supreme Court, 1948–1958. *Georgetown Law Journal, 68,* 1–96.

Richardson, E. R. (1979). *The presidency of Dwight D. Eisenhower.* Lawrence, KS: University Press of Kansas.

Silverman, C. (1959). *The Little Rock story.* Tuscaloosa, AL: University of Alabama Press.

Tushnet, M. V. (1994). *Making civil rights law: Thurgood Marshall and the Supreme Court, 1956–1961.* New York: Oxford University Press.

Before Free Agency in Major League Baseball

Flood v. Kuhn (1972)

GREGG IVERS

> The Sherman Antitrust Act of 1890 is a federal law designed to prevent monopolistic business practices that restrain the free flow of economic activity. In 1922, however, the Supreme Court exempted professional baseball from the law's requirements. As a result, baseball players did not enjoy the same freedom that others have to sell their labor to employers who might bid for their services. Fifty years later, when Curt Flood of the St. Louis Cardinals initiated a legal challenge to this exemption, the justices wrestled with the issue of whether the Court was the proper forum for resolving this question. Unwilling to reverse its earlier ruling, they concluded that it was up to Congress to make changes in the antitrust law and baseball's role within it. As Chief Justice Warren Burger explained, "Courts are not the forum in which this tangled web ought to be unsnarled."

In the late summer of 1968, *Sports Illustrated* anointed Curt Flood of the St. Louis Cardinals as major league baseball's premier center fielder by placing him on its cover and claiming in its feature story that his defensive skills now surpassed those of the great Willie Mays. By then, Flood was earning $90,000 per year, the highest salary of any nonpitcher, non–power hitter in major league baseball. But Flood's good fortune would soon change. In October 1969, just after the end of the season, Flood, a three-time All-Star, seven-time Gold Glove winner, and integral part of two World Series championship Cardinal teams, learned through a sportswriter's early-morning phone call that he had been traded to the Philadelphia Phillies. Flood, who was originally drafted in 1956 by the Cincinnati Reds and then traded to St. Louis before the 1958 season, had spent twelve of his fourteen major league seasons with the Cardinals. He did not want to uproot himself and his family to spend the next phase of his career with a team widely considered one of baseball's most poorly run franchises. So Flood did what was unthinkable in those days. He refused to accept the trade and said, in straightforward terms, that his annual one-year contract with the Cardinals had expired. Since he no longer had a contract binding him to the Cardinals, Flood believed that he should be free to negotiate with any team. Flood's decision soon led to a chain of events that would shake the rafters of the national pastime's business structure with an earthquake-like force that, up until then, was simply unprecedented.

Beginning in 1880, professional baseball incorporated what later became known as the "reserve clause" into the uniform contracts issued by each major league team to its players. The reserve clause permitted the owners to retain exclusive rights to the services of the players of their respective teams by forbidding them to negotiate with other teams after the expiration of their annual contracts for a period of one year. The practical result of the reserve clause was to bind a player to the team that first signed him into perpetuity, since refusing to sign an annual contract meant that a player would have to sit out a year before he could offer his services to other teams. Previous attempts by players to test the reserve clause's operation had resulted in their banishment from the game, the illegal but uncontested response of the owners to anyone who dared to challenge a system so favorable to their business interests (Heylar, 1994; Lowenfish, 1990; Goldstein, 1989).

Those who had observed Flood's career were surprised that this quiet man, a skilled portrait artist whose work hung in the offices of Cardinals' owner August Busch, would challenge the ancient business practices of the sport that, by his own admission, had paid him well. But Flood's reticence concealed a powerful intelligence and evolving social conscience, one whose values were shaped by the tumultuous events of the era in which he came of age. One such example was his decision to compose a portrait of Martin Luther King, Jr., after the civil rights leader was assassinated and present it to his widow, Coretta Scott King. Mrs. King was so moved by Flood's gesture that to this day it is the only portrait of her late husband she keeps hung in her home (Gildea, 1971, pp. 55–58). As a self-professed "child of the sixties," Flood decided he could not accept a business arrangement that denied him what he believed were basic civil rights in his own profession (Heylar, 1994; Miller, 1991).

After making clear to the Cardinals' management that he would not accept his trade to Philadelphia, Flood contacted Marvin Miller, the chief counsel and negotiator for the players' union, the Major League Baseball

Players Association (MLBPA), to inquire about a lawsuit attacking the reserve clause on antitrust grounds. The MLBPA had formed in 1954 to represent major league baseball players in labor and contract matters with the owners. Miller told Flood that the two previous such lawsuits that had reached the United States Supreme Court had been unsuccessful. The first, *Federal Baseball Club v. The National League* (1922), involved a challenge by a start-up professional baseball league to attract players from the established National and American Leagues. Federal League owners claimed that the reserve clause allowed the National and American Leagues to restrain trade in violation of the Sherman Antitrust Act of 1890, the first major congressional effort to prohibit and punish monopolistic business practices and price fixing. Justice Oliver Wendell Holmes, writing for a unanimous Court, rejected Federal Baseball Club's argument. Holmes held that professional baseball was not, in fact, interstate commerce subject to federal antitrust laws, but a series of intrastate "exhibitions" played for the public's enjoyment. Even though teams traveled across state lines to play in these exhibitions and were compensated for their efforts, Holmes nonetheless managed to conclude that professional baseball games were "purely state affairs" (*Federal Baseball,* 259 U.S. 200, 208–209 [1922]). Since professional baseball was not, according to Holmes, interstate commerce, it was not within the scope of congressional regulatory power.

Justice Holmes's ruling established a judicially created exemption to the Sherman Act that Congress had never contemplated when it passed the legislation.[1] The Court refused to disturb this exemption when it confronted the reserve clause for the second time in *Toolson v. New York Yankees* (346 U.S. 356 [1953]). In *Toolson,* the Court addressed the question of player mobility between teams under the reserve clause. George Toolson, a catcher stuck in the New York Yankees' minor league system, wanted the freedom to negotiate with other teams after the expiration of his one-year contract. But Yankees' management, following the accepted practices of the day, refused to allow Toolson to catch on with other minor league teams or play professional baseball in Mexico, where several major leaguers had gone to earn more money than they were making in big league jobs in the United States. Even though Toolson, like all players, was not paid by the organization to which he was under contract during the "off" season, he was still bound to the team under the reserve clause and prohibited from playing with any other team in any other league without the owner's permission.

This time, the Court, in a one paragraph per curiam opinion, said that Congress had had thirty years to repeal baseball's exemption and had chosen not to do so. If Congress had meant to subject professional baseball to federal antitrust laws, then surely, reasoned the Court, it would have done so by now. Moreover, the Court, despite the modernization of the game to include television and radio coverage and elaborate minor league or "farm" systems for each organization not only in the United States, but also in Cuba, Mexico, and Canada, did not budge from Holmes's conclusion in *Federal Baseball* that baseball was intrastate commerce. But unlike *Federal Baseball, Toolson* was not unanimous. Two justices, Harold Burton and Stanley Reed, dissented from the Court's conclusion that professional baseball was not interstate commerce. After reviewing the sources of revenue and organizational structure of major league baseball, Burton wrote that "it [was] a contradiction in terms to say that the defendants in the cases before us are not now engaged in interstate trade or commerce as those terms are used in the Constitution of the United States and in the Sherman Act" (*Toolson,* 1953).

What made *Toolson* even more perplexing, even bizarre, was that the justices deciding the case all came to the Court after the Constitutional Revolution of 1937, which rejected the old, parochial understanding of interstate commerce in favor of one that viewed the American economy as dynamic and interdependent. As illogical as the Court's decisions in *Federal Baseball* and *Toolson* appeared to those who understood the economics of professional baseball, Miller advised Flood that it was unlikely to reverse either decision on the principle of stare decisis, or the established judicial tradition of adhering to past precedent. Courts were reluctant to reverse prior holdings, even those that were considered flawed, because of the legal and societal disruption it would cause. Clear and unequivocal legal error was one thing, Miller said, but bad antitrust policy that did not raise substantial constitutional questions was another.

Undaunted, Flood, with the support of the MLBPA, pressed ahead. He informed the commissioner of major league baseball, Bowie Kuhn, in a letter addressed December 24, 1969, that he would not accept his trade to the Philadelphia Phillies. Wrote Flood: "After twelve years in the Major Leagues, I do not feel that I am a piece of property to be bought and sold irrespective of my wishes. I believe that any system that produces that result violates my basic rights as a citizen and is inconsistent with the laws of the United States" (Miller, 1991, pp. 190–191).

Flood also asked Kuhn to inform all the other major league teams that his services were available. Kuhn told him that he would not honor such a request because of the reserve clause. Flood then filed a lawsuit in federal court, naming the commissioner as the defendant, and charged that the Court's decisions in *Federal Baseball* and *Toolson* exempting major league baseball from federal antitrust law were erroneous and should be reversed. To reinforce the seriousness with which the MLBPA viewed this case and in anticipation that *Flood v. Kuhn* would reach the Supreme Court, Miller was able to persuade ex–Supreme Court justice Arthur Goldberg (1962–65) to represent Flood. Before entering public service in 1961 as President John F. Kennedy's secretary of labor, Goldberg had risen to legal prominence as a labor lawyer for the nation's largest automobile and industrial unions. Miller had an edge when he approached Goldberg—the two had worked together for over ten years dating back to the 1950s representing the United Steelworkers union.

Although the Court, by 1970, had declared horse racing, boxing, and football interstate businesses covered by federal antitrust laws, two lower federal courts rejected Flood's arguments (*International Boxing Club v. United States,* 358 F.2d 165 [CA9], cert. denied 385 U.S. 846 [1966]; *Radovich v National Football League,* 352 U.S. 445 [1957]; *Haywood v National Basketball Association,* 401 U.S. 1204 [1971]).[2] And not even the logic of the law and a former justice arguing his case could help Flood's chances before the Court. Although it found that professional baseball was in fact interstate commerce and called its exemption from the federal antitrust laws an "aberration," Justice Harry A. Blackmun, writing for a 5–3 Court, relied on stare decisis and ruled that Congress, not "this Court," should take appropriate corrective action (*Flood v. Kuhn,* 407 U.S. 258 [1972]). Blackmun even acknowledged that no special reason existed for baseball's exemption from the federal antitrust laws that applied to professional football, boxing, hockey, and golf other than what the Court had said in *Federal Baseball* and *Toolson.* And that was simply that baseball was special and thus permitted to retain an antitrust exemption to which no other sport and no other business engaged in interstate commerce was entitled. Wrote Blackmun: "It is an aberration that has been with us now for half a century, one heretofore deemed fully entitled to the benefit of stare decisis, and one that has survived the Court's expanding concept of interstate commerce. It rests on a recognition and an acceptance of baseball's unique characteristics and needs" (*Flood,* p. 282).

Among the dissenters in *Flood* was William O. Douglas, the only remaining justice from the *Toolson* Court. Commenting in a footnote that, "While I joined the Court's opinion in *Toolson* . . . and I would now correct what I believe to be its fundamental error," Douglas concluded that "[t]his Court's decision in *Federal Baseball* . . . made in 1922, is a derelict in the stream of the law that we, its creator, should remove. Only a romantic view of a rather dismal business account over the last 50 years would keep that derelict in midstream."

Douglas, who was appointed to the Court in 1939 by President Franklin D. Roosevelt in large part because of his commitment to the New Deal agenda, reminded his colleagues that under "modern decisions," such as *United States v. Darby* (1941) and *Wickard v. Filburn* (1942), "the power of Congress was recognized as broad enough to reach all phases of the vast operations of our national industrial system" (*Flood,* p. 287). Concluded Douglas: "[As] [a]n industry so dependent on radio and television as is baseball and gleaning vast interstate revenues [one] would be hard put today to say with the Court in the *Federal Baseball* case that baseball was only a local exhibition, not trade or commerce. There can be no doubt 'that were we considering the question of baseball for the first time upon a clean slate' we would hold it to be subject to federal antitrust regulation. The unbroken silence of Congress should not prevent us from correcting our own mistakes" (*Flood,* 1972, quoting *Radovich v. National Football League,* 352 U.S. 445, at 452 [1957]).

Also dissenting, Justice Thurgood Marshall wrote that, since it was the Court through its prior rulings that made the players "impotent" to confront the settled power structure of professional baseball, it was "this Court [that] should correct its errors" (*Flood,* p. 292).

But neither Douglas's nor Marshall's voice was powerful enough to carry the day. Thus, in the spring of 1972, just as the sights, sounds, and smells of another baseball season had eased their way back into the public's consciousness, Curt Flood would watch from afar, his career over.[3]

But Flood's decision to pursue his grievance with the economics of professional baseball all the way to the Supreme Court provided an excellent example of how litigation, even if unsuccessful, can raise public awareness and spur reform through channels outside the nation's courtrooms. *Flood v. Kuhn* generated unprecedented exposure of the economic and legal arrangements of professional baseball. As a result of Flood's lawsuit, the MLBPA, now much more aggressive and well educated about the infirmities of the owners' position, was able, through more sophisticated negotiating strategies, strike threats, and a superior legal position, ultimately to win major concessions from the owners on the reserve clause. The MLBPA's success soon resulted in much greater player mobility between teams and across leagues. This development led to unparalleled increases in salary and compensation, since most players were now free to entertain competitive bids from all major league teams after a certain period of service with one team. Change may well have come about at some point, but it would have happened much later had Curt Flood simply followed baseball custom and packed his bags and reported to the Philadelphia Phillies before the 1970 season.

But the *Flood* case is illustrative in another sense, for it demonstrates the extent to which conflicts from the most unlikely corners of American society ultimately find their way all the way to the Supreme Court. Like many individuals before him who had tried and failed to find a hospitable forum for their grievances, Curt Flood viewed litigation as the final means to overcome the legal barriers that stood in the way of what he believed were his rights under law. And like many such lawsuits, the *Flood* case stood to—and did— affect far more people than just one professional baseball player. In the end, major league players as a class were affected by Flood's suit. So too were baseball's owners, who, by 1975, saw their grip on the economics of the sport loosen considerably in a way that they never, before Flood's lawsuit, could have imagined. That year, the National Labor Relations Board (NLRB) ruled in favor of a reserve clause grievance filed by former Montreal Expo Dave Mc-Nally and the Los Angeles Dodgers' Andy Messersmith. The NLRB held that a player was bound to a team for the length of the contract only, after which the player was free to offer his services to another team. Thus, with the stroke of a NLRB arbitrator's pen, free agency in major league baseball was born. One year later, Messersmith signed a three-year contract with the Atlanta Braves worth $1 million, more than tripling what he received in compensation from the Dodgers the year before (Miller, 1991, pp. 238–253).

The *Flood* case, taken in context, can be understood as an exercise in legal reform. Trying to find a theoretical framework in which to understand and explain the *Flood* case is rather challenging, as it does not fall neatly into any category or type of case that so often occupies the attention of scholars who study reform politics and the courts.

The *Flood* Case and the Politics of Legal Mobilization

Where does the Flood case belong in the annals of the political science literature on the politics of legal mobilization? One place to look is the classic and well-established literature that deals with the constitutional politics of *public law litigation*. The other is the growing literature on the politics of reform through *civil litigation*, and how lawsuits can ultimately spur remedies from outside the courtroom.

CONSTITUTIONAL POLITICS AND THE COURTS

Scholars interested in the use of litigation to achieve legal reform have generally focused on the role of organized interests in bringing individual constitutional cases of great import or in a sustained campaign carried out with some overarching goal in mind. A prime example of the former is Clement Vose's pioneering study, *Caucasians Only*, which focused on the NAACP's efforts to have restrictive housing covenants declared unconstitutional (Vose, 1959).[4] Vose demonstrated how organized interests were able to provide the time, money, and skill to carry out complex litigation designed to achieve a specific policy goal in a way that individual attorneys or groups lacking such resources could not. Conceptually influenced by Vose and intellectually curious about the social and political dynamics of reform-minded constitutional litigation, more and more scholars examined the role of organized interests in individual cases that spanned the broad canvass of American constitutional law. Along the way, several scholars made important theoretical contributions that articulated a clearer picture of what kinds of organized interests were drawn to the litigation process and why.

By the end of the first important wave of such scholarly studies, the literature on organized interests in the litigation process was in accord. Organizational litigants most likely to turn to the courts to redress their grievances were, in Richard Cortner's words, "disadvantaged" in nature. That is, they were unable to secure their policy goals through the channels of majority politics.[5] Personified by such high-profile organizations as the NAACP, the American Civil Liberties Union, the American Jewish Congress, and the National Organization for Women, such litigants were overwhelmingly liberal in their political orientation and favored an expansive view of rights.[6] Moreover, reform-minded liberal litigants emphasized what Stuart Scheingold has called the "myth of rights," which suggests that a favorable Supreme Court decision was automatically followed by compliance, or, at worst, the "politics of rights," or the idea that judicial outcomes are the starting point for subsequent political conflict over implementation (Scheingold, 1974).

A second wave of literature examining interest group use of the courts found that not all such litigants were necessarily "disadvantaged" in the sense that Cortner had described, but historically quite "advantaged" in the ways and means of majoritarian politics. They were politically conservative as well, and, until the victories of liberal groups stemming from the 1930s through the 1970s, enjoyed a protected status in public law. In general, conservative groups did not represent racial, ethnic, and religious minorities; political dissenters; or women who believed they were politically and legally disenfranchised. They represented the status quo, and liberal groups skilled in litigation had succeeded in changing the scope and substance of constitutional law affecting the rights of individuals.

By the 1980s the social and political dynamics of the litigation process were very different than they were during the forty-year period that drew the attention of the first wave of scholarship on interest group use of the courts. This new environment was more ideologically plural and confrontational and no longer dominated by a single cause or by a small cadre of like-minded organizations (O'Connor & Epstein, 1983, pp. 479–489; Epstein, 1985; Ivers, 1992, pp. 243–268).

A third wave of literature sought to move beyond documenting and explaining the relationship between organized interests and the litigation process. In 1991 Gerald Rosenberg published *The Hollow Hope*, which challenged the very idea that the courts, without cooperation and enforcement from the political branches, were capable of bringing about social change through constitutional decisions. Beginning with Vose, scholars working in this area had *assumed* that a sweeping decision from the Supreme Court announcing a new rule of constitutional law would result in the social change desired by the parties bringing the lawsuits. Using racial desegregation, sex discrimination, abortion rights, environmental regulation, and criminal procedure as case studies, Rosenberg found that Congress, state legislatures, and other political bodies were much more effective in creating legal, and thus social, reform than the courts. Judicial decisions, noted Rosenberg, were not self-executing, and, citing *Roe v. Wade* (1973) as an example, often created a powerful opposition to a litigation-oriented reform movement. *The Hollow Hope* opened up a whole new debate on the efficacy of litigation as an instrument of reform, and one that continues, ten years after its publication, to occupy students of the subject (Rosenberg, 1991).

Shortly after *The Hollow Hope* appeared, Lee Epstein and Joe Kobylka published *The Supreme Court and Legal Change* (1992), which offered a different take on the power of organized interests to effect social change through the courts (Epstein & Kobylka, 1992). Using abortion and the death penalty as case studies, Epstein and Kobylka argued that the logic of law and the substance of legal argument ultimately determined the success or failure of a litigation campaign. External factors such as the political environment, the legal status quo, or the Court's ideological predisposition were fairly insignificant in explaining the success or failure of litigation. *The Supreme Court and Legal Change* challenged a different set of assumptions than *The Hollow Hope*, namely that judicial outcomes were less dependent on the attitudes of the justices and more influenced by legal argument than many scholars seemed to believe. Whether one was persuaded by these studies or not, they offered an important turn in the kinds of questions that scholars were asking about the politics of legal reform through litigation.

Other studies appeared around this time that focused more on the organizational dynamics of group participation in litigation and less on whether such lawsuits or the courts that decided them were "effective" tools of social change (although the assumption, again, is that they largely were). Numerous studies examining how individuals within groups interacted to decide tactical and strategic questions involved in bringing lawsuits found that organizations had far less control over the litigation environment than many scholars in the first and second waves of literature on the subject had assumed. Even for organizations with a clear long-term objective, the process of selecting cases and plaintiffs and developing tactics and strategies to carry out lawsuits was largely ad hoc in nature. How groups pursued their goals was heavily dependent on internal factors such as the personality forces within groups, congruence in leadership-membership goals, and how groups chose to respond to the events around them. Often, there was nothing "planned" about planned litigation. Moreover, as it turned out, many successful lawsuits that were described as part of a litigation campaign were more often a series of responses to new problems and issues generated by previous decisions or new laws and policies that required attention. In other words, there was no "campaign" in the sense that organizational leaders sat down and executed a carefully choreographed line of cases designed to achieve a clear goal (Tushnet, 1987; Ivers, 1995; Wasby, 1995).

Does the literature on interest group use of the courts offer a hospitable theoretical framework in which to place the study of the *Flood* case? Upon first glance, Flood's decision to challenge the reserve clause through litigation does share some fundamental characteristics with the cases studied in the aforementioned literature. Since *Federal Baseball* was decided in 1922, Congress had had almost fifty years to eliminate or modify professional baseball's exemption from the antitrust laws and failed to do so. The MLBPA had little or no interest in challenging the existing interpretation of the standard uniform contract, which the *major league owners, not an arbitrator or government board,* had interpreted to mean that players were "reserved" to a team into perpetuity. The only option that was left for Flood, or so it seemed, was to take his case to court and argue that no basis existed for baseball's exemption from antitrust law. And like many reform-minded cases that had come before, Flood faced an established body of legal precedent that was not favorable to his legal position. It is not unreasonable, then, to think of Flood as a classic "disadvantaged" litigant, in that the conventional channels of political access were closed tightly against his claim. Moreover, just like major constitutional decisions such as *Brown v. Board of Education* (1954) (striking down segregated schools) and *Engel v. Vitale* (1962) (banning state-mandated school prayer) affected all persons similarly situated to the litigants who actually brought the cases, the outcome in *Flood v. Kuhn* stood to affect *all* major league ballplayers. Depending on the scope of the Court's decision, players under contract currently assigned in a team's minor league system also stood to be affected.

But this is where the similarities between the *Flood* case and the examples mentioned above end. First, although Flood claimed in his letter to Bowie Kuhn that the reserve clause forced him to work in involuntary servitude, and would later claim in his court papers that the reserve clause violated the Thirteenth Amendment, *Flood v. Kuhn* went to the Court as a case about statutory construction. That is, the questions before the Court were if and how federal antitrust laws applied to baseball, not whether Flood's constitutional rights were being violated. The Court never even considered the Thirteenth Amendment claim, although Flood's attorneys did address it in their client's brief. In fact, no constitutional question was ever addressed by the Court in *Flood.* In the end, the Court affirmed *Toolson* and *Federal Baseball* for no other reason than that *Toolson* had affirmed *Federal Baseball,* which had established this uninterrupted "aberration" fifty years before. Second, Flood decided to challenge the reserve clause on his own and sought out the support of the MLBPA only after Marvin Miller agreed to raise the issue before the union. The MLBPA, as a union representing only one contour of the labor market, is not even similar to the business and governmental litigants studied by Richard Cortner during the first wave of studies on political jurisprudence. All ballplayers under contract to major league franchises were affected by the *Flood* case, but no other professional athletes were. Curt Flood's grievance, then, did not raise a constitutional question and did not attract the support of a classic public-interest law litigant. It did not affect a large class of similarly situated litigants and did not transform constitutional discourse or alter the meaning of the Constitution.

ALTERNATIVES TO THE PUBLIC-INTEREST LAW MODEL: CIVIL LITIGATION AND LEGAL MOBILIZATION

In *The Politics of Rights,* Stuart Scheingold pointed out that litigation can serve as a valuable mechanism in mobilizing people to stand up for their rights and find appropriate remedies for their grievances outside the courtroom. Almost twenty years later, Michael McCann described this view as "law as a catalyst," or the idea that judicial outcomes, whether successful or not, can provide people with the language to assess the nature of their problems and identify other institutions as responsible for solving them. In McCann's words, "legal rights discourse . . . provide[s] reform activists a compelling normative language for identifying, interpreting, and challenging the unjust logic [of a legal position]." Litigation, moreover, can be used "as a tactical resource to raise expectations" among aggrieved parties that legal reform is, in fact, possible (McCann, 1994, p. 48).

McCann also articulated another view of legal mobilization, which suggests that the mere *threat* of a lawsuit may compel concessions from a reluctant or hostile defendant, whether an individual or institution. McCann has described this view as "law as a club." It is important to note here that McCann does not use the word "club" in the associational sense, but as a metaphor for assault. A defendant might not want the publicity that comes with a very public lawsuit, even if the matter involves a civil law question. While a defendant might be able to prevail on the legal merits of a case, a calculation must be made of whether the nonlegal costs—negative public opinion, bad publicity, and so on—outweigh the advantages of a legal victory (McCann, 1994, pp. 138–179). Here, McCann's conceptualization of law as a club is similar to the argument that Karen O'Connor advanced in her 1980 analysis of women's rights organizations pursuing constitutional reform through litigation. Litigation might or might not succeed from a won-lost perspective, but it could be extraordinarily helpful in generating favorable publicity (O'Connor, 1980).

The confluence between McCann's observations about the utility of law as club in civil litigation and O'Connor's point about the power of litigation to generate positive publicity in a constitutional case demonstrates that approaches to understanding the politics of legal mobilization can and should be understood as complementary rather than at odds with one another. The *Flood* case is an effective illustration of "law as a catalyst" and "law as a club." Although Flood did not win his case, the three-year legal battle with major league baseball raised an awareness among ballplayers, sportswriters, union organizers, labor relations experts, and the owners over the reserve clause that did not exist before he decided not to accept his trade to the Phillies. As Marvin Miller later said, most of the players did not really care about Flood's case while it was in the courts, and not a single active player testified on his behalf during the trial phase of his lawsuit. Moreover, only a handful of retired players, with former Detroit Tigers great Hank Greenberg, baseball's first major Jewish star, and Jackie Robinson, who broke the color barrier with the Brooklyn Dodgers in 1947, the only true notables, testified on Flood's behalf. In 1970 the writers who covered baseball almost uniformly favored the owners' position and largely cooperated with the owners in portraying Flood in articles and profiles as an "ingrate" determined to undermine the sport (Miller, 1991, pp. 196–200). One only need look to the media coverage of the MLBPA's decision not to have ballplayers sign their contracts during the

1968–69 off-season until pension issues were settled for an idea of where the allegiances of writers were in those days (Heylar, 1994).

After the *Flood* case was decided and Curt Flood was out of baseball, Andy Messersmith and Dave McNally, under the direction of Marvin Miller and other labor lawyers for the MLBPA, brought their grievances over the perpetual reserve clause to the NLRB. The owners' representative in the collective bargaining process with the MLBPA, the Players Relations Committee (PRC), hired many of the same lawyers who represented the owners in the *Flood* case. For years they had placed the resolution of the reserve clause issue in a no-man's land between Congress and the courts, with each branch claiming it was the other's responsibility to resolve the issue. Since neither would, baseball continued to sit pretty. But in December 1975, almost six years to the day after Curt Flood had written his letter to Bowie Kuhn, the owners' luck came to an end. The NLRB ruled that nothing in the uniform player's contract permitted the team to hold a player perpetually in reserve and nothing in the contract prevented a player from negotiating with other teams after the expiration of the one-year contract (Lowenfish, 1990, pp. 207–221).

By the time the Court decided the *Flood* case, the MLBPA had become more assertive and its leadership more skilled in dealing with the owners. And by all accounts the players would have succeeded in establishing some sort of player mobility at some point by going through the collective bargaining process rather than through the courts. But all major accounts of baseball's labor struggles during this period agree that the *Flood* case served as the legal catalyst for the reform that came through the NLRB. Although a direct line cannot be drawn between the *Flood* case and the establishment of free agency in major league baseball—because the NLRB decision dealt only with the reserve clause—the rights consciousness established by the lawsuit is unmistakable. Moreover, *Flood v. Kuhn* also offers an interesting example of litigation as an exercise in reform politics, and one that defies simple categorization.

Today, major league baseball players earn the highest average salaries, $2,340,000 per season, of any professional athletes competing in team sports in the United States.[7] When Alex Rodriguez, a shortstop for the American League's Texas Rangers, signed a contract in May 2001 that would pay him a record total of $252 million over the next ten years—or the equivalent of $155,555.56 per game of each season's 162-game schedule—it is doubtful that Curt Flood was anywhere in the back of his mind. But had Curt Flood decided to report to the Philadelphia Phillies rather than challenge the power structure of major league baseball, Rodriguez may well never have had the chance to command this salary.

NOTES

1. For some of the earliest and most definitive commentary on the scope of the Sherman Act, see Neville, J. (1947) Baseball and the antitrust laws. *Fordham Law Review, 16,* p. 208; Eckler, J. (1949) Baseball—Sport or commerce? *University of Chicago Law Review, 17,* p. 56; Comment, Monopoly in manpower: Organized baseball meets the antitrust laws. (1953). *Yale Law Journal, 62,* p. 576.

2. The Court has also cited *Peto v. Madison Square Garden Corp.,* 1958 Trade Cases, 69, 106 (SDNY 1958), a lower federal court decision, as authoritative on the question of whether professional hockey is interstate commerce.

3. In 1971 Curt Flood signed a $110,000 one-year contract with the Washington Senators, which acquired his rights from the Philadelphia Phillies as part of a four-player trade after the 1970 season. Flood played thirteen games, hit only .200 in thirty-five at-bats, and decided to retire rather than diminish the legacy of his great playing career. In 1972 the Senators moved to Arlington, Texas, and became the Texas Rangers.

4. Vose also contributed several major articles shortly before *Caucasians Only* was published that set out many of the conceptual arguments developed more fully in his book. See, for example, The National Consumer's League and the Brandeis Brief, (1957), *Midwest Journal of Political Science 1,* pp. 267–290; and Litigation as a Form of Pressure Group Activity, (1958), *Annals of the American Academy of Political Science, 319,* pp. 20–31.

5. This idea was first introduced by Richard Cortner, Strategy and Tactics of Litigants in Constitutional Cases (1968) *Journal of Public Law, 17,* pp. 287–307.

6. The first wave of literature on interest group use of the courts is extensive. See, for example, Manwaring, 1962; Meltsner, 1973; Lawyers for Social Change. (1976). *Stanford Law Review, 28,* pp. 207–261; Kluger, 1977; O'Connor, 1980.

7. Salary figures are taken from the official website of Major League Baseball: http://mlb.mlb.com/NASApp/mlb/mlb/news/mlb_labor_salaries.jsp.

REFERENCES

Comment. (1953). Monopoly in manpower: Organized baseball meets the antitrust laws. *Yale Law Journal, 62,* 576.

Cortner, R. (1968). Strategy and tactics of litigants in constitutional cases. *Journal of Public Law, 17,* 287–307.

Eckler, J. (1949). Baseball—Sport or commerce? *University of Chicago Law Review, 17.*

Epstein, L. (1985). *Conservatives in court.* Knoxville, TN: University of Tennessee Press.

Epstein, L., & Kobylka, J. F. (1992). *The Supreme Court and legal change: Abortion and the death penalty.* Chapel Hill, NC: University of North Carolina Press.

Gildea, W. (1971, February). Curt Flood—Baseball's angry rebel. *Baseball Digest, 30,* 55–58.

Goldstein, W. (1989). *Playing for keeps: A history of early baseball.* Ithaca, NY: Cornell University Press.

Heylar, J. (1994). *Lords of the realm.* New York: Villard Books.

Ivers, G. (1992) Religious organizations as constitutional litigants. *Polity, 25,* 243–268.

Ivers, G. (1995). *To build a wall: American Jews and the separation of church and state.* Charlottesville, VA: University Press of Virginia.

Kluger, R. (1977). *Simple justice.* New York: Vintage Books.

Lowenfish, L. (1990). *The imperfect diamond: A history of baseball's labor wars.* New York: Da Capo Press.

Manwaring, D. (1962). *Render unto Caesar.* Chicago: University of Chicago Press.

McCann, M. W. (1994). *Rights at work: Pay equity reform and the politics of legal mobilization.* (1994). Chicago: University of Chicago Press.

Meltsner, M. (1973). *Cruel and unusual: The Supreme Court and capital punishment.* New York: Random House.

Miller, M. (1991). *A whole different ballgame.* New York: Simon and Schuster.

Neville, J. (1947). Baseball and the antitrust laws. *Fordham Law Review, 16.*

O'Connor, K. (1980). *Women's organizations use of the courts.* Lexington, MA: Lexington Books.

O'Connor, K. & Epstein, L. (1983). The rise of conservative interest group litigation. *Journal of Politics, 45,* 479–489.

Rabin, R. L. (1976). Lawyers for social change: Perspectives on public interest law. *Stanford Law Review, 28,* 207–261.

Rosenberg, G. N. (1991). *The hollow hope: Can courts bring about social change?* Chicago: University of Chicago Press.

Scheingold, S. A. (1974). *The politics of rights: Lawyers, public policy and political change.* New Haven, CT: Yale University Press.

Sunstein, C. (1993). *The partial constitution.* Cambridge, MA: Harvard University Press.

Tushnet, M. V. (1987). *The NAACP's legal strategy against segregated education, 1925–1950.* Chapel Hill, NC: University of North Carolina Press.

Vose, C. E. (1959). *Caucasians only.* Berkeley, CA: University of California Press.

Vose, C. E. (1958). Litigation as a form of pressure group activity. *Annals of the American Academy of Political Science, 319,* 20–31.

Vose, C. E. (1957). The National Consumer's League and the Brandeis brief. *Midwest Journal of Political Science, 1,* 267–290.

Wasby, S. L. (1995). *Race relations litigation in an age of complexity.* Charlottesville, VA: University Press of Virginia.

Political Questions and the Power of Impeachment

Nixon v. United States (1993)

DAVID YALOF

As Justice Felix Frankfurter once explained, "It is hostile to a democratic system to involve the judiciary in the politics of the people." Under the separation of powers, the Supreme Court can only resolve conflicts over the meaning of the law. Decisions about the direction of public policy are entrusted to elected officials. So, even though the Supreme Court addresses questions of great political consequence, it remains a judicial body, resolving strictly legal questions. A good illustration of this limit on the Court's power occurred when a federal judge, convicted of federal law violations, challenged the Senate's procedures for removing him from office. Because the Constitution entrusted the impeachment power to the Congress, the justices concluded that they had no authority to intervene.

On November 1, 1989, the full U.S. Senate convened as a court of impeachment for only the fourteenth time in its 201-year history. A mere two days later the Senate's president pro tempore, Sen. Robert Byrd (D-WV), read the Senate's verdict aloud to a packed legislative chamber:

> The Senate having tried Walter L. Nixon, Jr., U.S. District judge for the Southern District of Mississippi, upon three articles of impeachment exhibited against him by the House of Representatives, and two-thirds of the Senators present having found him guilty of the charges contained in articles I and II of the articles of impeachment, it is therefore, ordered and adjudged that the said Walter L. Nixon, Jr., be, and is hereby removed from office.

In a case that had featured a confusing morass of conflicting testimony from numerous individuals, the full Senate chose to hear testimony from only one witness: Judge Nixon himself. The ninety-seven Senators present had conducted just a single day of information gathering, and they had deliberated in closed session about the facts of the case for less than six hours. Still, the Senate had seen fit to exercise its power to remove Nixon from the judicial office he had occupied for over two decades. In search of vindication, Nixon was determined to challenge the process by which the Senate had so quickly and "summarily" ejected him from the federal bench. Yet a critical obstacle loomed in his path: even if Nixon's lawyers were able to mount a persuasive attack on the Senate's abbreviated proceedings for removal, would the federal courts—and in particular the U.S. Supreme Court—dare to intervene?

The Wiley Fairchild Affair

Walter L. Nixon grew up a part of the white political establishment that was entrenched in power in southern Mississippi for much of the early-to-mid twentieth century. Born in 1928, he was the son of a well-known politician who had served on the influential board of supervisors in Harrison County from 1923 to 1929. Like his father, Walter Nixon spent his entire life in Biloxi, Mississippi, save for time spent attending college and law school in Louisiana, and then a brief stint at the Marion Military Institute in Alabama.

Nixon was admitted to the Mississippi bar in 1952 and eventually built his own lucrative law practice handling personal injury cases in the area. Although his own bid for a seat on the board of supervisors ended in failure, Nixon's continued involvement in the local Democratic party placed him in good stead with Mississippi's political elite throughout the 1950s and early 1960s (Volcansek, 1993, p. 121). In fact, Nixon became a favorite of one of his father's long-standing friends, Senator James O. Eastland (D-MS), and in 1966 Eastland and fellow Mississippi senator John Stennis (D-MS) helped secure a judicial appointment for Nixon from President Lyndon Johnson (Peck, 1993, p. 57). On July 26, 1968, Walter Nixon officially took his seat as only the third federal judge to preside in the newly formed Federal District of Southern Mississippi.

Like many federal judges who come to the bench directly from private practice, Nixon was forced to take a substantial pay cut in his new position. From the more than $200,000 in annual earnings he had reaped in the late 1960s, Nixon's salary as a federal judge dropped to barely a quarter of that figure for most of the 1970s (Volcansek, 1993, p. 121). Saddled with hefty child support payments from his first marriage, Nixon eventually sought means of supplementing his limited judicial income. By Nixon's own admission, in 1979 or 1980 he asked a friend, Carroll Ingram, to make overtures on his behalf to Wiley Fairchild, the head of a multimillion-dollar oil and gas empire in Mississippi, about possible investments. Fairchild eventually agreed to sell three mineral properties with oil wells to Judge Nixon for $9,500; the financial deal was consummated on February 25, 1981. Prosecutors would later refer to the transaction as a "sweetheart deal" bestowed on an influential judge, but in comparison to the $250 per acre Fairchild originally paid for the three leases, he actually reaped some profit from the deal. As for Nixon, while one of the three wells was not "particularly good," the other two performed quite well, netting him royalties in excess of $62,000 in subsequent years.

Nixon's financial dealings with Fairchild provided the backdrop for events that led to the judge's arrest and subsequent conviction. In August of 1981 the district attorney of Forrest County, Mississippi, was Paul "Bud" Holmes, a colorful local figure who had amassed some regional fame as the agent of NFL superstar Walter Payton. Wiley Fairchild's frustration with the D.A. began when Holmes brought an indictment against the financial magnate's son, Drew Fairchild, for conspiring to smuggle drugs by plane into Hattiesburg, Mississippi. The case against Drew Fairchild dragged on for more than a year; Wiley Fairchild eventually complained to Nixon about the district attorney's handling of the case during a meeting between the two men at Fairchild's office. Later accounts of their discussion differ dramatically. Fairchild told Carroll Ingram that he explicitly requested that Judge Nixon intervene with Holmes concerning his son's case; Nixon disagreed with that version of events, although he conceded that the topic of Fairchild's prosecution did come up. Later that day Nixon traveled to Holmes's farm for a visit that Nixon claimed had already been scheduled before his meeting with Fairchild. While there, Judge Nixon allegedly broached the subject of "Holmes's black-mailing Fairchild" with the D.A. but declined Holmes's offer to explain the case to him. Apparently, Holmes then made a telephone call to Wiley Fairchild out of Nixon's immediate earshot in which he promised to bring an end to the case against Fairchild's son; according to Fairchild, Nixon got on the phone with him that same night and told him: "I've talked to [Holmes] and things are going to be all right." The case against Drew Fairchild was placed on inactive status on December 23, 1982.[1]

Based on a tip from a disgruntled employee of Fairchild's, the FBI officially commenced its investigation into the Nixon-Holmes-Fairchild affair in early 1984. Had Judge Nixon improperly tampered with the prosecution of Drew Fairchild as a payback for his father's financial generosity? On July 18, 1984, Nixon voluntarily appeared before a special grand jury and testified both that (1) Holmes had never discussed the Drew Fairchild case with Nixon; and (2) he himself had never discussed Drew Fairchild's case with any official involved in its prosecution. Nixon's testimony directly conflicted with that offered by Holmes and Fairchild, each of whom suggested that Nixon had actively interfered with the prosecution on Fairchild's behalf.

Over a year later, on August 29, 1985, Judge Nixon was indicted on one count of receiving an unlawful gratuity from Fairchild and two counts of perjuring himself before the special federal grand jury. Nixon's fate at his own trial in January of 1986 depended entirely on how the jury would choose to assess the competing accounts of Nixon, Fairchild, and Holmes. (The latter two had signed plea agreements with the government in advance of the trial). Holmes's colorful reputation made him a popular but controversial witness; meanwhile Fairchild, by then seventy-three years old, was sometimes "fuzzy in his recollection of dates" (Volcansek, 1993, p. 131). Nevertheless, on February 9, 1986, the jury returned its verdict: Nixon was acquitted on the illegal gratuity charge but convicted on the two perjury charges. Ironically, Judge Nixon had been found guilty of lying about a series of events that—at least in the eyes of that same jury—did not amount to acceptance of an illegal gratuity under the law.[2]

A Decisive Judgment in the House of Representatives

On March 23, 1988, Nixon reported to Eglin Air Force Base in Valaparaiso, Florida, to begin serving his two concurrent five-year sentences. From prison, Nixon's energies turned to how he might keep his judicial office. In 1982 he had been selected chief judge of the district by his judicial colleagues. Senator Thad Cochran (R-MS) and Representative Trent Lott (R-MS) had even offered to secure for him a nomination to the United States Court of Appeals for the Fifth Circuit back in 1982. Now a convicted felon, Nixon refused to resign his office and continued to collect his judicial salary of $89,500 per year. But given his criminal record, could his hold on judicial office really withstand the threat of impeachment and removal that was sure to follow?

Recent history offered Nixon little cause for optimism. Before his conviction in 1986, only one other federal judge in history had ever been convicted of a crime: Federal District judge Harry E. Claiborne of Nevada. Two years after Claiborne was convicted of income tax evasion in 1984, the Senate removed him from office. Meanwhile, four other federal judges from the nineteenth and early twentieth centuries (John Pickering, West Humphreys, Robert Archibald, and Halsted Ritter) had been convicted by the Senate and removed from office even though none of them had been previously convicted of a crime. And yet another federal judge, Alcee L. Hastings of Florida, was currently fighting impeachment efforts in the House even though he too had been acquitted of all criminal charges in a federal criminal trial held in 1983. Despite Hastings's favorable verdict, a federal judicial panel was so convinced that he had produced false documents to avoid conviction that it still recommended impeachment proceedings be commenced against him in 1987.

Once all of Nixon's appeals in his criminal case had been exhausted, the Fifth Circuit Judicial Council promptly certified that his conviction constituted potential grounds for impeachment. That certification was ratified by the U.S. Judicial Conference and forwarded to the House of Representatives on March 15, 1988. To many in the House of Representatives, Nixon's removal from office seemed almost a foregone conclusion; after all, Nixon was seeking to become the first jurist in American history to return to the bench after being convicted of a felony. Rep. James Sensenbrenner (R-WI) directly raised the question on the minds of so many of his colleagues: "What do you think the public's respect for the Federal judiciary is when a federal judge is incarcerated?" (Volcansek, 1993, p. 146). After two days of hearings in June and several more in July, a House subcommittee voted unanimously on July 12, 1988, to impeach Nixon on three separate articles: the first two restated the counts of perjury for which he had been convicted in his earlier trial, while a third alleged that Nixon's actions as a whole had "undermined confidence in the judiciary." After the full House Judiciary Committee approved the same three articles by a 34–0 vote the following spring, the House took up Nixon's case on May 10, 1989, and approved the impeachment resolution by a 417–0 vote.

Trial by Committee in the United States Senate

When the House managers appointed to prosecute the case transmitted Nixon's three articles of impeachment to the Senate for its consideration on May 11, 1989, the full Senate immediately passed Resolution 128, establishing an evidentiary committee to receive testimony and issue findings. In authorizing such a committee, the Senate was acting under authority of Rule XI of the *Rules of Procedure and Practice in the Senate when Sitting on Impeachment Trials,* which gave the Senate the option to hear witnesses in committee, with or without the defendant's consent. Passed by that body in 1935, the rule was not invoked for the first time until 1986, when Judge Harry Claiborne's impeachment articles were delegated to just such a committee. From the perspective of the Senate leadership, the rule had clear advantages: all pending business of the institution no longer had to be halted while all 100 senators sat through lengthy testimony. Yet the Senate had specifically refused to exercise Rule XI when trying the impeachment of Judge Halsted Ritter in 1936. At least one scholar has speculated that the Senate's refusal to do so was "due to doubts about its constitutionality." (Auslander, 1992, p. 68). But Judge Claiborne's objection to the committee format had made little headway when he first raised it in 1986.

Just a few weeks after Nixon's impeachment by the House, Alcee Hastings was busy with a lawsuit of his own. In June 1989, weeks before his own impeachment proceedings in the United States Senate were scheduled to begin, Hastings had brought suit in a federal district court in Washington contending that the contemplated impeachment hearing conducted under Rule XI was procedurally flawed because of the extensive delegation to a committee. This, Hastings contended, denied him due process under the Fifth Amendment. Nixon intervened in support of Hastings's primary claim, but the lawsuit was dismissed by the district court on July 5 in a ruling that was affirmed by a U.S. Court of Appeals three months later. Because the Senate was sitting in these cases as a "constitutionally-designated court of impeachment," the appeals court believed that interests of comity and deference dictated that it not "interrupt proceedings" already under way (*Hastings v. U.S. Senate*, 887 F.2d 332 [1989]).

Thus in September of 1989 Walter L. Nixon became only the third judge in history to be tried initially before a Senate panel convened under Rule XI. Although Nixon's trial record was fully incorporated into the Senate record, ten witnesses testified before the panel. Nixon's attorneys argued that the testimony of Holmes and Fairchild had been secured by government intimidation: "Give us Judge Nixon, or you're going to get indicted or we're going after you. So [both men] cut deals" (Bushnell, 1992, p. 316). They also argued that Fairchild had formally recanted his trial testimony at least once before. Additionally, each of the five witnesses called by Nixon testified to the judge's reputation for truthfulness.

The Senate impeachment Trial Committee's final report (filed on October 16, 1989) noted that the panel had "received dramatically inconsistent testimony concerning the substance, date, and result of [the disputed] conversations." Yet when the full Senate then met to decide the case in early November, Nixon was the only witness who appeared again to answer questions from the full Senate. Most of the Senate's deliberations on November 1—the only day allotted for the body's public inquiry into the matter—were taken up with speeches by the House managers summarizing the accusations made against Judge Nixon, as well as arguments from Nixon's lawyers. On November 2 the Senate met for six hours and privately deliberated on Nixon's fate. The next day the Senate came back and voted on removal. Nixon was ultimately convicted on Article I (lying to the grand jury about his discussions with Holmes) by a vote of 89–8, and on Article II (lying to the grand jury about his discussions with officials in general) by a vote of 78–19. In each instance, the vote against Nixon far exceeded the two-thirds requirement for removal from office. On the third article alleging Nixon had "undermined confidence" in the judiciary, just fifty-seven of the ninety-seven senators present voted to convict, well short of the two-thirds necessary. This last vote provided little solace for Nixon, however. Since being sentenced to five years in prison three years earlier, the judge had collected $324,321 in salary. But now, after two decades on the federal bench, his judicial career appeared to be over.

A Frontal Assault on the "Political Question Doctrine"

Nixon and his lawyers planned to mount a direct constitutional challenge to the Senate procedures that had led to his removal from office. The target of their attention was, of course, Rule XI. In early 1990 Nixon went to federal court seeking a formal declaration that the Senate's vote on his impeachment charges was void by law. Nixon's lead attorney, David O. Stewart, offered one central claim on his client's behalf. Article I, Section 2, Clause 5 of the Constitution, which vests in the Senate "the sole power to try all Impeachments," requires the Senate to "try" impeachments on the floor of the Senate so that all senators can (if present) see the witnesses, hear their testimony, and effectively appraise their credibility. In Nixon's case only the Senate special panel had examined the evidence and been privy to the testimony of witnesses. And the eighty-five senators not on the Rule XI committee had disproportionately favored the prosecution; if the full Senate's vote had reflected the distribution of votes from those senators who had heard the evidence, he would have been acquitted of Article II as well, as just seven of twelve panel members (58 percent) had voted to convict Judge Nixon on that article.[3]

Nixon was essentially asking the federal courts to define the term "try" in the context of Senate impeachment proceedings. Yet in seeking to accomplish this end, he revived for discussion what had seemed like a moribund feature of the Court's separation of powers jurisprudence: the Political Question Doctrine. The federal courts have long assumed that there exist certain constitutional questions that are inherently "nonjusticiable"—that is, inappropriate for resolution by a court of law. Such *political questions* normally invite government institutions other than the courts to exercise the *final say*. The Supreme Court first formally recognized the Political Question Doctrine in the case of *Luther v. Borden* (48 U.S. 1 [1849]). Although a rebellion of disenfranchised citizens in Rhode Island had created the specter of two competing governments in the state, the Court refused to determine which of the two was in fact the "true government of the state." In *Luther* the Court concluded that a federal court could not independently decide the issue because pursuant to the "Guaranty Clause" in Article IV, Section 4 ("The United States shall guarantee to every state . . . a Republican form of government . . .), Congress alone possessed that power.

The more modern landmark Supreme Court decision establishing more formal standards for identifying political questions was *Baker v. Carr* (369 U.S. 186 [1962]). Denying that the political question doctrine encompassed all "political cases," the Supreme Court held in *Baker* that it possessed the authority to determine whether a state's legislative districting scheme violated the Fourteenth Amendment's Equal Protection Clause by diluting the votes of residents in more populous districts. According to the Court, a controversy is nonjusticiable—and thus a "political question"—only when there is "a textually demonstrable constitutional commitment of the issue to a coordinate political department, or a lack of judicially discoverable and manageable standards for resolving it."

Critics of *Baker* warned that the case might open the door to unprecedented new levels of judicial supervision over the other branches of government. After all, in determining whether or not a political question even exists, a court might feel compelled to interpret the text in question, if only to determine whether and to what extent the text was "textually committed." Would such "first-level" inquiries only invite a more searching analysis on the merits? Just once in the first thirty years following *Baker* had the Supreme Court actually invoked the Political Question Doctrine to hold an issue nonjusticiable. That case was *Gilligan v. Morgan* (413 U.S. 1 [1973]), in which the Court refused to evaluate the training of the Ohio National Guard for constitutional deficiencies. By the High Court's reasoning, Article I, Section 8, appeared on its face to authorize Congress alone to engage in such supervision. Even more telling, the Court held that it would be "difficult to conceive of an area of government activity in which the Courts have less competence" (*Gilligan*, p. 10). By 1990 *Gilligan* stood alone as a symbol of Supreme Court deference to "political questions" in the years since *Baker* was handed down.[4]

Thus the Political Question Doctrine of the modern era did not appear to pose an insurmountable obstacle to Nixon's lawsuit at the time it was filed. Certainly Senate impeachment procedures were unlike the procedures used to train an army. And Nixon's chief attorney, David O. Stewart, had an especially favorable precedent to cite for judicial intervention into congressional procedures: in 1969 the Court had held in *Powell v. McCormack* (395 U.S. 486) that the Political Question Doctrine did *not* bar the courts from reviewing the House's power under Article I, Section 5, to judge the qualification of its own members. In Adam Clayton Powell's case, the class of procedural rules that would have denied him a seat in the House of Representatives was outweighed by the Court's interest in safeguarding his liberty. As Stewart later recalled: "We felt that if *Powell* was still good law, we would win" (Stewart, 2003, interview by author).

During the initial stages of federal court review, Nixon's case fared little better than Hastings's lawsuit had the previous summer. On August 10, 1990, U.S. District judge Louis Oberdorfer granted the federal government's motion to dismiss Nixon's case as not justiciable. The district court distinguished *Powell v. McCormack* as a case in which a congressman had met all the qualifications for House service established by the Constitution itself; by contrast, Nixon's denial of a full-fledged hearing before the whole Senate resembled more a "procedural ruling" than a denial of his constitutional rights. Eleven months later, on July 9, 1991, the Court of Appeals unanimously affirmed Oberdorfer's ruling and dismissed Nixon's claim. This time, however, Nixon's attorneys could find a glimmer of hope in the court's pronouncements, as only one of the appellate panel's three judges, Stephen Williams, invoked the Political Question Doctrine to rule against their client. The panel's junior judge, A. Raymond Randolph, specifically declined to rely on what he termed a "somewhat amorphous" doctrine. And Judge Harry Edwards held that *Powell* directly controlled Nixon's claim because there was no "textually demonstrable commitment" of the issue to a coordinate branch; notwithstanding that fact, he also determined that the Senate did in fact "try" Nixon within the meaning of the Constitution.

Before the United States Supreme Court

Not one of the four judges to hear Nixon's case to that point had ruled in his favor. Yet if the Supreme Court granted a writ of certiorari to review the case, it could conceivably side with two of the three appellate court judges and discard the political question doctrine as a barrier to Nixon's claim. Of course the Court might then go on to decide the case against Nixon on the merits. But for a judge who had already been removed from office, there seemed little to lose in spurring the Court to reconsider such an "amorphous" doctrine.

On February 24, 1992, the Court granted Nixon's petition for certiorari. Stewart's brief for the petitioner borrowed from Judge Edwards's opinion in analogizing Nixon's case to *Powell;* the language of the Constitution, he wrote, unmistakably directs the Senate itself to conduct a judicial-type trial in impeachment cases. Going on to the merits of the case, Stewart offered that without forcing senators to take testimony, "impeachment becomes easy, conviction is politically expedient, judicial independence is sapped, and the Constitutional balance of powers is tilted forever" (Brief of Petitioner, 1992). Not surprisingly the Solicitor General's Office, filing a brief on behalf of the U.S. government, hung its legal hat squarely on the Political Question Doctrine. The Framers of the Constitution, the government argued, chose the Senate to handle political impeachments because they wanted the process to be independent of the Courts. "The framers concluded that only politically accountable representatives—rather than a life-tenured judiciary—should exercise authority to remove from office those federal officers who have violated the public trust" (Brief for the Respondents, 1992). As for the merits of Nixon's claim, the government's brief reminded the Court that committees commonly put together evidence to be used by the Senate.

Each of these contentions resurfaced at the oral arguments held before a packed Supreme Court chamber on October 14, 1992.[5] Facing an especially heated interrogation by the justices, Stewart was continuously asked to grapple with other scenarios that might require judicial review under his theory of the case. "Could an interpretation by this Court [of the 'high crimes and misdemeanors' clause] supercede that of the Senate?" asked Chief Justice William Rehnquist. "What if the Senate did not allow the accused official to face and confront the witnesses against him?" queried Justice Anthony Kennedy. Stewart offered that in each of those instances an impeachment would be reviewable by the Court—"the court has to face up to that." Answering questions about the definition of "trial," Stewart was again put on the defensive. Justices Sandra Day O'Connor and Antonin Scalia asked whether such an abbreviated trial was materially different from the Supreme Court's use of a special master to "try" facts in certain cases. And what if a senator wasn't present at an impeachment trial to hear testimony—could that senator still participate in the final vote if there had still been a quorum?

Arguing on behalf of the federal government, Solicitor General Kenneth Starr faced much lighter questioning from the bench. The justices allowed Starr to review the events of the full Senate trial, in which Nixon himself had been allowed to testify. In asserting that the text of the Constitution contemplates finality, Starr was careful to distinguish Nixon's case from *Powell.* Unlike in that earlier instance, the *Nixon* case "satisfies at a minimum . . . criteria laid down in *Baker v. Carr* . . . a textual commitment [exists]." Citing Judge Randolph's lower court opinion, he posited that "as a matter of constitutional interpretation there is no role for the Court to play with respect to what procedures should be employed."

Constantly the justices raised fears about a slippery slope during the hour-long argument. "If we say that 'trial' does have a [technical meaning], there are all sorts of imaginable things that 'trial' ordinarily entails," exclaimed Justice Scalia. "Are we going to be reviewing all of those things too?" Justice Kennedy raised an even more haunting possibility: that a president removed from office might leave the country at a standstill for months while he appealed his conviction through the courts. He suggested that the nation would be at "grave risk" under those circumstances. Stewart's rebuttal was straight-forward: The Court cannot "shrink from deciding the constitutional issue that would be presented." Normally the tenor of oral arguments provides little indication as to how the Court might eventually rule in a particular case. Yet few present in the courtroom that day thought the proceedings had gone well for the former judge seeking his old office back.

A Breath of New Life for a Much-Maligned Doctrine

Three months later, on January 13, 1993, the Court ruled unanimously against Nixon. Writing for six members of the Court, Chief Justice Rehnquist held that because the meaning of the word "try" has never been limited to the judicial trial context, the use of the word in this instance was not so sufficiently precise to yield a "workable standard of review." Echoing the concerns of several justices at the oral argument, the chief justice expressed the fear that judicial review of impeachment procedures would threaten the stability of both the executive and judicial branches, and thus lead to "political chaos." Finally, Rehnquist distinguished Nixon's case from *Powell,* because the constitutional language at issue in the 1969 case—vesting Congress with the power to judge the qualifications its own members—was explicitly limited by the specific definition of those qualifications in Article I. No such limiting constitutional provision applied to the language of the Impeachment Trial Clause.

Nixon and his lawyers found little consolation from the three justices who wrote separately. Justice David Souter agreed with the majority that the claim was nonjusticiable; he refused to join the chief justice's opinion only to register his disagreement with the majority's view of how the Political Question Doctrine might operate in other instances. For example, if the Senate's behavior threatened the integrity of the results, Souter suggested, a judicial response might well be in order. Justice Byron White (joined by Justice Harry Blackmun) outright disagreed with the majority's analysis of the text. The case was justiciable despite the Political Question Doctrine, he argued, because the word "try" presents no greater interpretive difficulty than any other vague constitutional standards. Still, Justices White and Blackmun sided with the government on the merits of Nixon's claim: the scope of Rule XI did not exceed the Senate's procedural discretion under the Constitution.

Nixon v. United States thus assumes its place in the annals of constitutional law as a symbol of the Court's occasional willingness to invoke the Political Question Doctrine to deny review. Seven justices in all breathed life back into the much-maligned doctrine as a limitation on judicial authority. Additionally, the case holds significant implications for the prospects of courts reviewing future impeachment challenges. (Gerhardt, 1996, p. 120). As scholar Michael Gerhardt has argued, because it seems unlikely that a Court would ever abdicate an entire area of constitutional law, and because extreme abuses of congressional power (i.e., using a "coin flip" to render impeachment judgments) remain unlikely, judicial review of impeachment is now practically limited to violations of explicit constitutional restraints only. (Gerhardt, 1996, pp. 124–138). Other challenges grounded in vague provisions such as the Fifth Amendment due process clause presumably stand little or no chance of succeeding. In the case of presidential impeachments, the Senate's desire for finality probably counsels against the use of special panels or procedural shortcuts that might be objectionable to the president; although *Nixon v. United States* may well provide a legal basis for defending such shortcuts, the Senate would be acting on an uncertain political basis if it chose to do so.

Afterword

Four years after being removed from the bench, Walter Nixon was able to mount one final comeback of his own. In the years immediately following his formal removal from the bench, a disbarred Nixon had been reduced to doing paralegal work in Lake Charles, Louisiana, to make up for his lost judicial pension. Then, in May of 1993, the Mississippi State Supreme Court ruled that Nixon could be readmitted to the state bar after passing the exam. The following autumn, Nixon (by then sixty-four years old) took and passed the Mississippi State bar examination. Aided by enthusiastic recommendation letters from dozens of lawyers, judges, and law professors in the state, Nixon was formally reinstated to the bar later that same year.

During the ensuing decade, the one-time federal judge took full advantage of this new lease on his professional life, successfully rebuilding his own legal practice in Biloxi, Mississippi. Yet the capstone of this modest, but remarkable comeback may have occurred on August 25, 2001, when the D'Iberville, Mississippi, city council voted unanimously to hire Nixon, seventy-two, to serve as its new city attorney. "I did my time, I was reinstated to the bar . . . and I am now licensed to represent any client," Nixon declared. "The City of D'Iberville is my client. . . . I hope to be deserving of the job" (Winter, 2001). By the summer of 2002, Nixon had grown comfortable with his new responsibilities as city attorney; in one case he forcefully appealed a decision by a chancery court judge that had awarded part of a parcel of land D'Iberville wanted to annex to a nearby locality. Although no longer a federal judge presiding over important civil and criminal trials in his district, Nixon was finally back where he felt most comfortable—in the courtroom.

NOTES

1. Interestingly, Drew Fairchild's drug smuggling case was reactivated a few months later when, on January 26, 1983, the pilot of the plane that had flown the illegal drugs into Mississippi was extradited from Florida. Although the pilot skipped out of Mississippi again while on bond, as late as January 1, 1984, Drew Fairchild's case still remained "on active docket, waiting to be sentenced" (Volcansek, 1993, p. 125).

2. Over a decade later President Bill Clinton would find himself in the throes of a similar legal contradiction. On December 19, 1998, the House of Representatives approved two articles of impeachment against Clinton: one article charged the president with obstruction of justice in attempting to hide a sexual relationship he had maintained with White House intern Monica Lewinsky; a second article charged him with perjuring

himself in grand jury testimony provided four months earlier, when he had testified that he had never had sex of any kind with Lewinsky. To meet the legal definition of perjury, a simple act of making a false statement under oath does not suffice; rather, the statement must be *deliberately false,* and it must be *material* (in other words, not harmless or inconsequential) to some issue in the proceeding or context in which it was made.

Because a majority of the House of Representatives indicated that there was sufficient evidence to approve both of the above articles, President Clinton stood trial for impeachment before the United States Senate in February of 1999. Yet at no time did the president's accusers claim that his relationship with Lewinsky, if proven true, would itself constitute illegal or criminal conduct. Thus the president was essentially accused of hiding certain activities and lying before a grand jury about certain activities that—while perhaps unethical—were not in and of themselves illegal. Unlike Judge Nixon, President Clinton was ultimately acquitted by the United States Senate on both articles, and thus was not removed from office.

3. In fact, if all the votes in the Claiborne, Hastings, and Nixon impeachments are cumulated, Rule XI committee members voted to convict at a 53 percent rate, well short of the necessary two-thirds, while nonmembers voted to convict at a 71 percent rate. ("Committee Impeachment Trials," 1991, pp. 170–172).

4. Only four justices were willing to invoke the Political Question Doctrine in *Goldwater v. Carter* (444 U.S. 996 [1979]). President Jimmy Carter's highly controversial decision to unilaterally terminate a mutual defense treaty with Taiwan—taken to improve relations with the People's Republic of China—had instigated several senators to file suit on the theory that the Senate's constitutional power to approve and reject treaties had been circumvented. Although a majority of the Court did in fact defer to presidential power in that instance, only a plurality agreed that the abrogation of treaties represented a "nonjusticiable political question." Justice Powell concurred in the plurality's judgment on the theory that the controversy was not ripe, but he expressly disagreed with its invocation of the Political Question Doctrine.

5. All quotes from oral arguments found in this section were reconstructed by the author from actual tapes of the hearing in *Nixon v. United States* itself, archived on the *Oyez Project* Supreme Court multimedia database sponsored by Northwestern University (http://www.oyez.org/oyez/frontpage).

REFERENCES

Auslander, R. (1992). Note: Impeaching the Senate's use of trial committees. *New York University Law Review, 67,* 68–107.

Brief of Petitioner, *Nixon v. United States.* (1992). 91–740, filed in the United States Supreme Court, April 24, 1992.

Brief for the Respondents and Amicus Curiae United States Senate. (1992). 91–740, filed in the United States Supreme Court, June 10, 1992.

Bushnell, E. (1992). *Crimes, follies, and misfortunes: The federal impeachment trials.* Urbana, IL: University of Illinois Press.

Gerhardt, M. (1996). *The federal impeachment process: A constitutional and historical analysis.* Princeton, NJ: Princeton University Press.

Holleman, B. (2003, January 6). Telephone interview by author.

Luchsinger, D. (1991). Committee impeachment trials: The best solution? *The George-town Law Journal, 80,* 163–190.

Oral arguments from *Nixon v. United States* (October 14, 1992), found in the *Oyez Project* web site, http://www.oyez.org/oyez/frontpage.

Peck, R. (1993, February). Jurist before the bench: Challenging impeachment procedures for federal judges. *American Bar Association Journal,* 56–60.

Stewart, D. (2003, January 6). Telephone interview by author.

Volcansek, M. (1993). *Judicial impeachment: None called for justice.* Urbana, IL: University of Illinois Press.

Winter, R. (2001, August 26). Nixon proud of D'Iberville attorney post. *Biloxi Sun-Herald,* p. A2.

Constitutional Law as Hardball Politics

Bush v. Gore (2000)

HOWARD GILLMAN

The presidential election in November of 2000 was too close to call. The vote in Florida turned out to be crucial to determining the winner of the electoral college, and the popular vote in that state separated Democrat Al Gore and Republican George Bush by only a handful of votes. Not surprisingly, controversy immediately erupted over whether and how ballots were to be counted, and the opposing candidates took to the courts, seeking support for their interpretations of federal and state election laws. The conflict sped to the Supreme Court, where, depending on one's point of view, the case either allowed the justices to address important constitutional questions crying out for judicial resolution or marked an unprecedented venture by the Court to inject itself into the murky waters of electoral politics to determine the outcome of a presidential election.

None are more conscious of the vital limits on judicial authority than are the members of this Court, and none stand more in admiration of the Constitution's design to leave the selection of the President to the people, through their legislatures, and to the political sphere. When contending parties invoke the process of the courts, however, it becomes our unsought responsibility to resolve the federal and constitutional issues the judicial system has been forced to confront.

—From the per curiam opinion in Bush v. Gore *(2000)*

Everyone who lived through the 2000 presidential election dispute knew that they had witnessed an unprecedented and even momentous exercise of judicial power. Even at a time when the country had come to expect the Supreme Court to have something to say about almost every issue of public controversy, there was a consensus among scholars and political commentators during the early stages of the conflict that the justices had no legitimate role to play in the resolution of this dispute. It is not an overstatement to report that many were stunned when the five most conservative justices, over the persistent objections of their more moderate colleagues, not only became involved but went out of their way to issue a decision that handed the presidency to the conservative presidential candidate.

It is possible to analyze the case for what it says about the meaning of the constitutional provisions that were discussed in the decision. We could take seriously the question of how the equal protection clause regulates the counting of ballots, or whether Article II requires federal judges carefully to review how state judges interpret state statutes regarding the selection of presidential electors. It may also be worthwhile to ask what the decision says about the modern Political Questions Doctrine. But to subject *Bush v. Gore* (531 U.S. 98 [2000]) to a traditional legal-doctrinal analysis would be to miss what was most important about the decision, which was that it was a rare example of a case in which the justices seemed determined to reach an outcome without a sincere regard for the constitutional policy being announced in the case.

In normal circumstances the point of judicial review by the U.S. Supreme Court is to use the opportunity presented by a case to elaborate a constitutional policy that reflects their best understanding of the nature of our constitutional system. Of course, there is a political dimension to this process, in the sense that there are always competing views of the Constitution that more or less correspond to broad ideological debates in the political system. Political scientists sometimes refer to this as the "attitudinal model" of Supreme Court politics as a way of emphasizing the relationship between the justices' views of the Constitution and their more general political attitudes.[1] This is why we can recognize differences between John Marshall's Federalist vision and Roger Taney's Jacksonian vision, as well as between modern liberal and conservative understandings.

In *Bush v. Gore,* however, analysts will be hard pressed to link what the majority said to any constitutional view expressed by the same justices in other cases. The five most conservative justices were not known for their sympathy for civil rights claims, but in this case they associated themselves with an unprecedented and activist view of the protections of the equal protection clause. In other cases these same justices had developed a jurisprudence designed to force the federal government to show more deference to state governments; however, in this case they articulated a brand new understanding of Article II as a basis for second-guessing a state court's interpretation of state law and intruding into a sphere of decision making (the appointment of presidential electors) that had been reserved for states since the beginning of the Republic.

If there is a pattern to be found in the decisions of the conservatives in the election 2000 cases, it is to be found, not in their decisions in other cases, but by examining the practical consequences of their decisions for the outcome of this dispute. As we will see, these justices consistently adopted a view of the law that prevented any sort of ballot recounts that might jeopardize their favored candidate's claim to the presidency.

Why would these justices be so eager to deviate from the standard fare of good-faith constitutional interpretation and engage in something that looked more like result-oriented decision making? Some have argued that the justices were merely trying to perform a public service by efficiently ending a stubbornly persistent political crisis. Others have emphasized that, by the fall of 2000, the nine justices had settled into an enduring pattern of opposing coalitions. There had not been a new addition to the Court for seven years; in fact, it had been more than a century and a half since the same group of nine justices worked together for as long. The three justices with the most conservative voting record were Chief Justice William Rehnquist (appointed first by President Richard Nixon and again by Ronald Reagan for the chief justiceship) and Justices Antonin Scalia (Reagan) and Clarence Thomas (George H. W. Bush). Their allies on many constitutional disputes were the slightly less conservative Justices Sandra Day O'Connor (Reagan) and Anthony Kennedy (Reagan). A group of four justices, representing both political parties, had more moderate voting records: John Paul Stevens (Gerald Ford), David Souter (Bush), Ruth Bader Ginsburg (Bill Clinton), and Stephen Breyer (Clinton). Given the age and health of the some of the justices, it was widely assumed during the election that the next president would have a number of appointments; moreover, because the Senate was equally divided between Republicans and Democrats, the party affiliation of the vice president (as presiding officer of the Senate) would also determine which party controlled the institution that is responsible for confirming Supreme Court appointments.[2] Given how often these justices divided 5–4 on important constitutional matters, there was every reason to believe that these new appointments would determine which ideological wing on the Court would control constitutional policymaking for the foreseeable future—perhaps for decades. Thus, not only was there a lot at stake for the two presidential candidates; there was also a lot at stake for the justices themselves.

The 2000 Presidential Election Dispute

It has been 124 years since the country woke up the day after a presidential election without knowing who was president-elect. The two major-party candidates in the year 2000, Democratic vice president Al Gore and Republican Texas governor George W. Bush, were each painstakingly close to the 270 Electoral College votes needed to win the presidency, but it was mathematically impossible for either to get a majority until Florida's twenty-five electoral votes were decided. And there were problems.

First, the result in that state was astonishingly close. Almost six million votes were cast in Florida, and initial tallies indicated that Governor Bush led Vice President Gore by fewer than 1,800 votes, or around .03 percent of the total. Under state law, whenever results were this close, counties were required to run their ballots through the vote-counting machines one more time. These mandatory recounts further eroded Bush's lead; within a few days the formal tally indicated that Bush was ahead of Gore by just 229 votes. But that wasn't all. In a number of heavily Democratic counties, the machines that scanned the ballots failed to find a vote for president on thousands and thousands of ballots. For example, in Broward County there were almost 7,000 ballots in which the vote-counting machines detected no vote for president. In Palm Beach County machines failed to find a presidential vote in more than 10,000 ballots. Among election professionals ballots such as these were referred to as "undervote" ballots, and it was not unreasonable to assume that some of these "no vote" determinations were caused by a failure of the machines to detect the actual preference of the voter.[3] It was unacceptable to the Gore campaign that tens of thousands of discernible votes may have been cast but were nevertheless undetected by machines. And so, two days after the election, the vice president, following a provision of Florida's election law, formally requested a manual review of these undervote ballots in four heavily Democratic counties as a way of "recovering" votes that would otherwise remain unrecorded.

At the heart of the postelection battle in Florida was the question of whether these manual inspections of undervote ballots—these "recounts"—would be allowed to proceed. Bush supporters had a number of arguments for why they should not, and Gore supporters thought they had answers for every complaint. Bush supporters argued that the ballots had already been counted once on election night and then again after the mandatory machine recount; Gore supporters responded that the unreliable machines never actually counted these "undervote" ballots even once. Bush's advocates also pointed out that voters were instructed to verify that their ballots were prepared in a way that could be read by the machines (for example, by double-checking that "chads" on punch-card ballots were completely removed), and so if they submitted an unreadable ballot, it was their fault; pro-Gore advocates responded that Florida law required a ballot to be counted whenever the "intent of the voter" could be clearly discerned, whether or not voters followed directions in preparing the ballot. Most forcefully, the Bush camp argued that the manual inspection of ballots introduced a level of unacceptable subjectivity into the vote-counting process, in the sense that biased counters might say that a mark on the ballot should be treated as a vote for Gore even if the ballot was ambiguous. Gore's advocates responded that it was possible to develop vote-counting standards that would reduce or eliminate the subjectivity problem—for example, by requiring there to be a hole in the chad and not just a dimple, or requiring that one or more corners of the chad be dislodged—and besides, the manual recounting of ballots was a lawful feature of the Florida election system, as well as a long-standing feature of American elections from the beginning of the Republic.

This was the debate that captured the full attention of the country, and almost everyone quickly developed an opinion about each of these issues. Still, in the beginning, it seemed to be a debate that was going to be resolved by state election officials and judges charged with overseeing Florida election law—or, if worse came to worse, by the Congress. After all, the American Constitution appeared to give state governments the exclusive responsibility of choosing presidential electors. Article II, Section 1, indicates that "Each State shall appoint, in such Manner as the Legislature thereof may direct, a Number of Electors" for the Electoral College.

The state legislature of Florida had directed that presidential electors would be appointed on the basis of a statewide election, run under all the rules and regulation of the state's election statutes. What those rules and regulations permitted or prohibited were matters to be decided by state officials and, ultimately, the state's supreme court, which (as is the case with every state supreme court) is the final authoritative voice governing the meaning of state law. Moreover, under a federal law known as the Electoral Count Act of 1887, if states resolved disputes at least six days before the meeting of the Electoral College, on the basis of "laws enacted prior to" Election Day, "by judicial or other methods," then that resolution would be binding on the Congress, which has the responsibility of counting the Electoral College votes (*Electoral Count Act of 1887*, 24 Stat. 373, 3 U.S.C. § § 5, 6, and 15). If those disputes were not conclusively resolved by that date, then Congress would follow certain established procedures for resolving the issue and finishing the count of the Electoral College. Neither the Constitution nor federal statutes indicated any role for federal judges, including Supreme Court justices, in the resolution of such a supremely political controversy.

In light of all of this, when Bush's lawyers first went to federal court to challenge the constitutionality of the incipient recounts, it was not surprising to most observers that they were quickly sent away by the district court judge, who explained that "under the Constitution of the United States, the responsibility for selection of electors for the office of the President rests primarily with the people of Florida, its election officials and, if necessary, its courts." Moreover, the state's "manual recount provision . . . strives to strengthen rather than dilute the right to vote by securing, as nearly as humanly possible, an accurate and true reflection of the will of the electorate." The judge added, in a comment that was more prescient than he could have imagined, that he was not "the final word on this" (*Siegel v. LePore,* Case No. 00-9009-VCIV-Middlebrooks, Order on Plaintiffs' Emergency Motion for Temporary Restraining Order and Preliminary Injunction, Nov. 13, 2000).

The Supreme Court Takes On the Recounts

The Supreme Court's initial involvement in the election 2000 controversy, a few weeks before *Bush v. Gore,* came about after a dispute arose among state officials over the amount of time counties should be given to complete their recounts.

The Republican secretary of state, Katherine Harris, took the position that state law prohibited her from accepting any election results reported later than seven days after the election. Some large counties disagreed with her (as did Florida's Democratic attorney general), taking the position that the secretary of state should be required to accept results after this deadline if counties needed the extra time to complete legally authorized manual recounts.[4] In the case of *Palm Beach County Canvassing Board v. Harris* (772 So. 2d 1220 [2000]), the Florida Supreme Court, which was dominated by Democratic appointees, ruled that there was an apparent conflict between the deadline statute and the recount statute, at least in circumstances where larger counties were unable to complete authorized recounts within the seven-day time period. Those judges unanimously concluded that the conflict between the statutes should be resolved in favor of a more accurate tally of the voters' intent rather than a fixed deadline. To accommodate a little more time for counting without putting in jeopardy the state's participation in the Electoral College, the Florida justices ruled that the secretary of state had to accept the results of all recounts completed over the next five days, that is, by 5 P.M. on Sunday, November 26.

The Bush campaign immediately appealed that decision to the U.S. Supreme Court. They advanced two main arguments: first, that the Florida Supreme Court had changed the rules for elections in Florida in violation of the requirement in Article II that electors be chosen "in such Manner as the *Legislature* thereof may direct"; and second, that the resulting manual recounts violated the due process and equal protection clauses of the Fourteenth Amendment, because they resulted in the arbitrary and unequal treatment of ballots. When first developed, these arguments were widely viewed as long shots. Some sympathetic experts privately advised Bush's lawyers against including the Fourteenth Amendment arguments out of fear that they would seem too frivolous (Von Drehle, Nakashima, Schmidt, & Connolly, 2001, p. A1). The other argument was also unprecedented; worse than that, though, it seemed inconsistent with the long-standing presumption against federal court involvement in state disputes over the appointment of presidential electors and against the presumption that federal judges should not second-guess state court interpretations of state law. Nevertheless, three days after the Florida court's decision, the U.S. Supreme Court announced that it would hear Bush's appeal in the now-renamed case of *Bush v. Palm Beach County Canvassing Board.* However, the justices indicated that they wanted lawyers to focus on the Article II argument and to forget about the apparently groundless equal-protection claim.

While the justices contemplated these questions, events were changing quickly in Florida. The Florida court's extended deadline did little good for Al Gore. The U.S. Supreme Court's oral arguments came five days after the secretary of state had certified that George Bush had officially received 537 more votes than Al Gore. Only one county finished its recount, finding an additional 567 votes for Al Gore. Another shut down its recount after a boisterous demonstration by Bush supporters, and another finished two hours late and was told by the secretary of state that none of the almost 200 recovered votes for Al Gore would be included in the final tally.

The fact that the issue of the deadline extension no longer seemed central to the outcome of the election contest gave the divided justices some room to compromise, and three days after oral arguments they released a unanimous per curiam decision ordering the Florida justices to clarify whether they were interpreting Florida's election statutes or changing the statutes in potential violation of the U.S. Constitution.[5] In the meantime, though, the justices struck down the state court's decision allowing extra time for recounts (*Bush v. Palm Beach County Canvassing Board* [per curiam], 531 U.S. 70

[2000]). It was the Supreme Court's first antirecount decision during this presidential election dispute. It would not be its last.

This is because a new set of legal issues had been brewing while the Court was examining the deadline debate. After the final results were certified by the secretary of state, Gore's lawyers turned to provisions of state election law that permitted a candidate to contest an official election result if it could be shown that the certified vote totals rejected "a number of legal votes sufficient to change or place in doubt the result of the election" (Fla. Stat. § § 102.168[3][c] [2000]). The position of the Gore campaign was that the official results illegally ignored many legal votes, including (for example) a few hundred additional Gore votes found during the (two hours late) Palm Beach recount and some unspecified number of as-yet-unrecovered votes on ten thousand undervote ballots that were never reviewed after Miami-Dade canceled its recount.

On the same day the U.S. Supreme Court handed down its decision in *Bush v. Palm Beach County Canvassing Board,* a Florida trial court judge ruled against Gore on these new claims. This result was appealed to the Florida Supreme Court, and on December 8, by a vote of 4 to 3, the court ruled that the official election results ignored a number of legal votes in violation of the state's election statutes. While Gore had requested a recount of undervotes in certain selected Democratic counties, the majority on the Florida Supreme Court ruled that a selective recount would be unfair to the extent that it recovered legal votes in some parts of the state (Gore districts) but not others (Bush districts). Thus, they ordered a manual review of *all* undervote ballots throughout the state—approximately 60,000 ballots. As for the question of how these ballots should be evaluated, the judges insisted that "in tabulating the ballots and in making a determination of what is a 'legal' vote, the standard to be employed is that established by the Legislature in our Election Code which is that the vote shall be counted as a 'legal' vote if there is a 'clear indication of the intent of the voter'" (*Gore v. Harris* 772 So. 2d. 1243, p. 1262 [2000]). These state justices were careful not to go beyond the language of the statute by creating a brand new standard for reviewing ballots. After all, the Supreme Court had just warned them against making any changes in the state's election statutes.

Within a few hours a Florida judge was organizing the ground rules for a recount, including a process whereby he would ensure more uniformity in the treatment of ballots by personally making the final decision on any disputed ballot. If everything went according to plan, the statewide recount would be over by Sunday, December 10. Bush's lawyers prepared a hasty appeal to the U.S. Supreme Court, and on Saturday, December 9, less than twenty-four hours after the state supreme court's decision and a few hours after many counties had begun a surprisingly orderly recount process, a bare majority of the U.S. Supreme Court issued an injunction ordering a halt to all recounts. It was the first volley in the newly named *Bush v. Gore* case. And given that four members of the Court issued a strong dissent against the injunction, it was also the first official acknowledgment that the justices were deeply divided as to the appropriateness of the Court's involvement.[6]

The period of time from the Court's decision to hear the case to the release of the final opinion three days later represented the fastest turnaround in the history of Supreme Court decision making.[7] At around 10 P.M. on Tuesday, December 12, less than thirty-six hours after completing oral arguments, the Court distributed copies of its 5–4 decision to a pack of freezing reporters who were huddled on the courthouse steps. In a thirteen-page per curiam opinion, the five conservatives resurrected an argument that the Court refused to consider when the issue of recounts was first presented to the Supreme Court: that the recounts authorized by the Florida Supreme Court violated the equal protection clause. Specifically, the justices ruled that the legal standard used in evaluating the ballots—looking for "the clear intent of the voter"—allowed for too much variation in the treatment of ballots (in the sense that a dimpled chad may be treated as a vote in one county but as a nonvote in another), and that this "arbitrary and disparate treatment" of the ballots violated the constitutional principle that states cannot "value one person's vote over that of another." Apparently, in trying to avoid one constitutional mistake (associated with modifying the state statute to create a more specific standard for counting votes), the state justices had run smack into another constitutional mistake.

These five justices anchored their decision in the Court's famous apportionment decisions of the early 1960s, which stated that it was a violation of equal protection for states to create political districts with significantly different numbers of people in them (*Baker v. Carr*, 369 U.S. 186 [1962] and *Reynolds v. Sims* 377 U.S. 533 [1964]). However, they did not explain how this precedent was related to their completely innovative rule—unheard of and even unimagined by constitutional scholars before election day 2000—that manual recounts in statewide elections be guided by extremely precise criteria for evaluating ballots. The closest thing to an argument was that in both cases a form of vote "dilution" was taking place, but it was not explained why it was better for there to be widespread dilution of the vote throughout Florida (by not counting any of the undervote ballots) rather than run the purely hypothetical risk of there being some modest variation in the treatment of some ballots during a recount. These justices also did not explain

why the identical treatment of ballots was suddenly a constitutional requirement in the context of recounts but not in the context of the original vote on
election day, when the use of different voting technologies led to significant
county-by-county differences in the number of undervote ballots. They did
not explain why they assumed that the aborted recount was going to lead to
unacceptable variation even though it was overseen by a single judge who was
attempting to ensure statewide uniformity by personally evaluating all disputed ballots. All that the justices would say about the nature of their new
constitutional rule was that "our consideration is limited to the present circumstances, for the problem of equal protection in election processes generally presents many complexities."

To say the least, the equal protection argument at the heart of this decision was woefully underdeveloped, both as a matter of applying past precedent and as a matter of explaining the nature and scope of the new principle.
Still, why was it not possible for the Supreme Court to send the case back to
Florida courts so that the recount could be conducted in a way that was consistent with this newly developed constitutional standard? The reason given
by the five justices was that, in their judgment, the state of Florida wanted to
benefit from the federal law that ensured their electoral votes would be
counted if all disputes were resolved six days before the meeting of the Electoral College, or by December 12. "That date is upon us, and there is no
recount procedure in place under the State Supreme Court's order that com-
ports with minimal constitutional standards. Because it is evident that any
recount seeking to meet the December 12 deadline will be unconstitutional
for the reasons we have discussed, we reverse the judgment of the Supreme
Court of Florida ordering a recount to proceed." Even though this deadline
nowhere appeared in the state's election statutes, the conservatives were confident enough in their interpretation of state law that they felt no need to
verify this understanding with the state supreme court.

In their concurring opinion, Rehnquist, Scalia, and Thomas went further
and accused the Florida Supreme Court of changing the state's election law
in violation of Article II. However, they had a difficult time explaining what
it was about the Florida court's latest opinion that "impermissibly distorted"
the state's election statutes. For example, they argued that "the court's interpretation of 'legal vote' . . . plainly departed from the legislative scheme."
However, there was no attempt to reconcile the conclusion with the explicit
language in the very Florida statute that the state justices claimed to be
scrupulously following, namely, that "no vote shall be declared invalid or void
if there is a clear indication of the intent of the voter" (Fla. State § 101.5614[5],
[2000]). There were also statements in Florida case law, dating back to 1917,

to the effect that ballot inspectors must "examine each ballot for all evidence of the voter's intent and make its determination based on the totality of the circumstances" (*Darby v. State,* 75 So. 411 [Fla. 1917]). Instead of focusing on these state statutes and precedents, the concurring justices emphasized that voters in punch-card counties were given (nonstatutory) instructions by election officials to make sure that their ballot cards were punched "clearly and cleanly."

The dissenters made it clear that, from the beginning, they had opposed the Court's involvement in the presidential election dispute. Justice Souter, a Republican appointed by the first President Bush, opened his opinion by declaring that "the Court should not have reviewed either *Bush v. Palm Beach County Canvassing Board . . .* or this case, and should not have stopped Florida's attempt to recount all undervote ballots . . . by issuing a stay of the Florida Supreme Court's orders during the period of this review." Both he and Justice Breyer acknowledged that there may be some merit to the equal protection concerns expressed by the majority, but in their view state judges might have prevented or resolved these problems on their own "if the state proceedings had not been interrupted." If state officials did not avoid these problems, the issue should have been addressed by the Congress, which is given the responsibility under the Constitution for counting electoral votes. As Breyer put it, in drafting the Electoral Count Act of 1887, Congress was "fully aware of the danger that would arise should it ask judges, unarmed with appropriate legal standards, to resolve a hotly contested Presidential election contest. . . . In this highly politicized matter, the appearance of a split decision runs the risk of undermining the public's confidence in the Court itself." In their view, the best course of action would have been to send the case back to Florida with instructions that any recount should be guided by clearer standards for the review of ballots.

The two other dissenters, Ginsburg and Stevens, rejected the equal protection complaints completely, arguing that the legislature's "intent of the voter" standard for reviewing ballots was no more subjective than many other legal standards (such as "beyond a reasonable doubt") that are applied every day without anyone worrying that similar cases might be treated differently; it was also pointed out that the variations in ballot treatment resulting from the recount were no worse (and probably much more fair) than the county-by-county disparities that were built into the certified election results. However, they agreed with their other dissenting colleagues that the Supreme Court's persistent assault on the Florida courts was uncalled for. As Stevens (a Republican appointee) pointed out, underlying "petitioners' entire federal assault . . . is an unstated lack of confidence in the impartiality and capacity of the state judges who would make the critical decisions if the vote count were to proceed. Otherwise, their position is wholly without merit. The endorsement of that position by the majority of this Court can only lend credence to the most cynical appraisal of the work of judges throughout the land." In elaborating this point, Stevens penned one of the most enduring and widely cited passages in all of the *Bush v. Gore* opinions. "Although we may never know with complete certainty the identity of the winner of this year's Presidential election, the identity of the loser is perfectly clear. It is the Nation's confidence in the judge as an impartial guardian of the rule of law."

Lessons in Judicial Power and Constitutional Politics

The decision had its intended effect. The next morning Al Gore, citing his respect for the rule of law, conceded the election. Others were less willing graciously to move on. Stevens gave voice to the outrage of many Gore supporters, editorial writers, and law professors, more than 600 of whom lent their names to a full-page ad in the *New York Times* to tell the country that, in their professional judgment, "the U.S. Supreme Court used its power to act as political partisans, not judges of a court of law."

Nevertheless, as a general matter, the country did not respond in kind. Two days before the decision nearly three-quarters of those surveyed (73 percent) said they would accept as legitimate a decision by the U.S. Supreme Court that resolved the election controversy once and for all. When asked which institution they would "most trust to make the final decision on the selection of the next president," 61 percent said the Supreme Court, compared to 17 percent for the Congress, 9 percent for the Florida Supreme Court, and 7 percent for the Florida Legislature. More than six months after the decision, 62 percent of the public approved of the "way the Supreme Court [handled] its job," a figure that was essentially identical to polling numbers collected the previous year. As one commentator put it, "if . . . the Court was gambling that it could maintain broad public support even while throwing the election to George W. Bush and establishing ever-better relations with the congressional Republicans, it was a winning decision" (Levinson, 2002, pp. 7–39, 25).

It remains to be seen whether the constitutional principles announced in *Bush v. Gore* will have any lasting effect on the development of constitutional law or even on election practices in the United States. Some lawsuits were initiated in the wake of the decision, including one challenging the use of punch-card technology in some counties but not others in California (*Common Cause v. Jones,* 213 F. Supp. 2d 1110 [C.D. Cal. 2002]), but it is unclear whether other courts will build on the justices' decision. One federal judge dismissed one lawsuit by explaining that "the Supreme Court was cautious to limit its ruling in that case to the circumstances before it. . . . Therefore, its applicability to this or any other case involving concerns over voting rights and equal protection is dubious." The judge went on to point out that "numerous commentators and law professors have criticized the decision for its usurpation of state court power and its unjustifiable expansion of the Equal Protection Clause. . . . Whether the court was in fact guided more by personal preferences than by sound legal principles need not be addressed since the court has expressly indicated its intent to severely limit the case and the expert analysts suggest that the case has little or no value as precedent in the equal protection area."[8]

Even if the decision has no lasting effect on the development of American constitutional law, it will have a lasting effect on our view of Supreme Court politics. Needless to say, the Court's role in the political system becomes infinitely more problematic if its decisions seem motivated by a desire to manipulate constitutional doctrine for partisan advantage. Should such a practice become more commonplace, it is easy to see how it would place at risk the very project of constitutional law, as well as any chance for the Court to maintain bipartisan support in the political system.

Perhaps, then, *Bush v. Gore* is the anomaly that provides a perspective on the ways in which Supreme Court decision making is typically very different than the sort of hardball politics we wearily expect of power holders in other institutions. This may be another way of saying that, in order for the Supreme Court to establish and maintain its constitutional authority to exercise "the Judicial Power," it would be well-advised to act, as much as possible, like a court, just as Article III envisioned. As Justice Breyer put it in his dissenting opinion in *Bush v. Gore,* the country's confidence in the Court as an essentially nonpartisan institution "is a public treasure" that has been "built slowly over many years"; it is a "vitally necessary ingredient of any successful effort to protect basic liberty and, indeed, the rule of law itself."

NOTES

1. There are times when the "collegial" nature of Supreme Court decision making leads justices to support compromise versions of their preferred policies, and there are other times when the internal norms of the Court have led justices to suppress dissents they might otherwise have wanted to file. But it would be very difficult to find examples of justices who vote in favor of constitutional positions that do not essentially reflect their views. This is why the so-called attitudinal model is so effective at predicting the votes of Supreme Court justices based on their political ideologies.

2. The Republican Party controlled the Senate through March of 2001, when Republican senator Jim Jeffords of Vermont announced he was leaving the party because of

the conservative policies of the Senate leadership. By becoming an Independent, Jeffords gave Democrats a one-vote majority in the Senate up through the 2002 midterm elections, when Republicans won a majority.

3. How could this happen? Some of these counties used older "punch-card" ballots, whereby voters indicated their preferences by using a stylus to punch out a preperforated rectangular "chad" from an old-fashioned IBM computer card. The vote-tabulating machines only recorded a vote for a candidate if the chad had been removed enough to leave a hole through which light could be passed. In some cases, though, a person intending to vote for a candidate might push the stylus through the hole without completely removing the chad; instead, they might merely poke it and leave a dimple or (slightly more successfully) dislodge one or more corners but not the whole thing (thus creating what became known as a "hanging chad"). In punch-card counties machines reported that 3.9 percent of ballots included no vote for president; by contrast, only 1.4 percent of ballots were considered undervotes in wealthier counties that used more modern optical-scan systems. See *Bush v Gore,* at 126n.4 (Stevens dissenting).

4. The counties claimed they needed the extra time because of the structure of the recount statute, which gave candidates a few days to decide whether to request a recount, and then required counties to do a preliminary review of 1 percent of the ballots before making a final decision whether a full recount would be appropriate. Some counties had barely begun their recounts at the time that the secretary of state said she would not accept "late" results.

5. During oral arguments, two of the most conservative members of the Court, Chief Justice Rehnquist and Justice Scalia, strongly suggested that the Florida justices did something wrong when they referred to the right to vote in the state's *constitution* as part of their argument for why it might be inappropriate to enforce the deadline *statute.* Their novel constitutional theory was that Article II gave state *legislatures* unrestrained power over the appointment of presidential electors, even to the point of allowing them to pass a statute in violation of their own constitution.

6. Writing for the five conservatives in support of the injunction, Justice Scalia explained that the recount deserved to be stopped because there was a serious question whether the votes being counted were "legally cast" under Florida election law. "The counting of votes that are of questionable legality" threatens an "irreparable harm" to Bush "by casting a cloud upon what he claims to be the legitimacy of his election." There was no attention to the question of the irreparable harm to Gore by stopping the recounts. The four dissenting justices—Stevens, Souter, Ginsburg, and Breyer—could only complain that the Court's precipitous decision to intervene in the state recount "will inevitably cast a cloud over the legitimacy of the election" (*Bush,* 2000).

7. In the "Pentagon Papers" case, *New York Times v. United States* (403 U.S. 713 [1971]), decided during an unprecedented federal court order preventing a newspaper from publishing a story, the justices handed down their opinions (lifting the injunction) four days after oral arguments.

8. *Walker, et al v. Exeter Region Cooperative School District,* 157 F. Supp. 2d 156 (U.S. Distr. Ct. NH, 2001), 159n.6; the decision was affirmed by the First Circuit Court of Appeals at 284 F. 3d 42 (2002). Florida completed an overhauled of its election systems to re-

duce the likelihood that voters would have their intentions frustrated by error-prone machines. However, these reforms were caused by the debacle of the election dispute itself and would have taken place even without the Court's intervention.

REFERENCES

Levinson, S. (2002, Summer) The law of politics: *Bush v. Gore* and the French revolution: A tentative list of some early lessons. *Law and Contemporary Problems, 65,* pp. 7–39.

Von Drehle, D., Nakashima, E., Schmidt, S., & Connolly, C. (2001, January 29). In Florida, drawing the battle lines. *Washington Post,* p. A1.

Executive Power

Presidential Power in Times of Crisis

Youngstown Sheet & Tube Co. v. Sawyer (1952)

MAEVA MARCUS

> Presidents seem to exercise a great deal of authority, especially in the area of for-
> eign affairs, where they often order troops around the world, conduct various mili-
> tary actions, and engage troops in areas of conflict. When challenged, the Supreme
> Court has generally been reluctant to limit such actions by the commander in
> chief. In the area of domestic affairs, however, the chief executive has historically
> fared less well before the Court. President Harry Truman learned this lesson when,
> during the Korean War, he acted unilaterally to take control of the nation's steel
> production to avert a threatened labor strike and maintain the manufacture of
> military hardware. The justices concluded that, even during a time of national
> emergency, the Constitution limits the president's authority.

On April 8, 1952, in the midst of the Korean War, President Harry S. Truman
announced that, to forestall a strike, he was seizing the mills of the principal steel companies. At the time, he had no inkling that his action would
precipitate a major constitutional controversy. Overnight, however, the

president's attempt to encourage settlement of a labor dispute turned into a full-scale debate over executive power. The dramatic reaction of Clarence Randall, head of Inland Steel, to Truman's seizure speech captured the transformation: "There on the screen before me was [Truman's] tense face, speaking the firm crisp sentences that burned into my consciousness like the voice of doom. Seizure it was . . . with the same finality [as] a death sentence. . . . One man had coldly announced that his will was supreme, as Caesar had done, and Mussolini and Hitler" (Randall, 1956, p. 214). The entire nation was shocked. Although presidents had seized plants before, they had not taken over virtually an entire industry in what technically was peacetime. Moreover, to justify his action, Truman had invoked his inherent powers under Article II of the Constitution when several statutes gave him alternate, unquestionably legal means to prevent a strike.

President Truman's action touched off a constitutional and institutional crisis. Had Truman acted unlawfully? How should Congress have responded to the president's action? Is the judiciary the proper branch to deal with such questions?

Because Congress did nothing and the steel industry brought suit against Secretary of Commerce Charles Sawyer, the government official nominally charged with operating the mills, it fell to the Supreme Court to provide the answers. Against a backdrop of two decades of unprecedented employment of presidential power—which led Truman to believe that he had the authority to take over the mills—the Court invalidated Truman's seizure. The result in *Youngstown Sheet & Tube Co. v. Sawyer* (343 U.S. 579 [1952]), or the *Steel Seizure* case, as it has become known, while popular, stunned the nation. Why had the justices—all appointed by Roosevelt or Truman—chosen this moment to call a halt to the expansion of executive power? What elements were critical in shaping the Court's judgment? How did the *Steel Seizure* case affect the doctrine of separation of powers and the practice of presidential power? These questions cannot be answered without understanding the historical circumstances in which the case arose.

Three factors provided the framework in which the attempt to settle an ordinary labor dispute fueled a constitutional firestorm: the Korean War, problems with the economy, and the imperatives of an election year. The Korean War was the first of a number of armed conflicts following World War II in which the United States committed troops and armaments, but for which Congress never passed a formal declaration of war. After North Korea invaded South Korea on June 24, 1950, and the United Nations Security Council promptly called for the withdrawal of North Korean forces, the Truman administration moved immediately to come to South Korea's defense.

On June 27 the president ordered American troops into the fighting in Korea. Although Truman explained American policy to congressional leaders, he sought no explicit approval from the legislature for his actions. Expecting the conflict to be of short duration, he did not anticipate a great need for congressional cooperation. When the Chinese communists intervened on the side of the North in December 1950, however, and it seemed likely that hostilities would be protracted, the president declared a "limited" national emergency that triggered certain statutes giving him more authority to face the crisis in Korea. But as the fighting dragged on and public support waned, the administration found itself in the difficult position of prosecuting a full-fledged war without the wholehearted assistance of Congress, many of whose members became unwilling to act as if the country were involved in an acute wartime emergency. In the *Steel Seizure* case, Truman would face the consequences of his decision not to seek a formal declaration of war.

The military engagement in Korea caused serious economic dislocation at home. Congress initially indicated its approval of Truman's action in Korea by appropriating substantial funds for military needs and granting the president authority to put the nation's economy on a wartime footing. Immediately after the North Korean incursion, Congress passed the Defense Production Act, which gave the president the powers he had requested. He could establish priorities and allocate strategic materials, expand productive capacity and supply, and control consumer and real estate credit. The act gave the president authority, limited only by the requirement to pay just compensation in requisitioning property, equipment, supplies, materials, and facilities necessary for the national defense. Title IV of the act made explicit Congress's desire "to prevent inflation and preserve the value of the national currency; to assure that defense appropriations are not dissipated by excessive costs and prices"; and "to stabilize the cost of living for workers and other consumers." The act left the imposition of direct controls to the discretion of the president. But if mandatory price ceilings were needed in a substantial part of the economy, the act required the president to institute overall controls. If this became necessary, Congress directed the president to create a new independent agency to administer the task of economic stabilization (Defense Production Act, 1950, *Statutes at Large, 64,* pp. 803–804, 807).

The day after the Defense Production Act was passed, Truman, by executive order, set up the machinery to fulfill its directives (Executive Order No. 10161 [1950]). He created the Economic Stabilization Agency to administer the stabilization program. But the president did not share Congress's belief in the ability of a single agency to manage the regulation of both prices and wages. His order thus provided for the appointment of a director of price stabilization and a separate wage stabilization board composed of nine members equally divided among representatives of labor, management, and the public. Truman's action met the letter of the law but conflicted with Congress's single agency requirement, which was intended to force the consideration of the impact of wage increases on prices so as to limit the inflationary spiral. The administration did not think it would have to impose mandatory controls, however, because it anticipated that voluntary compliance by industry and labor with the administration's stabilization goals would be sufficient to regulate the economy.

But the Chinese intervention in Korea changed everything. Within two months prices had surged dramatically, and the president had to act. On January 26, 1951, Truman declared a general freeze on wages and prices. Sensitive to the inequities that such a total freeze perpetuated, he directed the stabilization agencies to seek to rectify injustices to businesses and workers that had been hurt unfairly by the imposition of mandatory controls. The standards the agencies devised, however, did not satisfy the labor unions, and their representatives withdrew from all government mobilization and stabilization offices. Administration officials soon realized that their problem stemmed from the fact that the Korean conflict was not an all-out war and the public did not perceive that there was any great danger. No one, least of all workers who saw industry profits growing, wanted to make sacrifices. President Truman needed the cooperation of labor, but he could not alienate business interests to obtain it.

In an attempt to regain labor support and participation, the president created a reconstituted Wage Stabilization Board (WSB) with eighteen rather than nine members, equally representing labor, business, and the public. To ease the threat of strikes and assist its wage stabilization duties, the board was given the authority, where labor disputes threatened the war effort, to make nonbinding recommendations on economic and other issues (Executive Order 10233 [1951]).

By the spring of 1951, the Truman administration faced additional problems that exacerbated the difficulties of dealing with industry and labor. The president's standing with the public had steadily diminished as the Korean conflict dragged on inconclusively and inflation eroded consumer purchasing power. Truman's difficulties were compounded by accusations that the administration was riddled with communism and corruption. Charges of communist infiltration of the government made by Senator Joseph McCarthy, which led to civil servants being denounced as disloyal, hampered efforts to govern effectively. Frequent disclosures of corruption further embarrassed the Truman administration. While the president himself was not implicated, some of his closest associates, including Attorney General J. Howard McGrath, were forced to resign. This unfortunate state of affairs led Truman to announce, on March 29, 1952, that he would not run for re-election (Marcus, 1977, pp. 1–37). A seasoned Washington reporter wrote on April 8, 1952 (the seizure was announced that night), "Under a parliamentary system of government, the Truman Administration would at this point of near collapse go out of office on a vote of no confidence. That would in all probability have happened months ago as the inability of the Administration to carry out even rudimentary policy was demonstrated over and over again" (Childs, 1952, p. 12).

The labor dispute that led to the seizure of the steel mills represented a clash between two powerful antagonists—the steel industry and the United Steelworkers of America—which had a long and bitter relationship. The steel companies believed the Truman administration did not understand their industry and was partial to the steelworkers. During the years following World War II, the steel industry had enjoyed its greatest profits since World War I, and the companies hoped to maintain this rate of return throughout the Korean conflict. They had learned an important lesson from their experience in World War II, when despite the tremendous growth in steel output during the war, the government would not permit a price increase to compensate for greater costs. The industry was determined not to allow this history to repeat itself. Conversely, the union, acutely aware of the extraordinary profits of the companies during the post–World War II years, thought that its members deserved to be rewarded for their part in the industry's success. From the union's point of view, only wages—not prices—were being effectively controlled during the Korean conflict. As 1951 ended, and the contract between the United Steelworkers of America and the steel industry expired, both parties realized that their differences would be settled only by decisions of the government's stabilization agencies and ultimately by the Truman administration.

President Truman grasped the urgency of successfully concluding contract negotiations between the companies and the union. Any interruption of the supply of steel—and a one-day strike caused a shutdown of steel furnaces for a week—would, he believed, impair the war mobilization effort. Furthermore, steel's central position in the nation's economy meant that the settlement of this dispute would prove whether or not Truman's overall stabilization policy worked. Thus, when 1951 came to a close without a contract, the president referred the labor dispute to the Wage Stabilization Board and got the union to agree to postpone a strike while the WSB considered the case.

The WSB's recommendations, which were finally made public on March 20, 1952, appeared to be very generous to the steelworkers. After some study the Truman administration concluded that the recommended wage increases were within stabilization guidelines, but the steel industry insisted on prices higher than the guidelines would permit and refused to come to terms with the steelworkers union unless such a price increase was allowed.

While attempting to settle the labor dispute, the president considered his options. The Pentagon bombarded him with dire warnings that any interruption in the production of steel would endanger the lives of the soldiers in Korea, slow down atomic weapons projects, and affect the domestic defense-related economy. Moreover, other sectors of the economy dependent on steel would suffer job losses that could lead to serious unemployment. Unwilling to accede to the companies' price demands, which Truman thought would destroy the administration's stabilization program, the president instead looked at other courses of action. All of the statutory routes open to him to avert a strike were unsatisfactory in his eyes. Government requisition of the steel mills under the Defense Production Act would take too long to meet the needs of the steel crisis. Seizure of the companies under section 18 of the Selective Service Act of 1948 (*Statutes at Large, 62,* p. 626), which allowed the president to take possession of any plant that did not fill orders placed by the armed forces or the Atomic Energy Commission, involved complicated and lengthy procedures that also would fail to ensure continued steel production.

The most obvious remedy—seeking an injunction against the strike under the Taft-Hartley Act—had no appeal for Truman. Before a Taft-Hartley injunction could be sought, a board of inquiry would have to be appointed and report to the president, and during that period the union would be free to strike. Furthermore, the president thought an injunction would be unfair to the steelworkers, who had cooperated with the government in its collective bargaining efforts, and would give the companies, the culprits in Truman's eyes, an undeserved advantage. Finally, Truman had a deep-seated reluctance to use the mechanisms of a statute he regarded as antilabor and that had been enacted over his veto.[1]

The White House staff considered two other alternatives: seeking seizure legislation from Congress or seizing the mills under the inherent powers of the president. They dismissed the first quickly because they thought it unlikely that Congress would pass such a measure promptly if at all. But seizure under the president's inherent powers attracted them. While seizure would not end the labor dispute, it would prevent an interruption in steel production and provide a new context in which the administration could pursue its goals of a fair settlement and reasonable price controls. Thus, on April 8, Truman issued Executive Order 10340, "Directing the Secretary of Commerce to Take Possession of and Operate the Plants and Facilities of Certain Steel Companies." The order authorized Secretary of Commerce Charles Sawyer to change wages and working conditions. Truman hoped that threatening to raise wages without any price increases would lead the steel companies to capitulate.

Any possibility of creating a favorable context for settling the dispute was eliminated, however, by Truman's vitriolic speech announcing the seizure. The steel companies, abetted by the press and Congress, charged the administration with dictatorship. They effectively changed the focus of discussion from the labor-management dispute to abuse of executive power.[2] The courtroom would be the crucial forum—a prospect that did not displease Truman and his staff, for they believed the seizure would be upheld by the courts.

Youngstown Sheet & Tube Co. v. Sawyer is noteworthy, from a procedural standpoint, in two respects: First, from start to finish, adjudication of the case took less than two months, an unusually rapid process. Beginning with a motion for a temporary restraining order twenty-seven minutes after Truman had ended his speech, steel company attorneys kept the pressure on for expedited treatment of the case, and the courts accommodated them. Second, this most important question of executive power was litigated as a matter of equity on a motion for a preliminary injunction. Justiciable controversies in which money would not be sufficient compensation for the wronged party are heard by courts of equity, but in the United States, the same federal courts discharge both equity and common law functions. The party seeking equitable relief must show that the action he wants enjoined would cause him irreparable injury and that the injunction will not unduly harm the interests of the other parties or the public. Should he prove this, the judge (no jury is required in equity proceedings) can issue one of three orders: (1) a temporary restraining order that prevents the challenged action from being put into effect until a full hearing can be held; (2) a preliminary injunction, which, after a hearing, enjoins the action until a final disposition of the case (at this stage, the party asking for relief has only to show that irreparable injury will be done to him and that he has a substantial likelihood of success when the legal merits of the controversy are determined); and (3) a permanent injunction, which will stem from a final decision on the rights of the parties involved.[3]

Judge Alexander Holtzoff denied the companies' motions for a temporary restraining order. He believed that in balancing the equities, more weight had to be given to the public's need, in a time of military conflict, for the continued production of steel. Moreover, he discerned no irreparable injury to the steel companies, because the government had stated that during the seizure, business would go on as usual with the mills being run by the same steel company executives and the steelworkers being employed by the government only as a technical matter. Beyond that, the judge had one larger concern. Even though a restraining order would be nominally directed to the secretary of commerce, in substance it would be against the president, and Holtzoff doubted whether a federal district court had the power to enjoin the president. The judge could find no previous case in which an injunction against the president had been issued by any court.[4]

When government attorneys would not agree to a shortened briefing schedule so that a hearing on the merits could be held as soon as possible, industry lawyers filed motions for a preliminary injunction, which were heard by Judge David A. Pine on April 24. If this had been a typical hearing on a motion for preliminary injunction, the opposing parties would have spent much, if not most, of their time arguing the equitable question: how do you balance injury to the public from a strike against injury to the companies from the seizure? But Holmes Baldridge, assistant attorney general in charge of the Claims Division, who led the government lawyers at this stage of the litigation, made a critical error of judgment that may have affected the outcome of the case in the district court and possibly the Supreme Court.[5] He chose to emphasize the president's constitutional power to seize private property—thirty-five pages of the brief were devoted to that question, while only eighteen discussed the equity issues—and thus invited the court to focus on the legal merits of the government's position rather than on the equitable question of injury, where the administration stood on firmer legal ground. Judge Pine took full advantage of Baldridge's miscalculation.

In two days of argument, the judge indicated time and again that he was ready to decide whether or not the steel seizure was valid. Counsel for the steel industry, steeped in the traditional practice that on a motion for preliminary injunction equity concerns take prominence over the legal questions involved, were slow to take Judge Pine's hints that he was ready to decide the merits. They concentrated on persuading Judge Pine that an order restraining the government from making any changes in the terms and conditions of employment in the mills was all they needed.[6] Pine finally got impatient with the steel company attorneys and told them he was willing to listen to extended discussion of the constitutional issues. After briefly listening to one company lawyer, the judge suggested that the government speak for itself.

Lower court arguments may be important, but they rarely have the consequences that attended Baldridge's appearance before Judge Pine. Baldridge began his presentation with the proposition that courts could not restrain the president; Secretary Sawyer was the "alter ego" of the president and therefore could not be enjoined. The president's power, Baldridge continued, was based on Sections 1, 2, and 3 of Article II of the Constitution and the inherent, implied, or residual powers that flowed from these. In plain language, Baldridge told Pine, that meant that in an emergency it was the executive's duty to protect the national security, and any action taken for that purpose was legal. The judge interrupted several times to ask what protections a citizen might have against such assertions of presidential power; Baldridge could identify none. He cited only two limitations on executive power: the ballot box and impeachment. Pine asked Baldridge if he meant that "when the sovereign people adopted the Constitution, it enumerated the powers set up in the Constitution but limited the powers of the Congress and limited the powers of the judiciary, but it did not limit the powers of the Executive." Baldridge responded affirmatively (U.S. Congress, House, 1952, p. 377). He explained why none of the pertinent statutes could have been used by the president on the night of April 8: the emergency was too great; use of any of them would have produced an interruption in steel production. Someone had to do something, Baldridge declared; he could not believe that the federal government was without power to act in a grave emergency. To Judge Pine that sounded like an argument for expediency. "Well, you might call it that, if you like," Baldridge replied. "But we say it is expediency backed by power" (U.S. Congress, House, 1952, p. 420). With that assertion, the government rested its case.

Judge Pine's opinion a few days later mirrored the reaction that had swept the country immediately after the hearing. Baldridge's argument, characterized as the "legal blunder of the century" by a member of the White House staff, had touched the "ever-sensitive nerve of 'constitutionalism'" by propounding a sweeping theory of executive power that no one in the White House had ever thought of (Enarson, 1952, p. 6, box 5). Newspapers across the nation warned that the president was asserting an unlimited power. In private, Truman disavowed that theory to Senator Hubert Humphrey and others and pointed out that the government's brief (as opposed to Baldridge's oral argument) espoused no such claim (*Congressional Record*, vol. 98, pp. 4472–4473). But the damage had been done. Judge Pine enjoined the seizure and ruled that every one of the government's positions was without legal justification (*Youngstown Sheet & Tube v. Sawyer*, 103 F. Supp. 569 [1952]). His opinion was more a statement of faith in the "immutable" principles of constitutional government than a carefully constructed legal document (U.S. Congress, House, p. 66–76). It struck a chord in the press and the public, however. The declaration in his opinion that he would prefer a strike "with all its awful results" to recognition of the unlimited power of the president reinforced suspicions in some quarters that the Truman administration was exaggerating the emergency that would occur if steel production were interrupted.[7]

The White House, meanwhile, was faced with the crisis it had tried so hard to avert, for as soon as Judge Pine announced his decision, the union went out on strike. To get the steelworkers back on the job as quickly as possible, the administration sought a stay of Pine's injunction from the United States Court of Appeals for the District of Columbia Circuit while going directly to the Supreme Court for a definitive review of Pine's ruling. The Court of Appeals granted the government's motion for a stay, giving the administration two days in which to petition the Supreme Court for certiorari (U.S. Congress, House, p. 444). And the steelworkers returned to the mills.

At its usual Saturday conference on May 3, the Supreme Court granted certiorari and set argument in the case for Monday, May 12. Along with the grant of certiorari, the Court stayed Judge Pine's preliminary injunction order until final disposition of the case, but with the critical stipulation that the government could not change wages or working conditions for the duration of the stay unless both the union and the industry agreed to it.[8] Eight days of feverish preparation led up to an oral argument that occurred over two days. John W. Davis, the seventy-nine-year-old distinguished advocate (the *Steel Seizure* case was his 138th argument before the Supreme Court), represented the steel industry, and Solicitor General Philip Perlman argued for the government. Davis's eighty-seven-minute argument, which concentrated on the arbitrary nature of Truman's seizure, was uninterrupted; Perlman, in contrast, was frequently interrupted with questions from the justices about the alternative procedures open to the president to resolve the steel dispute and the statutory and constitutional basis of Truman's claim of authority to seize the mills. When the argument ended, however, most informed observers expected that the Court would find a way to uphold the president's power or to avoid the constitutional question altogether (Marcus, 1977, pp. 179–194).

It came as a great surprise, therefore, when, more than two weeks later, the Supreme Court invalidated the presidential seizure of the steel mills. The 6–3 ruling produced a total of seven opinions (the opinion of the Court, five concurring opinions, and a dissent), which suggests that while the justices agreed on the result, they had great difficulty in achieving a consensus on a rationale to support that conclusion. The majority consisted of Hugo Black, who wrote the opinion for the Court, Felix Frankfurter, William O. Douglas,

Robert Jackson, Harold Burton, and Tom Clark, who concurred in the judgment but did not join the Court's opinion. Chief Justice Fred Vinson, Stanley Reed, and Sherman Minton dissented.

Justice Black, in a short and simple opinion for the Court, held that the seizure was fundamentally inconsistent with the Constitution's separation of powers. Truman, Black found, had not met the conditions set out in any of the statutes that permitted seizure, so he could not rely on them for authority. As for the Constitution, Black observed that there was no express language that gave the president the power to seize private property; the government's contention that the seizure authority stemmed from the aggregate of powers granted in the three principal sections of Article II could not be sustained. Presidential powers are distinct from the authority to make laws. Truman's seizure order was a piece of legislation. "The Founders of this Nation entrusted the lawmaking power to the Congress alone in both good and bad times," Black noted (*Steel Seizure,* p. 589). Thus, for Justice Black, the boundary between executive and legislative powers was fixed and exact. Not even in grave emergencies could one branch exercise the powers assigned to the other.

While four justices signed on to Black's opinion, only Justice Douglas shared Black's view that the separation of powers doctrine was absolute and inflexible. The other justices in the majority disagreed with this simplistic stance; experience had shown that the functions of the three branches of government did not fit into neat compartments. Nevertheless, although it was nonsense, as Justice Frankfurter put it, "to see a dictator in a representative product of the sturdy democratic traditions of the Mississippi Valley," it was necessary to check unauthorized, albeit well-meaning, assertions of power (*Steel Seizure,* p. 593). By differing routes, these justices generally reached the same conclusion: as Congress had enacted specific statutes applicable to the steel dispute, these statutes had to be followed by the president.

In his dissent, Chief Justice Vinson wrote a stirring defense of Truman's action. He rejected both the Black position that the president never could act in emergency situations without express statutory authorization and the view of the other majority justices that the existence of specific legislation precluded the seizure in this instance. Discussing previous examples of presidential emergency action in the absence of prior congressional authorization, Vinson demonstrated the Court's past approval of the Inherent Powers Doctrine. And he found the evidence of emergency in this case more than persuasive. From the statutes containing authorization for seizure in certain circumstances, Vinson drew a lesson different from the one favored by the majority justices: "Where Congress authorizes seizure in instances not necessarily crucial to the defense program, it can hardly be said to have disclosed an intention to prohibit seizures where essential to the execution of that legislative program." Truman's seizure of the steel mills was an act taken to prevent the destruction of the legislative defense programs until Congress could consider the crisis. The president had stated that he would abide by the directions of Congress—not the usual stance of a president bent on tyranny (*Steel Seizure*, pp. 702–704).

Why did the Court's majority, which in the past had upheld various uses of inherent executive power, rule against the president in this case? To begin with, the existence of Judge Pine's opinion, so widely acclaimed, made it imperative for the Supreme Court to determine the merits of the constitutional question. Moreover, the prospect of future international crises may have convinced the justices that the time had come for careful consideration of the powers of the president to take emergency action in the name of national security. Several opinions contain suggestions that the justices' views had been influenced by the events of World War II. The horrors wrought by the fascist governments in Europe were still fresh in their minds, highlighting the necessity for a firm foundation in law for all government action.

The specifics of the Korean conflict also undoubtedly influenced the justices. The United States entered the Korean conflict because of a presidential commitment of troops, with no declaration of war by Congress. A national emergency had been declared by the president—not Congress—after the hostilities had begun. Now, pointing to the harmful effects a strike might have on military forces in Korea, the president was asserting the power to seize the steel mills. As Justice Jackson stated in his concurring opinion: "No doctrine that the Court could promulgate would seem to me more sinister and alarming than that a President whose conduct of foreign affairs is so largely uncontrolled, and often even is unknown, can vastly enlarge his mastery over the internal affairs of the country by his own commitment of the Nation's armed forces to some foreign venture" (*Steel Seizure*, p. 642)

Even so, the Court might have ruled in favor of the president had the majority justices believed that a grave crisis in fact existed. But the majority of the Court appeared unconvinced that the necessity for the seizure was as great as the administration claimed. In the weeks between Judge Pine's decision and the Supreme Court ruling, it became clear that the administration was releasing steel for recreational purposes. The press had also revealed that large inventories of steel were on hand. It seemed doubtful, in short, that the nation's survival was dependent on an uninterrupted supply of steel.[9] In this context the Court could find no reason to sustain an exercise of inherent executive power.

The constitutional significance of the *Steel Seizure* decision lies not so much in the substance of its holding but in the fact that the decision was made. The Court served notice on the executive that its actions would be reviewed and would not always pass constitutional muster. Since 1952, the *Steel Seizure* case has been cited as a precedent for a great variety of legal points, not all dealing with executive power (Marcus, 1977, pp. 228–231). Its greatest influence, however, was felt during the presidency of Richard Nixon, when the courts struck down actions by the administration seeking to enjoin the publication of the "Pentagon Papers," place wiretaps without warrants in internal security cases, impound congressionally appropriated funds, and dismantle the Office of Economic Opportunity (Marcus, 1977, pp. 235–248). The most dramatic use of the *Steel Seizure* case precedent occurred as President Nixon tried to protect himself from the effects of the Watergate scandal. By taking personal possession of the Watergate tapes, which contained incriminating evidence, and asserting that the president was not amenable to court order, Nixon hoped to keep the tapes out of the hands of the courts and the special prosecutor. No court had ever issued an order directed to the president himself, and Nixon took the position that the separation of powers doctrine stood in the way of such judicial action. But the courts made short shrift of his argument. In a series of cases involving the tapes, the *Steel Seizure* decision provided the precedent on which the judges relied. As the Court of Appeals for the District of Columbia Circuit wrote: "There is not the slightest hint in any of the *Youngstown* opinions that the case would have been viewed differently if President Truman rather than Secretary Sawyer had been the named party. If *Youngstown* still stands, it must stand for the case where the President has himself taken possession and control of the property unconstitutionally seized, and the injunction would be framed accordingly. The practice of judicial review would be rendered capricious—and very likely impotent—if jurisdiction vanished whenever the President personally denoted an Executive action or omission as his own" (*Nixon v. Sirica*, 487 F. 2d 700, 709 [1973]).

With the advent of terrorism and the demand for executive action to combat it, the *Steel Seizure* case precedent may again play a role. After the destruction of the World Trade Center on 9/11, the administration of President George W. Bush took upon itself the power to decide which terrorists would be tried by military tribunals, thus depriving them of the rights of defendants in a civilian trial. In the search for terrorists, more than 1,000 aliens were detained, typically for minor immigration violations or as "material witnesses," and their names and places of detention kept secret. The president also claimed the power to arrest Americans as "enemy combatants" and hold them indefinitely without trial and without the right to consult a lawyer. Courts could not review such designations, his administration maintained. Whether the *Steel Seizure* decision will have any effect on the litigation flowing from challenges to these assertions of executive power remains to be seen.

NOTES

1. Defense Production Act, 1950, p. 812; Labor Management Relations Act. 1947. *Statutes at Large,* vol. 61, p. 136. This act, popularly known as the Taft-Hartley Act, was opposed by labor and was passed over Truman's veto.

2. Truman attempted to bring Congress into the picture to counter the steel industry's legal campaign. He sent a special message to the legislature the morning after his seizure order explaining the reasons behind his action and stating his willingness to abide by any further legislative mandate on the subject. Congress did nothing. Special Message to the Congress Reporting on the Situation in the Steel Industry, April 9, 1952, U.S. President, *Public Papers 1952–1953,* p. 251.

3. One more consideration comes in to play when the contested action is one that affects the public interest. In that circumstance a court of equity has more leeway to give or withhold relief than it would have when only private interests are at stake. *Virginian Ry. v. System Federation,* 300 U.S. 515 (1937).

4. A partial transcript of the record, beginning with the motion for a temporary restraining order and continuing through the Supreme Court adjudication, may be found in U.S. Congress. House. *The Steel Seizure Case.* H. Doc. 534. 82d Cong., 2d sess., 1952.

5. Baldridge, who had spent the major part of his career in the Antitrust Division of the Justice Department, had no familiarity with the law concerning the pivotal issues in the steel seizure case and was not prepared to discuss them.

6. Despite the huge public relations campaign undertaken by the steel industry claiming that the seizure was an act of dictatorship, the companies, at this hearing, revealed what they really cared about: the bottom line. If they could keep the government from raising wages, the seizure would be to the industry's benefit, because the union, which could not strike against the government, would have to continue working at 1951 wages.

7. See, for example, Cry wolf? Claim of "emergency" to justify seizure of steel plants was open to questioning. (1952, April 30). *Wall Street Journal,* p. 8. People suspected that if Pine really thought there was an emergency, he would never have enjoined the seizure.

8. Supreme Court of the United States, Journal of Saturday, May 3, 1952; U.S. Cong. House (1952). *Steel Seizure Case,* pp. 457–458. On the morning of May 3, President Truman had called representatives of the union and the industry to the White House and told them that if they did not come to an agreement, the government would raise wages. This was sufficient motivation for the companies to agree tentatively to a settlement, which was worked out by midafternoon. While the negotiators were out of the White House checking with their respective groups, word of the Supreme Court's action reached them, and when they returned no settlement was possible. Marcus, 1977, pp. 146–147.

9. In the event, this proved true, for the steelworkers went out on strike for fifty-three days after the Supreme Court decision, and neither the president nor Congress took any action to end it (Marcus, 1977, p. 249).

REFERENCES

Childs, M. (1952, April 8). *Washington Post*, p. 12.

Congressional Record, vol. 98. pp. 4472–4473.

Cry wolf? (1952, April 30).Claim of "emergency" to justify seizure of steel plants was open to questioning. *Wall Street Journal*, p. 8.

Defense Production Act. (1950). *Statutes at large, 61, 64.*

Enarson, H. (152, July 9). The steel strike—A modern tragedy. Enarson Papers, Truman Library, p. 6, box 5.

Executive Order No. 10161, 15. (1950). C.F.R. 6105.

Executive Order No. 10233. 16. (1951). C.F.R. 3503.

Executive Order No. 10340. 17. (1952). C.F.R. 3139.

Marcus, M. (1977) *Truman and the steel seizure case: The limits of presidential power.* (1994 reprint). Durham, NC: Duke University Press.

Randall, C. (1956). *Over my shoulder: A reminiscence.* Boston: Little Brown.

Selective Service Act. (1948). *Statutes at large, 62.*

Special Message to the Congress Reporting on the Situation in the Steel Industry. (1952, April 9). U.S. President, *Public Papers 1952–1953*, p. 251.

Supreme Court of the United States, Journal of Saturday, May 3, 1952.

U.S. Congress. House. (1952). *The Steel Seizure Case.* H. Doc. 534. 82d Cong., 2d sess.

The Limits of Presidential Immunity

Clinton v. Jones (1997)

KATY J. HARRIGER

One feature of the separation of powers is the ability of each branch of the federal government to function without the potential harassment of the others. Members of Congress, for example, cannot be prosecuted for any of their legislative actions. Similarly, presidents cannot be held liable in the courts for their official acts. But what about their unofficial acts? In 1994 President Bill Clinton was sued by a woman who claimed Clinton had made unwanted sexual advances toward her while he was serving as the governor of Arkansas. Clinton argued that, as president, he was entitled to immunity—if only temporarily—from the civil case filed against him. The Supreme Court had to decide whether the separation of powers would be violated by permitting the judicial branch to conduct proceedings that had been brought against a sitting president.

The legal parameters of presidential power were the subject of considerable litigation and change during the presidency of William Jefferson Clinton (1992–2000). Clinton's presidency was embroiled in scandal from its earliest days, and when he left at the end of his second term, he was only the second president in American history to have been impeached by the House of Representatives and to have kept his office because of the failure of the Senate to convict him.

In the meantime, a number of significant questions about the limits on presidential power, including questions of executive privilege and presidential immunity from lawsuit, were litigated (Fisher, 1999). At the center of the allegations that led to his ultimate impeachment was the lawsuit brought against him by Paula Corbin Jones alleging sexual harassment during Clinton's days as governor of Arkansas. How could allegations of sexual misconduct before Clinton's presidency lead to an attempt to remove him from office and a legal and political battle that would consume the latter years of his presidency? How could a lawsuit that, at its initiation, appeared to be a minor embarrassment brought by the president's political enemies, end up as a major Supreme Court precedent limiting presidential immunity? The answers to these questions lie in the story of *Clinton v. Jones* (520 U.S. 681 [1997]). The story is a fascinating and multilayered one, for it is not only about a president's personal failings but also about the state of American politics at the end of the twentieth century. The potential effect of this decision is significant, but it remains to be seen whether the combination of personal, political, and legal forces that brought it about will be repeated in subsequent presidencies or whether it stands merely as a monument to a unique period in presidential politics.

The Allegations and the Litigation

When Paula Corbin Jones filed her lawsuit against Clinton in 1994, he was already plagued by scandal. An independent counsel had been appointed in 1994 to investigate the Whitewater land deal in which he and his wife had invested during their days in Arkansas. From his earliest days as a candidate for the presidency, Bill Clinton was haunted by allegations about his private life. Gennifer Flowers, a nightclub singer in Arkansas, sold her story alleging a long-term affair with Clinton to a tabloid, and it was published just before the New Hampshire primary in 1992. He appeared with his wife Hillary on the television show *60 Minutes* to discuss the story, and that appearance was widely credited with saving his candidacy. Clinton came in second in the New Hampshire primary and went on to win the Democratic nomination that summer, and the presidency in November.

Jones's suit alleged that Clinton had violated her civil rights, inflicted emotional harm, and, along with a former state police officer Danny Ferguson, defamed her. She claimed that on May 8, 1991, when she was working as a state employee at the registration desk of a conference in Arkansas where Governor Clinton was speaking, she was told by state trooper Ferguson that Clinton would like to meet her. She was invited to his hotel room, where he allegedly made "abhorrent" sexual advances that she rebuffed. Subsequently, her complaint alleged, she was denied job advancement because of her rejection of the governor. Finally, Jones claimed that Ferguson's interview in an *American Spectator* magazine article about Clinton's Arkansas days defamed her by recounting a similar story but claiming that the woman named "Paula" had told Ferguson she was available to be the governor's girlfriend. She claimed that Clinton had defamed her by denying the allegations through a press release and his lawyer (Complaint, *Jones v. Clinton*, 858 F. Supp. 902 [E.D. Ark., 1994]).

In the district court, Clinton asked for dismissal of the suit based on a claim of temporary presidential immunity and asked that this question be addressed first before any other motions or pleadings were considered. Clinton did not claim that Jones could never sue him, but instead, that she should have to wait until he left office, when she would be permitted to refile her lawsuit without violating the statute of limitations. The district court judge, Susan Webber Wright, denied the president's request for temporary immunity, instead ordering that the discovery process go forward. She did, however, agree that the trial proceedings should be delayed until Clinton left office, finding that the public interest in having the president free to carry out his duties outweighed Jones interest in an immediate trial (*Jones*, 858 F. Supp. 902 [E.D. Ark. 1994]).

Both parties appealed the district court decision. A divided panel on the Eighth Circuit Court of Appeals overturned Judge Wright's decision to delay the trial until after Clinton left office. They held that this decision was an abuse of discretion by the district judge and amounted to "the functional equivalent" of a grant of temporary immunity (*Jones*, 72 F.3d 1354 [8th Cir. 1996]). Clinton appealed to the U.S. Supreme Court, and the Court granted certiorari, noting the importance of the issues raised.

The Supreme Court and the Law of Presidential Immunity

The question of presidential immunity was not a new one for the Supreme Court. Over the course of American history, the Court had developed a judicial doctrine of sovereign immunity, rooted in the English common law tradition that "the King can do no wrong" (Beaupre, 1995, p. 729). Evidence from early U.S. history, including Justice Joseph Story's Commentaries, an exchange between Vice President John Adams and Senator Oliver Ellsworth during the First Congress, and a letter written by Thomas Jefferson in 1807, all suggest that a similar rule should apply to the presidency. For example, Adams and Ellsworth contended that given the president's executive responsibilities, he should not be subject to any judicial process. To allow it, they argued, would be to allow a judge to "stop the whole machine of Government," a clear violation of the separation of powers doctrine. Again, using the separation of powers as his justification, Story also argued that the executive must "possess an official inviolability" (quoted in Beaupre, 1995, pp. 731–732).

Conversely, there is also evidence from the early days of the republic that many saw the presidency as very different from a king, and therefore rejected the notion that the office should have any special privileges that protected it from the law. James Wilson, a delegate to the 1787 constitutional convention, argued that the president had no special privileges, but instead, "far from being above the laws, he is amenable to them in his private character as a citizen, and in his public character by impeachment" (quoted in Weeden, 1999, pp. 374–375). Similarly, in rebuking Jefferson for refusing to turn over the commissions for new justices of the peace, Justice John Marshall wrote in the now-famous *Marbury v. Madison* decision that the government was "emphatically . . . a government of laws, and not of men. It will certainly cease to deserve this high appellation, if the laws furnish no remedy for the violation of a vested legal right" (*Marbury v. Madison,* 5 U.S. (1 Cranch) 163 [1803]).

The historical evidence thus conflicts on the issue of presidential immunity, and there is no specific textual provision to that effect in the Constitution. This is in contrast to the explicit immunity given members of Congress in the speech and debate clause of Article I. Instead, the notion of immunity for executive and judicial officers has evolved out of judicial doctrine. The Supreme Court has found that there are both absolute and qualified immunities for public officials. The first, absolute immunity, exists where the officers are carrying out their official duties, even if those actions may have been taken in bad faith. Qualified immunity requires an officer to prove that he or she did not know that the actions they took were illegal and that, instead, they had acted on the good-faith assumption that they were permitted to act as they had. When either form of immunity is granted, officials cannot be held liable for their actions through the civil law (Jeffery, 1996, p. 838).

The case law establishing absolute immunity started with questions of judicial immunity. In *Bradley v. Fisher* (80 U.S. (13 Wall) 335 [1871]), the court ruled that judges must be immune from civil suit in the exercise of their judicial duties. If judges were not immune from such suits, the court said, they would not be "free to follow their consciences without fear of litigation" and "the legal system could not function" (Beaupre, 1995, p. 733). The Court also worried that judges were particularly susceptible to suits because of the high stakes in many of the matters that came before them. Dissatisfied parties would have too great an incentive to sue.

Absolute immunity for executive officers was first recognized in *Spalding v. Vilas* (161 U.S. 483 [1896]). This case involved a civil suit against a post-master general, and again the Court found that in order for the official to be able to do his job, he must be free from the fear of lawsuit and the burden of financial liability for his official actions. This immunity was extended to executive officials below the top levels of government in *Barr v. Mateo* (360 U.S. 564 [1959]).

The Court did recognize that there may be actions taken by officials that should not enjoy the absolute immunity protection. In *Butz v. Economou* (457 U.S. 731 [1978]), the Court found that most executive officials enjoy only a qualified immunity when they are sued for constitutional violations. Whether or not they had immunity depended on whether or not they had acted in "good faith" and on the particular function they were performing. The Court had recognized in earlier cases and reiterated here that there were some particularly "sensitive" functions—especially those of judges and prosecutors—that required absolute immunity. But in *Butz* the Court found many other functions performed by many other executive branch officers to be subject to only a qualified immunity when the importance of remedying constitutional rights violations was weighed in the balance.

Nixon v. Fitzgerald (457 U.S. 731 [1982]) is the most important case to this discussion, because it dealt directly with the question of presidential, rather than executive branch, immunity. Fitzgerald was a "whistle-blower," whose job as an Air Force management analyst was eliminated after he testified before Congress about what he considered improper practices in defense procurement. He brought suit against President Richard Nixon and several of his aides, claiming that they had violated his First Amendment rights. The closely divided Court ruled against Fitzgerald, holding that the president enjoyed absolute immunity from civil suit for the same kind of "public policy imperatives that had governed earlier immunity cases" (Beaupre, 1995, p. 734). The Court found the need for the official to be able to act without fear of civil liability particularly compelling in the presidency. It held that the absolute immunity to which the president was entitled was a "functionally mandated incident of the President's unique office, rooted in the constitutional tradition of the separation of powers and supported by our history" (*Nixon v. Fitzgerald*, 457 U.S. 731, 749 [1982]). Fitzgerald argued that the president deserved no more than the qualified immunity of *Butz,* but the Court rejected this argument, focusing on the unique status of the president. "Because of the singular importance of the President's duties, diversion of his energies by concern with private lawsuits would raise unique risks to the effective functioning of government," the Court said. Noting the special functional exemption established for judges and prosecutors in *Butz,* the Court went on to argue that this exception was even more compelling in the case of the president, who "must make the most sensitive and far-reaching decisions entrusted to any official under our constitutional system" (*Nixon v. Fitzgerald,* 457 U.S. 731, 752 [1982]).

The *Fitzgerald* majority was also concerned about the president's particular susceptibility to lawsuit. They argued that "the sheer prominence of the President's office" could not be ignored. "In view of the visibility of his office and the effect of his actions on countless people, the President would be an easily identifiable target for suits for civil damages. Cognizance of this personal vulnerability frequently could distract a President from his public duties, to the detriment of not only the President and his office but also the Nation that the Presidency was designed to serve" (*Nixon v. Fitzgerald,* 457 U.S. 731, 753 [1982]).

Finally, the Court rejected the argument made by the four dissenters in the case, that the effect of this absolute immunity was to put the president "above the law." The majority noted that the president was still subject to the formal sanction of impeachment and the informal checks that came from congressional oversight, close media scrutiny, the desire for reelection, and concern about one's place in history. "The existence of alternative remedies and deterrents," argued the Court, "establishes that absolute immunity will not place the President 'above the law.' For the President, as for judges and prosecutors, absolute immunity merely precludes a particular private remedy for alleged misconduct in order to advance compelling public ends" (*Nixon v. Fitzgerald,* 457 U.S. 731, 758 [1982]).

In a concurring opinion that had particular relevance to the *Clinton v. Jones* dispute, Chief Justice Warren Burger emphasized the limits of the ruling. Rejecting the dissenters' argument that the decision would make the president free of legal constraints, Burger stated that "a President, like Members of Congress, judges, prosecutors, or congressional aides—all having absolute immunity—are not immune for acts outside official duties" (*Nixon v. Fitzgerald,* 457 U.S. 731, 759 [1982]).

Burger's opinion foreshadows the novel question raised by Clinton in the Jones lawsuit. Because Burger's opinion was a concurring one, his statement about the limits of absolute immunity held no force of law. Relying on the same public policy arguments used to justify absolute immunity for official acts, Clinton's argument was that presidents should have *temporary* immunity from civil suit for private actions until they leave the office. His lawyers relied on the same separation of powers concerns about judicial interference with the president and the pragmatic policy concerns about the president's particular vulnerability to harassing law suits and the unique responsibilities of the president to justify this extension of immunity to private action (*Clinton v. Jones*, 520 U.S. 681, 689–690 [1997]).

The Supreme Court rejected unanimously the president's arguments, agreeing with the lower courts that there was no temporary immunity from suits challenging private actions taken before Clinton's presidency and holding that the district court judge had abused her discretion in delaying the trial until after Clinton left office. First, the Court found that the historical evidence relied on by Clinton to justify the immunity was counteracted by the historical evidence used by Jones and did not offer a conclusive answer to the question (*Clinton v. Jones*, 520 U.S. 681, 695–697 [1997]). Second, the Court recognized the separation of powers argument offered by Clinton as his "strongest argument" but ultimately rejected its applicability in this case. The Court, acknowledging the unique burdens of the office, said that "It does not follow, however, that separation of powers principles would be violated by allowing this action to proceed." In this case the Court was not usurping executive power but instead simply responding to Jones's request that it exercise its Article III powers. "Whatever the outcome of this case," the Court said, "there is no possibility that the decision will curtail the scope of the official powers of the Executive Branch. The litigation of questions that relate entirely to the unofficial conduct of the individual who happens to be the President poses no perceptible risk of misallocation of either judicial power or executive power" (*Clinton v. Jones*, 520 U.S. 681, 697–701 [1997]).

The Court also rejected Clinton's argument that the burden of this case, and the likelihood of additional litigation should the lower court's decision be upheld, would impair his ability to carry out his official duties. It claimed that Clinton's prediction "finds little support in either history or the relatively narrow compass of the issues raised in this particular case" (*Clinton v. Jones*, 520 U.S. 681, 702 [1997]). The Court did leave open two possibilities that might give the president, or at least future presidents, relief. First, they noted the long-standing tradition that federal judges have discretion in deciding when discovery and trials should proceed and that, if the president could show a serious burden imposed on his ability to do his job, judges were empowered to accommodate the president's needs without a temporary immunity rule. Second, they noted that Congress was always free to create a statutory immunity rule if it deemed it important enough to the public interest, suggesting that there would be no constitutional problem with such a statute (*Clinton v. Jones*, 520 U.S. 681, 706–709 [1997]).

Of course, what the Court could not know was just how wrong it was about the likely burden this particular case would place on the Clinton presidency. When Clinton was deposed by Jones's lawyers, they asked many questions about his past alleged relationships with various women, including several questions about a possible liaison with a young White House intern named Monica Lewinsky. In his responses, Clinton denied any such relationship. When the news broke in January of 1998 that there was taped evidence that there had been a relationship between Clinton and Lewinsky, and the special prosecutor already investigating Clinton for the Whitewater and other matters successfully petitioned to have his jurisdiction expanded to encompass these allegations, the stage was set for the impeachment showdown that followed. For a year the president, his aides, Congress, and the country were consumed by fallout from the scandal. Clinton's alleged perjury in the Jones deposition, his alleged efforts to cover up the Lewinsky relationship, and his alleged repeated perjury before the grand jury in the investigation by Kenneth Starr, were used by the House of Representatives as the basis for his impeachment in December of 1998. The Senate acquitted Clinton in January 1999 of the two impeachment charges that passed the House. Interestingly enough, the House failed to pass the impeachment article that dealt with the alleged perjury in the Jones case.

The Political Context: Post-Watergate Washington and the Politics of Scandal

In their 1999 book, *Politics by Other Means*, Benjamin Ginsberg and Martin Shefter argue convincingly that during the last several decades of the twentieth century, political conflict was characterized by "postelectoral" politics. They assert that "[r]ather than engage in an all-out competition for votes, contending political forces have come to rely upon such weapons of institutional combat as congressional investigations, media revelations, and judicial proceedings to defeat their foes" (Ginsberg & Shefter, 1999, p. 16). They attribute these methods to the extended period of divided government, where no party was able to command the loyalty of the voting public. The twenty-four-hour media cycle also bred a climate of scandal, where media "feeding frenzies" could turn relatively minor accusations into full-blown scandals. In addition, the post-Watergate reform climate led to an increase in the use of the criminal justice system to ferret out and punish public officials accused of abusing their power (Ginsberg & Shefter, 1999, pp. 23–39).

One particular reform, the independent counsel statute first passed in 1978, was designed to try to avoid undue influence by the executive in cases involving high-ranking executive branch officials. During the Watergate scandal, President Nixon ordered the firing of a special prosecutor, Archibald Cox, who was investigating the scandal more vigorously than the president wanted. The event came to be known as the "Saturday Night Massacre." Cox had been appointed by the attorney general and could be fired by him. The public outrage that followed the firing was a turning point in the scandal. A new special prosecutor with more guarantees of independence was appointed, public opinion shifted against the president, and ultimately, the investigation led to the release of taped evidence that proved Nixon's complicity in the cover-up of the scandal. Congress's goal in creating the independent counsel was to avoid the possibility of another "Saturday Night Massacre" by providing for judicial appointment of an independent counsel who would investigate, and potentially prosecute, members of the executive branch accused of wrongdoing (Harriger, 2000).

The independent counsel arrangement was controversial throughout its existence, and its use and abuse by both parties gives considerable credence to the arguments of Ginsburg and Shefter. Although President Jimmy Carter supported its adoption in 1978 as part of his effort to improve government ethics, most presidents and their Justice Departments chafed under its limitations on their power and questioned its constitutionality. The Gerald Ford administration had effectively blocked its passage in the immediate aftermath of Watergate. The Ronald Reagan administration was openly hostile to it, testifying against it at the first reauthorization hearing in 1982. Nonetheless, its symbolic value in post-Watergate Washington meant that few were willing to vote against it, and Reagan signed it back into law twice during his presidency, in 1982, and again in 1987. There were two independent counsel appointed during the Carter administration and seven during the two terms of the Reagan administration, including two investigations of Attorney General Edwin Meese, and two indictments and convictions of close personal advisers Michael Deaver and Lyn Nofziger. The most significant investigation of this period was the Iran-Contra scandal, in which a large number of executive branch officials including the president, vice president, secretary of defense, national security adviser, and assistant secretary of state were investigated, and in some cases, prosecuted, for their role in a secret arms deal with Iran and a scheme to funnel money to a Nicaraguan rebel group in contradiction to congressional policy. This investigation extended throughout the presidency of George Bush and led to increased complaints about the costs and time allocated to independent counsel investigations. In 1992, when the statute was again considered for reauthorization, it was allowed to expire, largely because of the controversy surrounding this investigation (Harriger, 2000).

The first scandal of Clinton's presidency was labeled Whitewater, after a failed real estate project in Arkansas that garnered some national attention during the 1992 election but that became a central preoccupation of the press and Congress during Clinton's first term.

Both the president and the First Lady were alleged to have misused their influence in becoming partners in the land deal, and in covering up their role in its failure. Pressure mounted for an independent investigation of the allegations, but there was no longer an independent counsel statute requiring such an appointment. As media attention mounted and congressional investigations continued to prove embarrassing, Clinton asked Attorney General Janet Reno to appoint an independent counsel under her own authority. She did so, appointing former federal prosecutor Robert Fiske. He began his investigation, but the president's foes in Congress were not satisfied (Bartley, 1994).

Many congressional Republicans who had resented the independent counsel statute when it had been applied to a president of their party, began to see the value of an independent judicial appointment when the president was of the opposite party. Combined with the bipartisan good government coalition that had always supported the statute, they reauthorized the statute in 1994 and began pressing for Fiske to be replaced by a judicial appointment. Reno asked the judicial panel responsible for appointment to reappoint Fiske, who was well into his investigation. The investigation had expanded to include the circumstances surrounding the suicide of a close Clinton aide, Vince Foster, and Fiske had already found that there was no evidence of foul play in his death. The judicial panel rejected Reno's request, and instead appointed former solicitor general and federal appellate judge Kenneth Starr.

Starr's appointment was controversial from the start, both because the appointing judges were alleged to have been influenced by Clinton's enemies in Congress and because Starr himself was seen as more ideologically conservative than Fiske and had closer ties with major conservative groups opposed to Clinton's policy agenda. Starr reopened the Foster investigation and also had, at Reno's request, his jurisdiction expanded to include allegations that the Clintons had abused their authority in firing certain employees of the White House travel office. As the investigations dragged on through the 1996 election, public commentary became increasingly critical of the time and money being spent on allegations that appeared to have no basis for criminal charges against either of the Clintons. Starr did obtain convictions in Arkansas of several of the prominent figures in the Whitewater scandal, including the sitting governor, but he was unable to build a case against the president or his wife. When the Monica Lewinsky scandal broke in early 1998, he sought and obtained a further expansion of his jurisdiction to investigate Clinton's alleged perjury and efforts to cover up the relationship (Harriger, 2000).

This set up an epic struggle between the independent counsel and the Clinton administration. While Starr won most of the legal battles he fought with Clinton over claims of executive privilege (Miller, 1999), the president won the battle of public opinion. Encouraged by Clinton's apparent success in domestic policy, and put off by what they perceived to be an unfair investigation by an overly zealous prosecutor, the public appeared willing to forgive the president for his misdeeds. Clinton no doubt survived the impeachment effort because of the solid support he got from the public. Even though they found his private behavior reprehensible, they continued to give him high ratings for his general handling of his public responsibilities (Stuckey & Wabshall, 2000).

In 1998, in the midst of the Lewinsky scandal, the district court judge hearing the Jones case dismissed it, finding that Jones had not offered sufficient preliminary evidence that she could prevail at trial. Holding out the possibility that they would appeal the decision, Jones and her lawyers entered into negotiation with Clinton's lawyers for a settlement. Ultimately, in November of 1998, the president agreed to pay Mrs. Jones $850,000 but did not admit to the allegations she had made against him.

The climate of "revelation, investigation, and prosecution" (Ginsberg & Shefter, 1999, p. 39) that prevailed during the latter decades of the twentieth century and that were displayed so prominently in the Clinton years, was a breeding ground for a new group of litigants that emerged during this time. Just as the 1960s and 1970s were characterized by a growth in litigation strategies by civil rights, women's rights, and environmental groups, the 1980s and 1990s were a period in which groups with more conservative agendas found the courts to be an amenable place for fighting their battles (Epstein, 1985). One such group, the Rutherford Institute, provided the primary funding for the Jones lawsuit, as well as money for investigating Clinton's past in Arkansas. Another, Judicial Watch, led by attorney Larry Klayman, launched a barrage of law suits against the Clinton administration, including a defamation suit by another woman claiming to have had an affair with Clinton, a class action suit on behalf of former Republican White House staffers whose FBI files were acquired by the Clinton White House, and a Freedom of Information Act suit attempting to gain access to Commerce Department documents about the travels of the late secretary Ron Brown (himself the target of an independent counsel investigation before his death in a plane crash). While judges showed considerable impatience with Klayman's tactics, the resulting publicity drew substantial attention to his group, demonstrating that in the "postelection" climate, winning a suit could be less important than the damage done simply by filing a suit (Berkman, 1998).

Implications of *Clinton v. Jones* for the Presidency

The most immediate impact of the *Clinton v. Jones* decision was on the occupant of the White House, William Jefferson Clinton, rather than on the institution of the presidency itself. As outlined above, the public attention to the case contributed to the negative view that the public and political elites held about his personal character, and the outcome of the case led to the deposition in which his first alleged act of perjury occurred. There is little doubt that the decision had a devastating effect on Mr. Clinton and his legacy.

It is less clear what the long-term effect of the decision may be on the institution of the presidency. Critics of the opinion have called it "idiotic" (Bugliosi, 1998, p. 75), "the goof of the decade," "foolishly shortsighted," and "the stupidest decision in the court's history" (Miller, 1999, n. 6). Some of that criticism was based on the concern about the consequences for Clinton's presidency, some on the belief that the suit itself was an illegitimate effort by the president's enemies to ruin him, and some on the premise that it would undermine the institution of the presidency itself by exposing its occupants to harassing lawsuits in a political climate that encourages them. Whether or not this last concern bears fruit depends on the particular vulnerability of a president to allegations of misconduct in his or her private affairs, the likelihood of Congress taking up the Supreme Court's invitation to create statutory immunity for the president while in office, and the general climate of politics in the country.

The vulnerability of the presidency to lawsuit raises a related and important question fraught with complicated questions of political ethics. The cost to President Clinton and many of his aides of defending themselves was enormous. Supporters of Mr. and Mrs. Clinton created a legal defense fund to raise money to pay for the bills as they mounted through the various investigations. Given their prominence, they were able to raise the money they needed, but aides with less power and personal appeal had no such luxury. What are the ethics of the president soliciting money for such a fund? What are the consequences if you forbid such a fund but allow the president to be sued for private matters while in office? Is there a way to limit the fallout of such cases so that lower-level aides without the personal and political resources of the president are not ruined by the spillover of cases of this type onto them (Clark, 1997)? The questions were all raised by the Clinton experience, but remain unanswered.

Another as yet unanswered question is whether Congress will respond to the Court's suggestion that a statutory immunity for the president could be created. Critics of the Court's opinion think that Congress ought to do this, given the potential danger of exposing future presidents to suit in our increasingly litigious society. A statute might create a presumption of immunity based on the public interest in having the president able to focus on his executive responsibilities, but allow for that presumption to be overridden if the plaintiff can show that delay until the president leaves office would irreparably harm the plaintiff's case (Alexander, 1998). As of 2003 however, Congress had not taken up this invitation.

Some things have changed in the political climate as a result of the political bloodletting that took place in the late 1990s, and so it may well be that no future president will face the particular congruence of personal problems and contextual factors that led to Clinton's troubles. The independent counsel statute expired in June of 1999, with almost no one from either side of the political aisle any longer willing to defend it. The public's support for Clinton, despite their dislike of his personal character, suggests a public mood more willing to tolerate flaws in the president. In fact, several commentators have argued that this public mood reflects an altered and more mature view of the presidency (Stuckey & Wadshall, 2000; Miroff, 1999), which could lower the burdensome expectations on the office and may discourage partisans from using personal attacks as an alternative to electoral politics.

In other ways, the political climate that bred the *Clinton v. Jones* controversy remains intact. Ideological interest group litigation strategies remain a reality of the political and legal climate. Their ability to use the courts for cases of this sort may be restricted by judicial unwillingness to advance their cases, but given their general success in recent years in achieving political and policy goals through the courts, and the political advantages that can come from embarrassing one's political enemies even in defeat, it seems the incentives remain great for this kind of "politics by other means." Similarly, the influence of the mass media (particularly television and the Internet), the twenty-four-hour news cycle, the massive numbers of stations vying for an audience, and the continued saliency of political intrigue and scandal, all point to a Washington politics little changed by the Clinton scandals. Finally, as the elections of 2000 and 2002 appear to show, the country remains deeply divided with regard to partisan affiliation, and at least in the near future there appears to be no end to the fierce partisan struggles that have been at the heart of the post-Watergate political climate. The precedent set in *Clinton v. Jones* lies waiting, potentially dangerous, but on the surface standing largely for a particular dispute in a particular time, historically interesting but only vaguely threatening to future presidents.

REFERENCES

Alexander, D. D. (1998) In the aftermath of *Clinton v. Jones:* An argument in favor of legislation permitting a sitting president to defer litigation. *Southwestern University Law Review, 28,* pp. 71–92.

Bartley, R. L., ed. (1994). *Whitewater: From the editorial pages of the* Wall Street Journal. New York: Dow Jones and Company.

Beaupre, L. W. (1995, July). Note: Birth of a third immunity? President Bill Clinton secures temporary immunity from trial. *Boston College Law Review, 36,* pp. 725–767.

Berkman, H. (1998, November 9) Even if Starr disappeared, there'd be Klayman. *National Law Journal,* p. A9.

Bugliosi, V. (1998). *No island of sanity: Paula Jones v. Bill Clinton : The Supreme Court on trial.* New York : Ballantine Pub. Group.

Clark, K. (1997) Paying the high price for heightened ethics scrutiny: Legal defense funds and other ways that government officials pay their lawyers. *Stanford Law Review, 50,* pp. 65–138.

Complaint. *Jones v. Clinton.* U.S. Dist. Lexis 5739 (E.D. Ark 1994) (No. LR-C-94–290).

Epstein, L. (1985). *Conservatives in court.* Knoxville, TN: University of Tennessee Press.

Fisher, L. (1999, September). The law: Legal disputes in the Clinton years. *Presidential Studies Quarterly, 29,* pp. 697–707.

Ginsberg, B., & Shefter, M. (1999). *Politics by other means: Politicians, prosecutors, and the press from Watergate to Whitewater.* New York: W. W. Norton.

Harriger, K. (2000). *The special prosecutor in American politics,* 2nd ed., Revised. Lawrence, KS: University Press of Kansas.

Jeffrey, J. R. (1996, Summer). Temporary presidential immunity: Adhering to the Separation of Powers Doctrine and the will of the Framers in civil damages litigation involving the president—The *Jones v. Clinton* Case. *Saint Louis University Law Journal, 40,* pp. 833–864.

Miller, R. K. (1999, Spring). Presidential sanctuaries after the Clinton sex scandals. *Harvard Journal of Law and Public Policy, 22,* pp. 647–734.

Miroff, B. (1999, September). The contemporary presidency: Moral character in the White House: From Republican to Democratic. *Presidential Studies Quarterly, 29,* pp. 708–712.

Stuckey, M. E., & Wabshall, S. (2000, September). Sex, lies, and presidential leadership: Interpretations of the office. *Presidential Studies Quarterly, 30,* pp. 514–533.

Weeden, L. D. (1999, Winter). The president and Mrs. Jones in federal court: The litigation established no constitutional immunity for President Clinton. *George Mason Law Review, 7,* pp. 361–387.

Legislative Power

Policymaking Outside the Constitution

INS v. Chadha (1983)

AMY MCKAY AND MICHAEL MUNGER

Congress has long sought to monitor the effectiveness of its programs, and one of its most convenient tools of oversight has been a mechanism called the legislative veto. In countless pieces of legislation, Congress has provided for the ability to reverse the implementation of the law. To take one highly visible example, under the War Powers Act of 1973, Congress can recall troops committed to hostilities by the president. In a more unassuming instance, Congress used the legislative veto to overturn an executive branch decision to allow a foreign student named Jagdish Chadha to remain in the United States after his visa had expired. Chadha's challenge to this congressional action, however, resulted in one of the Supreme Court's most important decisions regarding the separation of powers.

What is the power to legislate? The answer seems obvious, but in fact it was not settled until 1983, when the U.S. Supreme Court decided *INS v. Chadha* (462 U.S. 919). Though important questions remain, *Chadha* is one of the key separation of powers cases in the last century.

In some ways, the most compelling part of this story is the human element: the international odyssey of Jagdish Chadha. But before we meet our protagonist, it is important that we describe the context in which the story takes place. In Article I, the U.S. Constitution asserts, "All legislative Powers herein granted shall be vested in a Congress of the United States, which shall consist of a Senate and House of Representatives." But any bill that passes "the House of Representatives and the Senate, shall, before it becomes a law, be presented to the President of the United States." This means that the president may use the veto power, a check on the Congress. Though vetoes can be overridden, this means that the power to legislate cannot really "all" be "vested" in the Congress.

As we will see, the *Chadha* case turned on the question of whether Congress could embed a "legislative veto" in laws that delegated rule-making authority to federal agencies. But the real question addresses the power to legislate: since Congress legislates, can Congress define the legislative power as it pleases, or is this power defined and circumscribed by the Constitution? Ultimately, as we shall see, the answer given by the Supreme Court echoes the claim made by John Marshall in *Marbury v. Madison* (5 U.S. [1 Cranch] 137 [1803]).

> The powers of the legislature are defined and limited; and that those limits may not be mistaken, or forgotten, the constitution is written. To what purpose are powers limited, and to what purpose is that limitation committed to writing, if these limits may, at any time, be passed by those intended to be restrained? The distinction between a governor with limited and unlimited powers is abolished, if those limits do not confine the persons on whom they are imposed, and if acts prohibited and acts allowed, are of equal obligation. It is a proposition too plain to be contested, that the constitution controls any legislative act repugnant to it . . . Certainly all those who have framed written constitutions contemplate them as forming the fundamental and paramount law of the nation, and consequently, the theory of every such government must be, that an act of the Legislature, repugnant to the constitution, is void.

It is possible to argue that the "balance of power" among the branches of government is a political, not constitutional, problem, and that the Supreme Court, itself having an interest in the balance, cannot be at once both party and judge. Nonetheless, it is settled law and practice that our Court possesses the authority to render such judgments. But it might have been otherwise: this idea of the court is a sharp break with the British tradition, where it is Parliament, not any court, that alone possesses the power to interpret, and in some cases define, the way the nation is governed.

In the American system, the Congress and the president cannot by law change the Constitutional balance of legislative power, even if both the Congress and president agree to the change. The tale of how this principle was reaffirmed in *Chadha* is one of the most interesting and complex stories of modern jurisprudence.

Background and Facts of the Case

Jagdish Chadha was born in 1944 in Kenya, of Indian parents. (His father moved to Kenya from South Africa, but was of Indian origin; his mother moved directly from India.) Kenya became independent from Great Britain in 1963 and moved to eliminate the vestiges of colonialism, particularly a race-based class structure in employment and government (Craig, 1988, pp. 4–35). Of course, in "Africanizing" the nation's workforce, Kenya in some ways replicated the injustices of race-based policies, with a particular bias against immigrants from other parts of the British Commonwealth (including Indians) who were not citizens at the time of independence.

Chadha had known several American Peace Corps volunteers in Kenya and had been friendly with them. They had suggested that he go to the United States to study, an idea that appealed to him, and he began the process of applying for a student visa. Of course, he faced the problem of needing a legal country of residence, and he also applied for citizenship in Kenya.

But Kenya was changing. The Immigration and Trade Licensing Acts, passed in 1967, severely restricted the ability of workers without permits to make a living, or even find a place to live. Work permits, however, were hard to obtain, and were good for only a few months. In 1968 the noose tightened still further: the United Kingdom announced it would accept only a strict quota of Asians from Kenya and other parts of formerly British East Africa. Then India and Pakistan imposed similar quotas, small enough to constitute virtual bans. South Asian residents of Kenya were in an impossible situation: they could neither stay nor leave legally. Threats of violence and open acts of discrimination were common. Between 1963 and 1968, 45,000 Asians did manage to leave Kenya for England, India, and Pakistan. Many others left for other countries, with their citizenship in a precarious state.

Chadha was but a mote in this surging tide of humanity, a case typical of the predicament in which Kenyan émigrés found themselves. Traveling with a British passport, he arrived in the United States in September 1966. When he contacted the Kenyan consulate, he was told unequivocally that he was a British subject and not a citizen of Kenya. Since he could under no circumstances travel to Great Britain because of the quota on immigrants there, his nationality was now ambiguous: he was not a permanent resident of the United States and was living there under a student visa, but he could not leave.

He had been accepted at Bowling Green State University in Ohio, and for the next six years he studied there, working a variety of jobs to support himself. After completing a BS in business, and an MA in political science and economics, he began job hunting in early 1972. Because his U.S. student visa was good only until June 30, 1972, he contacted the British Consulate to investigate the possibility of moving there to look for work. But in May 1972, less than two months before his student visa expired, he was informed by the British vice consul that his request for a voucher could not possibly be considered for at least a year, and probably much longer. He was advised to seek to "regularize" his residence in the United States, so he could find legal employment there.

Chadha was stuck. Kenya would not accept him, the British wouldn't claim him, but he could not legally remain in the United States. He moved to Los Angeles and interviewed for a variety of jobs but was always turned down when it was discovered that he was not a legal permanent resident of the United States. He approached the Immigration and Naturalization Service (INS) office in Los Angeles, but as soon as it was discovered that his visa had expired, and that he was no longer a student anyway, he was slated for a deportation hearing. The INS reaction was consistent with U.S. law, but Chadha was understandably upset at being treated like a criminal, since he had in fact made good-faith efforts to leave for Great Britain for most of the previous year.

After a series of hearings before INS administrative law judges, using attorneys with little experience in immigration law, Chadha did arrive at what seemed like a solution: he applied for an order of "suspension of deportation," based on an "extreme hardship" claim.[1] He claimed (plausibly) that he would face economic discrimination and political hostility in either Kenya or Britain. Judge Sipkin, after several hearings, denied the application for suspension of deportation. Chadha's lawyer immediately asked for asylum on behalf of Chadha. But Judge Sipkin appears to have had a change of heart, perhaps (though this is speculation) believing that a more experienced attorney could have presented the case much more effectively. Four months later, in June 1974, Judge Sipkin did order the deportation suspended.

So far, this is all just a sad story, one like literally thousands of other stories about immigrants. It was the two stipulations that closed the suspension of deportation order that matter, for our purposes.

> IT IS FURTHER ORDERED that if Congress takes no action adverse to the order granting suspension of deportation, the proceedings will be cancelled. . . .

IT IS FURTHER ORDERED that in the event Congress takes action adverse to the order granting suspension of deportation these proceedings will be reopened upon notice to the respondent.

Though this was perfectly standard language for administrative law decisions in the INS (in fact, the stipulations were required by law, in just this form), it seems odd. Why should an executive branch agency reach a conclusion in a judicial proceeding, only to be forced (in effect) to submit every one of those decisions to the Congress for approval?

The answer is that these boilerplate stipulations were the product of the "legislative veto" provision of the enabling statutes of many federal rule-making agencies. Authority to make administrative judgments about immigrants effectively resided in the INS, but this authority was delegated and contingent. Ultimately, the only power to regulate immigration in the U.S. government inheres in the national government. Article I, Section 8, Clause 4 of the Constitution clearly gives this power ("to establish an uniform rule of naturalization") to the Congress.

So, while Congress had formally delegated to the INS the power to make judgments in individual cases, and to promulgate general rules, this delegation was not complete, and it was not irrevocable. This revocability, or "veto" provision in the law, proved crucial in Chadha's case. Though the INS judge had granted a "suspension of deportation" order, it was still possible for Congress to take action.

And in December 1975 Congress did take action. Actually, it was something less than the whole Congress. Joshua Eilberg (D-PA), who chaired the Immigration, Citizenship, and International Law Subcommittee of the House Judiciary Committee, introduced a private bill on December 12. Because it was near the end of an exhausting and contentious session, and the bill was "private," it didn't attract much attention.

> H. RES. 926: RESOLVED, That the House of Representatives does not approve the granting of permanent residence in the United States to the aliens hereinafter named, in which cases the Attorney General has submitted reports to the Congress pursuant to section 244(a)(1) of the Immigration and Naturalization Act, as amended. . .

In the list of names that followed, Jagdish Chadha's name appeared second. On December 16, without either a debate or a formal vote, the House passed the bill on the Private Calendar.

And that was that. No explanation, and no recourse, was available to Mr. Chadha. According to the law, in immigration policy and dozens of other policy areas, a resolution passed by a majority of *either* chamber of Congress was sufficient to "veto" a policy of an executive agency.

We will now turn to a broader account of the legislative veto, though we will return to Chadha at the end. Larger forces were now at work, as foes of the legislative veto, stemming from a variety of different interests with the shared purpose of preserving or restoring the separation of power among the branches, took over the litigation and appealed it to the U.S. Supreme Court.

This aspect of the process is important to understand: Jagdish Chadha, on his own resources, could never have afforded the lengthy litigation and outstanding legal talent, such as Alan Morrison, then of the Public Citizen Litigation Group, required to bring the case up through the federal appellate system. The only reason that any of us now study *INS v Chadha* is that powerful groups seized on the case as a vehicle to fight the legislative veto, which they believed to be unconstitutional. We turn now to the other thread of our story, the legislative veto itself.

The Legislative Veto in the Law

Before *INS v. Chadha* (462 U.S. 919 [1983]), there had been no authoritative ruling on the legality of the legislative veto, even though this form of contingent delegation veto had been used for fifty years. It was first used as a result of a deal made in 1932 between Congress and President Herbert Hoover, who wanted to reorganize the federal government (Tolchin, 1983, p. 4). Since then, 350 legislative veto provisions had been enacted as a means for Congress to manage its oversight burden. Interestingly, though it would appear that the legislative veto limits powers of the executive branch, the inclusion of the veto provision was often accepted, or even advocated, by the executive. The reason is that Congress was guaranteed another chance at executive rule making, and so Congress wrote legislation that conferred broader powers on the executive. Without the legislative veto, the effective power of the executive would be reduced also.

Legislative vetoes are not mentioned in the Constitution, and there is no single definition of them. It is useful to consider the broad outlines and features of vetoes, however.

A legislative veto is any legislative provision that subjects actions taken by a federal agency to review by the legislative branch.

Legislative vetoes may stipulate that all of Congress, one house, or a certain committee, majority, or individual review the executive action.

The veto can be either affirmative (the agency must win approval for the action to stand, as was true for deportation suspension until 1962), or it can be negative (the rule is law unless Congress acts, as was the case for immigration rulings when Chadha's case was considered).

Congress assigns itself a period of time in which to act. Common examples include periods of thirty, sixty, or ninety days, but in immigration cases the period is up to two years.

The vetoes can apply to a one-time action, such as federal reorganization during the New Deal, or repeated acts, such as alien deportation.

The use of the legislative veto increased with the rapid growth in the size of the executive branch of government, arguably as a necessary response to it. It increased most rapidly in the years following Watergate, because Congress wanted greater control over the actions of the executive branch.[2] One of the most ardent supporters of the legislative veto was Elliot Levitas, a U.S. representative from Georgia. In testimony before the House Judiciary Committee, Levitas argued that

> If the founders of our nation could somehow return, 188 years after they wrote our Constitution, to see us engaged in a true, nonviolent revolution to get lawmaking power restored to Congress, they would be thunderstruck at the pass to which we have come. . . . They would ask, "How did it happen that the things we fought for—control over the executive power, power by the people through their representatives—should be the object of a revolution, albeit peaceful?" (Craig, 1988, p. 40)

Levitas was referring to what he saw as the increasing power of "nonelected" (and presumably, therefore, unaccountable) bureaucrats. To Levitas and other supporters of the veto, federal agencies had grabbed the power to enact regulations that controlled the lives and actions of citizens.

The truth is surely a bit more complicated. The legislative veto has always been used strategically: presidents and executive agencies comply with, and even advocate, the veto so that they can get greater discretion from Congress. Franklin D. Roosevelt, for example, purposely allowed for legislative vetoes in the New Deal legislation to extract more discretion from the Congress to do what he wanted (Fisher, 1993, p. 281).

Congress, too, has complex reasons for imposing legislative vetoes. On the high-minded side, Levitas's argument surely does have some merit. By checking the activities of bureaucrats whose actions are mostly hidden from view or appeal, members of Congress ensure responsiveness and accountability. Legislation with a veto provision can delegate greater latitude to the expert bureaucrats applying the laws, because Congress can always pull back on the reins if the authority is abused.

Supporters of the legislative veto argue that every day Congress engages in attempts to control agencies without making new public laws—informal contacts, Government Accounting Office studies, threats of budget reduction, and other means. To think otherwise "is a caricature of Congress, heretofore found only in the most sophomoric treatment" (Fisher, 1987, p. 214).

The claim that Congress constantly intervenes in executive action is surely correct, and it is hard to imagine our system without it. When Congress passes a law, it often leaves many of the details of implementation and enforcement, and perhaps even the specifics of the law itself, vague and unspecified. What Congress is doing is two things: (1) delegating the actual work of specifying details to experts in the relevant federal agency, and (2) preserving an ability to deny responsibility if the form of the "law" promulgated by the agency angers constituents. There is third aspect of the process that might not be obvious, but it is very important: (3) Congress also is delegating the "oversight" of the agency . . . to interest groups!

This last step is accomplished through the Administrative Procedures Act (1946), which requires that agencies publish proposed rules in the Federal Register, a government document that is read closely only by those whose activities would be affected by the proposed rule. The public then has at least thirty days, and often two months or longer, to object in the "comment period." The agency can amend, or withdraw, the regulation in response to these comments.

Together, these three elements (delegate the details, avoid the blame, invite feedback) constitute an extraordinarily efficient system from the perspective of members of Congress. As several political scientists have pointed out (Kiewet & McCubbins, 1991; McCubbins & Schwartz, 1984; McCubbins, Noll, & Weingast, 1987, 1989), members of Congress need never take specific action or perform active oversight, *yet the actual policy outcomes are very close to those that would have been observed if Congress had done all the work itself.* This frees up members of Congress to spend their time working on new legislation, or visiting their districts.

Still, the fact that Congress has designed a system where it has influence does not mean that Congress also needs a legislative veto. Further, and more important for our account, the real question about the legislative veto is not whether it is good or bad. Instead, we must focus on the question answered in *Chadha:* is the legislative veto *constitutional?* What are the limits of legislative action, and the beginning of executive authority? How can the authority to perform legislative action be delegated, and under what circumstances can it be taken back?

This was the question on which *Chadha* turned. Chief Justice Warren Burger, writing for the majority, argued that the attempt of Congress to override the INS violated the constitutional doctrine of separation of powers. Citing the majority opinion in *Buckley v. Valeo* (424 U.S. 1 [1976]), Burger claimed that the separation of powers doctrine was "woven in" to the Constitution, though the words do not appear. The legislative veto violated it, since it allowed a "legislative action" that was neither voted on in both houses, nor presented to the president for signature, as Article I requires.[3]

This decision was a landmark in constitutional law and had perhaps the largest impact of any decision in the twentieth century on the structure of government. Justice Byron White, one of the dissenters from the majority opinion, wrote that *Chadha* "strikes down in one fell swoop provisions in more laws than the Court has cumulatively invalidated in its history" ("Excerpts from Supreme Court decision," 1983, p. B5). Elsewhere in the dissent, he elaborated: "Our Federal Government was intentionally chartered with the flexibility to respond to contemporary needs without losing sight of fundamental democratic principles."

The question of which side is right in this debate is difficult, because there is merit in both arguments. Political scientist Jessica Korn argues that the separation of powers preserved by *Chadha* allows for an efficient division of labor in the government, which the founders thought was an important goal (Korn, 1996).[4] Constitutional scholar Louis Fisher suggests that Congress needs a way to keep the executive branch from writing its own laws (Fisher, 1993, p. 275). And Presidents Herbert Hoover, Dwight Eisenhower, Jimmy Carter, Ronald Reagan, and George Bush, Sr., at least, have publicly stated they believe legislative vetoes are unconstitutional, even though all have agreed to them at various times.

Since the landmark decision in 1983, little has actually changed in the way Congress and the executive branch use and accept legislative vetoes. In the ten years after the decision, more than 200 such vetoes were built into new statues (Fisher, 1993, p. 275). Supreme Court Justices have ruled that statutes with a legislative veto in them are still legal if the veto is "severable" from the rest of the law (Shirley, 1985), so why shouldn't members of Congress try to slip them in? Congress continues to control agencies' activities by preempting them, modifying their jurisdiction, limiting appropriations, and creatively using joint resolutions. They follow these formal approaches on "an ad hoc and piecemeal basis (as were legislative vetoes)" (Kaiser, p. 243).

It is clear, however, that even if *Chadha* is not enforced, it nonetheless has an important effect. *Chadha* requires all significant executive actions to be written into law—a heavy burden for many agencies as they go about their daily activities. In 1984 the National Aeronautics and Space Administration compromised with the House Appropriations Committee because it was easier than trying to pass a new law every time they needed to exceed a spending cap (Fisher, 1993, p. 289).

Korn asserts that legislative vetoes in appropriations bills have never had the force of law because congressional appropriations are continuously amendable and do not have the status of ordinary statues. Nevertheless, she quotes a congressional staffer as reporting that the veto possibility has the desired effect on agencies of keeping them in line with the committee's wishes, even though the veto often does not make it into the final bill (Korn, 1996, p. 40). Presidents, too, feel the weight of the threat of possible legislative vetoes, even after *Chadha*. Korn notes that the first President Bush continued to follow congressional procedures (even when they included a legislative veto) in trade agreements because it was easier than passing a new law (Korn, 1996, p. 117).

Three years later in the case of *Bowsher v. Synar,* the Supreme Court reaffirmed its opinion that after Congress passes a law, it must keep its hands off. But in 1996, on the heels of the so-called Republican Revolution, Congress passed and the president signed the Congressional Review Act (CRA), which gives members of Congress sixty days to revoke a rule made by an executive agency after it has been finalized. Both houses must vote and agree to the nullification, and the president must sign it for it to void the rule. This keeps it constitutional under the parameters of *Chadha*. While the law has only been used once to overturn an agency rule making,[5] the threat of CRA nullification may be enough to ensure that agencies are doing what the Congress wants (Pierce, 1997).

Supporters of the CRA say it allows Congress to delegate, which relieves some of its heavy workload, opens a dialogue on rules instead of keeping them hidden from public and congressional review (Korn, 1996, p. 13), and according to Korn, does not really give Congress very much power, though her argument on this point is unconvincing. As Justice Antonin Scalia has said, without legislative vetoes, the onus to oversee the actions of the agencies is left completely on the courts, who know little about the policies concerned, instead of the relatively knowledgeable Congress (Rosenberg, 1999, quoted from dissent in *Mistretta v. United States,* 488 U.S. 361 [1999]).

The CRA process mandates that agencies submit all of their rules—tens of thousands—to the presidentially controlled Office of Management and Budget (OMB). That organization then classifies each of them as either minor or major enough to warrant congressional review. Critics of the Congressional Review Act say that this process is a logistical impossibility and a highly politicized practice as well. Logistically, this burdensome requirement creates incentives for agencies not to report every rule to OMB, especially since, as written, the process is sheltered entirely from judicial review. And politically, it allows the president to exert pressure on his own OMB to favor or ignore certain rules as fit his agenda.

In sum, the Supreme Court will have a very hard time eliminating the legislative veto, if that is what it intends to do. Congress is nothing if not clever in its attempts to manipulate power. Much of the time executive agencies and the president find legislative vetoes more palatable than the alternatives. In spite of *Chadha,* therefore, the legislative veto and the CRA live on. Their purpose is mostly symbolic, but effective. *Chadha* keeps agencies under control by forcing them to comply with congressional wishes or have whole new laws passed. Congress need not reject rules it disagrees with. Instead, the threat of CRA nullification prevents agencies from making such rules in the first place.

Postscript: Jagdish Chadha

What about Mr. Chadha himself? We left his story just as the case was being appealed to the Supreme Court, because by that time the case was really about larger issues. Still, the particular outcome (as is true in all court cases) was still important for the litigant who had started it all.

In July 1977, the petitioner's (i.e., Chadha's) brief had been filed with the Ninth Circuit Court. The case was not argued before the Supreme Court until February 22, 1982. Finally, more than a year later, on June 23, 1983, the Court announced its decision: the congressional (H. Res. 976, passed in December 1975) action vetoing the suspension of deportation order had no legal force, because it was based on a constitutionally invalid portion of the Immigration and Naturalization Act. Chadha could not be deported.

By the time the case was decided, Chadha had married and was working at the Pacific Stereo Store in San Francisco. He had two daughters and had become an American citizen. On his "very, very small, insignificant case," Chadha had the following observation: "Justice at the higher levels in America, by my experience, seems uncorrupt and uncorruptible. At the lower levels, though, justice seems to be for the privileged; those who can afford the legal talent to get it. Legal rights and protections are worthless for those who cannot understand them, and they are so complicated that most can't" (Craig, 1988, p. 232).

The majority decision, written by Justice Burger, closed with an observation that seems a fitting end also for our account of Chadha's experience with the American government. Burger said, "with all the obvious flaws of delay, untidiness, and potential for abuse, we have not yet found a better way to preserve freedom than by making the exercise of power subject to the carefully crafted restraints spelled out in the Constitution."

NOTES

1. There was actually some confusion on the part of Chadha's attorney between suspension of deportation, which would have resulted in permanent resident status, and "withholding of deportation," which would have required a showing of an actual danger of persecution, not just discrimination or economic privation. For more specifics, see Craig, 1988, pp. 12–14.

2. For a review of the growth and use of the veto, see Bolton, 1977, or Lee, 1985. Between 1970 and 1975, Congress passed nearly ninety laws that contained some form of legislative veto provision.

3. This claim does have considerable modern scholarly support. See, for example, Sargentich, 1987.

4. For views of the founders, see Federalists 10 and 51.

5. This was the interesting case of the Occupational Safety and Health Administration's ergonomics standards. After being proposed under the Reagan administration, the Department of Labor worked on them for ten years. They were controversial and were adopted in the waning days of the Clinton administration. Two months after George W. Bush took office, Congress used the CRA to revoke them in March of 2000.

REFERENCES

Excerpts from Supreme Court decision on legislative vetoes. (1983, June 24). *New York Times,* p. B5.

Bolton, J. R. (1977). *The legislative veto: Unseparating the powers.* Washington, DC: American Enterprise Institute for Public Policy Research.

Craig, B. H. (1988). *Chadha: The story of an epic constitutional struggle.* New York: Oxford University Press.

Fisher, L. (1987). The administrative world of *Chadha* and *Bowsher. Public Administration Review, 47,* pp. 213–219.

Fisher, L. (1993). The legislative veto: Invalidated, it survives. *Law and Contemporary Politics, 56,* pp. 273–292.

Kaiser, F. M. (1984). Congressional control of executive actions in the aftermath of the *Chadha* decision. *Administrative Law Review, 36,* pp. 239–276.

Kiewiet, D. R., & McCubbins, M. (1991). *The logic of delegation: Congressional parties and the appropriations process.* Chicago, IL: University of Chicago Press.

Korn, J. (1996). *The power of separation.* Princeton, NJ: Princeton University Press.

Lee, W. P. (1985). FLPMA's legislative veto provisions and *INS v. Chadha:* Who controls the federal lands? *Boston College Environmental Affairs Law Review, 12,* pp. 791–821.

McCubbins, M., & Schwartz, T., (1984) Congressional oversight overlooked: Police patrols vs. fire alarms. *American Journal of Political Science, 28,* pp. 165–179.

McCubbins, M., Noll, R., & Weingast, B. (1987). Administrative procedures as instruments of political control. *Journal of Law, Economics, and Organization, 3,* pp. 243–275.

McCubbins, M., Noll, R., & Weingast, B. (1989). Structure and process, policy, and politics: Administrative arrangements and the political control of agencies. *Virginia Law Review, 75,* pp. 431–482.

Pierce, R. J., Jr. (1997, March 6). Testimony before the Subcommittee on Commercial and Administrative Law of the Committee on the Judiciary, U.S. House of Representatives: Oversight hearings on the Congressional Review Act.

Rosenberg, M. (1999). Whatever happened to congressional review of agency rulemaking?: A brief overview, assessment, and proposal for reform. *Administrative Law Review, 51,* pp. 1051–1092.

Sargentich, T. O. (1987). The contemporary debate about legislative-executive separation of powers. *Cornell Law Review, 42,* pp. 430–487.

Shirley, W. A. (1985). Resolving challenges to statues containing unconstitutional legislative veto provisions. *Columbia Law Review, 85,* pp. 1808–1832.

Tolchin, M. (1983, June 24). Hoover was first to let congress veto president. *New York Times,* p. B4.

Legislating the Links

PGA Tour, Inc. v. Martin (2001)

REGINALD S. SHEEHAN

Few people, even those who had taken an occasional whack at a golf ball at a driving range, had ever heard of Casey Martin. By the time the Supreme Court handed down its ruling in the spring of 2000, the American public had heard much more about this professional golfer who suffered from a rare degenerative blood disease that made walking a golf course a life-risking proposition. The Court's decision holding that the PGA Tour was not a private organization with a First Amendment claim to freedom of association but a public accommodation subject to the federal Americans With Disabilities Act meant that Martin was entitled to use an electric cart to get around the golf course. Although the constitutionality of this law was not at issue in this case, it nevertheless represents the considerable extent to which Congress can use its power to regulate interstate commerce.

The case of *PGA Tour, Inc. v. Martin* was one of the most highly publicized cases of the 2000 term of the U.S. Supreme Court. The Court heard arguments in the case on January 17, 2001, and delivered a 7–2 decision on May 29. The issue of protecting the rights of disabled athletes in professional sports caught the attention of the media and the American public in a way that is generally not seen in most Supreme Court decisions, not even most landmark decisions.

Golf is a sport with a history of elitism, and most Americans are not familiar with the rules of the game and do not actively participate in it for recreation. Nevertheless, when the controversy surrounding the PGA Tour's decision not to allow Casey Martin to use a golf cart erupted, people from all walks of life, golfers and nongolfers alike, had strong opinions on what constituted the fundamental rules of the game and what modifications to those rules would be acceptable. It fell to the Supreme Court to decide those questions and determine whether Casey Martin, a disabled athlete, could use the judicial system to alter participation rules in a professional sport.

Professional Golfers Association Tour and Casey Martin

The PGA Tour, Inc. of the Professional Golfers Association (PGA) is an organization founded for the purpose of sponsoring and cosponsoring professional golf tournaments in the United States. The PGA sponsors the PGA Tour, the Buy.com Tour (known as the NIKE Tour at the time of the case), and the Senior PGA Tour on an annual basis, with approximately 470 golfers participating in the three tours. The elite PGA Tour brings together the "best of the best" golfers in the United States, with only 200 players qualifying for play. When a player qualifies for the PGA Tour, he earns his "card" and is given the privilege to participate in tour-sponsored events.

There are several ways a player can qualify for tournament play on the PGA Tour. Each tournament event holds qualifying rounds the week before a tournament and any player can compete for the few slots that might be available. The PGA will also grant a "player card" to any player on the Buy.com Tour who wins three events in a season. But for the most part, players on the PGA Tour and the Buy.com Tour earn their playing privileges through a qualifying school known as "Q-School." The Q-School is a three-stage qualifying event that anyone can participate in if they are willing to pay the $3,000 entry fee and submit letters of reference, with the letters usually coming from members who already participate in the two tours.

Approximately 1,000 players attend the first stage of Q-School each year. The players participate in four rounds of eighteen holes of golf, and about half the players score low enough to progress to the second stage of qualifying. The second stage consists of another four rounds of golf, which results in cutting the field to around 170 players who will participate in the third stage. All of the players making it to the final stage are guaranteed a position on the Buy.com Tour, and about one fourth of the players in the third stage will receive the card that will allow them to play on the PGA Tour.

Obviously, this is a highly competitive process, and the player who makes it on either tour, but especially the PGA Tour, is in an elite class of golfers. Moreover, to maintain a card on either tour in the following year, the golfer will have to perform at a certain level in the current year or run the risk of having to attend Q-School again to qualify for the subsequent year.

During the first two stages of Q-school, players are permitted to use golf carts, but during the third stage, golf carts are prohibited. Additionally, golf carts are not allowed in PGA Tour and Buy.com Tour events. Golf carts are allowed in the PGA-sponsored Senior PGA Tour, but many of the players choose to walk anyway.

Casey Martin was a participant in the Q-school and qualified for the 1998 and 1999 NIKE Tour. Because he performed so well on that tour, he was granted his card for the PGA Tour in 2000. Martin is a very talented golfer, who played on the Stanford University golf team with Tiger Woods, a team that won the NCAA national championship.

Martin is also an individual who has suffered since birth from Klippel-Trenaunay-Weber Syndrome. This is a disease that affects the circulatory system, and in Martin's case it caused an obstruction of the blood flow in his right leg, which resulted in pain and fatigue. Moreover, walking for extended lengths and periods of time could lead to risks of hemorrhaging and blood clots and could even result in fractures in the leg. Stanford University requested from the NCAA that Martin be given an exemption from the "no carts" rule used in its events, and the NCAA granted the exemption, allowing Martin to play those events with a golf cart while competing in college at the amateur level.

When Casey Martin paid his fee and entered Q-school, he petitioned the PGA Tour for the same type of exemption so that he could use a golf cart in the third stage of qualifying and on the two tours for which he would subsequently qualify. The PGA refused to grant the exemption, and Casey Martin filed in district court for a preliminary injunction that would allow him access to a cart during the third stage of qualifying. The district court granted his request, making it possible for Martin to use a cart in the Q-school and on both the NIKE Tour and the PGA Tour.

The PGA appealed the district court ruling to the Ninth Circuit Court of Appeals, and the ruling was upheld at the circuit level. Meanwhile, a similar case was being appealed in the Seventh Circuit Court of Appeals that resulted in a decision inconsistent with the lower court ruling in Casey Martin's case, so the U.S. Supreme Court decided to grant certiorari when the PGA appealed the Ninth Circuit decision favoring Martin.

Americans With Disabilities Act of 1990

The severity of the disease afflicting Casey Martin qualified him for protection under the Americans With Disabilities Act (ADA) passed by Congress in 1990. The ADA was passed by Congress to address the long history of discrimination against disabled individuals in American society. It is a comprehensive and sweeping piece of legislation that is viewed by many civil rights advocates as pivotal in the development of American society. Justice Anthony Kennedy has written that the act serves as "a milestone on the path to a more decent, tolerant, progressive society" (*Board of Trustees of University of Alabama v. Garrett,* 531 U.S. 356, 2001).

During deliberations Congress found that "historically, society has tended to isolate and segregate individuals with disabilities, and, despite some improvements, such forms of discrimination against individuals with disabilities continue to be a serious and pervasive social problem" (Americans With Disabilities Act of 1990, 42 U.S.C. § 12101 [a] [2]). Moreover, Congress found that the discrimination existed in housing, employment, education, communication, transportation, public accommodations, voting, and health services and that it was prevalent throughout most of the institutions in American society. After a careful assessment of the scope of discrimination against disabled individuals, Congress decided there was a need for significant legislation that would be wide-ranging in its coverage and that would serve the purpose of removing discriminatory obstacles that were currently preventing disabled individuals from playing active roles in society.

The ADA prohibits discrimination against disabled individuals in three major areas. Title I of the act addresses discrimination in employment and Title II forbids discrimination in public services. Title III of the ADA prohibits discrimination in public accommodations and is the provision under which Casey Martin challenged the "no golf cart" rule of the PGA Tour. Title III states: "No individual shall be discriminated against on the basis of disability in the full and equal enjoyment of the goods, services, facilities, privileges, advantages, or accommodations of any place of public accommodation by any person who owns, leases (or leases to), or operates a place of public accommodation" (ADA of 1990, 42 U.S.C. § 12182 [a]).

The act went on to define the phrase "public accommodation" and identified twelve categories such as lodging facilities, restaurants, motion picture houses, museums, and so forth, and among those categories was one that included "gymnasium, health spa, bowling alley, golf course, or other place of exercise or recreation" (ADA of 1990, 42 U.S.C. § 12181 [7]).

Casey Martin based his legal claim on the argument that since the PGA

Tour was played on golf courses and the tournaments were open to the paying public, the Title III protections should be afforded to him and his request
to use a cart should be granted. According to Title III, discrimination against
disabled individuals occurred in public accommodations when there was: "a
failure to make reasonable modifications in policies, practices, or procedures,
when such modifications are necessary to afford such goods, services, facilities, privileges, advantages, or accommodations to individuals with disabilities, unless the entity can demonstrate that making such modifications would
fundamentally alter the nature of such goods, services, facilities, privileges,
advantages or public accommodations" (ADA of 1990, 42 U.S.C. § 12182
[b] [2]).

Martin argued that the failure to provide a modification to the "no golf
cart" rule was discrimination as defined under Title III of the ADA. The
PGA Tour claimed that it did not fall into the categories of Title III, because
it was a private entity providing entertainment to the public and did not own
the golf courses but rather rented them during the week for tournament play.
Moreover, it further argued that a change in its "rules of play" would be a
modification that would result in an fundamental alteration in the game itself and would provide an advantage to one player not enjoyed by the others
participating.

Supreme Court's Interpretation of the ADA

In the majority opinion of the Court, Justice John Paul Stevens identified
the two questions presented in the case of *PGA Tour, Inc. v. Martin*. (1) Does
the ADA "protect access to professional golf tournaments by qualified entrants with a disability"? and (2) "whether a disabled contestant may be denied the use of a golf cart because it would 'fundamentally alter the nature'
of the tournaments" (*PGA Tour, Inc. v. Martin*, 532 U.S. 661 [2001]).

The answer to the first question was dependent on how the Court would
interpret "public accommodation" under Title III of the ADA. It was clear in
the Court's reading of Title III that golf tours did fall within the defined coverage of a public accommodation. Justice Stevens argues, "petitioner's golf
tours and their qualifying rounds fit comfortably within the coverage of Title
III, and Martin within its protections. The events occur on 'golf course(s),' a
type of place specifically identified by the Act as a public accommodation. In
addition, at all relevant times, petitioner 'leases' and 'operates' golf courses to
conduct its Q-Schools and tours. As a lessor and operator of golf courses,
then, petitioner must not discriminate against any 'individual' in the 'full and
equal enjoyment of the goods, services, facilities, privileges, advantages, and
accommodations' of those courses" (*PGA Tour*, p. 675).

The majority went on to suggest that the privileges associated with the golf tournaments were twofold, with the public enjoying the privilege of viewing the performance of the golfers on the golf course and the prospective golf professional having the privilege of participating in Q-school and the golf tours. The latter was an important point for Martin, because the PGA Tour was arguing that the golfers who compete were not members of the protected class defined under the ADA. Specifically, they pointed to the language in Title III identifying "clients and customers" in places of accommodation as the class of disabled individuals the law was designed to protect. It followed from the PGA Tour's argument that Martin should not have argued his case under Title III but rather under Title I of the ADA, which prohibited discrimination in employment. Moreover, according to the argument, Martin was not employed by the PGA Tour but rather acted as an "independent contractor" and therefore could not be covered under Title I either.

The problem for PGA Tour was that the Court viewed Casey Martin as a "client and customer," because the golfers pay a fee of $3,000 to participate in the Q-School, and if they earn a place on one of the tours, they still are in the role of a client. The conclusion of the majority was that the public has the opportunity to watch the golf tournaments and the public also has the opportunity to participate in the golf tournaments, albeit, only a select few are good enough to take advantage of the latter opportunity. Nevertheless, these two "privileges" for the public exist together on the golf courses the PGA Tour uses for its tournaments, and therefore the audience and the participants are covered by the protections of Title III of the ADA.

Justice Stevens pointed to case law interpreting the Civil Rights Act of 1964 as supportive of the conclusion drawn with regard to public accommodations that discriminated. In *Daniel v. Paul* (395 U.S. 298 [1969]), the Court had held that public accommodations being used for public entertainment could not discriminate against "spectators," but it also could not discriminate against participants "in some sport or activity" on the basis of race. Similarly, the PGA Tour and its leased golf courses were places of public accommodation engaging in entertainment and therefore could not discriminate against spectators or golfers at the tournaments on the basis of disability.

The second question before the Court was the more critical issue, not only for this case, but for future cases involving the applicability of the ADA to professional sports. PGA Tour argued that allowing Martin to use the golf cart was a modification that would "fundamentally alter the nature" of the tournaments, and therefore the ADA did not require that the tour comply with the request. Justice Stevens pointed out that there were two ways a rule change could fundamentally alter the game of golf. The change could affect all players equally but alter the nature of the game. Steven's example of this would be to change the diameter of the golf hole so that it is more difficult for all the players to hit the ball in the hole. The second change would be one that affected an individual or small group of individuals only and gave a distinct advantage to those individuals in competition. The majority of the Court concluded that providing an exemption to the walking rule for Martin did not cause a fundamental alteration under either definition.

Historically, golf was a game in which players made their way around the course by walking. The majority of golf courses in Scotland, the birthplace of the game, still do not allow golf carts on the courses, and golfing traditionalists tend to criticize the proliferation of golf carts in the United States. But as the Court pointed out, early golfers only carried three or four golf clubs and did not use a golf bag. Over the years there have been significant improvements in equipment and golf course design. All of these changes affected the game of golf, but they did not fundamentally alter the nature of the game. The "essence" of the game of golf is to take a ball and hit it up the fairway until you reach the green and putt it in the hole in the fewest number of strokes possible. Under that definition of the game of golf, all the changes in equipment and course design may make it easier to play the game, but they do not alter the "essence" of the game—to hit the ball and put in the hole in the fewest strokes possible. For the Court, the same logic applied to the use of golf carts, which was nothing more than an advancement that made it easier to carry your clubs up the fairway. But the game was still played the same way golfers have played it for hundreds of years.

The rules of golf, written by the United States Golf Association and the Royal and Ancient Golf Club of Scotland, are the official rules governing the play of amateurs and professionals around the world. Justice Stevens pointed out in the majority opinion that there was no provision in those rules prohibiting the use of golf carts or proscribing a penalty for anyone playing with the aid of a golf cart. Again, this was further evidence that walking was not an essential attribute of the game of golf as defined by the ruling bodies of the game. In fact, the walking rule was established only in the "hard cards" used by the PGA Tour for each of its tournaments. The hard cards identified local rules of play for the various golf courses on which tournaments were held, such as out of bounds areas, hazard areas, and rules for penalties that should be incurred for conditions unique to a particular course.

Since the walking rule was unique to the PGA Tour and not a fundamental attribute of the game itself, the Court had to determine if it was an "indispensable" part of tournament golf. It was difficult for the PGA Tour to make this argument, because it allowed the use of golf carts on the Senior

PGA Tour it sponsored, and it also allowed the use of carts in the first two rounds of the Q-School. But the PGA Tour wanted to narrow this argument and in its brief suggested that a distinction had to be made between golf in general and golf played at the highest tournament levels, because the "goal of the highest level competitive athletics is to assess and compare the performance of different competitors, a task that is meaningful only if the competitors are subject to identical substantive rules" (*PGA Tour, Inc. v. Casey Martin*, No. 00-24, December 29, 2000, Brief for Petitioner, p. 13). According to the PGA Tour, the granting of an exemption to Martin would undermine this basic principle of competition by giving an advantage to one player in the tournaments and thus would undermine the fundamental nature of the highest level tournaments. This argument was based on the assumption that walking the golf course did "inject the element of fatigue into the skill of shot-making" (994 F. Supp., 1242, 1250 [D.Ore. 1998]). Removing walking from the competition for one player could result in an advantage of one or several strokes that could be critical to the outcome of the event.

To support its argument the PGA Tour brought in several world-renowned golfers, like Jack Nicklaus and Arnold Palmer, to testify that fatigue was a factor in golf and that the walking rule did inject an element of fatigue into the game. It should be pointed out that neither Nicklaus nor Palmer ever suggested that providing Martin with an exemption would unfairly advantage him in a tournament. Rather, they commented at a general level about the walking rule and fatigue as a factor in tournament outcomes.

While this argument seemed on its face to be strong, the Court countered that "golf is a game in which it is impossible to guarantee that all competitors will play under exactly the same conditions or that an individual's ability will be the sole determinant of the outcome. . . . A lucky bounce may save a shot or two. Whether such happenstance events are more or less probable than the likelihood that a golfer afflicted with Klippel-Trenaunay-Weber Syndrome would one day qualify for the NIKE Tour and PGA Tour, they at least demonstrate that pure chance may have a greater impact on the outcome of elite golf tournaments than the fatigue resulting from the enforcement of the walking rule" (*PGA Tour,* p. 686).

More important, the Court found that even if the outcome of a tournament could be affected at a general level by fatigue, the PGA Tour had erred in its decision not to grant Martin an exemption, because it did not "consider Martin's personal circumstances" in its decision to deny his request for a golf cart. Under the guidelines of the ADA, the PGA Tour was required to address discrimination against "individuals with disabilities" and must make modifications or accommodations in its "policies, practices, or procedures" to provide access to the disabled individual. It was clear to the majority of the Court that a correct interpretation of the ADA required that each case be examined on an individual basis and not as a general rule. An across-the-board refusal to allow the use of a cart would be a violation of the ADA. The denial of the request could occur only after an individual-level analysis of the nature of Martin's disability and the extent to which granting him use of the cart would affect the outcome of the tournaments.

The Court concluded that an individual-level analysis led to a conclusion that in the case of Martin, the granting of an exemption to the walking rule would have no substantial impact on the outcome of the tournaments. Martin suffered tremendous pain while playing golf, whether he walked or rode in a cart, and was often completely exhausted after playing a round of golf even with the assistance of a cart. In the district court, the judge had concluded that Martin "easily endures greater fatigue even with a cart than his able-bodied competitors do by walking" (994 F. Supp., 1242, 1252 [D. Ore. 1998]).

In the view of the majority, if the purpose of the walking rule was to inject fatigue into the contest, then granting the waiver for the rule for Martin would not have any effect on the role of fatigue in the outcome, because Martin was clearly still at a disadvantage in that regard. In fact, all the modification to the rule would have done was provide Martin the opportunity to qualify and play in the tournaments, and in the Court's view "That is exactly what the ADA requires" (*PGA Tour,* p. 690).

Justice Scalia and Justice Thomas Dissent

In the dissenting opinion of Justice Antonin Scalia, joined by Justice Clarence Thomas, Scalia took issue with the majority's classification of Martin as a "customer and client" and therefore subject to ADA protections. According to Scalia, Martin was not paying to be entertained by the PGA Tour, but rather Martin was providing the entertainment as an individual contractor who sold his services. It did not matter to Scalia that the services were paid for in winnings. He likened it to other contractors like real estate agents who were paid based on performance. Justice Scalia states:

> The PGA TOUR is a professional sporting event, staged for the entertainment of a live and TV audience, the receipts from whom (the TV audience's admission price is paid by advertisers) pay the expenses of the tour, including the cash prizes for the winning golfers. The professional golfers on the tour are no more "enjoying" (the statutory term) the entertainment that the tour provides, or the facilities of the golf courses on which it is held, than pro-

fessional baseball players "enjoy" the baseball games in which they play or the facilities of Yankee Stadium. To be sure, professional ballplayers *partici-pate* in the games, and *use* the ballfields, but no one in his right mind would think that they are *customers* of the American League or of Yankee Stadium. They are themselves the entertainment that the customers pay to watch. (*PGA Tour,* p. 661)

If in fact Martin was equivalent to an independent contractor, then Title III of the ADA would not be applicable to his circumstances and he would not be protected by its provisions designed to protect "customers and clients."

Justice Scalia further argues that after the majority erred in applying Title III to this case, it compounded the error by holding that the golf cart modification would not fundamentally alter the game. In Scalia's view, the Court should have declined to even try to answer the question of whether walking is "essential" to the game. "To say that something is 'essential' is ordinarily to say that it is necessary to the achievement of a certain object. But since it is the very nature of a game to have no object except amusement. . . . it is quite impossible to say that any of a game's arbitrary rules is 'essential'" (*PGA Tour,* p. 661). He solidifies this point by observing that eighteen-hole golf courses, ten-foot baskets in basketball, and one-hundred-yard fields in football are all the result of tradition and are not essential to the game but are generally provided for by ruling bodies of the sports. Scalia's point was that the Court should not become the ruling body of golf by trying to define what is and is not essential to the game.

Finally, Scalia was most concerned with the Court's application of an individual-level analysis in the case. The majority had attempted to maintain a narrow ruling by arguing that in the case of Martin, he would be more fatigued even while using the cart than other golfers, so granting him the exemption did not alter the outcome of the game. Justice Scalia believed that this was the critical mistake made by the Court, because this method of analysis would be the determinative factor in any future cases.

[In] determining whether waiver of the "nonessential" rule will have an impermissible "competitive effect" by measuring the athletic capacity of the requesting individual, and asking whether the special dispensation would do no more than place him on par (so to speak) with other competitors, the Court guarantees that future cases of this sort will be numerous, and a rich source of lucrative litigation. One can envision the parents of a Little League player with attention deficit disorder trying to convince a judge that their son's disability makes it at least 25% more difficult to hit a pitched ball. (*PGA Tours,* p. 661)

Scalia did not see any language in the ADA suggesting that cases of this type should be evaluated on an individual basis. His interpretation of the purpose of the statute was "to assure that a disabled person's disability will not deny him *equal access* to (among other things) competitive sporting events—not that his disability will deny him an *equal chance to win* competitive sporting events" (*PGA Tours*, p. 661).

Implications of the Decision

The decision in the *PGA Tour, Inc. v. Martin* case received a tremendous amount of attention in the media, with most journalists saying they believed the decision was correct. The most common critique in the press was that the case should have never made it to the Supreme Court and that it was a mistake for the PGA Tour to have ever appealed the case through the court system. Many observers pointed out that this was a decision that should have been made behind closed doors at the PGA Tour offices (Albom, 2001). It would have been in the best interest of the Tour to have just granted the exemption to Martin with the stipulation that it was a unique case and that future cases would be evaluated on an individual basis. The PGA Tour would have been viewed as accommodating a person with disability with little effect on its tournaments, and there would not have been a Supreme Court precedent involving the application of the ADA to professional sports ("PGA v. ADA," 2001).

The effect of the PGA Tour pursuing a strategy of litigation was to bring the issue to national attention, creating negative publicity for a tour that already was perceived as elitist and primarily the domain of white able-bodied male athletes who had primarily come from upper-class country club backgrounds. The legal effect of the strategy was to establish a precedent that raised the question of whether the ADA could be used in the future to accommodate disabled athletes in other professional sports (Davis, 2002).

It is difficult to judge the impact of the decision with regard to how it will affect sports and disabled athletes. The decision is so recent that we have not had the opportunity to observe similar cases matriculating into the appeals courts. There are very few cases that have applied the ruling using the protections of the ADA. But if Scalia is right, we should expect the floodgates to open in the coming years as disabled athletes apply the majority view that "whether a person is disabled under the ADA is an individualized inquiry based on the particular circumstances of each case." If we interpret this literally, it means that every single plaintiff can view her/his case as unique from any previous plaintiff who has been to court, and therefore, the language of rulings in other cases may not be relevant to his/her situation. While this may not result in a rush of cases to the Supreme Court, it is possible that it will lead to an increase in these types of cases in the lower district courts.

The decision of the Court also raises another problem for future cases of this type in that courts not only will have to examine the individualized disability of the plaintiff but also will have to focus on a specific aspect of a sport to determine if a modification is reasonable and will not fundamentally alter the nature of the sport. This analysis will become very complicated with the variety of sports, and rules governing sports, that may come into question in future litigation.

Some would argue that what the Court did was send a message that if you do not like the rules of a game, then litigate (see Coulter, 2001). This is probably too harsh in that the Court, in fact, tried to emphasize that the decision should be interpreted narrowly and that its effect should not go beyond Casey Martin. In essence the majority on the Court took the route that many critiques said the PGA Tour executives should have taken in that it granted an exemption to Casey Martin with the view that, in the future, golfers requesting the exemption would in all likelihood be denied. The majority viewed this as a unique and unusual circumstance that would not come along very often in professional sports.

Conclusion

In *PGA Tour, Inc. v. Martin* the Supreme Court was being asked by Casey Martin to take an expansive view of the Americans With Disabilities Act and extend its coverage into the area of professional sports. The extent to which this will become a "landmark case" in American law is still an open question because of how recent the decision is and the nature of the legal reasoning presented by the Supreme Court majority. It is not clear whether this will open the door for similar litigation in other professional sports and whether the ADA will find wide applicability in this new realm.

This case does demonstrate how a case can take on a life of its own as it matriculates through the judiciary. Litigants often have to make strategic decisions regarding appeals to higher courts, and this would seem to be one instance where the litigant may have been better served resolving the dispute early in the process and not continuing to appeal the case to higher courts. Allowing the issue to enter the judicial system and then continuing to give it life through the appeals process brought the issue to the attention of a wider audience, including interest groups, media, and other athletes.

It is unlikely that the majority of observers would disagree with the outcome in the case. After all, was it really going to matter if Casey Martin used a golf cart while playing in the tournaments? In fact, Casey Martin has not been very successful on the tours and is currently struggling to maintain his playing card. Most people would agree that the PGA Tour should have just allowed him to play with a cart and see what effect it had on the game. What probably concerned most observers was that an issue of this type could find its way to the Supreme Court and receive such attention from people across the country. In the end, what should have been a simple accommodation by the PGA Tour led to a Supreme Court decision that could have significant consequences in the future for disabled athletes, professional sports, and the interpretation of the Americans With Disabilities Act.

The author wishes to acknowledge the assistance of Layne Pethick and Valerie Stacy who assisted in collecting background information on the case.

REFERENCES

Albom, M. (2001). Mitch Albom: PGA Tour's fight vs. Martin shameful. *Knight Ridder Newspapers*. Accessed on 1 February 2003 at http://www.freep.com/sports/albom/mitch18_20010118.htm.

Coulter, A. (2001). Supreme Court conquers the PGA. Human Events Online. Accessed on 1 February 2003 at http://www.townhall.com/columnists/anncoulter/ac20010608.shtml.

Davis, C. W. (2002, January-February). *P.G.A. Tour v Martin:* Supreme Court issues Casey Martin his "ticket to ride," *Journal of the Missouri Bar, 58,* p. 1.

Ragone, N. (2001). Its common sense. Off the Fairway. Accessed on 1 February 2003 at http://www.golfsociety.com/cgi/viewcolumn.asp?editorialid'162.

Vicini, J. (2001). Supreme Court: Casey Martin can ride in cart. Accessed on 1 February 2003 at http://www.K-T.org/caseymartin.html.

Federalism

Our Towering Superstructure Rests on a Rotten Foundation

Hammer v. Dagenhart (1918)

JULIE NOVKOV

In the early 1900s, as the American economy became increasingly dynamic and complex, a serious debate took place between powerful corporate interests that insisted that the principles of laissez-faire capitalism had a legally protected home in the Constitution and the Progressive movement that sought social reform through legislation. Child labor was one of the major areas of dispute, and in *Hammer* the Court concluded that the regulation of child labor was a local matter, not within the reach of Congress's power to regulate interstate commerce. By the late 1930s, however, the Court had taken a remarkable turn and embraced the idea of the modern welfare state put forth by the New Deal. The decision to overturn *Hammer* in 1941 upheld the Fair Labor Standards Act and ushered in a new and unprecedented era of congressional power to regulate the economy.

Our towering superstructure rests on a rotten foundation. Not until we have done away with child labor completely, not until we have taken the blood and bones of babies out of the keystone, will our industrial arch know permanence.

—*Judge Benjamin Lindsey and George Creel,* Children in Bondage, *1914*

By the mid-1910s, Progressive activists who had focused on regulating and ultimately eliminating child labor could ruminate optimistically about their accomplishments and goals. Their concerted efforts, organized principally through the National Child Labor Committee (NCLC) in New York, had achieved systematic legislative regulation in most states. The NCLC had effective spokespersons in Alexander McKelway and Owen Lovejoy, who presented research on child labor in multiple forums and formats. Photographer Lewis Hine was dispatched to workplaces where children could be found across the nation and documented their labor copiously. While many regulations had been challenged in the state courts, almost all had been upheld as serving the states' interests in protecting future citizens. Even the conservative U.S. Supreme Court, still despised by Progressives for its ruling in *Lochner v. New York* that had invalidated protective labor legislation, had upheld the states' rights to regulate child labor in *Sturges and Burn v. Beauchamp* in 1915.

Advocates for legislation had begun making their public case before the turn of the century by detailing the evils of child labor in terms of the damage done both to the children themselves and to the body politic by depriving it of healthy, well-educated, prepared citizens for future democratic development (see, e.g., Trattner, 1970; Hindman 2002). Those fighting for regulation were a coalition of middle- and upper-class progressive reformers and union leaders (who saw child labor as a damper on wages). Their efforts centered on a highly organized public campaign seeking to raise awareness about the ill effects of child labor, thereby making the passage of legislation on the state level easily justifiable both politically and constitutionally as an exercise of the states' police power.

While individual manufacturers worked against the further regulation of child labor, they did not initially have a national organization comparable to the NCLC to guide their efforts. Most opposition came from chambers of commerce and individual manufacturers themselves (primarily textile manufactures). One example from the Department of Labor was opponent of regulation Thomas Dawley's influential study (and defense) of mill work published in 1912, lauding the better health of families in mill villages as compared to other poor families in the south. Industrialist John D. Rockfeller also funded a major campaign against hookworm, which Dr. George Stiles had identified as the major cause of poverty and ill health among southerners (Hindman, 2002, pp. 56–57).

Nonetheless, until the National Association of Manufacturers (NAM) and the Executive Committee of Southern Cotton Manufacturers, both southern-based organizations, adopted the issue as their own, the opponents found themselves on the losing end of the battle for public opinion. These organizations realized that the battle against regulation would have to be fought on multiple fronts and that it would require long-term commitments and strategizing. They worked to select the best arenas for the struggle and settled on the courts as an area where regulation could be thwarted. They simultaneously continued the struggle over public opinion, recognizing that simple opposition to limits on child labor was not a viable political position.

These oppositional efforts succeeded in extracting some concessions. The comprehensive legislative campaign had not eliminated child labor. Activists detailed the ways legislation was underenforced and evaded, particularly in the South, even though every state had limited the employment of children to those over twelve by 1907 (Davidson, 1939, pp. 12–13). Opponents of legislation sought exemptions and weak enforcement mechanisms in the drafting of legislation. They cautioned that limits on child labor had to be balanced against the states' interests in promoting effective and quick economic development. They also tried their hand at countering the pathetic image of the sweated child with their own imagery, presenting the specter of the child unable to help (usually) his widowed mother or invalid father and the positive image of the child who gained real-world experience in the workplace, rendering him more mature and ready to take his place as a citizen.

By the 1910s progressive opponents of child labor had thus won some significant battles. The national consensus had rapidly moved in favor of limiting children's work, as evinced by the nearly universal embrace of state-based legislation. The public, the legislatures, and the courts largely agreed that the state had the right and the duty to protect children as future citizens. The next step was obvious: use this broad consensus to ground national legislation that solved the problem of southern exemptions and lack of effective enforcement. The principle of the state's authority over child labor seemed to be firmly established both by multiple state supreme court rulings and by the U.S. Supreme Court itself.

The idea of establishing national legislation had been floating around progressive circles for several years. The first serious attempt was in 1906 by Senator Albert Beveridge (R-IN), who sought the NCLC's endorsement of his bill forbidding carriers of interstate commerce to handle goods manufactured by children (Davidson, 1939, p. 130). After a bitter struggle, the NCLC voted to endorse the bill, but Alabaman Edgar Murphy, who had been the motive force behind its organization in 1904, resigned over the endorsement. He and others believed that a struggle for national regulation would necessarily dilute the NCLC's work on securing statewide legislation and had serious reservations about the constitutionality of the national bill.

Murphy's public split with the NCLC is worth examining briefly, since the NAM and its allies ultimately took up his arguments against national regulation. As the motive force behind early legislation seeking protection for children, Murphy was clearly not opposed to laws limiting children's work. He argued, however, that the individual states were the best sites for such legislation. Sovereignty was most comprehensive and sensitive at the state level, in his view, and federal legislation would preempt the states' impulses to develop regulation. Further, he claimed, constitutional considerations prevented the Beveridge bill from regulating child labor directly, and the resulting indirect regulation was bound to be less effective than solid state-based legislation. Finally, he believed that the commerce clause did not authorize such legislation.

The Beveridge bill did not win passage, as Congress refused to take action on it (Davidson, 1939, p. 135). The NCLC soon discovered that one of its lasting effects was the hardening of hostility among southern elites toward the northern-based child labor reformers. Efforts for national reform became framed as attacks on the autonomy of southern states and surreptitious attempts to centralize power by curtailing state sovereignty. Ultimately, the NCLC continued its investigative efforts but opted not to lead the fight for national reform. With President Theodore Roosevelt refusing to support the bill, the NCLC pushed instead for federally conducted research on child labor, which the Bureau of Labor undertook (Hindman, 2002, pp. 64–65). The next national initiative it supported was in favor of the establishment of the federal Children's Bureau in 1912, which became the main institutional advocate for national regulation.

The bill that would give rise to the Keating-Owen Act and *Hammer v. Dagenhart* was introduced in Congress as the Palmer-Owen bill in the House of Representatives in 1914 (Hindman, 2002, pp. 64–65). It was substantially the same as the Beveridge bill in terms of the standards it set and in its use of the mechanism of prohibiting the transport in interstate commerce of items manufactured with child labor. In the House's consideration of the bill, only a few voices were raised in opposition, and it arrived in the Senate with a 237–45 endorsement in early 1915 (Hindman, 2002, pp. 65–66). In the Senate, North Carolina's Senator Lee Overman was able to block passage for a year, but President Woodrow Wilson ultimately received the bill, retitled the Keating-Owen Act, and signed it into law on September 1, 1916. His support for the bill likely helped him to win reelection by garnering the support of progressives and liberal Republicans (Trattner, 1970, p. 132).

The bill, as ultimately passed, clearly regulated commerce. It prohibited producers, manufacturers, or dealers from shipping in interstate commerce any product of a factory in which children under fourteen had been permitted to work or children between fourteen and sixteen had been permitted to work more than eight hours a day, six days a week, or at night (Act of September 1, 1916, c. 432, 39 Stat. 675). No one had argued seriously in favor of Congress's power to regulate directly, and all parties realized that the serious issue before the Court would be whether the indirect means of barring the movement of products of child labor in interstate commerce was permissible.

The opposition was prepared to move the conflict to the next forum, however. David Clark, publisher of the *Southern Textile Bulletin,* in early 1915 organized eight mill owners to finance and run the fight against national regulation. The Executive Committee of Southern Cotton Manufacturers hired two law firms, one in North Carolina to handle the initial challenge and a corporate firm in New York that would take the case to the U.S. Supreme Court. Even before President Wilson had signed the Keating-Owen Act, a suit had been created and was brought in the Western District of North Carolina, where a sympathetic hearing was all but guaranteed (Hindman, 2002, pp. 65–67).

The nominal plaintiff was Roland Dagenhart, suing on the behalf of his sons John (age thirteen) and Reuben (age fifteen), and the Executive Committee footed the bill for his legal expenses. After the initial filing and scripted response by the Dagenharts' employer, Fidelity Manufacturing, the legal battle was left to the real parties in interest: the Executive Committee and the United States (Hindman, 2002, pp. 67–68). Although the Dean of the Harvard Law School, Roscoe Pound, defended the law in the three-day trial, Federal District judge James E. Boyd, a known opponent of child labor legislation, permanently enjoined the law on August 31 (Trattner, 1970, pp. 134–35).

No written opinion issued from the court, but Boyd set forth three constitutional objections to the law. First and most predictably, he found that it violated Congress's scope of authority under the commerce clause. Second, he saw it as a violation of the Tenth Amendment's reservation of power to the states and the people. Finally, he claimed that it violated the Fifth Amendment's due process clause, using the language of property and liberty as articulated in *Lochner v. New York* (Davis, Frierson, & Szold, 1918, pp. 3–4). The law remained in operation everywhere but in Boyd's district, but its future was clouded.

The U.S. solicitor general, John W. Davis, undaunted by the defeat in the district court, appealed directly to the U.S. Supreme Court, where he no doubt expected a more sympathetic hearing. The NCLC and the Children's Bureau supported an immediate appeal, and the NCLC was charged with preparing a factual defense of the law's reasonableness for inclusion in the government's brief (Davis, Frierson, & Szold, 1918, pp. 136). Davis initially argued in his brief that the statute clearly regulated commerce by addressing the shipment of goods and then addressed the reasons for the regulation in an attempt to convince the Court that the statute was within the scope of national authority. The brief argued that child labor was an indefensible danger to the nation, as it deprived the United States of "that vigorous citizenship upon which the success of democracy must depend" (Davis, Frierson, & Szold, 1918, p. 14). The uneven nature of regulation on the state level was damaging in two ways: primarily, it meant that many children were not protected adequately, but it also meant that the states that regulated child labor stringently were at an unfair competitive disadvantage with states that regulated only minimally. History both in the United States and abroad had shown for the solicitor general that effective child labor regulation could only be implemented at the national level because of the threat of a race to the bottom (Davis, Frierson, & Szold, 1918, pp. 15–32). All of this implicated interstate commerce because of the emergence of a national economy for manufactured goods.

The argument on the basis of the Fifth Amendment was also framed in terms of the wrong that the legislation sought to rectify. Here (as with the direct question of the commerce clause's reach), Davis had a helpful precedent. In 1905 the Court had ruled in the *Lottery Case* (*Champion v. Ames*, 188 U.S. 321 [1905]) that Congress could exercise its power to prohibit the use of interstate commerce to facilitate a lottery. This power derived in part from a parallel to the states' power to prohibit intrastate trafficking relating to a lottery. Likewise, argued Davis, the well-established rule that the Fourteenth Amendment's protections for liberty and property did not prohibit state-based limits on child labor led logically to the conclusion that the Fifth Amendment operated in the same way. Child labor regulations had been validated repeatedly by the state supreme courts and once by the U.S. Supreme Court in the face of challenges based on the Fourteenth Amendment. The structure of analysis under the Fifth Amendment paralleled the reasoning in these earlier cases that the state's interest in the public health of its future citizens warranted the exercise of its police power, despite the limits on children's autonomy (Davis, Frierson, & Szold, 1918, pp. 38–41).

Even more to the point was the recent case validating the Mann Act (referred to popularly as the White Slave Act), which prohibited the transportation of women across state lines for immoral purposes (*Hoke v. United States,* 227 U.S. 308 [1913]). Likewise, the Court had ruled that Congress had the power to protect public health by regulating the shipping of impure foods and drugs (*Hipolite Egg Co. v. United States,* 220 U.S. 45 [1911]). As for the liberty of the manufacturers and transporters themselves, Davis quickly dispensed with this claim by citing the many ways Congress and the states had previously exercised constitutional authority over various elements of production and transportation to serve legitimate state interests.

With the principal objections addressed, Davis dedicated the remainder of the brief to answering the claims that he saw as less of a threat. The Ninth and Tenth Amendments were inapplicable because the Constitution had dedicated the power to regulate commerce specifically to Congress. Congress's authority to regulate was not limited to protecting consumers only. The second-to-last point was a brief explanation that Congress was not trying to do indirectly what the Constitution prohibited it from doing directly, as Davis read the act as preventing "the evil resulting from the interstate transportation of child-made goods" (Davis, Frierson, & Szold, 1918, p. 67). All of these arguments tracked faithfully the claims that public advocates for legislation and congressional actors had made in favor of the law.

The brief filed on the behalf of Dagenhart brilliantly marshaled earlier arguments in favor of child labor regulation and used them against the statute. This tactic was evident from the second page of the brief, which provided a narrative of Dagenhart's purported circumstances, paralleling regulatory advocates' use of stories about the real circumstances of child laborers. Dagenhart and his two sons were both employed by Fidelity Manufacturing when the act was passed. Fidelity advised the Dagenhart family that the younger boy would be discharged and the older boy would have his hours limited, "all to the pecuniary loss of the plaintiff father, who was a man of small means, with a large family, to whom . . . the compensation arising from the service of each of said minor sons was essential for the comfortable support and maintenance of the family, including said minors" (O'Brien, et al., 1918, p. 3). Part of the point here was to demonstrate that there was a real party in interest, but the brief also presented the virtuous children in question, injured not by work but by the federal government's action.

O'Brien and his fellow attorneys chose to stake their claim on the commerce clause, which they saw as the likeliest prospect for success. While they were undoubtedly gratified by the persuasiveness of the Fifth Amendment and Tenth Amendment claims in the district court, they did not pursue these claims seriously with the U.S. Supreme Court. The successful analytical shift they made was basically to agree with the government that child labor was an evil and to endorse the states' efforts to regulate it. The problem with the act was not its regulatory aim of limiting child labor per se, but rather its misplacement of the issue of child labor as a matter of national concern and control.

O'Brien, Manly, Bynum, Parker, and Hendren argued first that the regulation of child labor could only be calibrated properly on the local level, as national limits did not take into account the "infinite variations of climatic, social and other conditions" (1918, p. 9). Furthermore, they referred to the conceded existence of limits on child labor in every state as grounding for their argument that the states were addressing this question seriously already. The real threat to the nation was not the risk that overworked children would grow up to be poor citizens. Rather, it was the danger of congressional overreaching to achieve "the complete elimination of the States as political entities" (O'Brien, et al., 1918, p. 14). Filling in the outlines of this inflammatory statement, they argued that the Court had to set strict boundaries on Congress's authority under the commerce clause.

The primary limit they suggested was that congressional regulations of commerce had to be predicated on a real evil or injury inherent in commerce itself. Unlike lottery tickets, the products of child labor were not themselves deemed particularly dangerous or unwholesome. The use of channels of transportation were not directly tied to an evil intent of exploiting children, as they were tied to the intent of "stimulating and aiding prostitution" in the case of the upheld Mann Act (O'Brien, et al., 1918, p. 21). The purported evil in this case, claimed O'Brien and his associates, bore no real relationship to commerce and was itself far outside the scope of Congress's regulatory authority.

Further mirroring the earlier strategies of advocates for regulation, the attorneys for Dagenhart argued that the most influential scholars and politicians of the day believed the law to be unconstitutional. They cited the House Judiciary Committee's opinion that the earlier 1907 bill exceeded constitutional standards. They also cited "three other great Constitutional lawyers . . . each . . . a thoughtful and patriotic student of the Federal Constitution": President William Howard Taft, President Wilson,[1] and Senator Elihu Root, all of whom had cautioned against the expansion of federal power (O'Brien, et al., 1918, p. 56–58). Arguments based on the Fifth and Tenth Amendments were relegated to the last four pages of the brief.

The case was argued before the Court on April 15 and 16, and the Court issued its ruling on June 3, with a majority opinion written by Justice William Day (who had joined Justice John Harlan's dissent in *Lochner v. New York*). Six of the justices had been on the Court when it had upheld state-level child labor legislation and the White Slave Traffic Act in 1913. Nonetheless, the decision was a 5–4 ruling against the child labor law, which had been in effect nationally for only ten months. The five justices in the majority were Chief Justice Edward White and Justices Day, Willis Van Devanter, Mahlon Pitney, and James McReynolds.

The Court's analysis quickly signaled its acceptance of Dagenhart's attorneys' framing of the case as turning on the extent of Congress's power under the commerce clause. This analysis mostly ignored the dangers of child labor and the bars to the state-level regulation of it. The Court distinguished the regulation of lotteries, the passage of the Pure Food and Drug Act, and the prohibition of transporting women across state lines for immoral purposes from the bar on transporting the fruits of child labor largely in the terms set forth in O'Brien's brief. In the earlier cases, "the use of interstate transportation was necessary to the accomplishment of harmful results . . . that element is wanting in the present case" (*Hammer v. Dagenhart*, 247 U.S. 251, 271 [1918]). This reasoning formed the basis of the distinction between transport as a fit subject for national regulation and production as a quintessentially local phenomenon.

The Court did confront some of the arguments made by the solicitor general but refuted them quickly. The majority claimed that unfair competition among the states alone was insufficient to trigger Congress's regulatory authority; to embrace this principle could allow the fixing of national standards for wages and labor, at the time allowed only on the state level for women. The Court articulated a strong conception of the states' police power, bitterly ironic for supporters of regulation who had fought so hard to convince the states to exercise this power to establish enforceable laws. The Court freely owned "that there should be limitations upon the right to employ children in mines and factories in the interest of their own and the public welfare," but the only constitutional location for such limitations was in the states (*Hammer*, p. 275).

The most telling evidence of the Court's embrace of O'Brien's position came at the end of Day's opinion. There, he warned that allowing the national regulation of child labor by this route would start the United States down an apocalyptic path: "if Congress can thus regulate matters entrusted to local authority . . . all freedom of commerce will be at an end, and the power of the States over local matters may be eliminated, and thus our system of government be practically destroyed" (*Hammer,* p. 276). This language echoed O'Brien's fears of the destruction of federalism and demonstrated that the Court was determined to squelch any hint that the wartime expansion of national power would have lasting implications.

Justice Oliver Wendell Holmes wrote in dissent for himself and three other justices (Justices Joseph McKenna, Louis Brandeis, and John Clarke). He saw the law as being clearly regulatory and not prohibitive in its operation. The fundamental question for him and his colleagues was thus whether unconstitutionality resulted from the act's "possible reaction upon the conduct of the States in a matter upon which I have admitted that they are free from direct control" (*Hammer,* p. 279 [Holmes, J., dissenting]). Holmes then cited several examples of national laws that had regulated interstate commerce with significant effect on the states' domestic activities. In a classic Holmesian nod to external evidence while denying its persuasive effect in legal decisions, he acknowledged the NCLC's work:

> If there is any matter upon which civilized countries have agreed—far more unanimously than they have with regard to intoxicants and some other matters over which this country is now emotionally aroused—it is the evil of premature and excessive child labor. I should have thought that if we were to introduce our own moral conceptions where in my opinion they do not belong, this was preeminently a case for upholding the exercise of all its powers by the United States. (*Hammer,* p. 280)

He then expressed his long-held views about the Court's limited authority by suggesting that Congress, not the Court, was best situated to determine when prohibitive regulation was in the nation's interests.

Holmes argued that in the final analysis, Congress's act did not preempt the states' efforts to regulate child labor. They remained sovereign entities with the power to "regulate their internal affairs and their domestic commerce as they like" (*Hammer,* p. 281). The states were simply not situated to recognize and act in the national interest, tied as they were to their narrower scopes and need to compete with other states.

Both the majority opinion and the dissent, however, revealed the extent to which the manufacturers had succeeded in setting the terms of the debate (see, e.g., Novkov, 2001). The proponents of limits on children's work would have welcomed a battle that brought in the substantive conditions under which children were working. They encouraged the courts to consider whether child labor was analogous to or even worse than other evils regulated under the commerce clause: the traffic in women, lotteries, and impure foods and drugs. These arguments would have led the federal courts closer to the lines of reasoning that triumphed in *Ames, Hoke,* and *Hipolite Egg Co.*

The manufacturers refused to engage reformers on these grounds. They did not seriously contest the claims that child labor was bad and that it required regulation and eventual elimination. Instead, they embraced the earlier reformist enthusiasm for state-based regulation as the most appropriate and constitutional cure for the ills of child labor. The debate they wanted to have was over the federal government's propriety in interfering in the sovereign states' efforts to regulate, efforts that had been painstakingly justified by more than a decade of research and argumentation by those supporting limits on child labor. This debate pushed the factual circumstances of children's work to the sidelines and left little room for the reformers' efforts to question the efficacy of state-level regulation. Because both sides went into court assuming that no federal police power could be marshaled to address the local problem of child labor, the reformers' strongest and most empathetic lines of argument were unavailable.

The two immediate legislative reactions to the ruling in *Hammer v. Dagenhart* were efforts to secure more stringent laws on the state level and a renewed effort to solve the problem nationally. Some states that had initially adopted weaker standards strengthened their restrictions and investigative apparatuses to stave off a wave of public opinion in favor of national regulation. On the national level, many saw the problem of child labor as being particularly acute, because the invalidation of the Keating-Owens Act coincided with the rapid expansion of the wartime economy (Trattner, 1970, pp. 138–139). Thus, in 1919 Congress again attempted to regulate child labor, this time through its power to tax (Hindman, 2002, p. 70). The limits on children's working conditions paralleled the Keating-Owen Act, but the mechanism for enforcement was a 10 percent excise tax on products of children's work.

The Executive Committee, still under the direction of David Clark, again acted immediately, bringing suit before the same judge who had invalidated the Keating-Owen Act and securing an injunction rapidly. The suit, even more obviously arranged than *Hammer,* was initially rebuffed by a Supreme Court in the midst of replacing Chief Justice White with Chief Justice (and former president) Taft (Trattner, 1970, pp. 140–142). The Court finally ruled on the tax's constitutionality on May 15, 1922, invalidating the statute on the ground that it did not differ substantially from *Hammer.* This time, Taft wrote the majority opinion for eight members of the Court, and the single dissenter, John Clarke, did not write an opinion (*Bailey v. Drexel Furniture Co.,* 259 U.S. 20 [1922]).

Even long-time progressive ally Louis Brandeis and iconoclast Oliver Wendell Holmes agreed that the Court's message in *Hammer* had been a clear repudiation of national legislation. Frustrated reformers struggled to pass a constitutional amendment allowing the national regulation of child labor, but they ultimately were unable to muster the support of the necessary three quarters of the states, despite an initial burst of success immediately after the Court's second slap. The Depression-Era National Recovery Act was hailed as encompassing the abolition of child labor, but the Supreme Court invalidated it in *Schechter Poultry Co. v United States* just over a year after its passage.

Comprehensive national regulation was finally achieved in the Fair Labor Standards Act, signed into law by Franklin Roosevelt in 1938 and upheld by the U.S. Supreme Court in *United States v. Darby* in 1941. In fact, the strong sentiment against child labor was politically useful to encourage wavering legislators to sign on to an agenda of regulating wages and hours for all workers. The law had significant loopholes: agricultural workers were exempt, and the law's necessary reliance on the commerce clause left some major child-employing industries (message services and newspaper sales) unregulated. Nonetheless, in 1940 "the number of employed children ages fourteen to seventeen reached an all-time low while the high schools enrolled their all-time high" (Trattner, 1970, pp. 200–215). These gaps were eventually closed, and the most common forms of child labor in the present-day United States are babysitting and yard work.

Nonetheless, continued vigilance is warranted. Investigations conducted by the General Accounting Office have revealed persistent problems in agriculture, the continued existence of underground sweatshops, and children's excessive employment in industrial homework, and foster children remain significantly at risk of exploitation (Hindman, 2002, pp. 296–302). Internationally, child labor remains a harrowing and intractable problem for developing nations as well as for the developed nations that rely on a network of multinational corporate manufacturing for the provision of cheap goods.

When the Supreme Court ruled in favor of the Fair Labor Standards Act in 1941, it explicitly overruled *Hammer v. Dagenhart,* ushering in a new era of permissive readings of the commerce clause and an abandonment of the close scrutiny of Congress's regulatory motivations (*United States v. Darby,* 312 U.S. 100, 117 [1941]). *Hammer* seemed ready to sink into oblivion, to be cited only as an example of wrongheaded interference with Congress's power to create and implement national regulatory standards. Controversial and enraging to activists as it was in its heyday, by the late twentieth century, only law students with historically inclined professors knew much about it.

Since the William Rehnquist Court's revival of active limits on Congress's regulatory authority, however, the case has regained more than historic significance. In his concurring opinion (along with Justice Sandra Day O'Connor) in *United States v. Lopez,* Justice Anthony Kennedy cited the case as an experimental moment in the Court's struggles to develop workable boundaries for the regulation of commerce (514 U.S. 549, 571 [1995]). While he noted that the ruling was overturned, he joined the *Lopez* majority in rejecting *Darby's* significantly less searching mode of analysis. *Hammer v. Dagenhart* was not mentioned in the Court's 2000 ruling in *United States v. Morrison* invalidating part of the Violence Against Women Act. Nonetheless, the Rehnquist Court's rejection of Congress's attempt to build a factual legislative record of the direct effects of violence against women on the national economy bears significant parallels to the White Court's reluctance to consider the Bureau of Labor's evidence that the child labor problem of the 1910s could only be ameliorated through resort to national regulation.

Hammer v. Dagenhart stands as testament to several things. First, in any analysis of constitutional development, it highlights the significance of the federal courts, particularly the U.S. Supreme Court, in shaping the way that the modern welfare state emerged. Because of strong resistance to regulation by state and federal courts in the early twentieth century, reformers ultimately had to promote labor standards for workers who were seen as particularly vulnerable. By the 1910s, this meant that much of the struggle over establishing labor standards was about the appropriate protections for the bodies of women and children. Arguments for regulation depended on the existence of workers who could be framed as particularly needy and vulnerable rather than on the need for comprehensive standards for all workers. (See, e.g., Skocpol, 1992, Novkov, 2001).

Hammer and *Bailey* resoundingly slammed the courthouse doors to arguments about vulnerability and need, but reformers moved these arguments to the broader public sphere in their efforts to amend the Constitution to allow for regulation. The forging of the modern welfare state thus depended on the concept of dependence itself.

The struggle over child labor regulation also raises troubling questions about the core role of race as a political tool. Most contemporary analysts likely are sympathetic to the reformers who fought so hard and long to regulate child labor. This sympathy, however, should not blind us to the unsavory tactics that some used. The argument that educated, nonsweated children made better citizens depended on a background assumption of white citizenship. This assumption became explicit when advocates for reform discussed the situation in the South, deploring the fact that African American children were attending school while white children were working in the mills (Markham, et al., 1914, pp. 331–336). This discrepancy, claimed reformers, threatened the emerging modern nation because it would ultimately weaken the white race and strengthen the black race.

Reformers consciously and consistently used racially charged arguments to win southern elite support for regulation. The exclusion of agricultural and domestic labor from most state-based and national efforts to regulate were not just the result of strong lobbying efforts by the industry; rather, everyone understood that these types of work were most frequently performed by laborers of color (African Americans in the Southeast, Mexican immigrants and their descendants in the Southwest). The manufacturers also played the race card by noting that the large differences in the racial makeup of the states warranted local rather than national control (see, e.g., O'Brien, et al., 1918). This argument tied in with an emerging compromise that the "rebirth" of the American nation would be accomplished through allowing the South to exercise significant autonomy in structuring race relations. *Hammer's* background message endorsed this compromise.

In human terms, though, the case's most significant meaning was its thwarting of efforts to limit children's work. One of the real losers was *Hammer's* purported victor, Reuben Dagenhart, the fifteen-year-old boy on whose behalf the suit had been brought. As the campaign for the child labor amendment heated up in the early 1920s, a reporter for *The Nation* found him and interviewed him, asking him what benefits he had gained from winning in the U.S. Supreme Court. Dagenhart corrected him, saying "You mean the suit the Fidelity Manufacturing Company won?" He went on with evident bitterness:

> I don't see that I got any benefit. I guess I'd been a lot better off if they hadn't won it. Look at me! A hundred and five pounds, a grown man and no education. I may be mistaken, but I think the years I've put in the cotton mills stunted my growth. They kept me from getting any schooling. I had to stop school after the third grade and now I need the education I didn't get. . . . But I know one thing, I ain't going to let them put my kid sister in the mill. (Trattner, 1970, n. 49)

NOTE

1. This argument may seem odd, given that Wilson signed the child labor bill into law. He had, however, as a political scientist authored a book on the Constitution in 1908 that attacked the Beveridge bill as "a striking example of a tendency to carry congressional power over interstate commerce beyond the utmost boundaries of reasonable and honest interference" (Trattner, 1970, p. 122).

REFERENCES

Davidson, E. (1939). *Child labor legislation in the southern textile states.* Chapel Hill, NC: University of North Carolina Press.

Davis, J., Frierson, W. L., & Szold, R. (1918, March). Brief for appellant. Filed with U.S. Supreme Court.

Hindman, H. (2002). *Child labor: An American history.* London: M. E. Sharpe.

Markham, E., Lindsey, B., & Creel, G. (1914). *Children in bondage: A complete and careful presentation of the anxious problem of child labor—Its causes, its crimes, and its cure.* New York: Hearst's International Library Co.

Novkov, J. (2001). *Constituting workers, protecting women: Gender, law and labor in the Progressive Era and New Deal years.* Ann Arbor, MI: University of Michigan Press.

O'Brien, M., Manly, C., Bynum, W. P., Parker, J., & Hendren, W. M. (1918, April 5). Brief for appellees. Filed with U.S. Supreme Court.

Skocpol, T. (1992). *Protecting soldiers and mothers: The political origins of social policy in the United States.* Cambridge, MA: Harvard University Press.

Trattner, W. (1970). *Crusade for the children: A history of the National Child Labor Committee and child labor reform in America.* Chicago, IL: Quadrangle Books.

Smoking in the Courtroom

Cipollone v. Liggett (1992)

JOSEPH F. KOBYLKA

> Rose Cipollone's claim that tobacco companies failed to disclose the addictive nature of their product led to a Supreme Court decision—a holding that federal law mandating a warning label on the side of cigarette packages did not foreclose lawsuits under state liability law. As a technical matter, the case dealt with a somewhat obscure legal doctrine known as preemption. More practically, though, the Court's resolution of this question of federal versus state authority opened the door for a wave of lawsuits against major tobacco companies.

This case is about a lady who smoked cigarettes and died of lung cancer.
—Marc Edell, opening statement, February 2, 1986

Rose Cipollone did not set out to become a causist. In many ways, her sojourn was that of a typical American woman born in the years just before the Great Depression. One of four children born to a barber father and homemaker mother in New York City in 1926, she had a "normal" life in the city. Although her family scraped by during the Depression—unable to afford movie magazines new, she "caged" used ones from a junk collector in her neighborhood (Kluger, 1996, p. 645)—she was able to attend movies regularly, because her father received free passes to films in exchange for the movie posters he put up in his shop. The escapism of these films appealed to her, especially the heroines of the screen. She became enamored of "glamorous queens of the silver screen like Bette Davis, Joan Crawford, and Norma Shearer. Rose noticed two things in particular about her film idols: they always seemed to be wearing evening gowns, not regular dresses like she did, and they smoked a lot" (Kluger, 1996, p. 645).

Their dazzling lives and sophistication sharply contrasted with her stark working-class existence, and she sought to emulate them in manner and dress in a juvenile effort to transcend her own life. She soon outgrew the "dress-up" behavior, but the smoking was another matter.

Smoking began as a way out of the confines of young Rose Defrancesco's world. She initially rolled paper tube cigarettes for play. While her father smoked, her mother, thinking it not "ladylike," did not. Thus, by smoking, Defrancesco could emulate those in a world unlike her own and, at the same time, defy her parents. At sixteen she began sneaking smokes outside of their purview, buying "three Chesterfields for a penny apiece each morning at a candy store near the [elevated train] at 116th Street and Third Avenue on [my] way to Washington Irving High School. . . . I thought it was cool to smoke, and grown up, and I was going to be glamorous and beautiful" (Margolick, 1985a, B1). Never making it to Hollywood, she dropped out of high school; married Antonio Cipollone at twenty-one; worked as a packer for a scarf manufacturer, a secretary for the New York Philharmonic, and a billing clerk; bore and helped raise three children; served as a room mother for the PTA; threw dinner and card parties at her home; and generally moved between homemaking and labor for fee for the rest of her life (Kluger, 1996, p. 646). Although she left her youthful dreams behind, one lingering manifestation of them remained: her smoking.

Over the constant objections of her husband, Rose Cipollone continued her habit, seldom trying to kick it. As fashions and advertising campaigns changed, she moved from Chesterfields to L&Ms in 1955, to Virginia Slims in the late 1960s, to Parliament in the early 1970s, and finally True. When confronted with evidence that tied smoking to serious illness and death, she either made light of it or said that she was addicted. In 1981, at the age of fifty-five, her physical and medical problems began in earnest. That year she lost a part of her right lung; the next, the rest of it was removed, along with lymph nodes and some pulmonary arteries. Her first chemotherapy started then. In 1983 doctors removed a "ten-centimeter mass" from near her liver and kidneys. From there, the metastasized cancer spread—despite the doctors' treatments—to other organs. On October 21, 1984, after three and a half years of pain, treatment, and decline, Rose Cipollone died in a hospital room, in her husband's arms (Kluger, 1996, pp. 645–650).

This personal story, even in abbreviated form, is poignant but not unusual. Some 156,900 Americans died in 2000 from lung cancer or its complications; it kills more people than any other form of cancer (American Lung Association, n.d.). What made Cipollone unique was her decision to meet with Mark Z. Edell. Edell was an attorney and, ironically, a former smoker who had previously represented asbestos interests. That work suggested to him the "potential bonanza" of suing tobacco companies. After meeting with a New York physician who had treated Cipollone, Edell talked to Cipollone, and she invited him to her New Jersey home in August 1983. Sixteen months later she was dead, but Edell—with Tony Cipollone and, after his death, their son Thomas—pursued those he felt responsible for her death for eight more years. This pursuit led Edell, the Cipollone family, and a multitude of attorneys representing the tobacco companies whose products she smoked to federal district and appellate courts in Newark and Philadelphia; to the Supreme Court in Washington, D.C.; and finally back to the district court, where the legal saga—for the family—ended. Its postscript, though, changed the face of tobacco politics.

At trial, Edell and the Cipollones won the first-ever cash judgment against the tobacco companies for contributing to the death of a smoker. On appeal, they "won" some of the core elements of their case before the U.S. Supreme Court, which remanded the case for further litigation. After this, though, they dropped their suit on November 4, 1992. In summing up the litigation, a writer for the *New York Times* said "The court record will show that nobody won and nobody lost—the plaintiffs simply walked off the field" (Strum, 1992a, sec. 4, p. 4).

However, as the discussion that follows will make clear, the Cipollone saga was not a simple wash. Although Edell and the family experienced an ephemeral victory, it was an essential way station on the path to legal and policy change. The suit begun by a dying woman became a catalyst for the challenges brought shortly on its heels by state attorneys general. This shifted the direction of the conflict and culminated in the "tobacco settlement" of 1998. Rose Cipollone's case, *Cipollone v. Liggett Group, Inc.* (505 U.S. 504 [1992]), advanced a new strategic agenda, prompted a tactical shift, and, finally, forced tobacco companies to do something they avoided doing for over sixty years . . . admit that their products *caused* health problems in many of the individuals who used them.

A sixteen-year-old girl's dreams led her to addiction. Her addiction led her to a fatal disease. Her disease led her to file suit against the manufacturers of the cigarettes she had smoked for over forty-two years. Her suit altered legal terrain and set the stage for the defeat of a well-financed corporate giant. One woman helped change the scope and direction of the tobacco controversy. In the end, Cipollone's legacy may be greater than many of the movie stars she wished to emulate when she first put match to strike pad, then match to Chesterfield.

Politics, Players, and Policy

Harold Laswell defined politics as "who gets what, how" (Laswell, 1936). The "who" refers to the participants in the political contest, the "what" is the policy they seek, and the "how" describes the strategies and tactics they use to pursue their policy goals through the government. The systematic study of politics involves addressing and assessing the elements of this insight in the day-to-day world. Political science has led us to a general understanding of many of its essential elements. For example, from democratic theory and the study of interest groups, we know that a central factor in the struggle over public policy is organization (Truman, 1951; Schattschneider, 1960; Dahl, 1956; Olson, 1965). Political participants have to *organize* to pursue their goals, and the more effectively they do so, the greater their likelihood of achieving them. This "bias in organization" is the heart of Schattschneider's insight that politics is about "managing the scope of conflict" (Schattschneider, 1960, p. 5). Furthermore, victors achieve the advantage of perspective: as "winners" in this game, they are in a good position to develop the rules that govern how the game is subsequently played.

Schattschneider identified four manipulable components of conflict:

Scope: the number of people actively involved in the controversy

Intensity: the strength of feeling about or commitment to the controversy among those concerned with it; their willingness and capacity to pursue its resolution

Visibility: the profile of an issue; how many people were aware of it and aware that government could address it

Direction: the way the conflict divided those interested it, and the resulting position taken on it by the government

The better organized the players, the greater their capacity to manipulate these dimensions of conflict to their policy advantage. However, not all players are equally well organized, and organization certainly has its advantages. Among these are resources (i.e., financial, informational, political) and continued influence in the political system. C. Wright Mills (1956) argued that these resources are concentrated in narrow groups that dominate society, and scholars like Michael Parenti (1978) continue to advance this argument. One, though, does not have to be a devotee of elite theory to see a link between organization and resources: students of "ordinary" group and party politics have long held to this insight.

If in real estate the three most crucial things are "location, location, location," in politics, they are "resources, resources, resources." Possession of resources enables players to manipulate the dimensions of conflict to bias the political contest in their favor. This is obvious in the explicitly political world; for example, well-funded candidates usually prevail over those with less money because their resources enable them to set the issue agenda and draw the support of the public to them. "Staying on message" and "spinning issues" are merely new names for framing issues in the way best suited to advance the interests of a candidate or office holder: adjusting intensity and visibility to create a scope in which he or she can "win." Less obviously, these dimensions of politics also spill over into litigation undertaken to influence public policy.

A corollary to Schattschneider's "politics is the management of conflict" is that those who write the rules win the game. In the legal sphere of political life, "rules" are laws and how they are applied. American canons of legalism—symbolized by a blindfolded figure holding the scales of justice—foster the illusion that the law is just "out there," waiting to be applied impartially by courts. However, *someone wrote* those laws, and frequently those who fashioned the laws are the very same people who appear in court to litigate under them. These people—attorneys (McGuire, 1993), interest groups (Epstein & Kobylka, 1992), or corporations (Galanter, 1974)—not only *know* the rules, but also have the opportunity to guide their development and application by judges and juries. These "repeat players" (Galanter, 1974) have the advantages of organization: resources, contacts, and expertise. Not surprisingly, they often win public policy battles when they find their ways into the courts. Until Rose Cipollone's suit, tobacco companies enjoyed all the strategic policy benefits of being repeat players; they never lost.

Tobacco, Law, and the Courts

Tobacco and its use are as "American" as baseball, hot dogs, and apple pie; it fact, it predates all of these. Indigenous to the American continent, when Columbus came to the new world, its inhabitants used it. Not only did tobacco find its way back to Europe with returning explorers, but also plants followed and tobacco cultivation spread worldwide. Trade battles between

England and Spain sprouted from the roots of this plant, as each promoted tobacco growing in its colonies most favorable to it. Virginia became a primary source of the crop and fed English trade routes, the labor-intensive crop contributing to the growth of slavery there. By the middle of the nineteenth century, people were rolling tobacco into a *cigarito,* the forerunner of the cigarette. Soon thereafter, merchants like Philip Morris and Allen & Ginter began mass-producing cigarettes to meet the demands of soldiers returning home from the Crimean and Civil wars. With the rise of mechanization and the advent of national markets, American tobacco barons began to develop, and with them developed the concentrated organization and resources that Rose Cipollone took on 100 years later.

The early giant of the American tobacco industry was James "Buck" Duke, son of a former Confederate army officer and Durham, North Carolina, tobacco grower. He built an empire that began with the American Tobacco Company (ATC), ultimately taking over "some 250 companies." At the turn of the century, his holding company had sales of $125 million, employed over 100,000 people, and became global when it partnered with a British firm to create the British-American Tobacco Company (Kluger, 1996, p. 43). This commercial success turned out to be a mixed blessing in the trust-busting years of Teddy Roosevelt's administration. It filed a Sherman Anti-Trust action against Duke in 1907, and the Supreme Court held that the ATC "combination as a whole, involving all its co-operating or associated parts, in whatever form clothed, constitutes a restraint of trade . . . and an attempt to monopolize" (*U.S. v. American Tobacco Company,* 221 U.S. 106, 184 [1911]). Although the breakup of ATC was a loss for Duke, it was a boon for industry, because the newly divested firms joined other competitors such as R. J. Reynolds in expanding the market for their now-competitive products.

As the tobacco industry grew more expansive and profitable, it developed critics. Criticism at first came from religious figures, who found in it evidence of sinful moral decay (Kluger, 1996, p. 10), and it haltingly spread to the reformers of the Populist and Progressive eras, who focused on health concerns. Lucy Gaston, a teacher from Illinois and child of parents active in abolitionist and temperance movements, founded the National Anti-Cigarette League. While some states did ban cigarette sales (e.g., Washington, Iowa, Tennessee, and North Dakota), by the turn of the century, a more common governmental response was to tax tobacco for revenue.

This is not to say that tobacco's relationship with government was always smooth: as noted, some states prohibited its sale, others banned sales to minors, and taxation increased its cost. However, the "total prohibition of the product was a much graver matter, and the industry's operatives largely succeeded in preventing the passage of such measures in the populous Eastern states and the heavy-smoking South" (Kluger, 1996, p. 40).

In political terms, tobacco companies managed the scope of conflict, confined their "losses" to small states, and kept the national government at bay, while constantly expanding their markets. This had twin benefits: greater profits and more smoking voters (thus, less pressure for governmental regulation). Advertising was the leading edge of this campaign, but the resources generated by tobacco sales also allowed for campaign contributions and employment of top law firms and lobbyists. In an era when the national prohibition of alcohol became a reality, tobacco stayed largely under the regulatory radar. Even given increasing health concerns, it was left outside federal jurisdiction in the Pure Food and Drug Act of 1906. "The industry [argued] that tobacco was neither a food nor a drug . . . [but] others said the exemption was the result of pure economic and political might" (Kluger, 1996, p. 41). Those who write the rules win the game . . . as long as those rules hold.

Principles of separation of powers and federalism set the political field on which policy players run. Having insulated themselves from serious legislative regulation, tobacco companies remained potentially vulnerable to executive rule making and litigation at the national and state levels. The former was not particularly onerous, as the industry's organization and resources put it in a good position to coexist with bureaucracies. The latter, though, provided a potential opening through which to crack the industry's shell. Theoretically offering an equal footing before the law, courts give individual plaintiffs an opportunity to recover damages from defendants responsible for their injuries. As smoking-related health concerns grew in the aftermath of World War II, some people afflicted with diseases they attributed to smoking began to look to the courts for relief. However, the resource and organizational advantages held by the tobacco companies made this strategy a long shot.

Bryce A. Jensen (2001) and Martha Derthick (2002) see two phases to this litigation. The first ran from the mid-1950s through the late 1960s, and was composed of tort cases. Increasing public awareness of lung cancer and its equation with smoking spurred litigation, usually brought under theories of negligence and failure to warn (Derthick, 2002, p. 29). In essence, the claims boiled down to this: smoking cigarettes is dangerous; companies knew this and were negligent in selling their products to an unwitting public without frankly disclosing their attendant risks. The tobacco companies refused to settle these cases out of court—not wanting to admit to any link between smoking and cancer or to create incentives for other settlements. If plaintiffs pressed their causes, companies gladly went to court, where they had two strong allies. First, the law of product liability at that time required a product to be "defective" for its provider to be held liable for injuries. Second, they had armies of prestigious attorneys to defend them from the novice personal injury lawyers who brought the cases. In Galanter's terms, this was a classic example of litigation imbalance: "one-shotters" against "repeat players." It was David versus Goliath, and David had no slingshot.

Derthick captures the core of this strategy in quoting an industry insider: "To paraphrase General Patton, the way we won these cases was not by spending all of [tobacco's money], but by making that other son of a bitch spend all of his" (Derthick, 2002, p. 28). In addition to industry advantages in law and resources must be added one more: choice. Smokers choose to smoke, and the companies argued that in making that choice they assumed the consequences that flowed from it: smokers, not companies, were responsible for their illnesses.

Given the above, the conventional wisdom of political science would predict that the tobacco companies would prevail even before the "equalizing" eyes of the law. They did. "Rarely could the industry's opponents withstand this onslaught. The typical personal injury lawyer worked on a contingency basis and had to prepare his or her case with limited or no compensation" (Derthick, 2002, p. 29). The companies did not lose a single case.

Challenging Tobacco's Dominance

The 1980s saw a resurgence in litigation, though for the most part the results were the same as in the past: the companies continued to wear down plaintiffs or beat them in court. However, the context in which this litigation occurred had changed, and these changes emboldened some litigators. Marc Edell, Rose Cipollone's attorney, was one of them.

Three contextual changes, one political, one social, and one legal, altered the environment for tobacco litigation. Politically, smoking was coming under increasing fire. First, Congress answered the rise of concern about lung cancer by passing the Federal Cigarette Labeling and Advertising Act of 1965. This required cigarette packages to state: "Caution: Cigarette Smoking May Be Hazardous to Your Health." This warning was changed in 1969 to read: "Warning: The Surgeon General Has Determined that Cigarette Smoking Is Dangerous to Your Health." In 1970 Congress banned cigarette advertisements from broadcast media, and a year later the Federal Trade Commission (FTC) required print ads to carry the surgeon general's warning (Derthick, 2002, p. 14).

In the Congress, the House Commerce Committee's Subcommittee on Health and Environment began holding hearings on tobacco's effects in 1979. Antismoking advocates got assistance from an unexpected source when President Ronald Reagan's surgeon general, C. Everett Koop, called for a "smoke-free society" in a speech to the American Lung Association in 1984. That same year, Congress adopted an earlier FTC recommendation and required cigarette packages and advertisements to rotate four, much stronger warnings detailing risks to pregnancy, specific illnesses, and the carbon monoxide in smoke. As a result, the *visibility* of the smoking issue rose during this period, shifting the dimensions of politics.

Socially, consumer awareness and protection was in the ascendancy. Health concerns grew as people learned more about environmental risks and the relationship between certain behaviors and disease. To counter the claims of the Tobacco Institute (the industry's public relations arm), the American Cancer Society, the American Heart Association, and the American Lung Association founded the Coalition on Smoking OR Health to lobby and educate on antismoking issues (Kluger, 2002, pp. 509–510). The number of cigarettes sold in the United States was also in decline: a nearly 5 percent drop between 1982 and 1983 alone. This could have been the result of antismoking campaigns and some 45,000 scientific studies documenting the health effects of smoking (Margolick, 1985a, B1).

Legally, note two developments of consequence. First, the consumer movement had brought about a change in the product liability laws in many states. The rise of "risk-utility" analysis to prove "strict liability" allowed courts to "entertain the possibility that manufacturers could be held responsible for injury from products that were inherently dangerous even if they were not defective" (Derthick, 2002, p. 30). This wiggle in the law, along with an emerging doctrine of "comparative fault"—apportioning fault between litigants—gave plaintiffs attorneys more room to maneuver in their arguments. Second, recent court decisions held that companies that made asbestos were liable for the health consequences of exposure to it. Not only did these victories gain immense press, bringing the issue new visibility, but they also pointed the way for plaintiff lawyers in other areas: if courts could take on asbestos, why not tobacco? Further, the monetary awards that resulted were *huge,* and with lawyers taking cases on a contingency basis, 30 percent came to them! Kluger described Edell's initial interest in this litigation this way: "As the asbestos damage awards began to mount—seventeen companies would be made to pay out $7 billion over the dozen years following the *Beshada* verdict—Edell saw a potential bonanza in pressing similar liability actions against the tobacco companies as well as the chance of a lifetime to grab fame" (Kluger, 1996, 643). These forces set the stage for a second legal assault on the tobacco industry in the early 1980s.

Cipollone in Court

The task for plaintiff attorneys was to establish the *legal* culpability of tobacco companies for the illnesses suffered by their clients. Industry attorneys denied a *scientifically proven causal link* between smoking and lung cancer in general (not all people who smoked got lung cancer, and some who did get it did not smoke), emphasized the *choice* made—after 1965 with health warnings well known—by those who smoked, and pointed to the other factors associated with cancer. In a few well-publicized cases in the mid-1980s, industry lawyers succeeded in avoiding trial court judgments against their clients. *Galbraith v. R. J. Reynolds Tobacco Co.* (1985) and *Horton v. American Tobacco Co.* (1986) were two such, though in the latter the jury found ATC liable for Horton's death but did not award damages because he, in the face of warnings of risk, chose to smoke (Labaton, 1988, p. D2).

Another industry defense against legal liability was the constitutional doctrine of preemption. Preemption results from Article VI's "supremacy" clause. Under it, federal law trumps state laws contrary to it. In other words, if Congress passes legislation to address an area of public policy, and that legislation is considered comprehensive, state laws or court judgements to the contrary have no force. Ironically, given that the industry fought the package-labeling laws passed by Congress in the 1960s, they now used them as a shield. Federal law now helped them in two ways. First, it made it more difficult for a plaintiff to claim unawareness of the potential dangers of smoking. Second, it suggested that, because Congress had "occupied the field" with the 1965 and 1969 acts, states could not further regulate tobacco or cigarettes.

Edell had to contend with all of these legal arguments in bringing Cipollone's case to court in addition to dealing with the well-heeled repeat players against whom he would be arguing. At the outset of proceedings, the cards seemed stacked against him: legal know-how, resources, and the rules under which he had to convince first a judge and then a jury that the tobacco companies should be held legally responsible for Cipollone's death.

Fortunately for Edell, the federal district court judge assigned to the case, H. Lee Sarokin, proved sympathetic to his efforts. Sarokin had presided over a number of high-profile cases (Margolick 1985b, sec. 1, p. 30). He was no stranger to controversy, and an aggressive style suggested that he relished it. This style may have cost him, however, as the *New Jersey Law Journal* wrote that "Sarokin may be the most reversed federal judge in New Jersey when it comes to major cases" (Schroth, 1992b, p. 3).

Sarokin's early rulings afforded two openings for Edell at the outset: first, that the 1965 warning label act did not preempt negligence suits brought by smokers seeking damages under state law ("New Jersey Journal," 1984, sec. 11NJ, p. 3). This allowed the suit to move to trial. Second, he held in favor of broad discovery requests from the plaintiff (Rosen, 1986, A1). This allowed Edell access to many in-house company documents that he could use to argue that the companies were well aware of the danger of their cigarettes and thus bore responsibility for the illnesses they caused. Employing legal rules to tie up the proceedings—keeping the case from going to trial and eating up more of the plaintiff's resources—attorneys for the tobacco companies successfully appealed the preemption ruling to the Third Circuit Court of Appeals in Philadelphia. That court held that warning labels shielded tobacco companies from claims that they hid the dangers of smoking (Wright & Herron, 1986, sec. 4, p. 4). The Supreme Court denied certiorari to the case ("Cigarette Ruling Stands," 1987, p. D5).

The case could have ended there, with the repeat players using their resources—"at a recent federal court hearing . . . some 12 industry lawyers sat opposite Edell, who was alone" (Rosen, 1986, A1)—to again vanquish threats like a horse's tail does flies. Indeed, financial analysts said that "the decision was likely to put an end to the tobacco companies' legal problems" (Lewin, 1986, p. D1). Further, other cases around the country were folding: "In 1986 there were 78 cases filed against cigarette makers . . . This year there were only seven" (Labaton, 1987, p. D2). Yet, Tony Cipollone—Rose now dead for three and a half years—and Edell marched back into Sarokin's court.

The decision of the court of appeals left open the possibility that tobacco companies could be found liable for damages incurred before 1965. Edell sought to exploit this crack in the tobacco companies' appellate victory before a seemingly sympathetic judge in the trial that began on February 1, 1988. After four and a half years of poking through previously secret memoranda from the tobacco companies, Edell intended to put more than 200 of these secret memoranda into the trial record (Janson, 1988c, sec. 1, p. 34).

From these, he hoped to demonstrate that tobacco companies *knowingly* victimized Rose Cipollone: knowing their products dangerous, their advertisements played down or denied the danger, promoted smoking, and caused addiction. Telling jurors that no one outside of the industry had previously seen these documents, Edell opened his case noting, "This case is about a lady who smoked cigarettes and died of lung cancer. . . . We know the truth. This is an industry that sacrificed the lives of people like Rose Cipollone for one thing: money" (Pinsley, 1988, A1).

The opening response of the industry lawyers focused on Cipollone's decisions: "This case is about her knowledge, her awareness, and her decision to smoke cigarettes. . . . She had the information necessary to make an informed choice" (Pinsley, 1988, p. A1).

Deadly manipulation and personal choice framed the arguments tendered over the next four months. The stakes were high: no tobacco company had ever lost a liability case. Goliath was in court with David, and, although not yet armed, David was at least in the fight.

Edell's task at the trial was deceptively simple: to show that the tobacco companies *knew* that cigarettes caused cancer, *concealed* this knowledge, sought to *obscure* the dangers of smoking, and *misled* the public through a public relations blitz orchestrated by the Tobacco Institute, founded in 1958. Rose Cipollone—seduced by advertising—became first addicted to cigarettes and then the industry's victim. Under a "risk utility" theory of negligence, where the individual and societal benefits of smoking were weighed against its risks, Liggett & Myers, Philip Morris, and Lorillard should be held liable for damages.

Early in the trial, Edell introduced "secret" documents discovered against the defendants to establish their knowledge of smoking's risks (Janson, 1988c, sec. 1, p. 34), followed this with pathology experts to tie Cipollone's particular cancer with that caused by smoking (Janson, 1988e, sec. 1, p. 39), and called a participant in the surgeon general's 1964 and 1979 commissions on smoking to note that their reports were "unequivocal in determining that cigarette smoking causes cancer" (Janson, 1988d, sec. 1, p. 35). As the plaintiff's case moved to its conclusion, portions of Rose Cipollone's deposition were read, noting, in part, that "through advertising, I was led to assume that they were safe and they wouldn't harm me" (Janson, 1988g, B4). Tony Cipollone took the stand as the final witness to describe his wife's addiction, the travails it caused, and her death in his arms.

The goal of the tobacco companies was simply to avoid a judgment against them. As in other cases, they used their superior resources to drag out pretrial processes—motions, extensive depositions, background checks to turn up evidence and burn up time—to avoid going to trial by exhausting the plaintiffs. Failing this, they sought to discredit the plaintiff's witnesses and gain dismissal on grounds of prejudicial publicity.

After the plaintiffs concluded their arguments, the companies' lawyers immediately moved for a mistrial on the grounds that Sarokin had become "an advocate" for the plaintiffs. Alternatively, they asked for dismissal for lack of evidence ("Defendants Accuse Judge," 1988). Sarokin denied the motion for mistrial, dropped four allegations against the companies for want of evidence, but allowed the trial to continue on the question of a deliberate conspiracy to mislead people "in callous, wanton, willful, and reckless disregard for the health of consumers" (Janson, 1988f, p. A1). Failing to avoid trial on procedural grounds and forced to make an affirmative defense, the industry attorneys began their arguments to win it on substance.

Over the course of their five-week presentation, the defense team hammered three themes. First, smoking had not been scientifically proven to *cause* cancer. Second, smoking was not addictive in a strict sense, as many smokers did quit. Finally, Rose Cipollone was well aware of the possible health problems associated with smoking, but she *chose* to smoke regardless.

> She could have stopped smoking if she wanted to. She did not want to. She could control her smoking. She never smoked in the bedroom. She knew what she was doing. She was an intelligent, strong-minded person. She prayed that she would not get lung cancer, but she continued to smoke. It was a conscientious, reasoned decision. (Janson, 1988b, B2)

In his summation, attorney Donald J. Cohn even quoted Cipollone's deposition: "I liked to smoke. It gave me something to do." Her choice may have been ill fated, but it was *her* choice.

The jury, instructed by Sarokin that they were to only consider the pre-1965 behavior of the defendants—deliberated for five days and returned with a complicated verdict that left neither side happy but both claiming victory. It found that the companies were not liable for misrepresenting the dangers of smoking, but held that they had not adequately warned of the dangers of smoking before 1965. It found Cipollone 80 percent responsible for the behavior that led to her death and awarded her estate no damages. However, it awarded $400,000 in compensatory damages to Tony Cipollone. Tobacco's attorneys said that the lack of punitive damages showed that "the jury believed that the smoker was well-informed and responsible." Edell pointed to the damage award, said "this is only the beginning," and vowed to press on with other cases. Estimates of the plaintiff's cost to bring the suit this far ranged from $2 million to $2.5 million (Janson, 1988a, p. A1). By contrast, "in 1985, the tobacco industry's earnings were . . . $3.45 billion" ("Coffin Nails," 1988, p. A30). David had cut Goliath, but the wound was not fatal.

The litigation did not end there; Goliath feared the cut. The tobacco companies—in an effort to reverse the damages award and maintain their invincible litigation posture—appealed the decision less than a month after it was rendered. In this period—perhaps because of the unsettled nature of the decision, perhaps because of the paltry award to Cipollone—only one new suit was filed, while eleven were withdrawn (Glaberson, 1988, sec. 1, p. 33). The grind through which the companies were putting Cipollone and his attorneys was seemingly wearing down and scaring away other potential plaintiffs.

On January 5, 1990, the Third Circuit Court of Appeals overturned the $400,000 award, holding that Sarokin had not adequately instructed the jury. However, it also held that the "risk-utility" argument that Sarokin dismissed during the trial could be used by Cipollone to win damages regardless of the warnings on cigarette packages. This second, complex and ambiguous ruling begged further appeal, and in December 1990 Edell and Thomas Cipollone—Tony died five days after the appellate court decision—appealed to the U.S. Supreme Court, which granted certiorari and scheduled the case for argument in the fall of 1991. Edell took heart in a hearing before a court that looked favorably on "state sovereignty;" tobacco interests saw a court generally supportive of business with two (William Rehnquist and Antonin Scalia), and soon to be three (Clarence Thomas), smoking members. A watershed ruling seemed in the offing.

Of False Starts and New Beginnings:
Cipollone as a Catalyst for Strategic Change

A watershed ruling did not come. The confusion that colored the trial judgment and the appellate decision carried over to the majority's resolution—there was no majority opinion—of the case. Again, both sides could claim victory. In fact, though, both sides, whether they knew it or not at the time, had suffered serious wounds. From these wounds—from the denial of the clear victory that each side hoped for—came the impetus for a real revolution in the relationship between government and the tobacco industry.

The Supreme Court asked the parties to argue the issue of preemption: did the federal acts of 1965 and 1969 preclude state law judgments against tobacco companies that comply with the labeling requirements? Argued first before an eight-member Court (Thomas was awaiting confirmation), the arguments were "dry" (Greenhouse, 1991, p. A22). The justices "questioned Edell more intensely than they did Farr [representing the industry]," with Chief Justice Rehnquist suggesting the statutes could be read with a broad preemptive intent, and Justice Sandra Day O'Connor pressing him on the advertising burdens created by allowing damage judgments (Keily, 1991, p. A1). Justice Scalia expressed a clear leaning in favor of preemption (Mauro, 1991b, p. 5A). The Court's order for a reargument of the case, after discussion in at least two of its conferences, meant the sides would have to do it again, amidst speculation that the justices were deadlocked 4–4, with Thomas's vote necessary to break the tie (Mauro, 1992, p. 1A).

Beyond Thomas's elevation to the Court, the biggest change in the posture of the case was the decision to have Harvard Law professor Laurence Tribe reargue the case for Cipollone. Unlike Edell, who made his first appearance before the Court in the October orals, Tribe was a veteran of eighteen prior appearances before the Supreme Court, winning twelve of them, including successful arguments in five preemption cases (Schroth, 1991, p. 4)). Just why Edell stepped aside is not clear. He contended that it was a strategic decision: "They already listened to me, and I was only able to convince them to the point that they are at. I decided that a new voice, a new perspective was the best way to go. . . . Professor Tribe can provide a . . . perspective on the bigger global issue of federalism, and he has a lot more credibility than I do on that subject. He has a track record" (Schroth, 1991, p. 4).

Others contended that Edell was not up to the task and that his mock trial coaches urged him to step down. The *Baltimore Sun* wrote that he "was not equal to the emotional moment" of oral argument. *USA Today's* Tony Mauro thought that he "seemed ill-equipped to tackle the key questions before the high court, which had little to do with the nefarious history of the tobacco industry's knowledge of the link between cigarettes and cancer" (Mauro, 1991a, p. 6). Another observer thought him "generally nervous . . . he was shaken further by repeated interruptions by the justices, several of whom seemed unable to follow his argument" (Schroth, 1992a, p. 3).

Whatever the reason for the change, it was significant. For the first time, the plaintiffs had *their own* "repeat player." Now arguing against the tobacco industry's H. Bartow Farr III—a former Rehnquist clerk and attorney in the Office of the Solicitor General—was one of the leading academic constitutional authorities in the nation. During the reargument, Tribe—who took the case pro bono—never even mentioned Rose Cipollone's name, expanding the issue's scope: "It is certainly about them, the Cipollone family, but it is also about the 400,000 others who die annually," he told reporters after appearing before the Court (Kiely, 1992, p. A1). The plaintiffs now had *their* hired gun. For the first time, they were truly going toe-to-toe with the tobacco industry. This redressed one resource imbalance.

Tribe and Farr argued *Cipollone* before a full Court on January 13, and the feel and flow of the arguments was decidedly different from October. Where Edell had focused on legislative history and intent, Tribe examined the specific text of the labeling legislation. He contended that the acts limited states only insofar as regulating smoking and health, and prohibited them from requiring a warning statement beyond what the acts stipulated. A product liability action does not require a company to *make a statement,* but simply holds it accountable for the accuracy of what it does say. Farr essentially reiterated his earlier argument: the federal acts preempted *any* tort action that imposed liability on the companies (Greenhouse, 1992, p. A1).

The Court's decision, handed down on June 24, gave limited reason for joy to each side. Elite news coverage of it was seemingly contradictory, with the *New York Times* dubbing it "a surprisingly broad decision that rejected many of the industry's arguments," and the *Washington Post* stressing "Tobacco firms see little effect" (Marcus, 1992, P. A1). In fact, the ruling itself was ambiguous and the elite news corps simply reflected that. Two justices— Scalia and Thomas—held that federal legislation preempted *any* state suits; three others—Harry Blackmun, Anthony Kennedy, and David Souter— found it to preempt nothing. The justices holding the balance—Rehnquist, Byron White, O'Connor, and John Paul Stevens (writing for the plurality)— held that the 1965 Act did not preempt state damages actions, but that the 1969 Act did have some preemptive effect. "Petitioner's claims are preempted to the extent that they rely on a state law 'requirement or prohibition . . . with respect to . . . advertising or promotion.'. . . The Act does not, however, preempt petitioner's claims that rely solely on respondents' testing or research practices or other actions unrelated to advertising or promotion" (505 U.S., 504, 524–25 [1992]).

Tribe commented that "this is a major victory for all those who want to hold cigarette companies accountable, [but] anyone who thinks it's a slam-dunk victory for all plaintiffs underestimates how skeptical some juries will be and how resourceful the tobacco industry remains" (Marcus, 1992, p. A1). Philip Morris, however, saw the decision as "a significant victory [because] the court held that smokers can't sue cigarette companies claiming that after 1969 they weren't adequately warned of the risks of smoking" (Greenhouse, 1992, p. A1).

The Supreme Court decision remanded the case for "further proceedings consistent with this opinion." Edell said that in the new trial he "would introduce evidence demonstrating that the tobacco companies conspired to mislead the public and falsely advertised"—arguments he could make with the documents he received during earlier proceedings. However, five and a half months after the Court's decision, the plaintiffs dropped their suit against Liggett & Myers, Philip Morris, and Lorillard. The Cipollone chapter of the tobacco saga was over.

Consequences, Politics, and Policy

Assessing the consequences of the eight-year trek the Cipollones took through the court system is, like the court decisions they generated, messy. In one sense, they "won." Although ultimately overturned, they won the first personal injury damages ever awarded against a tobacco company. They also "won" at least modest legal victories before two appellate courts. Still, they spent eight years of their lives—and saw the death of Rose and Tony—to "win" these things, and yet the family had nothing tangible to show for it.

Why did the plaintiffs drop their case? In part, no doubt, it was a function of fatigue. Son Thomas lived in California, this fight was his parents', and they were now gone. In large part, though, it resulted from the colossal resources of the tobacco industry. With about $4.25 million in unrecovered legal costs to date, Edell's firm was understandably leery of another extended litigation—the industry's "strategy of attrition"—with no guarantee of victory and no chance of settlement (Frankel, 1993, p. 7). Indeed, the firm sought to get out of all of its pending smoking cases because they had "become an unreasonable financial burden" ("Law Firm Ordered to Stay," 1993, p. A15).

The tobacco industry was organized—organization has its benefits— and they translated into a legal force that could wear down the most committed individual adversary. The cost of defending the very existence of a $3.5 billion industry was grimly borne by its constituents as the cost of doing business (Olson, 1965). To protect it, they spared no expense in hiring the best attorneys, allowing them to conduct proceedings as they wished, and underwriting all attendant costs. Quitting was not an option, and they used all means available to protect themselves.

Indeed, in a preemptive action of its own, before Cipollone gave up the case, Liggett successfully moved to have Judge Sarokin removed from another of Edell's cases pending in the third circuit, *Haines v. Liggett Group*. Its claim, also made during the *Cipollone* trial, was that Sarokin's comportment demonstrated a bias against them that compromised his impartiality. This was no small accomplishment, as it is unusual to remove a case from a federal judge, and it necessitated the assignment of a new judge unfamiliar with the case record. As Tribe noted, "Judge Sarokin's familiarity with the details means that replacing him with a relative novice is likely to be good news for the industry, not because he is biased but because he's harder to deceive than someone who's new to this material" (Margolick, 1992, p. A1). Three days later, Sarokin recused himself from the remanded *Cipollone* case, saying "I fear for the independence of the judiciary if a powerful litigant can cause the removal of a judge for speaking the truth based on the evidence, in forceful language that addresses the precise issues presented for determination" (Sanderson, 1992, p. A1). Two months later, Thomas Cipollone dropped the case.

However, the history of litigation designed to prompt policy change is rife with winners who become losers, losers who become winners, and unintended consequences. *Cipollone* rearranged the dimensions of politics and catalyzed an expansion of the scope of the tobacco controversy. It received significant media coverage and close attention from attorney populations looking to expand the scope of tort victories beyond asbestos cases. Moreover, the once "internal documents"—now public because of the *Cipollone* trial—became grist for broad discussion and commentary. As such, *Cipollone* increased the visibility of the conflict and, especially for lawyers, its intensity as well. Moved out from smoky legislative corridors and denied absolute immunity from tort suits, the tobacco companies now had to maneuver in a new political space where their resources were less overpowering. This set the stage for the third phase of the smoking controversy.

Two years after *Cipollone,* class action suits making nicotine addiction their centerpiece were pending in Miami and New Orleans (Hilts, 1994, sec. 1, p. 42). Additionally, a growing coalition of states, led by Mississippi's attorney general, Mike Moore, sued to recover Medicaid funds paid out as a result of tobacco-related diseases (Derthick, 2002, p. 2). Though beyond our story here, the latter led to the $246 billion Tobacco Settlement Agreement of 1998 that frames the current state of tobacco politics. The "who" had changed, but the "what"—holding tobacco companies responsible for the effects of smoking—and the "how"—use of the courts—owed much to Rose Cipollone and her case.

That case, though, began unexceptionally with a sixteen-year-old girl who sought to escape her world and used cigarettes as a getaway vehicle. Ultimately, they led her out of this world, but not before she filed a suit that would consume her family for eight years. It did not forestall her death, nor did it ultimately help provide economic security for her family after she was gone. So, did the end of her case dash her latter-day dreams? One of Edell's associates put it this way:

> [T]he Cipollones always felt that they got what they wanted out of the case. . . . [Thomas] was always of the view that "I don't have to go back to court to get what I want." They were never sorry they got involved in it. Rose knew she would die long before the case got to court. She wanted to help people, and I think she did. (Strum, 1992b, p. B1)

One woman took on an industrial giant to hold it responsible for the pain and suffering it caused her. Her suit did not bring the industry to its knees, but it helped to change the direction of the conflict and create a new legal and political context. In giving the issue a new visibility and stoking its intensity, her suit changed the nature of the conflict and advanced "what [she] wanted out of the case." As one of her former neighbors said after the Supreme Court's decision, "Rose was an amazing woman, very smart. She was some lady. I sit back in awe of what she did. How did she accomplish all this? I mean, everybody has heard of the Rose Cipollone lawsuit" (Allen, 1992, p. A14).

REFERENCES

Allen, M. O. (1992, June 25). Years after her death, legacy of strength lives on. *Bergen Record*, p. A14.

American Lung Association (n.d.) Facts about lung cancer. Retrieved March 14, 2003, at http://www.lungusa.org/diseases/lungcanc.html.

Cigarette ruling stands. (1987, January 13). *New York Times*, p. D5.

Coffin nails. (1988, June 15). *New York Times*, p. A30.

Dahl, R. (1956). *Preface to democratic theory.* Chicago, IL: University of Chicago Press.

Defendants accuse judge of bias in suit on smoker's death. (1988, March 21). *New York Times*, p. B3.

Derthick, M. (2002). *Up in smoke.* Washington, DC: Congressional Quarterly Press.

Epstein, L., & Kobylka, J. F. (1992). *The Supreme Court and legal change.* Chapel Hill, NC: University of North Carolina Press.

Frankel, A. (1993, July 12). Was Budd Larner another smoking victim? *New Jersey Law Journal*, p. 7.

Galanter, M. (1974). Why the "haves" always come out ahead: Speculation on the limits of legal change. *Law and Society Review, 9,* pp. 95–160.

Glaberson, W. (1988, September 10). Surprise tobacco data: suits fail. *New York Times*, sec. 1, p. 33.

Greenhouse, L. (1991, October 9). Court hears debate on suits against makers of cigarettes. *New York Times*, p. A22.

Greenhouse, L. (1992, June 25). Court opens way for damage suits over cigarettes. *New York Times*, p. A1.

Hilts, P. J. (1994, November 6). Lawsuits against tobacco companies may be consolidated. *New York Times*, sec. 1, p. 42.

Janson, D. (1988a, June 14). Cigarette maker assessed damages in smoker's death. *New York Times*, p. A1.

Janson, D. (1988b, June 2). Cigarette maker blameless in death. *New York Times*, p. B2)

Janson, D. (1988c, March 13). Data on smoking revisited at trial. *New York Times*, sec. 1, p. 34.

Janson, D. (1988d, February 27). Delay on smoking risk research is faulted. *New York Times*, sec. 1, p. 35).

Janson, D. (1988e, March 20). Doctor links smoking to cancer in woman. *New York Times,* sec 1, p. 39.

Janson, D. (1988f, March 22). End to suit denied in smoking death. *New York Times,* p. A1).

Janson, D. (1988g, March 7). The husband of a smoker testifies on her death from lung cancer. *New York Times,* p. B4).

Jensen, B. A. (2001). Note: From tobacco to health care and beyond—A critique of lawsuits targeting unpopular industries. *Cornell Law Review, 86,* p. 1334.

Kiely, E (1991, October 9). Justices hear case of N.J. smoker. *Bergen Record,* p. A1.

Kiely, E. (1992, January 14). N.J. smoking case reheard. *Bergen Record,* p. A1.

Kluger, R. (1996). *Ashes to ashes.* New York: Alfred A. Knopf.

Labaton, S. (1987, August 31). Business and the law: Untested issues on smoking. *New York Times,* p. D2.

Labaton, S. (1988, January 18). Business and the law: Expectations in cigarette case. *New York Times,* p. D2.

Laswell, H. (1936). *Politics: Who gets what, when.* New York: McGraw-Hill.

Law firm ordered to stay on case. (1993, January 29). *Bergen Record,* p. A15.

Lewin, T. (1986, April 11). Tobacco companies' victory. *New York Times,* p. D1.

Marcus, R. (1992, June 25). Tobacco firms see little effect. *Washington Post,* p. A1.

Margolick, D. (1985a, March 15). Antismoking climate inspires suits by the dying. *New York Times,* p. B1.

Margolick, D. (1992, September 9). Judge ousted from tobacco case over industry's complaint of bias. *New York Times,* p. A1.

Margolick, D. (1985b, November 9). Man in the news: Judge with acerbic pen, Haddon Lee Sarokin. *New York Times,* sec.1, p. 30.

Mauro, T. (1992, January 14). Thomas may decide smoke case. *USA Today,* p. 1A.

Mauro, T. (1991a, October 14). Blowing smoke. *Legal Times,* p. 6.

Mauro, T. (1991b, October 9). Tobacco industry future on line. *USA Today,* p. 5A.

McGuire, K. (1993). *The Supreme Court bar.* Charlottesville, VA: University Press of Virginia.

Mills, C. W. (1956). *The power elite.* New York: Oxford University Press.

New Jersey Journal (1984, October 7). *New York Times,* sec. 11NJ, p. 3.

Olson, M. (1965). *The logic of collective action.* Cambridge, MA: Harvard University Press.

Parenti, M. (1978). *Power and the powerless.* New York: St. Martin's Press.

Pinsley, E. (1988, February 2). Tobacco is put on trial in Newark. *Bergen Record,* p. A1.

Rosen, B. (1986, February 2). Tobacco's defense may go up in smoke. *Bergen Record,* p. A1.

Sanderson, B. (1992, September 12). Judge erupts. *Bergen Record,* p. A1.

Schattschneider, E. E. (1960). *The semi-sovereign people.* Hinsdale, IL: The Dryden Press.

Schroth, T. (1992a, January 20). Cipollone reargued, with new look—and outcome? *New Jersey Law Journal,* p. 3.

Schroth, T. (1992b, September 14). Sarokin off tobacco case after circuit's rare move. *New Jersey Law Journal,* p. 3.

Schroth, T. (1991, November 21). Tribe to argue Cipollone before U.S. justices. *New Jersey Law Journal,* p. 4.

Strum, C. (1992a, November 8). Cipollone v. Liggett: Legal costs doom suit against tobacco industry. *New York Times,* sec. 4, p. 4.

Strum, C. (1992b, November 6). Major lawsuit on smoking is dropped. *New York Times,* p. B1).

Truman, D. (1951). *The governmental process.* New York: Alfred A. Knopf.

Wright, M., and Herron, C. R. (1986, April 13). A victory for tobacco industry. *New York Times,* sec. 4, p. 4.

Judicial Decision Making as Legal Debate

Printz v. United States (1997)

NANCY MAVEETY

Since 1995, the Supreme Court has issued several decisions directly challenging the New Deal approach to economic regulation. One of the most important came in the context of the Brady Handgun Violence Prevention Act, a law sparked by the 1981 assassination attempt on the life of President Ronald Reagan. Under this law, Congress ordered states to conduct background checks on gun purchasers, but some local law enforcement officials regarded this law as a violation of their sovereignty. As the Court explained, despite Congress's broad discretion in regulating economic affairs, it cannot compel state officials to execute national laws.

Under the Tenth Amendment of the U.S. Constitution, "the powers not delegated to the United States by the Constitution, nor prohibited by it to the States, are reserved to the States respectively, or to the people." Its description of the federal relationship departed from the understanding provided in the Articles of Confederation, that "each State retains its sovereignty, freedom and independence, and every power, jurisdiction and right not expressly delegated to the United States, in Congress assembled" (Article II). Nevertheless, the meaning of American federalism was far from settled by the ratification of the Constitution and its Bill of Rights. State sovereignty, and its restriction on exercises of power by the national government, continued to be exerted by defenders of states' rights throughout the nineteenth and early twentieth centuries.

Such debates continued in the post–New Deal period of "cooperative federalism," even as the Tenth Amendment was viewed as simply reaffirming the Constitution's structure and limitations of federal powers to those specifically granted. Such debates were fueled in part by the increasingly complex and interdependent nature of public policy making and implementation. As a practical matter, "the states have a crucial role and responsibility in the administration of [governmental] services[, and] Congress and the federal government depend heavily on them in sharing the burdens of governing" (O'Brien, 2003, p. 626). The constitutional politics of federalism thus concern controversies not only over the power of the states, but also over intergovernmental relations generally. This controversy, and debate, was renewed in the contemporary era of the U.S. Supreme Court by two closely divided and opposing Burger Court rulings in 1976 and 1985. In *National League of Cities v. Usery* (426 U.S. 833 [1976]), a five-member majority led by then-Associate Justice William Rehnquist invalidated the 1974 amendments to the Fair Labor Standards Act (FLSA) that extended minimum-wage and maximum-hours standards to state and local government employees.

Rehnquist relied on what some considered a novel reading of the Tenth Amendment as prohibiting Congress from regulating "the States as States" or interfering with states' "freedom to structure integral operations in areas of traditional governmental functions." While this doctrine was utilized by the court in a series of decisions in the early 1980s, it was not employed to further limit Congress's regulation of state and local government employees. Then, in 1985, in *Garcia v. San Antonio Metropolitan Transit Authority* (469 U.S. 528 [1985]), Justice Harry Blackmun—who had been part of the five-member majority in *Usery*—"changed his mind about the wisdom of judicial line drawing in defense of interests of the states as states" (O'Brien, 2003 p. 668). The new five-member majority, led by Justice Blackmun, overruled *Usery*— a precedent of less than ten-years' vintage.

The justices' debate in *Garcia* was less about the application of FLSA standards to municipal transit workers than it was about whether federalism as a political structure, and its national political process, adequately safeguards states' "sphere of inviolable sovereignty" against the encroachments of federal regulatory activity. The view of the *Garcia* majority was that it does, and that no constitutional provision barred that case's exercise of congressional commerce power. The dissenters, conversely, saw in the ruling an "emasculation of the powers of the States" and the "bare[st] acknowledg-[ment] that the Tenth Amendment exists" (Powell, J., dissenting). More prescient even were the final words of recently appointed Justice Sandra Day

O'Connor's dissent: "this Court will in time again assume its constitutional responsibility."

By the late 1980s and early 1990s, the Supreme Court's membership was partially reconstituted by new appointments by President Reagan, including the elevation of sitting-associate justice Rehnquist to the chief justiceship. In 1992 the Rehnquist Court decided the case of *New York v. U.S.* (505 U.S. 144 [1992]), holding that Congress could not compel state legislatures to enact a federal program for disposal of radioactive waste, pursuant to its conditional exercise of authority under the Spending Clause of Article I of the Constitution.

At the time of the decision, the ruling—the O'Connor-majority opinion suggesting but not declaring an infringement of states' rights guaranteed by the Tenth Amendment—received only muted fanfare. While the *New York Times* provided the case with front-page coverage in its late edition of June 20, 1992, the *Washington Post* consigned coverage of the case to "below the fold" status in its final edition of the same date. Yet by 1995, with the Court's decision in *U.S. v. Lopez* (514 U.S. 549 [1995]) (and with the placement of two Bush appointees), Court observers clearly sensed that a majority supportive of states' rights concerns had emerged on the high bench. In a five-to-four ruling, the Court in *Lopez* invalidated the Gun-Free School Zones Act of 1990 as an unconstitutional exercise of congressional power to regulate interstate commerce. This marked the first time since the New Deal era that the Supreme Court had overturned an act of Congress under the Commerce Clause.

Unlike the 1992 *New York* case, the *Lopez* decision generated tremendous press and learned commentary and featured the judicial lineup that would come to be the Rehnquist Court's configuration in its subsequent federalism decisions. The five justices voting to restore what some legal scholars considered an outmoded and defunct states' rights jurisprudence were Chief Justice Rehnquist and Justices O'Connor, Anthony Kennedy, Antonin Scalia, and Clarence Thomas. All were Reagan and Bush, Sr., appointees. The four dissenting justices—John Paul Stevens, David Souter, Ruth Ginsberg, and Stephen Breyer—constituted the moderate bloc, opposing such radical, or in their view conservatively activist, constitutional change.

The rulings in *New York* and *Lopez* seemed to presage a dramatic (and enduring) change in federalism jurisprudence, because they so strongly suggested a reappraisal of New Deal–era constitutional doctrine. With the infamous "Switch in Time that Saved Nine" in 1937, the Supreme Court had vindicated FDR's constitutional vision of national supremacy, federal predominance in economic regulation, and the preeminence of congressional commerce power over the "reserved" powers of the states. The Tenth Amendment became once again, much as it had been during the Federalist era of Chief Justice John Marshall, "but a truism" (*U.S. v. Darby Lumber Co.,* 312 U.S. 100 [1941])—without independent force in constraining the federal government's powers.

While neither *New York* nor *Lopez* rested the decision on and thereby resuscitated the Tenth Amendment, both rulings unambiguously held that Congress had exceeded its constitutional powers and intruded on those of the states. Moreover, Thomas's concurring opinion in *Lopez* frankly stated that the Court's case law on the scope of congressional authority had drifted far from original understandings of the commerce clause and the Tenth Amendment, and that the Court's opinion in *Lopez* was neither radical nor wrong but a needed corrective with respect to the federal-state balance.

Testing the Court's New Federalism

Among the Court watchers taking notice of the Rehnquist Court's turn toward a "new federalism" were critics of federal gun-control legislation. In 1993, in the wake of the attempted assassination of President Ronald Reagan and the critical wounding of his White House press secretary, Jim Brady, President Bill Clinton signed into law the Brady Handgun Prevention Act. To address what a House of Representatives report termed the national epidemic of gun violence, the act sought to enhance the enforcement of existing federal regulations of gun dealers—regulations that included bans on the sale of firearms to convicted felons, minors, and others prohibited by state or local law from possessing a firearm. The Brady Act mandated, among other provisions, a background checking procedure for gun purchases that involved the participation of local law enforcement agencies. Such local involvement in the federal program was an interim enforcement measure, to be utilized until a Department of Justice national database was created that made instant, electronic background checks by firearms dealers feasible.

Lobbying efforts over the legislation were intense—most particularly, lobbying by the National Rifle Association (NRA) against the passage of the act and its alleged infringement on the rights of gun owners and enthusiasts. When two local sheriffs in Montana and Arizona, Ray Printz and Richard Mack, objected to their compulsory performance of background checks on prospective gun buyers in their jurisdictions, their suit in federal court challenging the Brady Act on federalism grounds had the support of the NRA. As Gregg Ivers comments, the *Printz* case was selected and funded by the

NRA "to test the [Supreme] Court's sympathies toward greater state autonomy in the federal system," and would demonstrate the success of "a carefully crafted litigation campaign in a sympathetic judicial environment" (Ivers, 2001, p. 396).

Initially, the campaign was of limited success. Although both district courts held that the interim background-checking provisions of the act's requirements contravened the Tenth Amendment's protection of state sovereign authority, neither was willing to invalidate the Brady Act's notice and waiting period for gun purchases in its entirety. A divided panel of the Court of Appeals for the Tenth Circuit upheld in 1995 all provisions of the act, concluding that nothing in it transgressed any implied limitation on federal power. The court of appeals particularly rejected the notion that, under *New York v. U.S.,* the federal government is flatly precluded from requiring state officers to assist in carrying out a federal program. The federal mandate condemned in *New York* was thus distinguished from the Brady Act program. Moreover, the Tenth Amendment's reservation to the states of powers not delegated to the federal government did not bar Congress from imposing on a state officer a duty and compelling him to perform it. Indeed, the circuit court found that the act's requirement that local law enforcement officers make "reasonable efforts" to ascertain if there is a legal impediment to a handgun sale "represent[ed] a minimal interference with state functions," and "[was not] the kind of interference with state functions that would raise Tenth Amendment concerns."

At the Supreme Court level, the *Printz* litigation marked not only the participation of the NRA as a sponsor of the case, but also the participation of numerous gun rights, gun control, and other interest group organizations as amicus curiae petitioners. The Pacific Legal Foundation, a conservative public interest group, filed an amicus brief in support of the petition to grant certiorari in the case. Amicus briefs filed at the certiorari or access stage of Supreme Court proceedings are argued to function as cues to the justices regarding case salience, influencing the likelihood of the cert petition's acceptance for oral argument and a decision on the merits (McGuire, 2002, p. 80).

The Rehnquist Court accepted the petition in *Printz* in June of 1996, but there is, of course, no publicized accounting of why or how many justices chose to hear the case. By the time of the filing of the petitioners' and the respondent U.S. government's briefs, twelve amicus curiae briefs were filed in support of the petitioners and the respondent, by organizations as diverse as the Gun Owners Foundation and the AFL-CIO and by governmental or individual actors ranging from the Council of State Governments to members of Congress. Many of these briefs were cosponsored or jointly authored by like-minded interest group organizations. Public interest in the *Printz* case, as measured by the number of these amici filings, was high.

The amicus briefs filed by the NRA and the Pacific Legal Foundation merit special attention for their arguments that the challenged provisions of the Brady Act violated "the standards of federalism" previously set out by the Supreme Court. The NRA's brief explicitly noted (however immodestly) that the Court would be assisted by the expertise the association had developed on the constitutionality of the sale and transfer of firearms. Such informational cues from briefs filed by organized interests are often significant in judicial proceedings, facilitating the justices' making of efficacious policy as close as is possible to their ideal preferences (Epstein & Knight, 1999, p. 215). This amicus brief presented three legal arguments—some echoing, others expanding on the arguments made in the briefs of the petitioners.

First, drawing heavily on *New York v. U.S.,* the NRA brief asserted that the Brady Act shifted the primary burden of enforcing the federal statute onto state officials, "commandeering" them to administer a federal program in violation of the Tenth Amendment. Additionally, and relying on the decision in *U.S. v. Lopez,* the brief argued that Congress had transgressed its own commerce powers under Article I by attempting to regulate a state activity— indeed, by compelling a state activity—that does not "substantially affect" interstate commerce. At this point, the brief's Tenth Amendment–based argument explicitly evoked a concurring statement by moderate conservative Justice Kennedy, from his *Lopez* opinion, to the effect that exercises of national power cannot intrude on areas of traditional state concern. This federalism argument, and the reliance on the key precedents of *New York* and *Lopez,* reiterated the legal position taken in both petitioners' briefs. Second, but in a departure from the content of the latter two briefs, the NRA amicus brief asserted that the statute violated the Eleventh Amendment by authorizing a civil cause of action against a state law enforcement official's political subdivision, constituting an attempt to abrogate the sovereign immunity of states. Finally, speaking against the position taken by the district courts and again echoing petitioners' arguments, the NRA brief argued that the unconstitutional provisions of the act could not be severed from the statute, requiring that the gun control legislative scheme be invalidated in toto.

Ranging somewhat more broadly, from an interpretive perspective, was the amicus brief filed by the Pacific Legal Foundation. It asserted that "the letter and *spirit* of the Tenth Amendment" and "the federal *structure* protected by the Tenth Amendment" was violated by the act's federal co-option of local law enforcement mechanisms. This brief, too, relied heavily on the "guidance" provided by the *New York* and *Lopez* rulings. Also, it ended its argument with an explicit overture to moderate conservative Justice O'Connor, appealing to a position taken in her dissent in the Tenth Amendment *Garcia* case: that in reconciling congressional commerce power with the constraints of the Tenth Amendment, the means to the end chosen by Congress "must not contravene the spirit of the Constitution." Like the NRA amicus brief, the brief filed by the Pacific Legal Foundation was clearly aimed at those justices who might be swing votes in the case, tailoring its legal arguments to them accordingly.

The respondent in the *Printz* case was the U.S. government, with the acting solicitor general presenting the government's brief. Judicial process studies often note that the solicitor general is an influential litigant in Supreme Court proceedings, with petitions filed from this office enjoying disproportionate success in both case selection and decisions on the merits (Baum, 1997, pp. 52–53).

In *Printz*, the U.S. government's brief took great pains to limit the ruling of *New York* and render inapplicable the holding in *Lopez*, aiming its efforts to appeal to the same median justice position targeted by the NRA and Pacific Legal Foundation amicus briefs. The respondent brief stressed the interim, limited, and nonpolicymaking aspects of state officials' implementation of the Brady Act provisions, emphasizing that scheme's comportment with the constitutional principle of federalism as espoused in the Tenth Amendment.

Tellingly, the brief called the constitutional inquiries under the amendment and the commerce clause "mirror images of one another," clearly hoping to play down the separate and independent force of a commerce clause/ *Lopez*-based challenge to the act. Once again, Justice Kennedy's concurring opinion in *Lopez* was cited as instructive, and the U.S. government's brief warned against endorsing an "absolutist position [that] finds no basis in this Court's jurisprudence of federalism or in the constitutional tradition that it reflects." This statement appeared geared toward those moderate conservative justices who recoil from the establishment of "bright-line," absolute rules in constitutional jurisprudence.

Finally, in a failsafe measure, the brief by the solicitor general argued that the challenged provisions of the act were severable, and their invalidation would leave the remainder of the act's restrictions on gun transfers fully operative and the background checking by local officials purely voluntary. Amicus briefs filed in support of the respondent U.S. government echoed the importance of such severability and of retaining the option of voluntary compliance with the background-checking provisions.

The Justices Debate the Tenth Amendment

The Rehnquist Court's 5–4 decision on June 27, 1997, reflected the diversity and intensity of opinion represented by the multiple amici. The court's multiple opinions—the majority opinion, two concurrences, and three dissents—constituted a heady interpretive debate among the Rehnquist justices. Implicit in this interpretive debate was the interpretive position of the Pacific Legal Foundation brief that the protection of state sovereignty could be discerned from the Constitution's structural principles. Moreover, the overtures in this brief and in the NRA brief to the more moderate conservative members of the court did correlate with their support of the majority's Tenth Amendment argument—but not without generating a cautionary and seemingly responsive separate statement by Justice O'Connor. Finally, the litigants' and amici quarrels as to how and with what weight to construe the historical record and relevant Supreme Court precedents carried over into the justices' policy debate in the case.

For those familiar with the jurisprudence of Justice Scalia, his opinion for the court in *Printz* was a curious departure from his oft-stated textualism. Finding that there was no constitutional text that spoke to the precise question of whether congressional action compelling state officers to execute federal law was unconstitutional, he stated that the answer to the petitioners' challenge must be sought in "historical understanding and practice, in the Constitution's structure, and in this Court's jurisprudence."

After extensively reviewing the historical record on federal legislative and executive actions imposing obligations on state officials and assessing the relevant papers of *The Federalist,* Scalia concluded that the historical constitutional practice tended to negate the congressional exercise asserted in the Brady Act but was not conclusive. He turned to consideration of "the structure of the Constitution" to see if could be discerned among "its essential postulates a principle that controls the present cases." The chain of connection between structure, postulates, and principle is a rather more tenuous one, interpretationally, than Scalia's textually grounded constitutional arguments usually feature. Nevertheless, he found varied and multiple sources for the Constitution's establishment of "a system of dual sovereignty" and separate spheres of national and state authority, including Court precedent, *The Federalist,* and various constitutional passages, among them the Tenth Amendment.

"Finally and most conclusively," Scalia rested his argument on the prior jurisprudence of the court. Explaining that the court concluded categorically, as it concluded categorically in *New York v. U.S.,* that the "principle of separate state sovereignty" must be adhered to, Scalia used the language of that precedent to speak to the present case. "The Federal Government may not compel the states to enact or administer a federal regulatory program," he repeated. But his construction of *New York* was heavily influenced by a much earlier precedent: that of *Texas v. White* (7 Wall 700 [1869]), from the nineteenth-century era of "dual federalism." That influence is evident in the following passage from the opinion for the Court, with the portion quoting *Texas* italicized:

> Even assuming that the Brady Act leaves no "policymaking" discretion with the States, we fail to see how that improves rather than worsens the intrusion upon state sovereignty. Preservation of the states as independent and autonomous political entities is arguably less undermined by requiring them to make policy in certain fields than by reducing them to puppets of a ventriloquist Congress. *It is an essential attribute of the States' retained sovereignty that they remain independent and autonomous within their proper sphere of authority.* It is no more compatible with this independence and autonomy that their officers be dragooned into administering federal law, than it would be compatible with the independence and autonomy of the United States for its officers to be impressed into service for the execution of state laws.

For Scalia, *New York* not only spoke authoritatively and unambiguously, but also was supported by history, practice, and constitutional structure.

Scalia's interpretive tour de force occasioned an extended legal debate and discourse among the justices over these several points. The principal dissent by Justice Stevens began with the interpretive proposition that "the text of the Constitution"—or, more properly, its silence—"provides a sufficient basis for a correct disposition of the case." Stevens's dissent also lengthily engaged the Scalia majority opinion on how to construe precedent. Stevens went so far as to call the Court's decision "*un*precedented," as the "conclusive" "prior jurisprudence of this Court" cited by the majority was limited to *New York v. U.S.,* which was itself not conclusive—unless the dicta of this opinion was read as binding.

Souter's dissent devoted most of its discussion to challenging Scalia's reading of the *Federalist*—an analytic endeavor perhaps more appropriate to a political theory seminar than a judicial opinion, but both Souter's and Scalia's opinions responded directly to arguments based on this source made in the petitioners' briefs.

Two dissents, by Stevens and Breyer, took on the Scalia majority opinion for its assertion of an activist judicial role in discerning constitutional structural principles. Stevens objected to "the Court's newly defined constitutional threshold" for congressional action, noting the possibility "that the

Court's holding [is] rooted in a 'principle of state sovereignty' mentioned nowhere in the constitutional text." Breyer commented that there was no need for the Court to interpret the Constitution as containing an "absolute principle" forbidding the assignment of virtually any federal duty to any state official, citing in part the instruction provided by the comparative experience with federalism. (This comparative constitutional exegesis earned a dismissive rebuke from the Scalia majority opinion, in a footnote.)

Finally, Thomas's concurrence commented separately to emphasize the need for the "revisionist" jurisprudence of the Tenth Amendment, and of the federal balance generally. In addition to reaffirming the position he asserted separately in *Lopez,* Thomas took the occasion of his *Printz* concurrence to sow the seeds for further reconsideration of the Constitution's "plac[ing of] whole areas outside the reach of Congress's regulatory authority." The Second Amendment's right to "keep and bear arms" was his target.

Only O'Connor's brief concurring opinion added little in the way of jurisprudential substance to the judicial debate. She limited herself to limiting the Court's holding by rephrasing it as refraining from presenting an absolute rule regarding ministerial reporting requirements imposed by Congress on state authorities, pursuant to its commerce clause powers. Her short concurring statement also made clear that she would not be party to ending the objectives of the Brady Act, including local law enforcement personnel's voluntary participation in the federal program—an option defended with force by several amicus briefs filed on behalf of the respondent U.S. government. Interestingly, from the perspective of judicial process scholarship, the *Printz* majority did vindicate one position argued by the solicitor general's brief: that the constitutionally suspect background-checking provisions of the Brady Act were severable from the rest of the statute.

It is impossible to know from the justices' final opinions themselves, but this compromise position on the act and on congressional power exertions may have been the price of O'Connor's concurring vote. Clearly, the solicitor general's warning in his brief against absolutist constitutional doctrine was not lost on this member of the majority coalition.

Conclusion

As a result of the decision in *Printz v. U.S.,* the Tenth Amendment has once again galvanized legal debate over federalism.[1] Although the Court has, in some subsequent instances, declined the opportunity to extend the decision—in *Reno v. Condon* (528 U.S. 141 [2000]), for example, the Court upheld a federal law prohibiting states from selling the personal information contained on drivers' license to marketers—the *Printz* ruling has nevertheless been cited as an authority in a number of decisions, including a 5–4 ruling prohibiting the national government from using statistical estimates of the population when allocating a state's number of congressional representatives (*Department of Commerce v. U.S. House of Representatives,* 525 U.S. 316 [1999]). More significant, the federalism stance of the Rehnquist Court in *Printz*—and its majority's reliance on "the structure and history" of the Constitution—has continued in a series of narrowly decided rulings resurrecting the Eleventh Amendment's protection of state sovereign immunity as a limitation on congressional power under Article I (O'Brien, 2003, p. 672; Pellicciotti, 2001).

Similarly, traditional state concerns in the area of criminal law were the rationale for a 5–4 majority invalidating the civil cause of action remedy of the Violence Against Women Act of 1994, as an unconstitutional exercise of congressional commerce power (*U.S. v. Morrison,* 529 U.S. 598 [2000]). *Printz* is therefore emblematic of a jurisprudential journey by the Rehnquist Court, back to a states' rights philosophy and a constitutional principle of federalism that has not commanded a majority of the U.S. Supreme Court since before the New Deal era.[2]

Printz is also indicative of a decision-making convention that increasingly describes the modern Supreme Court, and certainly describes the many closely decided, highly salient cases of the Rehnquist Court. That convention is ruling on the law by issuing multiple, separate opinions (O'Brien, 1999). So, rather than relying on the single voice of a unified, majority opinion, the justices will frequently write separate opinions that express their own distinctive views. Here, for example, in addition to the five-member majority opinion of Justice Scalia, concurring opinions were filed by Justices O'Connor and Thomas, and three dissenting opinions were filed, by Justices Stevens, Souter, and Breyer.

According to Justice Scalia, these divisions among the justices are common, because "[t]he Court itself is not just the central organ of legal *judgment;* it is center stage for significant legal *debate*" (1994, p. 39). In other words, the Court is as much a forum for simply contemplating legal issues as it is for resolving them.

Of course, these various separate opinions signal ideological division and jurisprudential disagreement on the Supreme Court. Whether such decisions are genuinely the product of an orientation toward an institutional goal of legal debate, however, remains to be seen. All of the Rehnquist Court's "revisionist" federalism rulings—*Printz* included—have been decided by minimum-winning majority coalitions, often framed by concurring commentary. This has doubtlessly contributed to the continuing debate, among the justices and in American political society, about the legal and political correctness of the policy espoused by the *Printz* majority. If informing the country of the state of the court's collective mind was the goal of the Rehnquist Court in *Printz,* then the justices surely achieved it. In this sense, the many opinions written in the case serve as testimony to the intellectual engagement with which the justices perform their judicial job. If, however, the debate over federalism within *Printz* was intended to constitute a more intellectually persuasive and jurisprudentially convincing argument, this has not been achieved. The decision may very well mark constitutional change, but it is a change in process rather than a change in outcome that the decision most tellingly indicates.

NOTES

1. The legal literature on the case has been voluminous. For a representative, early analytic commentary, see Woods, 1998.

2. For a critical analysis of this development, particularly its historical justification, see Dervan, 2001.

REFERENCES

Baum, L. (1997). *The puzzle of judicial behavior.* Ann Arbor, MI: University of Michigan Press.

Dervan, L. E. (2001). Selective conceptions of federalism: The selective use of history in the Supreme Court's states' rights opinions. *Emory Law Journal, 50,* pp. 1295–1317.

Epstein, L., & Knight, J. (1999). Mapping out the strategic terrain: the informational role of amici curiae. In C. Clayton & H. Gillman (Eds.), *Supreme Court decision making: New institutionalist approaches.* pp. 215–235. Chicago: University of Chicago Press.

Ivers, G. (Ed.). (2001). *American constitutional law, power and politics: Constitutional structure and political power.* Boston: Houghton Mifflin Co.

McGuire, K. T. (2002). *Understanding the U.S. Supreme Court: Cases and controversies.* Boston: McGraw Hill.

O'Brien, D. M. (Ed.). (2003). *Constitutional law and politics: Struggles for power and governmental accountability.* New York: W. W. Norton and Co.

O'Brien, D. M. (1999). Institutional norms and Supreme Court opinions: On reconsidering the rise of individual opinions. In C. Clayton and H. Gillman. (Eds.). *Supreme Court decision making: New institutionalist approaches.* pp. 92–113. Chicago: University of Chicago Press.

Pellicciotti, J. M. (2001). Redefining the relationship between the states and the federal government: A focus on the Supreme Court's expansion of the principle of state sovereign immunity. *Boston Public Interest Law Journal, 11,* pp. 1–62.

Scalia, A. (1994). The dissenting opinion. *Journal of Supreme Court History, 19,* pp. 33–44.

Woods, D. T. (1998). A step toward stability in modern Tenth Amendment jurisprudence: The Supreme Court adopts a workable standard in *Printz v. U.S. St. Louis University Law Journal, 42,* pp. 1417–1443.

Establishment
of Religion

Funding Religion and Free Speech

Rosenberger v. University of Virginia (1996)

KEVIN T. MCGUIRE

When a religious group at the University of Virginia sought student funds to pay for the publication of a newsletter, the university balked, owing to a concern about the state funding of religious activities. The Supreme Court had consistently ruled that, once the state makes its resources available to different organizations, it cannot deny those resources on a selective basis, but this case did not involve access to classrooms, auditoriums, or other facilities. The state would be giving money directly to a religious group to spread its message. At the same time, though, the university gave its funds to other university student groups. Could it discriminate against a religious viewpoint? Weighing two provisions of the First Amendment—the establishment clause and the free speech clause—the justices concluded that funding campus speech, even if some of it is religious in nature, does not amount to an establishment of religion.

One of Thomas Jefferson's proudest achievements was founding the University of Virginia. After having served the nation as president, he retired to Monticello, where he planned, developed, and oversaw the construction of his "academical village" in nearby Charlottesville (Ellis, 1996, p. 335). The care and interest he devoted to the project reflected Jefferson's strong belief in state sponsorship of education as a means of promoting an informed citizenry and responsible policymakers. "Jefferson believed that, to preserve republican government and prevent tyranny, it was necessary 'to illuminate, as far as practicable, the minds of the people at large'" (Randall, 1993, p. 305). Education promoted enlightened leaders, free from irrational passion or prejudice, who would guard against the potential abuses of power.

To serve those ends, a state-controlled school was seen as especially critical. Jefferson, devoted to freedom of thought, believed that a principal impediment to academic inquiry was the control that organized religion exercised over institutions of learning. As he explained, students at his university would enjoy "the free range of mind encouraged there [without] the restraint imposed at other seminaries by the shackles of a domineering hierarchy and a bigoted adhesion to ancient habits" (Randall, 1993, p. 588). So, to ensure that the university's students would be able to pursue knowledge in an atmosphere of tolerance and respect, Jefferson took special care to deny any type of religious influence over the course of study. "One of the most distinctive features of the University of Virginia was its disavowal of any religious affiliation . . . [Jefferson] was extremely sensitive to the way boards of trustees at other American colleges, usually dominated by the clergy, imposed restrictions on what could be taught or what books could be read. He was absolutely insistent that his university not succumb to such forms of censorship" (Ellis, 1996, p. 339). To guarantee free expression of ideas, Jefferson aimed to keep religion out of the program of education at the University of Virginia.

Nearly two hundred years later, educational sponsorship of religion and freedom of speech would clash at Mr. Jefferson's university in a conflict that would eventually be settled by the U.S. Supreme Court. The case, *Rosenberger v. University of Virginia* (515 U.S. 819 [1995]), involved a student Christian group that sought university funds to help pay for the publication of a magazine. Inasmuch as the First Amendment forbids the state from creating "an establishment of religion," the university balked at providing money to promote an avowedly religious point of view. Because the First Amendment also prohibits government from "abridging the freedom of speech," however, the student group believed that denying funds for the dissemination of their message—while actively underwriting the views expressed by other student groups—violated their rights of expression. How did the Supreme Court resolve this tension between a university founded on the principle of academic freedom and a university designed to educate its students in an environment removed from religious doctrines?

The Background

Across the United States, colleges and universities sponsor a variety of activities that are designed to enrich the educational experience of their students. Concerts, plays, speakers, public forums, and the like all serve to give students the chance to supplement their academic pursuits with opportunities to challenge and expand their outlooks. One of the ways schools most frequently pursue this goal is by encouraging students of similar interests to form associations, student groups that enable individuals to discover and pursue their common goals.

These student organizations exist in considerable variety. They consist of traditional groups, such as fraternities and sororities; glee clubs; rugby, skiing, and fencing clubs; and professional organizations, including law and business associations and societies of scientists and engineers. Some groups are defined by a common race or ancestry; thus there are organizations for African Americans, Filipinos, Mexicans, Native Americans, Israelis, Italians, and Vietnamese, to name only a few. Even students with more obscure interests manage to find clubs devoted to such passions as French film, bagpipe bands, cattle roping, pheasant hunting, and Chinese yo-yos.

Among the most common are religious organizations. Groups such as Campus Crusade for Christ, Hillel, and the Muslim Students' Association are found on countless campuses across the country. These groups typically help to care for the spiritual needs of their student members, promoting fellowship within the context of their individual religious traditions.

In 1990, at the University of Virginia, an undergraduate named Ronald Rosenberger, together with several fellow students, formed one such organization, a group called Wide Awake Productions. Seeking to promote Christian values among students of different cultural backgrounds, the group published a magazine entitled *Wide Awake: A Christian Perspective at the University of Virginia*. Drawing its title from St. Paul's letter to the Romans—"The hour has come for you to awake from your slumber, because our salvation is nearer now than when we first believed"—its aim was "to challenge Christians to live, in word and deed, according to the faith they proclaim and to encourage students to consider what a personal relationship with Jesus Christ means."[1]

To that end, Rosenberger sought to have Wide Awake Productions recognized as a bona fide campus organization. Such a designation was significant, because Virginia's official student organizations were permitted access to the university's facilities, including meeting rooms and computer resources. In addition, they were also permitted to apply to a Student Activities Fund, which allocated money to groups that would use that money to pursue legitimate educational activities. Supported by mandatory student fees, the Student Activities Fund helped to underwrite the projects of a good many different organizations.

Recognized campus groups were not always eligible for these funds, however. The university placed some restrictions on how the money from the Student Activities Fund could be utilized. Among other things, it did not permit the money to be used for purely social entertainment. Nor could a group receive money that would, in turn, be used as a charitable donation. Similarly, while the university was certainly willing to support the educational activities of groups with political views—it might, for example, fund a voter registration drive by the Young Democrats or a Young Republican's public debate on an issue of public concern—it would not permit such groups to use the state's money to pursue their public policy goals directly, through such programs as political campaigning during elections or lobbying governmental decision makers.

One other noteworthy restriction was placed on the use of the money: it could not be used for religious activities. The university's guidelines defined a religious activity as one that "promotes or manifests a particular belie(f) in or about a deity or an ultimate reality" (*Rosenberger v. University of Virginia*, 515 U.S. 819 [1995]). This meant that *Wide Awake*—a magazine that sought to offer "a Christian perspective on both personal and community issues, especially those relevant to college students at the University of Virginia"— was not entitled to the University's financial support (*Rosenberger*, pp. 819, 826).

Rosenberger learned this shortly after *Wide Awake* began publishing, carrying articles of both religious and secular orientation. Since the university's guidelines permitted funding for "student news, information, opinion, entertainment, or academic communications media groups," Rosenberger submitted an application to the Appropriations Committee of the Student Activities Fund, after the first issue was published, seeking roughly $6,000 to cover its printing costs. After examining the magazine, however, the committee turned down this request, because it regarded *Wide Awake* as a "religious activity" and therefore ineligible for financial support. From the University of Virginia's perspective, *Wide Awake* was merely one of several different types of activities that it regarded as inconsistent with its educational mission.

From Rosenberger's perspective, however, the university was being selective about what types of ideas it would subsidize. The fund had helped pay the costs of numerous other student publications on a wide variety of subjects—politics, literature, science, and the like—and Rosenberger believed that *Wide Awake* should not be denied the same support that was available to other organizations. As he explained, "I was very disturbed by what I thought was a double-standard" (Biskupic, 1995). Following established guidelines, he appealed the committee's decision, but at each turn the answer was the same: the University of Virginia would not authorize its resources to support the dissemination of a religious message on campus.

The willingness of the university to subsidize some publications but not others seemed to Rosenberger to be a violation of the First Amendment. Its guarantee of freedom of expression, he believed, did not permit the state (i.e., the University of Virginia) to treat some ideas more favorably than others. To discriminate against a religious viewpoint, while providing active support for nonreligious ideas, violated the constitutional guarantee of free expression; the state could not take sides on matters of public debate by helping some speakers or hindering others. On that basis, Rosenberger and his fellow editors filed a legal suit against the university in federal court, arguing that its refusal to fund *Wide Awake* violated the First Amendment.

In its defense, the university argued that it was not discriminating against a particular religious view. Stated differently, it was not demonstrating hostility toward *Wide Awake*'s Christian message. Instead, it was simply refusing to support *any* religious message, Christian or otherwise. Not only that, the university feared that to offer financial support to help propagate such ideas would violate the Constitution. After all, the First Amendment forbids government from establishing religion, and the university was concerned that state funds being given to promote a religious message might amount to an unconstitutional endorsement of religion.

Persuaded by the university's arguments, the federal trial court rejected Rosenberger's claims. He appealed the decision to the U.S. Court of Appeals for the Fourth Circuit. The appeals court acknowledged that the University of Virginia had, in fact, discriminated against *Wide Awake* and that the state could not fund some viewpoints while denying funding to others, unless it had an exceptionally strong reason for doing so. In this case, the court concluded that the university did have a compelling interest that justified its action; by refusing to fund *Wide Awake*, it was "maintaining strict separation of church and state" (*Rosenberger*, p. 828). As the appeals court explained, "Because *Wide Awake* is a journal pervasively devoted to the discussion and advancement of an avowedly Christian theological and personal philosophy, for the University to subsidize its publication would, we believe, send an unmistakably clear signal that the University of Virginia supports Christian values and wishes to promote the wide promulgation of such values" (*Rosenberger v. University of Virginia,* 18 F. 3d 269 [1994]). Having been rebuffed again, Rosenberger had no place left to turn, except the U.S. Supreme Court.

Decision Making in the Supreme Court

Cases of civil liberties almost always involve competing arguments over the meaning of a single constitutional provision, with an individual interest on one side and a governmental interest on the other. Disputes over the free exercise clause of the First Amendment might involve a state governmental policy—a tax, a health policy, a military regulation—that arguably interferes with the practice of one's religious faith. Conflicts over the First Amendment's free press provision will often place some legitimate state goal— guarding national secrets, protecting vulnerable children, regulating the public airwaves—against the interests of the media.

What made *Rosenberger* especially unusual was that it pitted two different constitutional safeguards of civil liberties—the free speech clause and the establishment clause—against one another. On the one hand, *Wide Awake* argued that its right to free expression was being violated by the university's decision to pick and choose, among the various voices on campus, those that would receive subsidies from the state. On the other hand, Virginia argued that to pay a student organization to spread a religious message would constitute an establishment of religion.

This unusual conflict brought together an interesting mix of legal and political forces. The justices had to weigh a series of competing arguments over both public policy and legal doctrine, weighing them all against their own individual orientations about how best to craft the law.

LEGAL CONTEXT

Judging strictly by the Court's relevant precedents, the arguments for Rosenberger looked fairly favorable. At least since 1981, the Supreme Court had supported the idea that religious groups were entitled to equal access to educational facilities. In *Widmar v. Vincent* (454 U.S. 263 [1981]), the Court reviewed a policy at the University of Missouri at Kansas City, which allowed its recognized student organizations to hold their meetings within the facilities of the university. Despite this otherwise open policy, however, the university maintained a rule prohibiting religious worship and religious teaching. When a campus group of evangelical Christians was told it could no longer hold meetings at the university because of this policy, it challenged its exclusion and prevailed on free speech grounds.

Much like the *Rosenberger* case, *Widmar* highlighted the tension between free expression and the establishment of religion. In resolving that tension, the Court ruled that, since it opened its doors to campus groups in general, the university could not then close those doors to some groups based on the content of their expression. The exclusion of religious expression might be justified, the justices reasoned, if the policy had the effect of advancing religion, but since there were so many different campus groups making use of the university's facilities, the Court saw no such complication posed by an equal-access policy.

A similar question arose in the public secondary schools in *Board of Westside Community Schools v. Mergens* (512 U.S. 687 [1990]), a case in which a Nebraska school allowed students with similar interests to form clubs and meet on school property. Concerned that approving a request for a club devoted to prayer and Bible study would unconstitutionally advance religion, the principal denied students the right to form their group. A nearly unanimous Supreme Court held that a policy of excluding religious clubs interferes with the speech rights of those who are excluded.

In its most recent related decision, the Court again sustained the right of access for religious groups in *Lamb's Chapel v. Center Moriches Union Free School District* (508 U.S. 384 [1993]). Just as in *Widmar,* where the state permitted access to its university facilities, the state of New York authorized local school boards to permit after-school use of its facilities for social, civic, and entertainment programs. Meetings for religious purposes, however, were not permitted under the law, and when a church group sought permission to use a local school to show a religious film series, it was denied. Since the regulation permitted nonreligious views to be expressed on a subject—in this case, family and child raising—but excluded religious views on the same subject, this law also violated the church's speech rights.

As far as Rosenberger and the other editors of *Wide Awake* were concerned, these cases provided every reason to believe that the Court would find in their favor. Their general teaching was fairly clear. Whenever the state sets out to make its facilities available to individual groups, it cannot exclude those with a religious message without violating their rights to free speech. In this case, the Student Activities Fund had underwritten other publications. Academic journals, such as the *Journal of Law and Politics,* and journals that featured original creative works, such as the *Virginia Literary Review,* received money. The Court's cases suggested that, if the University of Virginia were going to support student publications, it could not single out *Wide Awake* without violating freedom of expression.

Didn't such funding unconstitutionally further religious interests, though? It would not seem so. The justices had considered such practices as granting tuition tax deductions for parents who sent their children to both nonreligious and religious private schools or sending state interpreters for the deaf into parochial schools (*Mueller v. Allen,* 463 U.S. 388 [1983]; *Zobrest v. Catalina Foothills School District,* 509 U.S. 1 [1993]). In these cases, the conclusion was largely the same: whatever benefit religion receives is merely incidental to the state's pursuit of its nonreligious purposes, which include promoting a well-educated citizenry or providing assistance to the disabled.

Of course, the University of Virginia was not without legal foundation for its position. In its written arguments before the Court, it placed considerable reliance on the case of *Regan v. Taxation with Representation of Washington* (461 U.S. 540 [1983]). This decision provided ammunition for the university, since it represented a decision in which the Court upheld the denial of a government benefit to a speaker based the content of the speech. At issue was a provision of the federal Internal Revenue Code that provides tax exemptions to nonprofit organizations, provided that those organizations do not engage in lobbying activities. The justices concluded that, although the government could not prevent nonprofits from lobbying for law reform, it did not have to provide them with the funds to do so.

Perhaps even more compelling, Virginia noted that the Court had upheld the federal government's decision to fund certain ideas on a selective basis. In *Rust v. Sullivan* (500 U.S. 173 [1991]), the justices faced a federal law that forbade the government to make public health grants that would be used to counsel abortion as a method of family planning. Here the Court ruled that, since the government had the right to make policy that discourages abortion, it could certainly require that its money be spent in a manner consistent with that aim. Health officials still had a First Amendment right to counsel abortion, but the government was simply not going to pay to help them exercise that right.

Drawing on these two precedents, the University of Virginia argued that "*Regan* and *Rust* state the principle on which this case should be decided: The First Amendment does not forbid reasonable content-distinctions in the distribution of public funds. There is simply no precedent to the contrary" (Brief for the Respondent, *Rosenberger v. University of Virginia,* 515 U.S. 819 [1995]). When allocating government money, the university argued, it had the right to restrict to whom the money was granted and to dictate the terms of its use. It was justified, therefore, in refusing to underwrite activities that it concluded were inconsistent with its educational mission. Moreover, *Wide Awake* was still perfectly free to publish its student magazine through private resources and advertising.

The University of Virginia emphasized that this case did not involve the state denying speech on a street, in a park, or in any other public space where individuals have historically had great freedom to express their views. In other contexts where there is no general expectation of a right to unfettered speech—for example, the office mail system within a public school—the Court had upheld the exclusion of certain opinions (*Perry Education Association v. Perry Educators' Association*, 460 U.S. 37 [1983]). The Student Activities Fund, the university argued, was not a public forum established to allow students to express ideas. It was simply a mechanism to support the various activities of student organizations.

Of equal concern for the university was its potential violation of the separation of church and state. In previous cases, the justices had been skeptical of turning the state's resources over to religious groups, something Virginia was keen to avoid (see, e.g., *Board of Education of Kiryas Joel Village School District v. Grumet*, 512 U.S. 687 [1994]; *Roemer v. Board of Works of Maryland*, 426 U.S. 736 [1976]). True, the university had given financial support to the Muslim Students Association, the Jewish Law Students Association, and a group of gospel singers, all organizations with an explicit religious orientation. But the university argued that these were cultural, not religious organizations. These groups did not engage in devotion or other religious activities. Rather, they fostered social ties among students with common customs and heritage.

In sum, Rosenberger and the university both had substantial legal precedent to support their respective arguments, and the justices would have to decide whether and to what extent they were relevant to this case. The law was hardly the only consideration for the justices, however. A mix of political forces sought to shape the Court's decision, as well.

POLITICAL CONTEXT

Since the election of Ronald Reagan in 1980, many observers had anticipated a change in the Supreme Court's approach to cases involving religion. The liberal Warren Court had been quite skeptical of permitting government involvement in religious activities—cases involving prayer in the public schools were perhaps the most visible example—and many expected that the conservative president would seek to appoint justices who would be more accommodating of an active relationship between church and state (Ivers, 1993). Reagan's decision to elevate William Rehnquist to the position of chief justice, as well as his nominations of vocal conservatives, such as Antonin Scalia and Robert Bork, reflected the president's ambition to reverse the Court's liberal doctrines. Similarly sympathetic, George Bush pursued a comparable course as president, and by the time he left office in 1993, Republican presidents were responsible for eight of the nine members of the Court. Although these justices did not furnish the major legal change the many anticipated, they were certainly more supportive than their predecessors of public policies that benefited religion (Kobylka, 1995).

Organized interest groups had followed the Rehnquist Court's church-state litigation with considerable interest, and in *Rosenberger* many of the groups that had been active in earlier cases filed amicus curiae briefs, "friend of the court" briefs in which affected interests can support and amplify the arguments of the litigants. So, for example, Jewish groups that have historically sought to separate religious and secular affairs—such as the American Jewish Committee and American Jewish Congress (Ivers, 1995)—joined together with groups like the American Civil Liberties Union and Americans United for the Separation of Church and State. At the same time, the Religious Right had become quite active in advocating governmental accommodation of religion in the Supreme Court (Fisher, 2002, pp. 76–80). In this instance, the Christian Legal Society, the Christian Life Commission of the Southern Baptist Convention, and the National Association of Evangelicals voiced their support for *Wide Awake.*

For almost all of the interest groups who participated, *Rosenberger* represented a conflict over the meaning of the establishment clause, not freedom of expression. In their view, the question was simply whether student funding of a religious group was an unconstitutional endorsement of religion. According to the American Center for Law and Justice, a conservative Christian organization, James Madison—who wrote the First Amendment—opposed government placing special burdens on religion. The Catholic League for Religious and Civil Rights also observed that Thomas Jefferson believed that religious speech deserved as much protection as any other form of expression. This group also noted the historical value of religious speech in American life, citing the spiritual views of Abraham Lincoln and Martin Luther King, Jr., and their effect on policymakers.

By contrast, Americans United for the Separation of Church and State offered competing historical perspectives, noting that Madison, as well as fellow Virginians Jefferson and George Mason, were opposed to state money being used to fund religious groups. Another coalition of separationist groups, including the National Council of the Churches of Christ and People for the American Way, cited Jefferson's "Bill for Establishing Religious Freedom," in which he argued that "to compel a man to furnish contributions of money for the propagation of opinions which he disbelieves and abhors, is sinful and tyrannical" (Amicus Brief of Baptist Joint Committee on Public Affairs, et al., *Rosenberger v. University of Virginia,* No. 94–329, January 13, 1995).

Only two amicus briefs fully addressed the issue of freedom of expression. The American Civil Liberties Union devoted much of its brief to acknowledging that a university's selective funding of ideas violated the freedom of expression. In the context of funding religious speech, however, the group concluded that such funding was prohibited by the establishment clause. The principal advocate in favor of Rosenberger's speech rights was, ironically enough, the state of Virginia, whose brief regarded the university's policy as a direct violation of the group's speech rights. The state's brief noted that Jefferson actually hoped that religious ideas would be actively expressed at his university, to compete with secular views on the pursuit of truth. Jefferson believed that "by bringing the sects together, and mixing them with the mass of other students, we shall soften their asperities, liberalize and neutralize their prejudices, and make the general religion a religion of peace, reason, and morality" (Amicus Brief of Gov. Allen). The state argued that, in fact, its own university did not correctly comprehend the intention of its founder, who supported the open expression of all ideas, including religious ones.

These briefs provided the justices with an array of historical considerations. No less than the competing legal precedents of the Court, these briefs provided alternative (and yet highly plausible) interpretations of how best to evaluate state support for religious organizations.

THE DECISION

The Supreme Court often saves the announcement of its most important cases until the last day of its term. It was no surprise therefore that the Court waited until the closing day of its 1994–95 term to issue its decision in *Rosenberger v. University of Virginia.* In a 5–4 decision, the Court ruled that the University of Virginia had violated the First Amendment's guarantee of free speech by discriminating against the viewpoints expressed by *Wide Awake.* Citing the opinion from the *Lamb's Chapel* case, Justice Anthony Kennedy explained that, while the university provided financial support for discussion of a wide range of subjects, it refused to provide that support if a group's views on a subject happened to have a religious perspective. As Kennedy explained, "[T]he University does not exclude religion as a subject matter but selects for disfavored treatment those student journalistic efforts with religious editorial viewpoints." By this logic, the university would fund all groups that wanted to express ideas on a particular subject—say, politics, the arts, or campus life—unless the ideas were motivated by religious conviction, and "the University may not silence the expression of selected viewpoints" (*Rosenberger,* 1995, p. 835).

Even if the subject were religion—something the university claimed it wanted to avoid—Virginia would still fund some views on religion over others. The university's guidelines prohibit money from going to groups that "promote or manifest a particular belief in or about a deity or an ultimate reality." Under those rules, student groups that espoused precisely the opposite view, by promoting skepticism or denial of a deity, would be entitled to financial support. That meant that if famous atheistic thinkers, such as Karl Marx, Bertrand Russell, or Jean-Paul Sartre, were undergraduates at Virginia, their publications criticizing religious faith could receive money from the Student Activities Fund. Undergraduates who acknowledged some form of divine belief in their writings—even one named Thomas Jefferson, who asserted that all individuals "are endowed by their Creator with certain unalienable Rights"—would be denied the university's support. Government cannot, the Court said, agree to support speech on a particular subject and then favor some viewpoints on that subject over others.

Furthermore, the funding of *Wide Awake* posed no church-state problems. The fund was quite neutral with regard to the speech it funded. Underwriting the publication of a religious point of view was only one of many activities that were supported by the Student Activities Fund. It was hardly designed to support or endorse a religious idea. In earlier cases, the Court had upheld policies allowing groups access to school facilities on a neutral basis, and Kennedy's opinion underscored that, through their tuition and fees, students paid for the general maintenance of those facilities. So, whether student funds paid for the construction and upkeep of the buildings used by religious groups or for the publications of those groups, the university is still devoting its resources to support religion. What makes it constitutionally permissible is that the university makes those resources available to all student organizations, religious or otherwise.

The Court's Consequences

Across the country, public universities offering financial support to campus groups had to reevaluate their procedures. The rector of the University of Virginia, Hovey Dabney, regarded the decision in *Rosenberger* as "far-reaching . . . because so many other colleges and universities fund [groups] exactly the way we do" (Goodstein & Biskupic, 1995). In earlier cases, state colleges and universities that allowed student organizations access to their facilities could not deny access to religious groups. Now, those state institutions of higher learning that offered financial assistance would likely be obliged to ensure that groups with religious views received money, too. So, just as public schools had been obliged to open their doors, those same schools would now have to open their wallets.

For the longer term, however, the decision represented something more substantial. By expanding religious access, Justice Kennedy, along with Justices Sandra Day O'Connor, Rehnquist, Scalia, and Clarence Thomas, provided a policy that accommodationists had long sought and that separationists had long feared. Those who had believed the Constitution did not forbid general governmental support of religion hailed the decision as path breaking. Jay Sekulow of the American Center for Law and Justice announced, "We have crossed a critical threshold in the fight for religious liberty." As representing one of the most active groups among the Religious Right, he saw little ambiguity in the Supreme Court's policy. "The message is clear: Religious speech or speakers must be treated exactly the same way as any other group. The content of that speech does not disqualify them from funding" (Goodstein & Biskupic, 1995). Indeed, as Ronald Rosenberger himself observed after the decision, "We're finally beginning to move away from government hostility to religion, and going in the direction of neutrality" (Mauro, 1995).

By emphasizing that religious groups have the same free speech rights as secular interests, the Court has replaced some of its traditional "wall of separation" logic with a standard of equal access derived from the free speech guarantee of the First Amendment. This means that cases that might previously have been decided in a liberal direction under the Establishment Clause now tend to favor conservative legal interests. In *Good News Club v. Milford Central* (533 U.S. 98 [2001]), for example, the majority ruled that the principle of equality required a pubic grade school to open its doors to a Christian children's group for it after-school meetings.

Groups, such as Americans United for the Separation of Church and State, that had argued against funding religious expression were sharply critical of the majority. This group's executive director complained, "Evangelism should be supported by the voluntary donations of the faithful, not extracted forcibly from other Americans who don't share those beliefs" (Greenhouse, 1995). Counsel for the Baptist Joint Committee on Public Affairs was similarly sullen, lamenting that it was "a sad day for religious liberty. For the first time in our nation's history, the Supreme Court has sanctioned funding of religion with public funds" (Goodstein & Biskupic, 1995).

If there was some consolation for separationists, it was the that the

Court's decision seemed to be limited to the question of student fees. "[F]or- tunately for us, the majority opinion spends a long time explaining that this is not tax money, that this is student money," said August Steinhilber of the National School Boards Association. "If there should be an attempt to move toward aiding of church-related schools, we have more than enough room to file suit, and a reasonable chance of success" (Goodstein & Biskupic, 1995).

What organizations like the National School Boards Association feared was that the *Rosenberger* majority was laying the groundwork for the Supreme Court's eventual approval of school vouchers, a highly controversial policy that would permit parents with children in the public schools to send their children to private school with financial support from the state's general rev- enues. Since school vouchers would offer a substantial benefit to private reli- gious schools—religious schools would, after all, be receiving tuition money directly from the state—opponents regarded the policy as a clear violation of the establishment clause.

For those who supported school vouchers, the *Rosenberger* decision cer- tainly suggested that the Court would look favorably on such programs. Speaking in support of vouchers, one public-interest lawyer announced, "This settles the matter that if public benefits are distributed neutrally, it is irrelevant whether people choose to spend them for religious purposes" (Greenhouse, 1995), a forecast the proved to be quite accurate. Almost seven years to the day after the justices announced their decision in *Rosenberger,* the Court decided the highly watched case of *Zelman v. Simmons-Harris* (536 U.S. 639 [2002]). In it, the same five justices who constituted the *Rosenberger* majority joined together to approve the use of tuition vouchers, even when the overwhelming beneficiaries were religious schools.

By providing the intellectual connections between a state's grant of neu- tral access to active government involvement in and support for religious in- stitutions, *Rosenberger* represented a critical link in the process of legal change. Seen in this way, the decision presaged an important transformation in the Court's interpretation of the meaning of religious establishment. By chipping away at the wall of separation in *Rosenberger,* the justices provided both an incentive and a rationale for religious interests who have sought an increased role for religion in American life.

NOTE

1. *Ronald W. Rosenberger v. The Rector and Visitors of the University of Virginia.* 1995. 515 U.S. 819, pp.826, 865. Unless otherwise noted, the factual circumstances of the case are drawn from the U.S. Supreme Court's opinion, as well as the written briefs filed at the merits stage.

REFERENCES

Biskupic, J. (1995, February 26). Court to tackle religious issues. *Washington Post,* p. A10.

Ellis, J. J. (1996). *American sphinx: The character of Thomas Jefferson.* New York: Vintage Books.

Fisher, L. (2002). *Religious liberty in America: Political safeguards.* Lawrence, KS: University Press of Kansas.

Goodstein, L., & Biskupic, J. (1995, June 30). In two rulings, high court refines relationship between church, state. *Washington Post,* p. A1.

Greenhouse, L. (1995, June 30). The Supreme Court: Church-state relations; Justices, in 5–4 vote, reject districts drawn with race the "predominant fact"; Ruling on religion. *New York Times,* p. A1.

Ivers, G. (1993). *Redefining the first freedom: The Supreme Court and the consolidation of state power.* New Brunswick, NJ: Transaction Publishers.

Ivers, G. (1995). *To build a wall: American Jews and the separation of church and state.* Charlottesville, VA: University Press of Virginia.

Kobylka, J. F. (1995). The mysterious case of establishment clause litigation: How organized interests foiled legal change. In L. Epstein (Ed.), *Contemplating Courts.* Washington, DC: Congressional Quarterly, Inc.

Mauro, T. (1995, June 30). Debate widens over religion in public life. *USA Today,* p. 8A.

Randall, W. S. (1993). *Thomas Jefferson: A life.* New York: HarperPerennial.

Free Exercise
of Religion

Blood and Precedent

Church of the Lukumi Babalu Aye v. City of Hialeah (1993)

STEVE BROWN

> The ritual sacrifice of animals is not widely practiced in the United States, but it is
> more common in other parts of the world, such as the Caribbean, where some re-
> ligious traditions incorporate it into their worship. When a church for one such re-
> ligion, the Santeria faith, opened in a suburb of Miami, Florida, the city became
> concerned about the public health risks associated with this practice and enacted
> rules banning the ritual killing of animals. At the same time, it made exceptions
> for others in the city, such as slaughterhouses and restaurants, to engage in similar
> practices and to dispose of animal waste. Was this a legitimate public health mea-
> sure, or did it interfere with religious freedom guaranteed by the First Amendment?

The rather exotic-sounding name of the petitioner alone signified that
Church of the Lukumi Babalu Aye v. City of Hialeah would be unique among
the dozens of free exercise of religion cases ever decided by the U.S. Supreme
Court. With its combination of animal sacrifice and Afro-Caribbean mysti-
cism, this case would enlighten both the Court and the nation to an ancient
religion that had somehow persisted through the centuries, enduring inter-

tribal warfare in Africa, the Atlantic slave trade, forced submission to a state-sponsored church, and the Cuban Revolution, only to be challenged by a series of local public health and animal cruelty ordinances in southern Florida. And yet, as fascinating as its background issues were, much of the significance of *Lukumi* lay in the question of whether the Court would use this case to clarify or possibly even refute the controversial standard for assessing free exercise claims it had erected just three years earlier in the landmark decision *Employment Division, Department of Human Resources of Oregon v. Smith* (494 U.S. 872 [1990]). Whether *Lukumi* was viewed as a prime example of "religious gerrymandering," as Justice Anthony Kennedy would somberly intone for the Court, or "the war of the chickens," as Hialeah residents somewhat less seriously referred to it (Resnick, 1989), the overriding question remained the same: To what extent may government burden the free exercise of religion?

Santeria: The Way of the Saints

The *Lukumi* case originates centuries ago and a continent away with the Yoruba of southwestern Nigeria, a people who wielded a tremendous amount of political and commercial influence on Western Africa until the end of the eighteenth century, when the loose confederation of city states that composed their empire collapsed. Wracked by civil war from within and territorial advances from enemies without, the Yoruba, who had extracted tribute from surrounding states for a hundred years, found themselves without a country, enslaved en masse, and bound for the Americas (Murphy, 1988).

Many of the Yoruba were sent to Cuba, where there was a seemingly insatiable demand for slaves whose lives were quickly worn out in the harsh working conditions that accompanied the labor-intensive requirements of planting, harvesting, and refining sugar, a booming international commodity in the first half of the nineteenth century (Klein, 1999). Like other slaves who survived the Middle Passage, the Yoruba brought little more than their language and beliefs to the New World, and normally even those would be lost through forced cultural assimilation and the passage of time. But in Cuba the religious beliefs of the Yoruba persisted, ironically, because of the Spanish establishment of the Roman Catholic Church (Klein, 1986, p. 193).

Although early Cuban laws mandated that slaves receive religious instruction and be baptized into the Catholic faith, there was relatively little opportunity for the church generally to have much of an effect on the lives of plantation slaves. In the city, however, the church dominated. Due in part to the efforts of the Catholic Church, slaves in the cities were permitted to work for set hours with wages, rent out their free time to other owners to earn additional money, and even open their own businesses (Brandon, 1993, p. 69–70). Cuba's urban areas saw slaves freely intermix with former slaves who had purchased their freedom, Creole blacks who had never been enslaved, and others who had been liberated from slave ships by the British. Encouraged by the Catholic Church, this diverse mixture of people formed their own social and fraternal clubs along African ethnic lines known as *cabildos*. In their urban cabildos, the Yoruba (known in Cuba as *Lucumi*) sought recreation, fellowship, and mutual aid (Scott, 1985). It was here as well that they participated in and perpetuated their ancient religion, even as they were being instructed in the Catholic tradition.

Although the outright practice of native African religions was prohibited in Cuba, the Catholic Church took a softer stance in the cabildos. "Under the direction of a diocesan priest the cabildo allowed for the accommodation of African customs to the church's worship. Through this guided syncretism the priests hoped that the Africans would be swept up into the mainstream of Cuban Christianity, in time forsaking African customs" (Brandon, 1993, p. 71). What emerged instead from this "guided syncretism" was a new religion that borrowed elements of both Catholicism and traditional Yoruba religious belief. It was called Santeria, "the way of the saints."

Santeria takes its name from the devotion followers pay to Yoruba orishas, divine spirits who oversee some aspect of human life, and whose identity in Cuba became fused with that of Catholic saints. Thus, for example, the orisha Ogun, the deity of iron, is depicted using the Catholic iconography of Saint Peter, Agayu with that of Saint Christopher, and Babalu Aye with Saint Lazarus. Although this syncretism may have started out as an attempt to pay superficial homage to Catholic icons while masking a genuine expression of reverence for the ancient Yoruba spirits, it "became a genuine universal religious vision in which a Catholic saint and a Lucumi orisha were seen as different manifestations of the same spiritual entity" (Murphy, 1988, p. 32).

While the syncretism of Catholicism with native African beliefs is one of the many unique characteristics of Santeria, it is far from the most controversial. Undoubtedly, the most widely discussed but least understood aspect of the religion is its practice of animal sacrifice. Animal sacrifice has long been a central element of Santeria and is performed in association with birth, marriage, and death rites as well as on certain holy days as a way of acknowledging dependence on as well as symbolically feeding the orishas (Murphy, 1988, p. 41). Although most of the rituals require fowls to be sacrificed such as chickens, pigeons, doves, and ducks, special occasions require four-legged animals such as guinea pigs, goats, sheep, and turtles (Gonzalez-Wippler, 1989, p. 156). During their eight-day initiation ceremony, new priests being received into Santeria will see a combination of several of these animals sacrificed.

Because the public practice of Santeria was forbidden in Cuba, its traditions and rituals, including animal sacrifice, were perpetuated in individual homes through small group, often family to family, interaction, eventually spreading throughout the Caribbean. With the Cuban Revolution, large numbers of Cubans fled to America, where Santeria continued to prosper, particularly in south Florida, where, by the mid-1980s, some 60,000 practitioners resided. An accurate count was impossible to obtain, however, because of the still-secretive nature of the religion even in the United States. Mindful of the historic discrimination against their beliefs in Cuba, practitioners of Santeria continued to shield their religion from public scrutiny, further entrenching the home-based nature of their rituals and ceremonies. One influential leader within the religion, however, believed that such practices were unnecessary and even detrimental to the growth of the movement itself.

Ernest Pichardo, a ranking high priest within Santeria known as an *italero* and president of the Church of the Lukumi Babalu Aye sought to bring about greater understanding of the beliefs and practices of Santeria by establishing a branch of the church in the southern Florida city of Hialeah. In the spring of 1987 Pichardo announced that land had been secured for a church where all of the rites of Santeria, including animal sacrifice, would be performed publicly. He also envisioned a cultural center, school, and museum that would interpret many of the controversial and misunderstood aspects of the religion. By promoting the religion publicly, Pichardo believed Santeria would take its place among the accepted faiths in religiously diverse south Florida. As it turned out, his actions had almost the entirely opposite effect.

Immediately upon Pichardo's announcement, hundreds of concerned citizens as well as a wide range of organizations from traditional Christian churches to animal protection groups came out vocally against his efforts specifically and Santeria in general. The director of the southeast regional office of the Humane Society, for example, decried Santeria as "a bloody cult" and its deity a "god of pestilence" (Resnick, 1989).

Regulating Religious Expression

Within days of the church's application for operational licenses, the Hialeah City Council convened in emergency session and passed the first of several ordinances expressing the council's determination to prohibit "any and all acts of any and all religious groups which are inconsistent with public morals, peace and safety" (*Church of the Lukumi Babalu Aye v. City of*

Hialeah, 508 U.S. 520, 548 [1993]). To that end, the council passed several ordinances over the next few months regulating the killing of animals within its borders. Four were particularly troubling to the church. Ordinance No. 87-40 adopted the state of Florida's animal cruelty statute verbatim but added an additional local penalty of up to sixty days in jail. Ordinance No. 87-52 banned the possession of animals for slaughter or sacrifice, except in slaughterhouses as designated by law. Ordinance No. 87-71 made it unlawful to sacrifice any animal within Hialeah's city limits, defining sacrifice as "to unnecessarily kill, torment, torture, or mutilate an animal in a public or private ritual or ceremony not for the primary purpose of animal consumption" (*Lukumi,* 508, p. 551). Ordinance No. 87-72 authorized animal protection groups to investigate and report violations of the animal cruelty and slaughter ordinances. In accordance with statewide practice, it also exempted from penalty people and organizations that slaughtered and sold small numbers of hogs and cattle weekly. Upon their adoption and noting the apparent targeted nature of the ordinances, Ernesto Pichardo and the Church of Lukumi Babalu Aye filed suit in federal court claiming the city had violated their free exercise of religion.

In his October 1989 ruling, U.S. District Court judge Eugene Spellman detailed the testimony that had been presented during the nine-day trial held the previous summer. Pichardo had recounted his own experience with animal sacrifice, pointing out the specific procedure followed by Santeria priests for killing an animal so that its blood would drain into clay pots to be used later in the ceremony. On some occasions, the animal was decapitated, with the head also being reserved for later use. Pichardo testified that after most ceremonies, the sacrificed animal was cooked and eaten by participants (the exceptions being healing and death rites) and that, to his knowledge, the remains were disposed of properly.

In addition to Pichardo's matter-of-fact description of the sacrificial act, he also gave some indication of the sheer number of offerings that were involved. According to the district court's opinion, "Pichardo estimated up to 600 initiations per year are performed in private homes in Dade County. . . . [He also] testified that between 20 and 30 animals are usually sacrificed during an initiation rite. That means that between 12,000 and 18,000 animals are sacrificed in initiation rites alone, during a one year period" (*Lukumi,* 723 F. Supp., p. 1474). It is likely that the number of sacrificed animals was even higher than Pichardo had estimated, given the secretive, individualistic nature of the religion and the fact, as he acknowledged at trial, that he could not account for the number of animals sacrificed by Santeria practitioners outside of his own church.

In defending the city's ordinances, lawyers for Hialeah produced evidence that the remains of a number of animals bearing marks of ritual killing had often been found in public places. While these remains obviously could not be traced directly to Santeria (the court noted the existence of other religions in the area that practiced animal sacrifice), the public health risks to such dumping were considerable. The testimony of expert witnesses in veterinary medicine and psychology further buttressed the city's position with their opinion that the method of sacrifice practiced by Santeria priests was neither painless nor particularly quick as had been indicated previously and could in fact traumatize children who happened to view the act.

In upholding the constitutionality of the ordinances, Judge Spellman found the public health, animal cruelty, and child welfare interests asserted by the city compelling. While the Church of the Lukumi Babalu Aye would undoubtedly be affected by the ordinances, they were not, he wrote, "aimed solely at [the church], but [were] an attempt to address the issue of animal sacrifice as a whole" (*Lukumi,* 723 F. Supp., p. 1484). In short, the city had properly identified and dealt with an issue it saw as a threat to the health and welfare of both its citizens and animal population. That the free exercise clause might be implicated was irrelevant, according to Judge Spellman, because "nothing in the First Amendment prevents a municipality from specifically regulating such conduct when it is deemed inconsistent with public health and morals" (*Lukumi,* 723 F. Supp., p. 1484). The decision was affirmed in a one-paragraph per curium opinion of the U.S. Court of Appeals for the Eleventh Circuit and the church appealed to the U.S. Supreme Court.

The Shadow of *Smith*

Upon the Court's granting of certiorari to the case on March 23, 1992, a wide range of organizations from across the religious and political spectrum waded into the dispute. On behalf of the city, a number of animal rights groups filed amicus briefs contending that the city's interests in public and animal welfare were compelling enough to permit an admitted infringement on the Santeria religion. The briefs filed in support of the Church of the Lukumi Babalu Aye represented a coalition of disparate interests (including Americans United for Separation of Church and State, the Christian Legal Society, the Mormon Church, and People for the American Way, among others) that had marshaled their support behind the church's free exercise claim. That these same organizations would vigorously oppose each other in most establishment clause litigation, but find common ground with the Church of the Lukumi Babalu Aye, clearly speaks to the unifying nature of the free exercise clause.[1]

Although amici briefs for both parties obviously differed as to how the Court should resolve the dispute, a consistent theme (even among amici supporting the city) was concern about the Court's application of its own standard for acknowledging free exercise claims against governmental regulation. Indeed, although the *Lukumi* case arose out of the controversial nexus of religious belief and animal sacrifice, the constitutional questions it raised were tied to a three-year-old Supreme Court decision that was no less divisive.

In *Employment Division, Department of Human Resources of Oregon v. Smith* (494 U.S. 872 [1990]), the Supreme Court confronted a state agency's denial of unemployment benefits to two Native Americans, who had been fired from the private drug rehabilitation clinic where they worked, for ingesting peyote, a controlled substance under Oregon law. The two maintained that they only used the drug in connection with the worship and sacramental rituals of their Native American religion within which peyote played a central role. They further claimed that the state's denial of employment benefits on the basis that the possession and ingestion of peyote was illegal infringed on their free exercise of religion. The state of Oregon argued that its ban on peyote was applicable against all state citizens, not just Native Americans, and reflected a compelling governmental interest on its part to protect its citizens by regulating drugs.

Writing for a 6–3 majority in *Smith,* Justice Antonin Scalia enunciated a new constitutional standard for resolving claims arising under the free exercise clause. For nearly thirty years, albeit with varying degrees of fidelity, the Court had embraced the two-part *Sherbert* test that required that any governmental action infringing on the free exercise of religion be justified by a compelling government interest and use the least restrictive means possible for accomplishing that interest (*Sherbert v. Verner,* 374 U.S. 398 [1963]).

Although the *Sherbert* test was not expressly jettisoned in *Smith,* the Court held that Oregon's ban on peyote and the denial of unemployment benefits to people fired for such use did not infringe on the free exercise rights of the Native American workers. The Court noted that many of its landmark free exercise decisions had also involved substantial issues of freedom of speech and press and had received additional protection corresponding to those rights under the First Amendment as well. But where no such "hybrid rights" exist (as the Court put it), and where no direct regulation of belief was undertaken, individuals could not claim an exemption from government regulations because of their religion and on that basis alone.

The Court went on to announce that a neutral, generally applicable law that happened to burden the free exercise of religion could, in fact, survive constitutional challenge. "To make an individual's obligation to obey such a law," Scalia wrote, "contingent upon the law's coincidence with his religious beliefs, except where the State's interest is 'compelling'—permitting him, by virtue of his beliefs, to become a law unto himself—contradicts both constitutional tradition and common sense" (*Smith*, p. 885, internal citations omitted).

While this clear break with the free exercise jurisprudence of the past was of grave concern to the dissenting justices, it was the practical effect of *Smith* on the free exercise of religion to which they and even Justice Sandra Day O'Connor, who had concurred in the majority's decision, were most opposed. To substitute the neutral, generally applicable law standard for the government's burden of demonstrating a compelling interest to justify its infringement on religious belief, she maintained, was to presume that "the First Amendment never requires the State to grant a limited exception for religiously motivated conduct" (*Smith*, p. 900). And that presumption, according to Justice O'Connor and the three dissenters, was simply incompatible with the historic role of the free exercise clause.

Although there were some who saw the Court's action as the proper corrective to a decision that never should have created a religious exemption to legal requirements in the first place (see, e.g., Cruz, 1994), *Smith* was generally greeted by criticism from conservatives and liberals alike, who decried the loss of the compelling interest standard, and Congress rushed to respond. The combined efforts of organized interest groups (including many of the organizations supporting the church in *Lukumi*) and Congress would eventually yield the Religious Freedom Restoration Act of 1993 (RFRA). Passing with nearly unanimous support in Congress, RFRA used the Court's words in *Sherbert* as the basis for a statutory standard that prohibited government from burdening the free exercise of religion unless it was "in furtherance of a compelling governmental interest; and . . . [was] the least restrictive means of furthering that compelling governmental interest."[2]

As a free exercise case involving an unpopular minority religion, the *Lukumi* case was important. But as the first free exercise case to be decided by the Court since *Smith,* it took on even greater significance. Notwithstanding the 6–3 decision in the peyote case, four justices were clearly dissatisfied with the notion that religion could be properly burdened by government so long as its regulations were neutral and generally applicable.

The Court, *Santeria,* and *Smith* as "Settled Law"

In their oral arguments before the Court on November 4, 1992, lawyers for the church immediately questioned the constitutionality of the ordinances under the *Smith* standard. The city's efforts failed the neutrality test, they argued, because in making it unlawful to "unnecessarily kill" an animal, the city had put itself in the position of adjudging when animal killing was necessary or not. "The only way to prove that sacrifice is unnecessary," argued Douglas Laycock for the church, "is to prove that Santeria is a false religion. To believers in Santeria, sacrifice is directly commanded by the gods. . . . To prove it unnecessary, you must prove the religion false, and when the prosecutor has to prove a religion false, the prosecutor is engaged in a heresy trial" (Oral argument by Douglas Laycock, Esq. on behalf of Petitioner [1993], at 5).

The targeted nature of the ordinances, however, was even more troubling than their discriminatory wording. On what basis, the church questioned, could Hialeah permit hunters within its borders to kill their prey, farmers to slaughter their cattle or hogs for market, and veterinary offices, animal control authorities, and pet owners to euthanize their animals and yet still forbid practitioners of Santeria from doing the same thing? In other words, Laycock argued, "You must ban all killing of animals or you must permit religious killing of animals" (Oral argument by Douglas Laycock, Esq. on behalf of Petitioner [1993], at 12). Attorneys for Hialeah responded that the neutrality principle had been satisfied, because animal killing generally was not the purpose of the ordinances; animal sacrifice as a category was. Hunting was not the problem, noted Richard Garrett for the city, "it isn't euthanasia, it's not pest control, it is the problem with animal sacrifice, all the way from the beginning of the process and the damage to the animals to the end of the process and the disposal of the remains" (Oral argument by Richard G. Garrett, Esq. on behalf of Respondent [1993], at 18).

The ordinances were generally applicable to groups that practiced animal sacrifice, something that Garrett was careful to note included more than just the Church of the Lukumi Babalu Aye: "There is evidence in the record which has not been mentioned that [other] groups engage in this activity—malevolent magic is mentioned by one of their witnesses to describe what existed with respect to a goat that was cut in half and found on Miami Beach. . . . [T]here's also evidence in the record with respect to the fact that this particular type of practice is engaged in by Satanists, by witchcraft, [and] voodoo" (Oral argument by Douglas Laycock, Esq. on behalf of Petitioner [1993], at 5). Aside from meeting the *Smith* test, Garrett also argued that the human health hazards associated with the unregulated slaughter and disposal of animals used in the sacrificial rites of any group constituted a compelling governmental interest that the city should be permitted to address.

To the surprise of many observers, the Court's June 1993 judgment in favor of the church was unanimous. The unanimity of the decision, however, masked serious differences among the justices regarding the value of the *Smith* decision on which it was predicated. After recounting the facts and procedural history of the case, Justice Kennedy considered each disputed ordinance in turn against the neutrality requirement of *Smith*. The Court found that Ordinance 87-40, which incorporated Florida's animal cruelty statute, had been selectively misinterpreted by the city. "The city, on what seems to be a per se basis, deems hunting, slaughter of animals for food, eradication of insects and pests, and euthanasia as necessary. . . . [It] devalues religious reasons for killing by judging them to be of lesser import than nonreligious reasons" (*Lukumi*, p. 537).

The Court found that Ordinance 87-52, which prohibited the sacrifice or slaughter of animals for food (with several significant exemptions), also seemed to fall "on Santeria adherents but almost no others." The prohibition on animal sacrifice set by Ordinance 87-71 (again with several exemptions) led to a result where "few if any killings of animals are prohibited other than Santeria sacrifice" (*Lukumi*, p. 536). The Court did acknowledge that Ordinance 87-72 permitting animal rights groups to monitor and report animal cruelty and sacrifice could, in fact, be neutral, but given its passage at the time of the three other ordinances, it was found to be invalid, "because it functions, with the rest of the enactments in question, to suppress Santeria religious worship" (*Lukumi*, p. 540).

Having dispensed with the city's neutrality argument, the Court turned to the general applicability requirement of *Smith*. Given the many exemptions stated within the ordinances themselves, as well as situations where the ordinances simply were not deemed to be applicable, the Court found Hialeah's action not only far from generally applicable but also vastly underinclusive. As Justice Kennedy noted, "Despite the city's proffered interest in preventing cruelty to animals, the ordinances are drafted with care to forbid few killings but those occasioned by religious sacrifice. Many types of animal deaths or kills for nonreligious reasons are either not prohibited or approved by express provision. For example, fishing . . . is legal. Extermination of mice and rats within a home is also permitted. Florida law incorporated by Ordinance 87-40 sanctions euthanasia of stray, neglected, abandoned, or unwanted animals; destruction of animals judicially removed from their owners for humanitarian reasons or when the animal is of no commercial value; the infliction of pain or suffering in the interest of medical science; the placing of poison in one's yard or enclosure; and the use of a live animal to pursue or take wildlife or to participate in any hunting, and to hunt wild hogs" (*Lukumi*, pp. 543–544).

The Court also held that the ordinances were not only underinclusive in their targeted ban on animal slaughter but also in the city's purported interest in public health. Although the district court found this argument persuasive, the Supreme Court questioned how compelling the public health interest could really be when it was only selectively invoked. For instance, although Hialeah had cited the improper disposal of animal carcasses as a reason for passing the ordinances, it did not prohibit hunters from bringing their kill home to be boned and skinned and did not regulate how those animal remains should be disposed of. The Court noted that restaurants in Hialeah also disposed of organic garbage, perhaps even improperly, but were not regulated to the extent that the church was.

Having concluded that the city's ordinances were neither neutral nor generally applicable, the Court proffered one last hope for Hialeah's actions. *Smith* held that in the rare event, such as in this case, that governmental action burdening religion failed to meet the neutral and generally applicable requirements, it might still be subjected to strict judicial scrutiny and, in the event that it stood up to such scrutiny, be permitted. In essence, the *Sherbert* test still applied, permitting governmental infringement on religion so long as it was governed by a compelling interest and used the least-restrictive means possible but only after the action had failed the *Smith* requirements. As the Court explained further, however, "A law that targets religious conduct for distinctive treatment or advances legitimate governmental interests only against conduct with a religious motivation will survive strict scrutiny only in rare cases. It follows from what we have already said that these ordinances cannot withstand this scrutiny" (*Lukumi,* p. 546).

Although the Court unanimously struck down the Hialeah ordinances, at least three justices strongly disagreed with the Court's reliance on *Smith* to reach its decision. In his concurring opinion, in which Justice O'Connor joined, Justice Harry Blackmun expressed his dismay at the Court's striking down of the ordinances on the basis of *Smith*. To him, any law that burdened religion should be justified by a compelling governmental interest right from the beginning, because, unlike the Hialeah ordinances, few laws would so specifically target a religious practice as to fail the neutral and generally applicable prongs of *Smith*.

Justice David Souter carried this theme even further. In a concurring opinion that was nearly as long as the Court's ruling, Justice Souter expressed his doubts as to the precedential value of *Smith*. Given the stark contrast between the *Smith* requirements and the *Sherbert* test and the fact that none of the Court's pre-*Smith* free exercise cases had been overturned by the decision, Justice Souter believed that the Court had created a "free exercise jurisprudence in tension with itself" (*Lukumi,* p. 565, J. Souter concurring). After surveying the Court's free exercise cases, Justice Souter opined that the proper resolution of that tension lay in abandoning *Smith:* "Since holding in 1940 that the Free Exercise Clause applies to the States, the Court repeatedly has stated that the Clause sets strict limits on the government's power to burden religious exercise, whether it is a law's object to do so or its unanticipated effect. . . . I would have trouble concluding that the Court has not meant what it said in more than a dozen cases over several decades. . . . In sum, it seems to me difficult to escape the conclusion that, whatever Smith's virtues, they do not include a comfortable fit with settled law" (*Lukumi,* pp. 570–571, J. Souter concurring).

Although the Court has considered free exercise cases since its 1993 decision in *Lukumi,* none has played as important a role in buttressing the Court's post-*Smith* free exercise jurisprudence in which (despite Souter's consternation) *Smith* has indeed become "settled law."

Aftermath

The *Lukumi* decision has had an important influence outside the courtroom as well. Joining New York, Chicago, and Los Angeles, such cities as Charleston, Virginia Beach, Denver, and San Jose are seeing an upsurge of Santeria activity in their communities. There are now nearly 100,000 practitioners of Santeria in South Florida alone (Riley, 2002). In Hialeah, things are very much like they were before the passage of the ordinances. The city chose not to respond to the Court's decision by passing a general ban on animal killing within its borders, and the Church of the Lukumi Babalu Aye faded from public view when it closed its public buildings in 1999. Ernesto Pichardo, however, maintains that the closure "does not hinder our ability to operate."[3] And law enforcement officials continue to find animal remains in public places on a regular basis.

NOTES

1. The church enjoyed the amicus support of other groups as well, including the American Jewish Committee, Anti-Defamation League of B'nai B'rith, Home School Legal Defense Association, General Conference of Seventh-Day Adventists, and National Association of Evangelicals. Only animal rights groups submitted amici in support of the city. The U.S. Catholic Conference submitted an amicus brief in direct support of neither party, but encouraged the Court to abandon *Smith.*

2. Religious Freedom Restoration Act of 1993, 42 U.S.C. § 2000bb (1993). The Supreme Court would later strike down RFRA as it applied to the states, saying that it exceeded Congress's power under Section 5 of the 14th Amendment (*Boerne v. Flores,* 521 U.S. 507 [1997]).

3. Personal e-mail from Ernesto Pichardo to author, December 24, 2002.

REFERENCES

Brandon, G. (1993). *Santeria from Africa to the new world.* Bloomington, IN: Indiana University Press.

Cruz, R. (1994, Winter). Animal sacrifice and equal protection free exercise. *Harvard Journal of Law and Public Policy, 17,* pp. 262–273.

Gonzalez-Wippler, M. (1989). *Santeria: The religion.* New York: Harmony Books.

Klein, H. S. (1986). *African slavery in Latin America and the Caribbean.* New York: Oxford University Press.

Klein, H. S. (1999). *The Atlantic slave trade.* New York: Cambridge University Press.

Marshall, W. P. (1991, Winter). In defense of Smith and free exercise revisionism. *University of Chicago Law Review, 58,* pp. 308–328.

Murphy, J. M. (1988). *Santeria: An African religion in America.* Boston: Beacon Press.

Oral argument by Douglas Laycock, Esq., on behalf of Petitioner. *Church of the Lukumi Babalu Aye v. Hialeah,* 508 U.S. 520 (1993), in vol. 218, *Landmark Briefs and Arguments of the Supreme Court of the United States: Constitutional Law.* Bethesda, MD: University Publications of America.

Oral argument of Richard G. Garrett, Esq., on behalf of Respondent. *Church of the Lukumi Babalu Aye v. City of Hialeah,* 508 U.S. 520 (1993), in vol. 218, *Landmark Briefs and Arguments of the Supreme Court of the United States: Constitutional Law.* Bethesda, MD: University Publications of America.

Resnick, R. (1989, September 8). To one city, it's cruelty. To cultists, it's religion. *National Law Journal, 11.*

Riley, M. (2002, April 14). Cuban healer works magic. *Denver Post,* p. L8.

Scott, R. J. (1985). *Slave emancipation in Cuba.* Princeton, NJ: Princeton University Press.

West, E. (1990). The case against a right to religion-based exemptions. *Notre Dame Journal of Law, Ethics, and Public Policy, 4,* pp. 591–638.

Freedom of Speech

Abortion Protests, Abortion Rights, and the Regulation of Speech

Hill v. Colorado (2000)

KAREN O'CONNOR

The Supreme Court usually permits the state to regulate the time, place, and manner of speech, provided it does not target the content of the message. When Colorado enacted a law restricting how close abortion protesters could get to health-care clinics, some protesters regarded the statute as designed not to merely regulate where they could express their view but also to stifle their views altogether. This case demonstrates how the Court must balance competing interests in cases involving individual liberties. It also illustrates the power of different personalities and interest groups to shape the dynamics of the contemporary debate over abortion rights through Supreme Court litigation.

On January 22, 1973, the United States Supreme Court invalidated the laws of forty-eight states when it issued its landmark 7–2 decision in *Roe v. Wade* (410 U.S. 113 [1973]). Although the news about *Roe* wasn't the lead story that night, *Roe*'s guarantee of the right of women all over the nation to obtain an abortion in the first two trimesters of pregnancy quickly became the catalyst of a growing conservative movement that eventually stymied ratification efforts of the proposed Equal Rights Amendment; created a powerful antiabortion, pro-life movement; forced the Republican and Democratic parties to the right and left, respectively; helped to create the Moral Majority, which led to the election of Ronald Reagan in 1980; and made abortion a defining political issue throughout the 1980s and the 1990s.

Hill v. Colorado (2000), which involved a challenge to the constitutionality of a Colorado statute that made it unlawful for any person within 100 feet of a heath-care facility's entrance to "knowingly approach" within eight feet of any person, without that person's consent, in order to pass "a leaflet or handbill to, display a sign to, or engage in oral protest, education, or counseling with [that] person . . . ," is illustrative of the kinds of corollary issues that arose in the wake of the Court's decision in *Roe*. In this case the Court had to decide how to weigh the rights of protesters to voice their opposition to abortion versus the rights of women to exercise their constitutional right to obtain an abortion.

A Short History of Abortion in the Court

In the aftermath of *Roe v. Wade*, antiabortion forces went on the offensive to try to limit abortion in a variety of ways. Both pro-choice and antiabortion forces view the courts, especially the Supreme Court, as an important arsenal in their efforts to maintain or restrict access to abortion. But, once the Court had spoken in *Roe*, antiabortion activists quickly turned to Congress, the states, and even local governments to try to obtain limits on *Roe* legislatively. As attempts to obtain a constitutional amendment to end abortion proved futile, antiabortion activists were able to convince Representative Henry Hyde (R-IL) to take up their cause. By 1976 Hyde convinced Congress to pass what is known as the Hyde Amendment, which prohibits the use of federal Medicaid funds for abortion. The constitutionality of this act was upheld by the Supreme Court in 1977 and again in 1980.

Antiabortion activists, who by the late 1970s had renamed themselves pro-life activists, also successfully lobbied a wide array of state legislatures as well as city councils to enact a host of abortion restrictions ranging from spousal, parental, and informed-consent laws, to regulations concerning where abortions could and could not be performed. In *Akron v. Akron Center for Reproductive Health, Inc.* (462 U.S. 416 [1983]), for example, pro-life activists convinced the City Council of Akron to enact myriad abortion restrictions including:

(1) a ban on performing second trimester abortions in outpatient clinics rather than hospitals;
(2) a requirement that physicians provide detailed information about abortion to women before they signed consent forms; and,
(3) a twenty-four-hour waiting period between signing the consent forms and obtaining the abortion.

In 1983 the majority of the Supreme Court found that all of these regulations failed to meet the Court's allowance of reasonable state regulation as articulated in *Roe*. The clinic was represented by lawyers from the ACLU's Reproductive Project; the U.S. government as amicus curiae urged the Court to abandon the trimester approach articulated in *Roe* and to replace it with a test that allowed states and local governments to regulate abortion so long as the restrictions were not "unduly burdensome," a position the Court declined to adopt.

Similar restrictions were at issue in *Thornburg v. American College of Gynecologists and Obstetricians* (476 U.S. 747 [1986]), which involved a challenge to the Pennsylvania Abortion Control Act. Among them was a mandate that physicians give women seeking abortions detailed information on fetal development as part of giving informed consent. Again, the Court struck down all of the provisions, this time, however, by a 5–4 vote.

Clinic Violence and Protest

Frustrated by their inability to win major reversals of *Roe,* as well as the Supreme Court's continued votes against the constitutionality of most abortion restrictions worked so hard for by pro-life activists, a small segment of the pro-life community turned to a range of other activities from legal protest to illegal violence, and even murder. As early as 1976, a seminar on "How to Disrupt an Abortion Clinic," was held at the annual meeting of the National Right to Life Committee (O'Connor, 1996). According to the National Abortion Rights Action League (Now NARAL-Pro-Choice USA), the seminar was the catalyst for a host of activities aimed at disrupting clinics that ranged from picketing and sit-ins to blockades, which effectively eviscerated women's ability to obtain legal abortions at targeted clinics.

Some of these protests escalated to violence. In 1977 several clinics were bombed, and in 1984, after *Akron,* the number of clinic bombings skyrocketed as more and more clinics reported a variety of activities including:

Picketing clinics and physicians offices, . . . appealing to women entering them not to kill their babies, . . . [placing] epoxy cement . . . in clinic locks; stink bombs were ignited in clinic bathrooms by bogus patients; bomb threats were called into clinics; clinic employees received threatening calls at home; patients were followed home or traced through license tags and loudly denounced in their own neighborhoods or before their family; judges conducting trials for anti-abortion activists . . . were threatened; court trials of arsonists and bombers were picketed; . . .[and] several clinic personnel were injured during incursions by protestors. (Blanchard, 1994, pp. 53–54)

By 1986 the National Organization for Women (NOW) had filed a lawsuit to end clinic violence, charging that the militant Pro-Life Action League and several other, new, antiabortion groups were engaged in a private conspiracy in violation of the federal Ku Klux Klan (KKK) Act of 1871. And in 1987 the actions of the Pro-Life Action League, which actively promoted violence to stop abortions, became the model for a nationwide series of "rescues," when Pope John Paul II toured the United States. Leila Jeanne Hill, who came to be the named plaintiff in *Hill v. Colorado,* was first arrested for trespassing at an abortion clinic in 1987. Her arrests and the course of the litigation that led her to the Supreme Court, provide the backdrop for, as well as illustrate, how political the abortion debate became as interest groups on both sides sought to advance their positions and lawmakers and the courts responded to their actions.

HILL V. COLORADO

In 1980 Leila Jeanne Hill, known to her friends as Jeanne, was sitting at her kitchen table in the very comfortable brick home she shared with her gynecologist/obstetrician husband, in Wheat Ridge, a suburb just west of Denver. Hill, a nurse, was reading an article that suggested abortions were becoming safer for women. As she pondered the newspaper article, Hill thought: "It's not safe. It kills at least one person when it's done" (Gorski, 2000).

Hill wasn't a likely activist. Born in Texas in 1948, Hill moved to Colorado in the 1960s with her parents so her father could continue ranching. Hill went on after high school to become a nurse and specialized in obstetrics and gynecology at a Wheat Ridge Hospital, where she was later to settle permanently. She left Wheat Ridge, however, to join the Air Force. As a nurse, she was stationed at Luke Air Force Base in Arizona, where she met her husband, a physician on base.

It was at the base that Hill's antiabortion sentiments first emerged. As an obstetrics nurse, she was assigned to a floor where nurses were required to act as witnesses to the surgical consent forms women signed just before their abortions. Hill refused to do it, citing her opposition to abortion.

When Hill and her husband left the service, they settled in Wheat Ridge, where Hill raised three children. The 1980 news article awakened her concern about abortion, an issue that was receiving widespread attention in the media. Ronald Reagan was waging a campaign for the presidency as the first staunchly pro-life president, and the issue was constantly in the media as pro-life groups sought to limit the reach of *Roe* through a variety of actions. It wasn't until 1985, however, that Hill formed Sidewalk Counselors for Life (Gorski, 2000). She also penned a short, fifty-three-page workbook for other counselors. With verses from the Bible peppered liberally throughout the work, Hill (who declines to reveal her faith, saying only that she is Protestant and that her "faith influences her activism" [Gorski, 2000]), offers all kinds of suggestions to other sidewalk counselors. "Be short and to the point." If a patient won't listen, tell them: "This isn't Disneyland! They kill kids in there!"

The Sidewalk Counselors for Life routinely picketed Denver area abortion clinics just as other groups picketed and blockaded clinics around the nation. The first reported arrest of Hill, herself, was 1987, but these charges were quickly dropped. This experience, however, served only to heighten her resolve. On June 26, 1988, Hill and a friend, Joan Cannon, were among several protestors gathered outside the office of the Rocky Mountain Planned Parenthood office in Denver, Colorado, where abortions, in addition to routine women's reproductive health care, were offered. Both women carried signs labeling the clinic "The Killing Place" (Sotos, 1993).

Staff and patients entering the clinic were disturbed by the signs and the shouts of the protestors. At one point, one individual began yelling at the protestors and was restrained by an off-duty Denver police officer (whom the clinic had been forced to hire). The officer was assisted by another off-duty officer who happened to be passing by. These two police officers then asked Cannon and Hill to cover the offending parts of their signs, which appeared to be inciting clinic patients. Cannon and Hill refused, undoubtedly having been prepped about what to do by their lawyers from the Free Speech Association, a conservative, Kentucky-based public-interest law firm devoted to protecting the rights of unpopular protesters such as Hill and Cannon. At that point, both women were arrested for disturbing the peace and each spent about eight hours in jail. Later, the charges against both of them were dropped (Sotos, 1993).

In 1988, however, assisted by lawyers from the Free Speech Association—whose lawyers included Jay Sekulow, who ultimately was to work for Pat Robertson's American Center for Law & Justice (ACLJ)—Cannon and Hill sued the officers who arrested them and the City of Denver, alleging that their arrests violated federal civil rights laws and the First Amendment. In

1991 a federal district court judge dismissed their complaint, saying that the contours of the First Amendment are very "difficult, if not impossible to pinpoint." Thus, the judge extended qualified immunity to the officers whom he viewed as operating within the scope of their jobs, and the plaintiffs appealed.

As the case known as *Cannon v. City and County of Denver,* involving Joan Cannon and Leila Jeanne Hill, was wending its way through the federal court system, the Supreme Court was beginning to get several appeals involving clinic violence litigated from a variety of perspectives. Interestingly, most of them involved Free Speech Advocates (FSA), or the American Center for Law & Justice, which was quickly moving to the fore in abortion litigation, overshadowing other groups such as the Americans United for Life Legal Defense Fund, which had been involved in many of the earlier cases (Epstein, 1985).

Bray v. Alexandria Women's Health Clinic (506 U.S. 262 [1993]), was the first clinic violence case fully litigated before the Supreme Court. There, the U.S. Supreme Court ruled against NOW's contention that the KKK Act could be used to enjoin antiabortion demonstrations at clinics. Jane Bray and several other pro-life activists were represented at every stage of the litigation by the same lawyers who were also representing Cannon and Hill—FSA and Jay Sekulow, who argued the case before the U.S. Supreme Court (Henderson, 2003).

Pro-choice activists and clinics were in a dilemma. At the same time several states were enacting more and more restrictions on abortion, women were finding it much more difficult to secure abortions. Some providers were being put out of business by the effective protesting of pro-lifers, and the courts seemed unwilling to support a woman's right to hassle-free, safe access to a clinic over protestors' First Amendment rights.

In response to *Bray,* and the violence and protest that was taking place nationwide against clinics, several things were happening simultaneously. As pro-lifers were becoming more and more successful in their efforts to affect entrance and egress from clinics—in 1991 over 2,770 arrests of Operation Rescue protestors were made in Wichita, Kansas, alone—pro-choice activists continued to try to get injunctions against them in court, and they began to lobby Congress and state legislators to enact legislation to protect clinic access. On September 24, 1990, for example, in western New York, pro-choice activists and area physicians, including Dr. Bernard Slepian (who later was shot and killed in his home by a militant pro-lifer), asked for an injunction to stop a planned "rescue" blockade of local clinics. Similarly, Congress began debating the Freedom of Access to Clinics Act (FACE). And, on February 12, 1993, just one month after *Bray,* out of frustration with Congress's failure to pass FACE and continuing clinic protests in Colorado (many of them led by Hill and Cannon), liberal Democratic state representative Diana DeGette introduced a bill to limit clinic violence and the harassment of women.

The purpose of her bill, modeled after pending federal legislation, said DeGette, was to protect patients from protesters who "would literally, physically block them, scream at them, call them names, spit on them, (and) shove posters in their faces" (O'Driscoll, 2000). "Women who are going into a clinic to have an abortion—which is still a legal procedure in this country—are really traumatized by these tactics," said DeGette. "Even if they go through with the abortion, they are still traumatized" (Pankratz, 2000). DeGette, the married mother of two, later was to run for the U.S. House of Representatives, heavily supported by pro-choice groups, including EMILY's List and the National Abortion and Reproductive Rights Action League. (EMILY's List was DeGette's top contributor.)

The DeGette bill, which was signed into law in April 1993, quickly became known as the first "bubble law" in the nation. Planned Parenthood (PP) spokeswoman Ellen Brilliant said that PP didn't push for the bubble law "to prevent women from changing their minds, or even to restrict freedom of speech. It was to protect women seeking health care from the bullying and intimidation" ("Protesters Want Freedom to 'Counsel,'" 1999). While courts around the nation had been ordering bubble, or buffer, zones in response to clinic protest activity, Colorado's was the first legislation creating these kinds of zones where free speech was limited. Specifically, the Colorado statute created a 100-foot zone around all health-care facilities from doctor's offices to hospitals. Within that zone, protesters could get no closer than eight feet ("the bubble") to nonconsenting targets or persons entering or leaving the facility without risking a $750 fine and six months in jail. The new law prompted Hill and two others, again with the legal assistance of Jay Sekulow, to file a lawsuit in state court arguing that the bubble law violated their First Amendment rights.

Five months after the law was passed, Jeanne Hill and two other anti-abortion protestors filed suit in Jefferson County Court arguing that section three of the statute was facially invalid. (The other two sidewalk counselors, Audrey Himmelmann, and Everitt W. ["Boe"] Simpson, Jr., preferred to let Hill be the public face of the case.) They also requested declaratory and injunctive relief. They believed that "Many women who abort their children do so because no one has offered them information about alternatives to abortion." As self-described sidewalk counselors, they routinely stood outside of clinics around the state, offering women entering the clinics information about alternatives to abortion as part of their education and counseling mission. In the documents filed in the court, they stated that these efforts included the use of leaflets, signs, conversation, and a life-size model of a ten-week fetus, which they referred to as an unborn child. These activities routinely occurred closer than eight feet to their desired targets, and they alleged that the eight-foot bubble would make it very difficult for them to engage in meaningful conversation with those entering or exiting a clinic while staying on public sidewalks or driveways, staying more than eight feet away from patients not granting assent to their approach, and conducting their conversational and political leafleting activities. They maintained that they did not engage in any dangerous or harassing conduct as part of their speech activities but that after passage of the act, out of fear of criminal prosecution, they were forced to abandon their sidewalk counseling, or these activities were curtailed in such a way by the statute as to make them ineffective. As the base of their claim was their belief that the bubble law violated their First Amendment rights.

On April 25, 1994, a Jefferson County District Court judge dismissed their lawsuit, saying that the act "helped give people access to health clinics" and protected them from being "threatened and harassed or assaulted by forced confrontations with demonstrators." Moreover, said the trial court judge, the law protected patients who were seeking health care.

Hill continued her work as a sidewalk counselor nearly every day, rain or shine, through her 1987 and 1988 arrests, while her lawsuit with Cannon and her challenge of the bubble law were pending. Rocky Mountain Planned Parenthood continued to be her major focus. Her favorite signs continued to call the clinic "The Killing Place." Another favorite had a picture of a fetus. Hill insists that even before passage of the bubble law, she never was violent or threatening. Instead, she claims that she approached women "quietly" and "politely," as she offered them "literature that had our telephone number and resources . . . whatever they needed we'd try to provide for them." Said Hill:

> We want to draw them to us, not push them away. . . . Ordinarily they didn't have a husband, they didn't have somebody who really cared. We served more or less to provide for information that Planned Parenthood refused to provide. We were successful, we were. This is why Planned Parenthood, they didn't want us talking to their clientele because we were changing minds. ("Protesters Want Freedom to 'Counsel,'" 1999)

Hill went on to admit that sometimes, however, when she was farther away and needed to get their attention, she did use a bullhorn to implore patients to let the counselors help them. And when all else failed, she and other counselors did use the bullhorn to implore clinic entrants not to "let them kill your baby" (Gorski, 2000).

Although Hill insists that, before the bubble law, she never shoved, pushed, or threatened any women seeking access to the Planned Parenthood facility or any other clinics where she engaged in sidewalk counseling, Planned Parenthood says that many protestors did their best to intimidate patients entering or leaving the clinic.

Interestingly, shortly after the Colorado District Court judge dismissed Hill's challenge to the new Colorado law, on July 23, 1993, the Tenth Circuit Court of Appeals reversed the federal district court ruling in the Cannon and Hill case in favor of the protestors and remanded the case back to the district court for trial, saying "The First Amendment means that government has no power to restrict expression because of its message, its ideas, its subject matter or its content. . . . For the state to enforce a content-based exclusion, it must show that its regulation is necessary to serve a compelling state interest and that it is narrowly drawn to achieve that end" (*Cannon and Hill v. City and County of Denver,* 998 F. 2d 867, 871–872 [1993]). The federal appeals court went on to discuss the words on Cannon and Hill's posters and found "no assault or threatening of bodily harm, no truculent bearing, no intentional discourtesy, no personal abuse." Thus, the court concluded that these were not "fighting words," which could have given the officers the authority to arrest the protesters. Said the court, "(A)lthough the words 'killing' or 'murder' are certainly emotionally charged, it is difficult to conceive of a forceful presentation of the anti-abortion viewpoint which would not assert that abortion is the taking of human life" (*Cannon and Hill v. City and County of Denver,* p. 873).

As Hill had two cases pending in the state and federal courts, in 1994 the U.S. Supreme Court upheld the constitutionality of a court-ordered protest-free buffer zone of thirty-six feet surrounding the entrance to a Florida abortion clinic that had been obtained by the Feminist Majority Foundation (FMF). FMF provides lawyers for clinics that are targets of protests, in addition to lobbying for a wide array of women's issues, including for laws such as FACE. In *Madsen v. Women's Health Center* (512 U.S. 753 [1994]), however, the Court also found that a more sweeping ban that prohibited protestors from approaching staffers and patients within 300 feet of a clinic was unconstitutional. The 6–3 decision appeared to give lower courts considerable authority to check protests. This triggered strong objections from Justice Antonin Scalia, who, in an impassioned dissent from the bench, noted that the Court "has left a powerful loaded weapon lying about today," which

TABLE 1 Supreme Court Justice Votes in Key Clinic Protest Cases

	Pro-Choice				Pro-Life		
	Hill	*Schenck*	*Madsen*		*Hill*	*Schenck*	*Madsen*
JUSTICES							
Rehnquist	X	X	X				
Blackmun	X	left Court					
Stevens	X	X	X				
O'Connor	X	X	X				
Souter	X	X	X				
Ginsburg	X	X	X				
Breyer		X	X				
Scalia					X	X	X
Thomas					X	X	X
Kennedy					X	X	X

could be used to limit all kinds of speech about any kind of issues. Ellie Smeal, the president of FMF, said that "the decision was a good omen for the 40 other local and state injunctions in place" around the nation. "Having Chief Justice (William H.) Rehnquist hand down the decision makes it stronger" (Biskupic, 1994). As underscored by Smeal, and as revealed in table 1, *Madsen* produced an interesting lineup. Chief Justice Rehnquist, one of two dissenters in *Roe v. Wade*, wrote the *Madsen* majority opinion, in spite of having ruled against NOW's attempts to limit clinic protesting in *Bray*.

Shortly after *Madsen*, and with several protest cases pending in federal court, including the case from western New York, discussed below, Congress passed the Freedom of Access to Clinics Act. The act made it a federal crime either to block access to a reproductive health clinic or to harass or use violence against women seeking reproductive health or those providing it. As *Madsen* and *Hill v. City of Lakewood* (as *Hill v. Colorado* initially was known), were wending their way through the courts, so was the case from western New York that later was to end up at the Supreme Court. In 1990, when pro-life activists announced they would blockade and protest at area clinics, pro-choice activists immediately went to court to obtain an injunction to prevent the protestors from closing down area clinics.

While this injunction was being challenged in the federal courts, Hill and the other two sidewalk counselors, aided by their attorneys from the American Center for Law & Justice, appealed the state district court dismissal of their challenge to the Colorado bubble law. One of their lawyers, James Henderson, told the Colorado Court of Appeals that the law "tramples their right to free speech," and further contended that the act was "one of the most sweeping criminalizations of First Amendment activities in Colorado's history" (Pankratz, 1995). In response, the state argued that the First Amendment "does not guarantee the right to communicate at all time in all places," noting that the district court judge's dismissal of the case came after weighing the free speech issues involved (American Political Network, 1995). Interestingly, the state attorney general at the time was Gale A. Norton, who went on to head the Department of the Interior in the current, pro-life, Bush administration.

After hearing these arguments, on July 13, 1995, the Colorado Court of Appeals upheld the bubble law, concluding that it did not violate the petitioners' free speech rights. Moreover, said the court in justifying the act, the law is "content neutral," because the political beliefs of any protesters are "not relevant to a determination of whether a violation of the law occurred," rejecting the plaintiffs arguments that the law was directed only at them and was "more than necessary to accomplish the goal of providing access to health care facilities" (*Hill v. City of Lakewood*, 911 P.2d 670 [1995]). DeGette was gratified by the court's action. "This is cutting-edge legislation. Colorado is the only state with this bubble concept added to clinic-access law. . . . It's a reasonable restriction on free speech in order to protect patient's rights," said DeGette ("Appeals Court Upholds 'Bubble Law,'" 1995).

Hill immediately pledged that she and the others, while "disappointed," would not give up. "The middle court is a means to an end. This will go higher. I don't see that either side will stop until we reach the U.S. Supreme Court. The women in crisis pregnancy in Colorado will not have the right to receive the constructive-type help we can give them. That's the bottom line" ("Appeals Court Upholds 'Bubble Law,'" 1995).

On August 17, 1995, the Court of Appeals denied Hill's request for a rehearing, and her lawyers appealed the case to the Colorado Supreme Court. On February 26, 1997, the state supreme court refused to hear their appeal, prompting Hill's lawyers to petition the U.S. Supreme Court for a writ of certiorari.

Ultimately, three years after *Madsen,* and after Hill's lawyers had requested that the Supreme Court hear their appeal, the question of the constitutionality of the judicially imposed fixed and floating buffer zones ordered by the federal district court judge in Buffalo, New York, reached the Supreme Court. In *Schenck v. Pro-Choice Network* (519 U.S. 357 [1997]), the Court upheld a fifteen-foot buffer zone around the clinic building but found that a fifteen-foot "floating" buffer zone around individual staff members and patients as they entered and exited the clinic was unconstitutional. Floating buffer zones, which surround the targets of the speech (from protestors), burdened "more speech than is necessary," concluded the 6–3 majority. The Court seemed especially concerned with the difficulty that demonstrators might have in continually correctly gauging the buffer zones. Thus, the lower court injunction that created the floating buffer zone placed a far too great impediment on the protesters' First Amendment free speech rights, concluded the Court, noting that "(L)eafleting and commenting on matters of public concern are classic forms of speech that lie at the heart of the First Amendment." As is revealed in table 1, Justice Rehnquist again wrote for the majority in *Schenck,* and Justice Stephen Breyer, who succeeded the retired Justice Harry A. Blackmun, replaced him in the six-person majority.

Less than one week later, on February 24, 1997, the U.S. Supreme Court granted certiorari in *Hill,* vacated the judgment, and remanded the case back to the Colorado Court of Appeals. It is not all that common for the U.S. Supreme Court to direct lower state courts to reevaluate their decisions in light of recent Supreme Court cases, but that is what the Court opted to do when the challenge to the Colorado law first reached the justices. Specifically, in the wake of its decision in *Schenck,* in lieu of accepting the Colorado case for review, the Court asked the Colorado Court of Appeals to reconsider its decision upholding the buffer zone in light of *Schenck,* which invalidated a similar, but larger (fifteen- versus eight-foot) buffer zone.

Four months later, the court of appeals, after reconsidering the issues presented, again upheld the bubble law. On January 12, 1998, the Colorado Supreme Court agreed to review the court of appeals decision, becoming the first state supreme court to address the question of the constitutionality of a statewide bubble law.

In *Hill v. Thomas* (973 P. 2d 1246 [1999], which later would be called *Hill v. Colorado*), the Colorado Supreme Court noted that it "Must decide whether a legislative enactment designed to protect the privacy rights of citizens entering and leaving Colorado health care facilities unduly burdens the First Amendment rights of other citizens. We conclude that it does not."

In highlighting that the provision in question was the result of legislative deliberation and action, and not a judicially constructed mandate as was the case in *Schenck,* the Court underscored that the restrictions on speech were (1) content neutral; (2) narrowly tailored to serve a significant governmental interest; and (3) open to ample alternative means for communication of information that the petitioners seek to place in the marketplace of ideas. The Court looked to another U.S. Supreme Court case, *Ward v. Rock Against Racism* (491 U.S. 781 [1989]), to support its conclusion that *Ward* permits greater deference to legislative enactments limiting speech than to the *Schenck* standard, "which places greater limitations upon the judicial regulation of speech through injunctive proceedings." Thus, several Colorado courts consistently upheld the constitutionality of the law as a narrowly tailored approach to meet a pressing problem—one that the legislature identified as "a history of obstructive demonstrations" that negatively affected the efforts of others to exercise other constitutionally protected rights (Mauro, 1999). Moreover, all of the courts found that the buffer zones were a "fair accommodation of two fundamental rights," recognizing the competing interests at stake in the case.

In the Supreme Court

In May 1999 the American Center for Law & Justice asked the U.S. Supreme Court to review the action of the Colorado Supreme Court. Four months later, before the official beginning of the Court's October 1999–2000 term, on September 28, 1999, the U.S. Supreme Court agreed to consider the constitutionality of the Colorado law. "This could very well be a defining moment in First Amendment law," said Jay Sekulow, chief counsel and founder of the ACLJ, which was continuing to represent the three sidewalk protesters. "There is no abortion speech exception to the First Amendment on sidewalks surrounding abortion clinics," noted Sekulow. "Sidewalk counselors . . . should not have to surrender their constitutionally protected First Amendment rights because some people disagree with their message," continued Sekulow in heralding the Court's decision to accept the case (ACLJ, 1999).

THE ROLE OF INTEREST GROUPS

As veteran Supreme Court reporter Tony Mauro noted in reporting on the Court's acceptance of *Hill v. Colorado* for review, "(w)hen it comes to setting limits on aggressive protests around abortion clinics, the Supreme Court apparently hopes that the third time is a charm" (Mauro, 1999). But, its decision to accept *Hill* for review quickly became a flash point for many groups on both sides of the abortion struggle. It also proverbially produced some strange bedfellows, pairing the liberal, often radical animal rights group People for the Ethical Treatment of Animals (PETA) with conservative pro-life groups. To many pro-life groups, as well as groups such as PETA, *Hill* was simply another in a series of cases designed to limit the right of citizens to exercise their rights of free speech and assembly to focus attention on their respective causes. For the sidewalk counselors, it entailed the right to free speech in a public place, where they could, they hoped, persuade women not to go through with their decision to have an abortion. In the case of groups such as PETA, an adverse decision in *Hill* could affect its rights to protest outside department stores and furriers, as well as at universities and labs where animals are used for research. As table 2 below highlights, not only did the sidewalk counselors have the support of the American Center for Law & Justice, but they also were supported by PETA, Liberty Counsel, and the Life Legal Defense Foundation.

Political scientist Richard C. Cortner has written that "cases do not arrive on the doorsteps of the Supreme Court like orphans in the night" (1975). Given the resources of the three counselors, it is unlikely that, despite their commitment to their work as demonstrated by their daily protests at area clinics, they might have had the resources to sustain a challenge all the way to the U.S. Supreme Court. Not only did this case go up and down the Colorado Court system, but it also took savvy, committed lawyers to stay the course throughout the complicated and constantly changing legal doctrines surrounding access to clinics.

Jay Sekulow, who acted as Hill's lawyer since her original arrests in 1987, first litigated as the lawyer for Jews for Jesus and later became the chief counsel for the Christian Advocates Serving Evangelism, which worked closely with Free Speech Advocates, a project that was founded in 1984 by Catholics United for Life (Horne, 1991). Sekulow and James Henderson, who graduated from law school in 1987 but who was representing Hill and Cannon along with Sekulow the next year, eventually became affiliated with and then merged with Pat Robertson's ACLJ in 1994 (Henderson, 2002). All of these groups that ultimately merged in the ACLJ were united by their belief that the free speech rights of clinic protesters were violated by most of the restrictions levied on protestors by the courts or legislatures (Ivers, 1995).

AMICUS CURIAE

As is revealed in table 2, the American Center for Law & Justice was not the only interest group concerned with the issues in *Hill v. Colorado*. Not only were Hill and her colleagues represented by the ACLJ, but many of the groups that had been involved in other cases involving clinic protests also filed amicus curiae briefs in *Hill*. Liberty Counsel, PETA, and the Life Legal Defense Foundation filed in support of the sidewalk counselors. On the other side, Colorado was defending the constitutionality of its statute supported by seven briefs written by four groups representing twenty-three organizations, and an additional three groups representing twenty local and state governments, as well as the United States. New York and seventeen other states

TABLE 2   Interest Group Participation in *Hill v. Colorado*

On Behalf of Sidewalk Counselors	On Behalf of Colorado
REPRESENTING COUNSELORS:	REPRESENTING COLORADO:
American Center for Law and Justice	State Attorney General
AS AMICI:	AS AMICI:
Liberty Counsel	ACLU
PETA	AFL-CIO
Life Legal Defense Foundation	American College of Obstetricians and Gynecologists and the American Medical Association
	City of Boulder and the city and county of Denver
	NARAL, NAF, and the NOW LDEF, American Jewish Committee, American Jewish Congress, Center for Constitutional Rights, Center for Reproductive Law and Policy, Colorado NARAL, Colorado Women's Bar Association, Connecticut Women's Education and Legal Fund, Feminist Majority Foundation, National Center for the Pro-Choice Majority, National Women's Health Network, Northwest Women's Law Center, Planned Parenthood Federation of America, Planned Parenthood of the Rocky Mountains, Inc., Planned Parenthood of the Rocky Mountain Services Corp., Republicans for Choice, The Women's Law Project
	State of New York and the attorneys general of Arizona, California, Connecticut, Hawaii, Kansas, Maine, Maryland, Massachusetts, Missouri, Montana, Nevada, New Mexico, Oklahoma, Oregon, Rhode Island, Vermont, Washington
	United States

urged the court to uphold the Colorado law to give states the much-needed flexibility "to deal with serious public safety issues by appropriate means."

ORAL ARGUMENT

Political scientists often have questioned how much can be implied from the course of oral argument of any cases heard by the Supreme Court. Still, reporters and other Court watchers regularly dissect every exchange to glean insights as to how the individual justices, in particular, lean in any case. *Hill v. Colorado* was no exception. And, again, appraisals of the oral argument, ultimately, were similarly uninstructive. "The Supreme Court seemed skeptical yesterday of a Colorado law aimed at restricting aggressive demonstrations around abortion clinics and other health care facilities," wrote court reporter Tony Mauro (2000), for example, for the Freedom Forum.

In evaluating the law that applies to all medical facilities and to all types of unsolicited communication, during oral argument Chief Justice Rehnquist offered that "You're curtailing a lot of other activity. . . . If you're restricting speech, you can't be vague." Jay Sekulow then noted that a pizza delivery employee trying to hand out discount coupons outside of a Denver hospital would violate the law. "The Colorado statute converts protected speech into a crime," he told the justices. Sekulow was not challenging the constitutionality of the provision of the law that banned blocking a clinic's entrance or hindering anyone from entering or exiting the clinic. Thus, said Sekulow, "the case concerned only speech in a public forum" (Greenhouse, 2000a). Justice Sandra Day O'Connor noted that "You can convey anything you want at eight feet." And, Justice Breyer asked "What's the problem?" several times.

But, according to Mauro's appraisal, the problem became apparent to several of the justices when Colorado solicitor general Michael McLachlan began to defend the provision (Mauro, 2000). The justices were all ears when Justice Anthony Kennedy asked how the law would act if a physician's office was on the sixth or seventh floor of a building where other nonmedical businesses were housed. The Colorado solicitor general replied that "the law would apply to anyone entering such a building, so long as a public sidewalk or thoroughfare was within 100 feet of the entrance" (Mauro, 2000). According to Mauro, most of the justices seemed stunned that a single physician's office in a large building could provide a wide zone where a wide range of speech would be unlawful, and in fact, criminalized. "In a public forum, can we have to turn off unwelcome speech?" asked Justice Antonin Scalia quite incredulously.

Sekulow and the Colorado solicitor general were not the only attorneys who appeared during the *Hill* oral argument. Also arguing as an amicus curiae in favor of the constitutionality of the law was Deputy U.S. Solicitor General Barbara Underwood. The solicitor general is not a frequent participant in oral argument as amicus curiae; thus, its position often is given more weight than that of others and the Solicitor General's Office enjoys a close relationship with the Court.

A moment of humor was interjected into the proceedings when McLachlan interrupted Justice Scalia to note that "Everyone you communicate with is a willing listener." This was met with a "Don't be too sure" one liner from Justice O'Connor.

The Opinion

The basic issue before the justices in *Hill* was whether the Colorado law prohibiting demonstrators from coming within eight feet of anyone seeking to enter or exit a medical facility violated the First Amendment. Unlike *Roe,* or many subsequent cases, it had nothing to do with whether or not a woman had a constitutionally protected right to obtain an abortion or under what circumstances she could do so. Instead, it involved a basic First Amendment issue that pitted the rights of those seeking to stop women from securing abortions against pro-choice activists who viewed clinic protest as just another way of intimidating women who sought to exercise a constitutionally protected right. And, from the point of view of abortion providers, including the National Abortion Federation, it added an unwelcome and often costly addition to their efforts to provide services to women in a safe and comfortable environment.

"This could very well represent a defining moment in First Amendment law, " said Jay Sekulow upon hearing of the Court's decision to review the case (ACLJ, 1999). This was probably an overstatement given how the Supreme Court treated the case. The *Hill* decision was announced on the last day of the Court's 1999–2000 term along with another abortion case, *Stenberg v. Carhart* (530 U.S. 914 [2000]), which attracted far more attention from the press. In *Stenberg,* a 5–4 majority of the Court ruled that Nebraska (and by implication thirty other states), could not ban physicians from performing a procedure known as "partial birth abortion," because it may be the most medically appropriate way of terminating some pregnancies (Biskupic, 2000).

In *Hill,* where the "floating buffer zone" was narrower than the one struck down in *Schenck,* the Court seemed to be swayed by the content neutrality of the Colorado provision. Thus, six justices found no constitutional violation in the law, because antiabortion speech had not been singled out for special treatment because of its message and the eight-foot floating bubble provided adequate opportunity for speech.

Writing for the majority. Justice John Paul Stevens wrote "The right to free speech, of course, includes the right to attempt to persuade others to change their views, and may not be curtailed simply because the speaker's message may be offensive to his audience. But the protection afforded to offensive messages does not always embrace offensive speech that is so intrusive that the unwilling audience cannot avoid it." Justice Stevens then went on to say that the eight-foot floating bubble zone "leaves ample room to communicate a message through speech." More specifically, the majority also found that:

(1) States have a strong interest in protecting the health and safety of their citizens that "may justify a special focus on unimpeded access to heath care facilities and the avoidance of potential trauma to patients associated with confrontational protests."
(2) The right to free speech includes the right to try to persuade others, but "the protection afforded to offensive messages does not always embrace offensive speech that is so intrusive that the unwilling audience cannot avoid it."
(3) An eight-foot bubble is not a regulation of speech, but "a regulation of the places where some speech may occur."
(4) The statute offered ample opportunities for oral statements, displaying signs, and leafleting (if a person chooses to accept the leaflet).

In a stinging dissent, both Justices Scalia and Kennedy read their dissents aloud for more than a half hour (Biskupic, 2000). Scalia called it "one of the many aggressively pro-abortion novelties announced by the Court in recent years." "Does the deck seem stacked? You bet," said Scalia in frustration. Justice Kennedy added that "the Constitution doesn't permit criminalization of peaceful dissemination of unpopular views."

The Reaction

Diana DeGette, now a representative in the U.S. Congress, hailed the Court's decision, saying that "This law was written to protect First Amendment Rights as well as the patient's right to get into a clinic without being harassed. The Supreme Court's decision was a resounding affirmation of that restrained approach" (O'Driscoll, 2000). Not surprisingly, Jim Henderson had a different perspective, commenting, "Justice Stevens has torn out of our United States Constitution the right to freedom of speech" (O'Driscoll, 2000).

Hill and many of the cases before it, with the exception of the votes of Chief Justice Rehnquist, are probably best viewed as surrogates for the Court's ongoing debate concerning abortion. On many occasions since *Roe,* the Court has waited until the last day of its term to hand down cases involving a host of issues surrounding abortion even if they don't have the public attention generated by *Roe* or, later, *Planned Parenthood of Southeastern Pennsylvania v. Casey* (505 U.S. 833 [1992]), which actually was the last major case heard by the Supreme Court involving major abortion restrictions and the appropriate level of scrutiny given to state abortion restrictions. *Hill* was no exception. It weighed First Amendment rights and a woman's right to secure an abortion, as well as a state legislature's right to legislate for the health and safety of its citizens and determined that the Free Speech infringements were insignificant, because the restriction went more to the regulation of the time, place, and manner of speech.

REFERENCES

ACLJ. (1999, September 29). ACLJ pleased Supreme Court to hear landmark case involving First Amendment rights of pro-life sidewalk counselors. The American Center for Law and Justice.

American Political Network. (1995, June 22). Colorado: Lifers challenge constitutionality of bubble law. *Abortion Report,* State Reports.

Appeals court upholds state's "bubble law": Abortion foes vow to press fight. (1995, July 14). *Denver Post,* p. B1.

Biskupic, J. (1994, July 1). Court allows abortion clinic buffer zones; Scalia sees threat to free speech rights. *Washington Post,* p. A1.

Blanchard, D. (1994). *The anti-abortion movement and the rise of the religious right: From polite to fiery protest.* New York: Twayne.

Cortner, R. C. (1975). *The Supreme Court and civil liberties policy.* Palo Alto, CA: Mayfield.

Epstein, L. (1995). *Conservatives in court.* Knoxville, TN: University of Tennessee Press.

Gorski, E. (2000, January 18). Court to hear abortion activism appeal. *Times-Picayune,* p. 12E.

Greenhouse, L. (2000a, January 20). Free speech or interference? Abortion case is argued. *New York Times,* p. A14.

Greenhouse, L. (2000b, June 29). The Supreme Court: The Nebraska case: Court rules that governments can't outlaw type of abortion. *New York Times,* p. A1.

Henderson, J. M., Sr. (2003). Résumé, accessed on July 19, 2003, at http://www.geocities .com/thetruthserum/words/resume.html.

Horne, W. W. (1991, November). Defending the disobedience. *The American Lawyer.* Accessed on July 18, 2003, from NEXIS database.

Ivers, G. (1995). *To build a wall: American Jews and the separation of church and state.* Charlottesville, VA: University Press of Virginia.

Mauro, T. (2000). Supreme Court appears leery of Colorado's buffer-zone law. Accessed on July 18, 2003, at http://www.freedomforum.org/templates/document.asp? documentID=4307&printerfriendly=1.

Mauro, T. (1999). Supreme court gives itself another chance to clarify abortion-protest limits. Accessed on July 18, 2003, at http://www.freedomforum.org/templates/document.asp?documentID=4301&printerfriendly=1.

O'Connor, K. (1996). *Neutral ground: Abortion politics in an age of absolutes.* Boulder, CO: Westview Press.

O'Driscoll, P. (2000, June 29). Ruling upholding "bubbles" at clinic hailed, denounced. *USA Today,* p. 9A.

Pankratz, H. (2000, January 17). Big test for "bubble law": Limit on abortion clinic protests heads to high court. *Denver Post,* p. A1.

Pankratz, H. (1995, June 21). Clinic "bubble" statute debated; appeals court hears free speech case, *Denver Post,* p. B2.

Protesters want freedom to "counsel" women at clinic; Patients were harassed rights supporters say. (1999, September 29). *Rocky Mountain News,* p. 5A.

Sotos, J. G. (1993, September 23). Arrest of abortion protestors violates First Amendment. *Chicago Daily Law Bulletin,* p. 6.

Freedom of Association

Competing Constitutional Claims

Boy Scouts of America v. Dale (2000)

ERIN ACKERMAN AND JOEL B. GROSSMAN

> Like many organizations, the Boy Scouts maintain certain standards of member-
> ship. Among other things, Scouts must be "trustworthy," "cheerful," "brave,"
> "courteous," "physically strong," and "mentally awake." Because the organization
> regards homosexuality as inconsistent with some of its standards—that scouts be
> "clean" and "morally straight"—it dismissed an openly gay scoutmaster. The scout-
> master sued, alleging a violation a state antidiscrimination law, but the Supreme
> Court determined that, as much as any other group that expresses ideas, it has a
> constitutional right to determine who can and cannot be among its members.

Some of the most perplexing issues before the Supreme Court arise when
competing constitutional rights claim precedence over each other. Such a
conflict is all the more difficult to resolve when the decision will have important secondary effects on the nation's cultural divide. *Boy Scouts v. Dale* (530
U.S. 640 [2000]) is such a case. On the surface it is about the limits of the
constitutionally protected association of a private group and the right of an
individual to be treated in a nondiscriminatory fashion. This is in itself an

issue—a continuing issue—of great importance, because both claims, in the abstract, have valid title to constitutional protection. Freedom of association is part of the "expression bundle" of rights in the First Amendment, and that alone attests to its significance. But it is also a doctrine that provides important protections linked to privacy—the rights of individuals to join together for private purposes.

The right to nondiscriminatory treatment is also deeply embedded in our constitutional and social fabric. But there is an important twist that makes this a special case. The development of equality law in the United States, and the public's perception of the nondiscrimination principle, is based largely on the familiar trio of race (including ethnicity), religion, and gender. But other rights claims have also been asserted, and these have met, both on and off the Court, with uneven approval. "Sexual orientation" is an evolving right that is only slowly gaining acceptance. It is more than merely a theoretical proposition but certainly not yet a right that is fully protected or recognized as legitimate. The ambivalence of the Supreme Court's decisions on homosexuality bear witness to this division of opinion, as do surveys that clearly show the public's ambivalence over recognizing the legitimacy of the gay, lesbian, and bisexual community. *Boy Scouts* is thus not just about the formally pleaded constitutional issues, but also about the progress and status of the movement to give full legal recognition, and protection, to the gay community. It is thus at the volcanic center of what Justice Scalia once deprecated as the "culture wars" (*Romer v. Evans,* 517 U.S. 620, 652, [1995]).

The Boy Scouts of America

The Boy Scouts of America (BSA) is a private-membership organization offering educational and recreational activities for boys and young adults to "build character, to train in the responsibilities of participating citizenship, and to develop personal fitness." The BSA was founded in 1910 and was chartered by an act of Congress in 1916. It is governed by a National Council based in Irving, Texas. The organization is divided into three membership divisions: Cub Scouting for boys seven to ten; Boy Scouting for boys eleven to seventeen; and Venturing for young men and women fourteen through twenty. At the age of eighteen, a Boy Scout may apply for adult membership. All adult members are designated as "leaders." Most serve as scoutmasters, assistant scoutmasters, troop committee members, and merit badge counselors.

As of the end of 2001, BSA national membership was 3,325,500, divided into 125,800 units, and supported by 1,200,000 adult members. Since its inception, the BSA has enrolled approximately 90 million members. While the

BSA's corporate structure is centralized, at the operational level it is highly decentralized. Each of the divisions is divided into smaller units (packs, troops, and crews, all of which are subdivided into dens or patrols), and then organized into regional councils. Community-based organizations that are deemed to have goals compatible with those of the BSA (including religious, educational, civic, fraternal, business and labor organizations, governmental bodies, corporations, professional associations, and citizens' groups) receive national charters to sponsor Scouting programs. The largest sponsors of Scouting are the United Methodist Church (417,000 youth participants), the Mormons (411,000), public schools (361,000), and the Roman Catholic Church (351,000).

Financial support for BSA programs comes from a variety of sources. The National Council is supported by members' annual registration fees, local councils' charter and service fees, fund-raising campaigns, income from the sale of publications and equipment, and bequests and special gifts. The local councils are supported by fund-raising campaigns, local United Ways, foundation grants, investment income, and bequests. The chartered organizations provide meeting places and often furnish materials and other facilities. Youth members pay dues to their unit and often participate in fund-raising activities.

The ideals of Scouting are spelled out in the BSA oath, law, motto, and slogan, which are further explained and interpreted in handbooks and BSA publications. Boys earn merit badges and awards for learning skills and various achievements. The rank of Eagle Scout, awarded to fewer than 4 percent of all Boy Scouts, is Scouting's highest honor.

James Dale, Eagle Scout

James Dale became a Cub Scout at age eight in Mattawan (Monmouth County), New Jersey, and progressed through the ranks with distinction. He became an Eagle Scout, was chosen for the Order of the Arrow (the Boy Scout honor society), and was by all accounts an exemplary scout. In 1988, at age eighteen, he became an adult member and assistant scoutmaster.

Dale attended Rutgers University. Having previously come out to friends and family, he spoke at a seminar addressing psychological and health concerns of gay teenagers. A local paper ran a story about the seminar, including an interview with Dale and his picture; he was identified as the copresident of the Rutgers Lesbian Gay & Bisexual Alliance. A month later, Dale received a letter informing him that his BSA membership had been revoked. The letter stated that membership "is a privilege" that may be denied "whenever there is concern that an individual may not meet the high standards of membership which the BSA seeks to provide for American youth" (*Boy Scouts,* p. 665). Surprised and upset by his sudden expulsion, Dale requested an explanation. The Monmouth Council responded that "the standards for leadership of the Boy Scouts of America . . . specifically forbid membership to homosexuals" (*Boy Scouts,* p. 665).

Dale sought the assistance of Lambda Legal, a national organization advocating "full recognition of the civil rights of lesbians, gay men, the transgendered, and people with HIV or AIDS." In addition to its educational and public policy activities, Lambda pursues "impact litigation" through test cases chosen for their "likelihood of success in establishing positive legal precedent" (Lambda Legal, 2002). Lambda attorney Evan Wolfson, who would take the case all the way to the Supreme Court, was particularly impressed with Dale as an "intelligent, self-possessed . . . representative of gay youth" (Wolfson telephone interview, 2002).

Lambda assisted Dale in seeking review of his expulsion within the BSA governing structure. When this failed to win Dale reinstatement, Wolfson filed a complaint in New Jersey Superior Court, under the state's public accommodations statute (the New Jersey Law Against Discrimination, or LAD), seeking reinstatement. New Jersey is one of twelve states prohibiting discrimination in public accommodations on the basis of sexual orientation. The law provides that "all persons shall have the opportunity . . . to obtain all the accommodations, advantages, facilities, and privileges of any place of public accommodation . . . without discrimination because of affectional or sexual orientation." But the law exempted "distinctly private entities, religious educational facilities, and parents or individuals acting in loco parentis in respect of the education and upbringing of a child (*Dale v. Boy Scouts of America,* 160 N.J. 562, 584 [1999]; hereafter *"Dale NJ"*).

Freedom of Association v. Nondiscrimination: The Threshold Issue

The threshold issue in Dale's case in the trial court was whether the BSA was an exempted private entity or a place of public accommodation under New Jersey law. The answer depended primarily on how the courts would construe and apply the right to "freedom of association" protected by the First and Fourteenth Amendments. Although the First Amendment does not explicitly refer to association, judges have long believed that the amendment necessarily protects private or group activities that encourage and protect individual liberty, the freedoms of speech and religion, and political participation through the rights of assembly and petition. Freedom of association was fully recognized as a constitutional right by the Supreme Court in *NAACP v. Alabama* (357 U.S. 449 [1958]). The Court held that "freedom to engage in association for the advancement of beliefs and ideas is an inseparable aspect of the 'liberty' assured by the due process clause of the Fourteenth Amendment, which embraces freedom of speech," and that "[e]ffective advocacy of both public and private points of view, particularly controversial ones, is undeniably enhanced by group association."

Subsequently the Court has recognized two distinct types of freedom of association claims. The first is freedom of *intimate* association. This involves "choices to enter into and maintain certain intimate human relationships," which "must be secured against undue intrusion by the State because of the role of such relationships in safeguarding the individual freedom that is central to our constitutional scheme" (*Roberts v. U.S. Jaycees,* 468 U.S. 609, 617–618 [1984]). Freedom of intimate association is characterized by its private, nonpolitical nature. It marks off the boundaries of personal liberty, in which government may not interfere with personal choices such as marriage, family, and procreation. Intimate associations are "distinguished by such attributes as relative smallness, a high degree of selectivity in decisions to begin and maintain the affiliation, and seclusion from others in critical aspects of that relationship" (*Roberts,* p. 620). Determination of an intimate association entitled to constitutional protection includes consideration of "size, purpose, policies, selectivity, congeniality, and other characteristics that in a particular case may be pertinent (*Roberts,* p. 620). By these standards, the BSA would not appear to be an "intimate association."

The Court has also recognized a "right to associate for the purpose of engaging in those activities protected by the First Amendment—speech, assembly, petition for the redress of grievances, and the exercise of religion . . . as an indispensable means of preserving other individual liberties" (*Roberts,* pp. 617–618). This freedom of *expressive* association implies the right *not* to speak, including the right to be able to control political, religious, or cultural messages attributed to the group or its members. It is at this point that freedom of association comes into tension with the social and legal goal of nondiscrimination. The case law on freedom of expressive association attempts to balance these often-competing claims—the right of a group to control its image or message versus the right of individual or potential group members to be judged or treated without prejudice, including the right of access to public facilities and organizations.

The two key cases that articulate the main concepts and principles at issue in *Boy Scouts* are *Roberts v. Jaycees* (1984) and *Rotary International v. Rotary Club of Duarte* (481 U.S. 537 [1987]). Each case involved attempts by a national civic organization to keep local chapters from admitting women. In both cases, those chapters, seeking to comply with state laws that prohibited discrimination against women in public accommodations, had admitted women to full membership and had been censured by their national boards. The national organizations had argued that the admission of women as full members would hinder their group right to communicate their message.[1] The Supreme Court agreed that admitting women might have some effect on the message the groups wished to disseminate, but in both cases found that the admission of women as members would not "impose any serious burdens" on its "collective effort on behalf of [its] shared goals" (*Roberts,* pp. 609, 622, 626–627; *Rotary,* pp. 548–549). Nor, the Court said, would it force the clubs to communicate any message they did not wish to endorse. The impact of the admission of women on the First Amendment protected speech of the club members was too slight to permit either the Jaycees or the Rotary Club to use expressive association claims to trump antidiscrimination measures. "The right to associate for expressive purposes is not . . . absolute. Infringements on that right may be justified by regulations adopted to serve compelling state interests, unrelated to the suppression of ideas, that cannot be achieved through means significantly less restrictive of associational freedoms" (*Roberts,* p. 623).

Dale v. Boy Scouts of America: New Jersey Courts

In November 1995 a New Jersey Superior Court granted summary judgment to the Boy Scouts. The trial judge concluded that Dale was "a sexually active homosexual" and found that the BSA had always had a policy of excluding "active homosexuals" (*Dale NJ,* pp. 580–581). He concluded further that the "BSA considered homosexual conduct neither 'morally straight' under the Scout Oath, nor 'clean' under the Scout Law" (*Dale v. Boy Scouts of America,* 308 N.J. Super. 516 [1995]). The judge argued that homosexuality is not only immoral, but also criminal, and presumed that the BSA shared that understanding. He held that the LAD was not applicable because the "BSA was not a 'place of public accommodation,' or alternatively, that it was exempt under the 'distinctly private' exception in the statute." Since the court believed that the BSA's moral position regarding homosexuality was clear, it found that it had a right of expressive association and could protect that right by refusing to allow Dale to continue as an adult leader (*Dale NJ,* pp. 580–583).

The New Jersey Superior Court, Appellate Division, however, reversed the trial judge's ruling. It held that the BSA was indeed a place of public accommodation, and that revoking Dale's membership solely because of his sexual orientation constituted a LAD violation. Addressing the public-private distinction, the appeals court held that the BSA was a public accom-

modation because of its large size, its lack of selectivity in membership policies and procedures, its openness to and reliance on participation by the general public, its advertising and public promotions, and its sponsorship of
activities and recruitment in public schools and other public forums (*Dale
NJ*, pp. 581–582).

In a unanimous decision, the New Jersey Supreme Court agreed, holding
that LAD imposed on the BSA the duty not to discriminate against Dale because of his sexual orientation, and that to reinstate Dale would not violate
the BSA's right of expressive association. The court also noted the policy of
inclusiveness in the BSA's membership recruitment, its emphasis on individual choice in morality and religion, and its failure to articulate a position on
homosexuality that would place such behavior outside of its emphasis on tolerance and diversity:

> The LAD . . . does not have a significant impact on Boy Scout members'
> ability to associate with one another in pursuit of shared views. . . . Boy
> Scout members do not associate for the purpose of disseminating the belief
> that homosexuality is immoral; Boy Scouts discourages its leaders from dis-
> seminating any views on sexual issues; and Boy Scouts includes sponsors and
> members who subscribe to different views in respect of homosexuality. (*Dale
> NJ*, 612)

The court noted that the BSA's litigation argument "appears antithetical to
the organization's goals and philosophy. . . . We are satisfied that Boy Scouts'
expulsion of Dale is based on little more than prejudice, and not on a unified
Boy Scout position; in other words, Dale's expulsion is not justified by the
need to preserve the organization's expressive rights" (*Dale NJ*, p. 618).

In a strongly worded concurrence, Justice Alan Handler focused on the
"significance of the connection between the individual's speech and his identity when both relate to his sexual orientation" (*Dale NJ*, p. 625). There is a
difference between an individual's identity as a homosexual and his conduct,
and there is, Handler wrote, a distinction between self-identifying speech
and the realization of identity. To merely identify oneself as a homosexual is
not action; indeed, as with religion, homosexuality is an attribute that is
often unknown unless and until the individual self-identifies. "Dale's statement of his identity does not express a view about homosexuality generally
or specifically advocate that homosexuality is moral" (*Dale NJ*, pp. 642–643).
The Boy Scouts' position that gay status is tantamount to gay action,
Handler argues, is tenable only by reliance on outmoded stereotypes of
homosexuality as immoral and deviant. Stereotypes based on sexual orientation, like those based on race or sex, are "false and unfounded, and reveal

nothing about that individual's moral character, or any other aspect of his or her personality" (*Dale NJ*, p. 651).

The Context of Cultural Change

Supreme Court decisions are not delivered by constitutional storks, and they are not made in a vacuum. As Dale's case approached the Supreme Court, changing public attitudes about the acceptability of homosexuality, and indeed some changing attitudes on the Supreme Court, provided new context. In a major decision on homosexual rights, *Bowers v. Hardwick* (478 U.S. 186 [1986]), the Court, in a 5–4 decision, held that the constitutional right to privacy should not be extended to acts of adult consensual homosexual sodomy performed at home. At that time, twenty-four states and the District of Columbia had laws criminalizing sodomy, although they were rarely enforced.[2]

Notwithstanding the *Bowers* decision, and perhaps because of it, public acceptance of homosexuality continues to grow. Today only thirteen states still have antisodomy laws.[3] Twelve states and many municipalities have enacted or expanded antidiscrimination laws to protect sexual orientation in public accommodation. The Gallup polling organization has consistently surveyed public attitudes on whether homosexuality should be legal, and whether it is an acceptable alternative lifestyle. Through the 1980s, about one-third of the public answered affirmatively. The numbers began to climb in the 1990s, however; and in the most recent polls for 1999, 2000, and 2002, more than 50 percent of Americans accepted consensual homosexual relations between adults. And more than two-thirds responded positively to questions about whether homosexuals should have equal employment rights (Newport, 2002).

The Supreme Court itself has already veered away from the *Bowers* decision, holding in *Romer v. Evans* (1995) that a Colorado constitutional amendment prohibiting municipal gay rights ordinances was unconstitutional. Strangely, the Court made no reference to *Bowers* in its opinion, holding instead that the referendum revealed an "animus" toward gays that was prohibited by the equal protection clause of the Fourteenth Amendment. It is true that, technically speaking, *Bowers* was a right to privacy decision, and *Romer* was based on the equal protection clause. But in social and political context they are essentially incompatible with each other. Clearly the Court was responding to, or sharing, the public's growing sentiments of tolerance.[4]

In 1995 the Court had also decided another gay rights case, but did so in a way that subordinated the homosexuality issue to other constitutional concerns. The issue in *Hurley v. Irish-American Gay, Lesbian and Bisexual Group of Boston* (515 U.S. 557), was whether the sponsors of the annual St. Patrick's Day parade in Boston, a private group, could prohibit the display of banners identifying the marchers carrying them as Irish gay men, lesbians, and bisexuals. The decision, a harbinger of the result in the *Boy Scouts* case, was that to require the parade organizers to permit these banners violated *their* First Amendment right to free speech. In a unanimous opinion, Justice David Souter wrote that a parade is an instance of speech, a communicative event, and not a public accommodation to which a denial of access constituted an act of discrimination. One of the central questions in *Boy Scouts* was whether the denial of membership in the Scouts was also protected speech and association, or whether, unlike *Hurley,* it was less that than a matter of discrimination. Although the Court's holding in *Boy Scouts* would place the majority's rationale close to the unanimous *Hurley* decision, only five of the justices believed the two cases were similar. Justice Souter, the author of the unanimous opinion in *Hurley,* was a dissenter in *Boy Scouts.*

James Dale Goes to the Marble Palace

Dale's case was already well known as it wended its way up to the Supreme Court. Popular sentiment was distinctly divided. Dale's supporters cited other youth organizations with explicit nondiscrimination policies, such as the Girl Scouts, Boys and Girls Clubs, 4-H, and Camp Fire USA, as examples the Boy Scouts could follow. Religious organizations were divided. The National Catholic Committee on Scouting, the General Commission on United Methodist Men (which oversees Scouting in the United Methodist church), the Mormons, and other religious groups, filed an amicus brief on behalf of the BSA. They argued that homosexuality was inconsistent with their religious principles and would compromise their involvement in Scouting. They claimed that the New Jersey Supreme Court decision, if upheld, had the potential to "fracture the Scouting movement." The Mormons said they would leave the BSA if the Court decided in Dale's favor (National Catholic Committee on Scouting, et al., p. 25). Conversely, the General Board of Church and Society of the United Methodist Church, the Religious Action Center of Reform Judaism, and the Unitarian Universalist Association, among others, argued that to permit the BSA to exclude homosexuals nationally would betray the BSA's nonsectarian and diversity policies.

The Supreme Court granted certiorari. Oral argument was held on April 28, 2000, and the decision was handed down just two months later. Dividing along familiar lines, the Court held, 5–4, that the forced inclusion of homosexuals as BSA members would significantly alter the Boy Scouts' message, and therefore impair their First Amendment right of "protected association."

Chief Justice William Rehnquist wrote for the majority; Justices John Paul Stevens and David Souter authored dissents, joined by Justices Ruth Ginsburg and Stephen Breyer.

The majority accepted the Boy Scouts' assertion that it is a private and not-for-profit association, and that it "teaches that homosexual conduct is not morally straight," and therefore that it is at odds with the Boy Scout oath. The Court found it indisputable that an organization in which "scoutmasters and assistant scoutmasters inculcate [boys] with the Boy Scouts' values" was engaged in expressive association. Ignoring evidence in the written record that the Scouts' opposition to homosexuality was internally inconsistent, the Court deferred to the BSA's professed characterization of its official stand (*Boy Scouts*, p. 651). It relied instead on various executive committee communications, and on the BSA's stance in previous litigation, most notably the *Curran* case decided in 1998 by the California Supreme Court (17 Cal. 4th 670; 952 P.2d 218).

The fact that the BSA may have been internally inconsistent on this matter, or that it was not formed *for the purpose* of opposing homosexuality, did not undermine its constitutional claim. The Court did not formally take issue with the New Jersey decision that the BSA was "a place of public accommodation," but merely concluded that the state's interests, embodied in its public accommodations law, "did not justify such a severe intrusion." The Court noted, pointedly, that of the four state courts and one federal court that had considered whether the BSA was a public accommodation, only New Jersey had determined that the BSA qualified as such. The Court further noted, somewhat disapprovingly, that as the term "public accommodation" expands in meaning and coverage (the LAD listed more than fifty examples of "public accommodations"), it increasingly threatens First Amendment values: "As the definition of 'public accommodation' has expanded from clearly commercial entities, such as restaurants, bars, and hotels, to membership organizations such as the Boy Scouts, the potential for conflict between state public accommodation laws and the First Amendment has increased" (*Boy Scouts*, p. 657).

Each side sought support from the *Hurley* case. The majority supported the BSA's right not to be compelled to send a message they did not want to send. To them, Dale's presence, "as an avowed homosexual and gay rights advocate in an assistant scoutmaster's uniform," would send a symbolic message at variance with BSA values. And it rejected Dale's argument that his dismissal was inconsistent with the BSA keeping other adult members who, though heterosexual, had publicly disagreed with the Scouts' policy. The BSA, the Court said, has a "right to choose to send one message and not the other" (*Boy Scouts*, p. 656). Thus, for the majority, there was little difference, in constitutional terms, between a public parade and a denial of individual membership.

The dissenters, however, like the New Jersey Supreme Court, noted such a distinction. The New Jersey Court had distinguished between sexual *orientation* and sexual *conduct*. This distinction, they argued, makes the *Hurley* example inapposite. The parade's exclusion was one of message, not orientation; there was, in fact, no effort to exclude homosexuals from marching in approved parade units: "Dale's status as a scout leader is not equivalent to marching in a parade. . . . [He] does not come to Boy Scout meetings 'carrying a banner'" (*Dale NJ*, p. 623). There was also no evidence that Dale had used his leadership position to proselytize, or even to contest Scout policies. According to Justice Stevens in dissent, Dale's mere membership could not be construed as Boy Scouts' own speech, unless one concludes that "homosexuals are simply so different from the rest of society that their presence alone . . . should be singled out for special First Amendment treatment" (*Boy Scouts*, p. 696).

Perhaps the most difficult challenge for the majority was to distinguish *Boy Scouts* from the *Roberts* and *Rotary* precedents. Among the justices sitting in the *Roberts* and *Rotary* cases, only Chief Justice Rehnquist, and Justices Stevens, Sandra Day O'Connor, and Antonin Scalia remained on the Court. In *Roberts*, Rehnquist had concurred in the judgment of the Court, but not the majority opinion (although three years later he did join the majority in *Rotary*). Scalia, likewise, concurred in the judgment in *Rotary* without joining the Court's opinion. In *Roberts*, O'Connor concurred in the judgment, but in a concurring opinion disagreed with the majority's rationale for determining whether violations of expressive association had occurred. "Whether an association is or is not constitutionally protected in the selection of its membership should not depend on what the association says or why its members say it," O'Connor wrote (*Roberts*, p. 633). Instead, she proposed that the determination be made whether a group is primarily or exclusively engaged in protected, as opposed to commercial, expression. One of the examples of possible expressive association that O'Connor used was the BSA: "Even the training of outdoor survival skills or participation in community service might become expressive when the activity is intended to develop good morals, reverence, patriotism, and a desire for self-improvement" (*Roberts*, p. 636). To the extent that the majority justices in *Boy Scouts* did not examine the connection between BSA membership and its message, they seemed to have actually moved closer to O'Connor's suggested rationale of "implicit expression."

The majority in *Boy Scouts* thus rejected *Roberts* and *Rotary* as controlling precedents. To be sure, both of those cases had involved discrimination against women, rather than sexual orientation. But this was not a tenable distinction under First Amendment law, whatever the distinction that might have been drawn if these were equal protection cases.[5] The majority, however, held that the key to those earlier decisions was that the enforcement of those statutes "did not materially interfere with the ideas that the organization sought to express."

In *Rotary,* for example, the Court wrote that "the evidence fails to demonstrate that admitting women to Rotary Clubs will affect in any significant way the existing members' ability to carry out their various purposes" (*Rotary,* p. 548). The majority opinion in *Dale,* however, accepts the *Roberts/Rotary* conclusion, without any new evidence, that membership policies favoring women have no significant effect on protected associational values, while membership policies affecting homosexuals necessarily have a destructive effect. In *Roberts/Rotary,* the Court sided with local chapters seeking to depart from discriminatory national organizational policies; in *Boy Scouts,* however, there is no evidence that the local troop or council sided with Dale, although it is unlikely that troop-level support would have swayed either the BSA's National Council or the Supreme Court majority.

Aftermath

Legal victories do not necessarily bring about change or settle political conflicts. It is almost axiomatic that courts—even the Supreme Court— don't always have the last word. Sometimes decisions have the unintended effect by engendering complacency in the victors and energizing the opposition. In the aftermath of the Supreme Court's decision in *Boy Scouts,* the BSA has been subject to increasing and substantial grassroots opposition—both from within and outside its ranks. There are continuing efforts to change the BSA's exclusionary policies through petitions, protests, legislative measures, and withdrawals of organizational and monetary support. Public reaction has not been so negative; many communities have increased their support for Scouting. The national debate over homosexuals' exclusion from Scouting reveals that the nation, very much like the Supreme Court itself, is divided. A review of reactions to the decision reveals the complex cluster of issues that is involved in this clash of important constitutional rights.

SCHOOLS AND OTHER PUBLIC FACILITIES

Spearheaded by Lambda Legal, one attempt to pressure the BSA to change its policy has been to end preferential relationships between BSA units and government entities in jurisdictions that prohibit sexual orientation discrimination. Unlike many other youth groups, Boy Scout units require a sponsor or chartering organization; most of these are private businesses and organizations. In some cases, however, units are sponsored directly by public schools, police precincts, or other governmental entities. The BSA's critics have sought to terminate these sponsorships and the preferential access to public facilities that is often involved. They are not seeking to bar Scout troops altogether, but to require them to abide by the same fee and procedural requirements that other community organizations must meet. Tucson, Chicago, San Diego, San Francisco, and San Jose have, in response to these efforts, ended free use of public parks and schools (France, et al., 2001). These efforts have also resulted in litigation challenging the new policies in San Diego and San Francisco (Egelko, 2002; Taylor, 2003). A change of policy has also been debated in the New York City and Miami area school districts (France, et al., 2001).

PUBLIC OPINION

A Pew poll conducted in July 2000 found that 56 percent of Americans agreed with the *Boy Scouts* decision, and a June 2000 Gallup poll found that 64 percent of the respondents believed that the BSA "should not be required to allow openly gay adults to serve as leaders" (Newport, 2002). Asking more generally about the same issue, however, a *Los Angeles Times* poll came up with different results. Asked to agree or disagree with the statement, "A Boy Scout leader should be removed from his duties as a troop leader if he is found out to be gay, even if he is considered by the Scout organization to be a model Boy Scout leader," 36 percent of those interviewed agreed, while 54 percent disagreed (Newport, 2002). *Newsweek* reported that the BSA's own internal polling showed that 30 percent of Scout parents don't support the current policy of excluding homosexuals from membership (France, et al., 2001).

MEMBERSHIP

Membership in both the Cub Scouts and Boy Scouts has been decreasing, although this decline had begun before the *Boy Scouts* decision. Using totals from the BSA's own website, we estimate that Cub Scout membership has declined 6 percent since 1999, and Boy Scout membership has declined 2 percent. There is some regional variation, with the greatest declines in the Northeast and on the West Coast (France, et al., 2001). We are not able to relate this downward trend in membership to the Court's decision or the exclusion debate. The BSA attributes some of the decline in membership to poorly timed recruitment drives in September 2001 and notes that the decrease in membership is consistent with overall membership trends. BSA members who disagree with the exclusionary policy seem divided on whether to withdraw from Scouting or to remain and work for change from within (Cohen, 2000; France, et al., 2001).

To the extent that members choose the latter, they represent Scouting's most difficult public relations problem. In response to the *Curran* and *Boy Scouts* cases, for example, California Boy Scout Scott Cozza, his father, and Dave Rice, another longtime Scouting adult volunteer, founded "Scouting for All." This organization has collected more than 75,000 signatures so far on a petition to end BSA discrimination against homosexuals. It uses Scouting's own professed values—tolerance, justice, and citizenship—in calling for change. The BSA's response was to revoke Rice's membership. Scott Cozza was the subject of the PBS documentary, "Scout's Honor," which won awards at the 2001 Sundance Festival. It appears that he and his father have started their own Scout troop, which will model openness and tolerance as a Boy Scout policy. Scouting for All's website implies that this troop has been chartered, although troops in other areas that have indicated that they will not abide by national policy have had their charters revoked ("Scout's Honor" 2001).

BOY SCOUTS AND GIRL SCOUTS

A comparison is inevitable. Membership in the Girl Scouts is increasing, reaching a recent high of 2.8 million members. Changes in the Girl Scouts program have de-emphasized traditional stereotypes such as "cooking, cleaning, and cookies" in favor of more rugged adventures and travel, and gender-neutral skills (Foderaro, 2002).

The Girl Scouts' national policies allow more flexibility in its members' beliefs on sexual orientation and religion, thus enabling them to avoid the problem raised in the *Boy Scouts* case. Lesbians are not prohibited from being members or becoming leaders in the Girl Scouts. The only policy is that *no* member or leader may promote a particular sexual orientation, or display any sexual behavior (Foderaro, 2002).

The Girl Scouts are also more flexible with regard to religion. When reciting the Girl Scout promise, another word can be substituted for God. An atheist who was not comfortable reciting the promise would not be met with an inquisition into her beliefs. This openness policy, however, is not perfectly inclusive of homosexuals and atheists. The GSA allows each of its 317 local councils some discretion in membership policy, and a few councils *have* included heterosexuality as a requirement for their adult leaders (Tyre, 2001).

MONEY

Forty-four of the most affluent chapters of the United Way have withdrawn or modified their BSA contribution policies. A few have augmented their funding (France, et al., 2001). The *Chronicle of Philanthropy* surveyed the nation's 400 largest United Way chapters and reported that twenty-five have dropped the Boy Scouts from their rosters of member agencies; an equal number have taken steps to assure future allocations to the Boy Scouts (Williams, 2001). During oral argument in the Supreme Court, the BSA's attorney said that "the Scouts have said many times that their policies are not for sale . . . if it costs sponsorship . . . so be it." The evidence so far suggests that while the BSA may have to make some strategic funding reallocation decisions, it has not suffered a catastrophic dollar drain. Some regional councils, however, have been hit especially hard by the antidiscrimination backlash.

JAMES DALE

Today, James Dale lives in New York City and is the vice president of a health-care publishing company. He continues to speak to organizations nationwide about the gay civil rights movement and the controversy generated by his case (Keppler Associates, 2003).

Constitutional and Social Implications

It is unlikely that *Boy Scouts* will be the last word on the subject, but, assuming no major ideological shifts in the composition of the Supreme Court, it will probably govern the disposition of similar disputes in the short term. Where to draw the line between protecting expressive association and prohibiting discrimination, and how to enforce it, remain enduring problems. Each of these constitutional concepts remains a safe harbor for certain sets of interests, and there is no agreed principle as to which should prevail in every case, or what compromises can be struck. Thus, at least in the immediate future, contests of this kind will be determined as much by principle as by situational perceptions and subjective ascriptions.

In today's America, it is much easier (though less than it used to be) to discriminate on the basis of sexual orientation than by gender or race, which are, themselves, treated under different constitutional understandings. We have suggested that the Boy Scouts prevailed, while the national Rotary and Jaycees organizations did not, at least in part because of the respective issues in those cases. *Boy Scouts* involved issues of personal association and contact between boys and older men that allegedly posed threats to the boys and the teachings of the BSA. While there is no evidence to warrant this fear, it is nonetheless widely believed.

Admitting women to Rotary Clubs could not be interpreted in the same way. The interpretation of the threat in the *Boy Scouts* case bears an eerie resemblance to the attitudes of white southerners toward racial segregation before the *Brown* case. In a classic 1944 study of race in the American South, Gunnar Myrdal and his colleagues reported that there was an informal "pecking order" of beliefs that determined how southerners responded to integration efforts. Those that involved less-intimate contact, Myrdal reported, such as segregation in transportation or the workplace—though strongly opposed—were nonetheless more acceptable than those, such as integrating public schools, that created the possibility of social and sexual contact between children.

James Dale lost his case, but the litigation nevertheless contributed to changing attitudes on the acceptance of homosexuality. Litigation is not only about victories; it is also about education and symbols and organizational development, and it can be of strategic importance (McCann, 1994). Even losing cases can be part of a social change process. People who had not given much thought to the matter of discrimination against homosexuals took notice. And a large number of BSA members and other concerned citizens failed to discern why sexual orientation should matter so much to the BSA. Dale's attorney, Evan Wolfson, regards the case as a victory even though his client lost, because of its impact on the ever-more-public debate about homosexuality. "We lost the case, but we won the cause," he said (Wolfson telephone interview, 2002). The case, he believed, brought a lot of public attention and acceptance to gay youths, and thus further strengthened a cultural shift already in progress. Almost everyone has heard of, and knows something about, the Boy Scouts. They are a pervasive presence in our national popular culture, and their central role brought not only this case but the issues of fairness and tolerance to new levels of visibility.

NOTES

1. In both *Roberts* and *Rotary,* the BSA filed amicus briefs supporting the national organization's membership policies excluding women. This indicates that the BSA was concerned about the precedential effect of these cases on its own ability to restrict or define its membership. The amicus participation is an early indication that the BSA had thought about these policies before the *Dale* case. Indeed, at the time *Roberts* and *Rotary* were before the Supreme Court, the BSA was involved in a case in the California state courts that challenged its dismissal of Tim Curran, an assistant scoutmaster and gay man.

2. Bowers was not the first decision on "homosexual rights." In *Boutilier v. Immigration Service* (387 U.S. 118 [1967]), the Court upheld the denial of immigration rights

to homosexuals on the grounds that homosexuality was among the "psychopathic" disorders Congress included in the immigration laws. The Court had also upheld the denial of security clearances in federal employment to gays, as well as termination from federal employment on the basis of their gay status (*Carlucci v. Doe,* 488 U.S. 93 [1988]).

3. Four of those states punish only homosexual sodomy; the others do not distinguish between homosexual and heterosexual sodomy.

4. In June 2003, after this essay was written, the Supreme Court took a major step to further this growing tolerance. In *Lawrence v. Texas* (123 S. Ct. 2572 [2003]), it held the remaining state antisodomy laws unconstitutional and took the further step of formally overturning *Bowers.*

5. In the *Lawrence* case, cited in note 4, the primary rationale used in Justice Kennedy's majority opinion for overturning the challenged state sodomy laws was the protection of privacy, although in a concurring opinion, Justice O'Connor suggested an equal protection analysis holding that sexual orientation discrimination is a form of prohibited sex discrimination.

REFERENCES

The Boy Scouts. (2001). First broadcast April 1, 2001, by CBS on television series *60 Minutes.*

Cohen, R. Demerit badge. (2000, July 23). *New York Times Magazine,* p. 19.

Coyle, M. (2003, March 24). Gay rights are at the center of the sodomy case at the Supreme Court. *National Law Journal,* p. A1.

Egelko, B. (2002, November 26). Court of appeal rules against Berkeley Sea Scouts. *San Francisco Chronicle,* p. A18.

Foderaro, L. W. (2002, December 25). Beyond crafts and cookies, Girl Scouts are prospering. *New York Times,* p. A1.

France, D, et al. (2001, August 6). Scouts divided. *Newsweek,* pp. 44–51.

General Board of Church and Society of the United Methodist Church, et al. (2002). Amicus curiae brief to the U.S. Supreme Court in *Boy Scouts v. Dale.* Available as of November 20, 2002, at the Findlaw Supreme Court Center website at http://supreme .lp.findlaw.com/supreme_court/docket/aprdocket.html#99-699.

Keppler Associates. (2003). James Dale. Available as of May 1, 2003 at http://www .kepplerassociates.com/speakers/dalejames.asp?2.

Lambda Legal. (2002). About Lambda Legal. Accessed on October 28, 2002, at http:// www.lambdalegal.org/cgi-bin/iowa/about.

McCann, M. W. (1994). *Rights at work: Pay equity reform and the politics of legal mobilization.* Chicago: University of Chicago Press.

McGowan, D. (2001, Spring). Making sense of Dale. *Constitutional Commentary, 18,* p. 121–175.

Mechling, J. (2001). *On my honor: Boy Scouts and the making of American youth.* Chicago: University of Chicago Press.

Myrdal, Gunnar. (1944). *An American dilemma: The Negro problem and modern democracy.* New York: Harper & Brothers.

National Catholic Committee on Scouting, et al. (2002). Amicus curiae brief to the U.S. Supreme Court in *Boy Scouts v. Dale.* Available as of November 20, 2002, at the Findlaw Supreme Court Center website at http://supreme.lp.findlaw.com/supreme_court/ docket/aprdocket.html#99-699.

Newport, F. (2002, September). In-depth analyses: Homosexuality. The Gallup Organization.

Scouting for All. (2002). About Us. Available as of November 20, 2002, at http://www .scoutingforall.org.

Shepard, T. (Director). (2001). Scout's honor (short shown on *60 Minutes*). Hohokus, NJ: New Day Films.

Taylor, M. (2003, March 11). Judge says decision near on ACLU's Scouts lease lawsuit. *San Diego Union-Tribune,* p. B3.

Tyre, P. (2001, August 6). Where the girls are. *Newsweek,* p. 51.

Williams, G. (2001, April 19). Divided in support of Scouts. *Chronicle of Philanthropy,* pp. 1, 31, 34.

Wolfson, E. (2002, December 12). Telephone interview with authors.

Freedom of the Press

National Security vs. Freedom of the Press

New York Times v. United States (1971)

JOHN ANTHONY MALTESE

> Can the government ever censor the press? During the era of the Vietnam War, the federal government sought to do just that. The *New York Times* and the *Washington Post* began publishing excerpts from a top-secret Defense Department document known as the "Pentagon Papers." The papers invoked the First Amendment's guarantee of freedom of the press. The United States invoked its inherent power to protect national security. In one of the Court's most famous and deeply resonant opinions of the twentieth century, the justices weighed compelling arguments for the constitutional exercise of government power against equally compelling claims to individual rights found in the Bill of Rights and the Fourteenth Amendment.

On Monday, June 14, 1971, William Rehnquist went back to work at the Justice Department for the first time since his recent back surgery. At the age of forty-six, he was assistant attorney general for the Office of Legal Counsel—a post he had held since 1969. Just over four months later President Richard Nixon would nominate him to be an associate justice on the United States

Supreme Court. That Monday, Attorney General John Mitchell asked Rehnquist to research the law on prior restraints. Mitchell and Robert Mardian, assistant attorney general in charge of the Internal Security Division of the Justice Department, were considering an injunction against the *New York Times* to cease publication of future installments in its planned series of articles on the so-called "Pentagon Papers"—a massive forty-seven-volume, 7,000-page top-secret Pentagon study about U.S. involvement in the Vietnam War.

President Lyndon Johnson's secretary of defense, Robert McNamara, had commissioned the study in June 1967 (without Johnson's knowledge) to trace the history of U.S. involvement in Vietnam. McNamara had become increasingly disillusioned with U.S. policy in Vietnam. By 1967 he believed the war was unwinnable and that the United States should seek a negotiated settlement rather than escalate the conflict. That view was out of step with the one held by President Johnson and his other top advisers. Although his precise motivations are unclear, McNamara appears to have believed that the "Pentagon Papers" could be used to bolster his argument that government policy in Vietnam had been misguided and to convince Johnson to change U.S. policy (Rudenstine, 1996, pp. 18–23).

Some 4,000 pages of the "Pentagon Papers," officially entitled "History of U.S. Decision Making Process on Vietnam Policy," consisted of copies of classified documents from such sources as the White House, the State Department, the Defense Department, the Joint Chiefs of Staff, and the CIA. The remaining 3,000 pages were a historical analysis and summary of U.S. policy based on classified government documents. Daniel Ellsberg, who had helped to prepare the "Pentagon Papers" (and who had come to oppose U.S. involvement in the Vietnam War) leaked all but the most sensitive final four volumes to *New York Times* reporter Neil Sheehan in March 1971. The *Times* had published its first installment in the series as a front-page article by Sheehan on Sunday, June 13.

Publication of the first *New York Times* article caught President Nixon and his administration by surprise. No one within the administration knew that the *Times* possessed the "Pentagon Papers," nor did Nixon even know of the study's existence until the *Times* broke the story. The president was preoccupied that weekend with the White House wedding of his daughter Tricia on Saturday. Aides to Secretary of Defense Melvin Laird learned about the story during the wedding reception on Saturday from the *Times* news wire. They immediately informed both Laird and Alexander Haig, assistant to National Security Adviser Henry Kissinger. Laird, Haig, and Kissinger were among the few in the Nixon administration who knew that the "Pentagon

Papers" existed. Leslie Gelb—a former student of Kissinger's at Harvard who led the staff of thirty-six that assembled the "Pentagon Papers" in the 1960s—had approached both Kissinger and Haig about helping to prepare the study. Both declined to participate, but Gelb gave Kissinger access to some parts of the study during the Johnson administration, and Kissinger later obtained a copy of the entire study and kept it in his White House safe when he went to work for the Nixon administration. Kissinger and Haig both immediately suspected that Ellsberg, whom they both knew, had leaked the papers (Rudenstine, 1996, pp. 68–70).

From all indications, Nixon's first reaction to the publication was not one of great alarm. Nixon met with his chief of staff, H. R. "Bob" Haldeman, at 10:00 A.M. in the Oval Office on Sunday—the day the *Times* published its first installment. Haldeman's notes show Nixon saying that it was "criminally traitorous" for someone to turn over the documents to the *New York Times,* but that the White House should "keep clear of the *Times*'s series." Emphasizing again in his notes that the "key is for us to *keep out of it,*" Haldeman quoted Nixon as saying that the publication "doesn't hurt us" (quoted in Rudenstine, 1996, p. 71). All of the documents contained in the "Pentagon Papers" preceded the Nixon administration. If anything, they made Presidents Kennedy and Johnson look bad. Haig emphasized that point to Nixon when he spoke with him on the phone at 12:18 P.M.: "It's a tough attack on Kennedy," Haig told him, "It shows that the genesis of the war really occurred during '61, and it's brutal on Johnson" (June 13, 1971, 12:18 P.M.).[1]

Conventional wisdom has long been that Kissinger goaded Nixon into changing his view that the White House should keep out of the "Pentagon Papers" dispute during a telephone conversation at 3:00 P.M. on Sunday (e.g., Rudenstine, 1996, chapter 4). The release of the tape of that conversation in 1999, however, refutes that view. Nixon told Kissinger that Haig was very disturbed by the publication and agreed that both the leak and the publication were "unconscionable." Kissinger said that he was certain that the leak of the papers violated security laws. "It's treasonable, there's no question—it's actionable," he told the president, but their concern seemed to be centered on the person who leaked the documents. As Nixon told Kissinger: "I think you should call [Attorney General] Mitchell and ask him about his just calling this—getting this fellow in, on the purpose of this was a national security leak, and we want to know what does he have, and did he do it, and put him under oath." Kissinger agrees with Nixon's statement to Haldeman that morning that the publication "doesn't hurt us." As Kissinger tells Nixon: "In public opinion, it actually, if anything, will help us a little bit, because this is a gold mine of showing how the previous administration got us in there [into the war]. . . . It just shows massive mismanagement of how we got there, and it [unclear] pins it all on Kennedy and Johnson. . . . This in an indictment of the previous administration. . . . They have nothing from this administration, so actually—I've read this stuff—we are, we come out pretty well in it" (June 13, 1971, 3:09 P.M.).

Attorney General Mitchell had learned about the *Times* article late Saturday night from Secretary of Defense Laird. He, too, seemed unalarmed by the publication. He took no action on Sunday to learn more about the "Pentagon Papers," nor did he investigate what action the government could take against the *Times* for its publication. Not until Assistant Attorney General Mardian became involved on Monday morning did the issue of injunction against the *Times* become an important issue. Mardian was a hard-liner in the Justice Department. As David Rudenstine has written, Mardian "was a controversial figure inside and outside the administration. He was excitable and coarse (even Bob Haldeman, whose abrasiveness was legendary, found Mardian difficult) to the point that he was tagged with the nickname 'crazy Bob.' His aggressive investigation and prosecution of left-wing political activists and antiwar demonstrators earned him a reputation for disregarding civil liberties and civil rights" (Rudenstine, 1996, p. 78). But Mardian had the ear of Mitchell, and he convinced Mitchell that there needed to be a thorough Justice Department review of legal and national security consequences of the *Times* article. Mitchell instructed Mardian to lead the review. So it was, that Rehnquist found himself investigating the law on prior restraint.

Rehnquist focused most of his attention on the 1931 Supreme Court decision in *Near v. Minnesota* (283 U.S. 697). By a 5–4 vote in that case, the Court struck down a 1925 law passed by the Minnesota legislature that allowed prior restraint. Under the law, a judge could enjoin future publication of any material deemed "malicious, scandalous, and defamatory." In his opinion for the Court, Chief Justice Charles Evans Hughes concluded that the "chief purpose" of the First Amendment to the U.S. Constitution had been "to prevent previous restraints on publication." This interpretation followed English common law. In his famous *Commentaries on the Laws of England* (1765–69), the British legal scholar, Sir William Blackstone, wrote that liberty of the press "consists in laying no previous restraints upon publication." Until 1694, Parliament had required government licensing of all publications. Prior official approval of publications meant that the government could control the content of the material the public read. This provoked great opposition in England, including John Milton's famous *Areopagitica—A Speech for the Liberty of Unlicensed Printing* (1644). Parliament chose not to renew the licensing system in 1694, and the principle of no prior restraint subsequently became an accepted part of English common law.

Still, Hughes did not believe that the ban on prior restraint was absolute. This is what Rehnquist focused on. As Hughes wrote, "the protection even as to previous restraint is not absolutely unlimited. But the limitation has been recognized only in exceptional cases." Hughes than proceeded to give some examples of such cases. These included troop movements during wartime and obscene publications. Despite the categorical nature of the First Amendment—"Congress shall make no law . . . abridging the freedom of . . . the press"—Hughes did not believe that it prevented Congress from passing libel laws that punished publication after the fact. On this issue, Hughes seemed to be in accord with the views of the Framers of the First Amendment. As Thomas Jefferson put it in a letter to James Madison on July 31, 1788, "A declaration that the federal government will never restrain the presses from printing anything they please, will not take away the liability of the printers for false facts printed" (quoted in Levy, 1988, p. 200).

In short, Hughes's opinion in *Near v. Minnesota* suggested that national security could trump the presumption against prior restraint (making it possible for the government to seek an injunction against future publication of the "Pentagon Papers"), and that the government might also be able to punish the *New York Times* for its publication after the fact. If it chose to do the latter, however, the Justice Department felt that it had to give the *Times* fair warning—notify it before publication of future installments that it might be violating federal law by publishing the contents of classified documents.

John Ehrlichman, the president's chief domestic affairs adviser, informed Nixon of this in a phone conversation at 7:13 P.M. on Monday, saying that Mitchell had been "advised by his people that unless he puts the *Times* on notice, he's probably going to waive any right of prosecution against the newspaper." Nixon seemed surprised: "You mean prosecute the *Times?*" "Right," Ehrlichman replied. Nixon still thought that the administration should not interfere with the publication. "Hell, I wouldn't prosecute the *Times,*" he said. "My view is to prosecute the goddamn pricks that gave it to them." But Ehrlichman pointed out that failure to put the *Times* on notice might prevent the government from bringing any action against the newspaper, adding, "I'd hate to waive something as good as that," and suggesting that Nixon call Mitchell (June 14, 1971, 7:13 P.M.).

Nixon called Mitchell as soon as he finished speaking with Ehrlichman. The two never discussed an injunction to stop publication. Instead, the emphasis was on giving the paper fair notice that they might be violating federal law and requesting that they refrain from publication. Nixon still seemed hesitant. "Has this ever been done before?" he asked. "Has the government ever done this to a paper before?" Mitchell was reassuring: "Oh yes—advising them of their—yes, we done this before."

> NIXON: Have we? Alright.
>
> MITCHELL: Yes sir. I would think that—
>
> NIXON: How do you go about it? You do it sort of low key?
>
> MITCHELL: Low key. You call them, and then, uh, send a telegram to confirm it.
>
> NIXON: Uh-huh, uh-huh—say that we're just—uh, we're examining the situation, and we just simply are putting you on notice.
>
> MITCHELL: [unclear] we're putting them on notice that they're violating a statute, because we have a communication from Mel Laird as to the nature of the documents, and they fall within a statute (June 14, 1971, 7:19 P.M.).

Ironically, the decision to seek an injunction to stop publication of the "Pentagon Papers" seems to have occurred almost by chance. At no time in either his conversation with Ehrlichman or Mitchell did the president ever authorize an injunction. An injunction was not even discussed. As Daniel Ellsberg wrote in his recent memoir: "Not once during the first three days of publication, in any of the transcripts available, did the president or any White House aide, including Kissinger, show any interest in stopping publication by injunction; the impetus for this seems to have come exclusively from Mitchell and the Justice Department" (Ellsberg, 2002, p. 424). The fact that Mitchell and Mardian instructed Rehnquist to investigate the law on prior restraint showed that they had considered an injunction before Mitchell spoke with Nixon. And once Mitchell put the *Times* on notice that they might be violating federal law by continuing to publish the documents, an injunction became a logical next step.

In fact, one could argue that there were national security grounds for seeking an injunction. Publication of the classified documents came less than four weeks before Kissinger's highly sensitive secret trip to China that would eventually lead to a breakthrough in relations with that country and culminate in Nixon's historic summit meeting there the next year. Kissinger was also engaged in secret peace talks with the North Vietnamese in Paris. It was not unreasonable to fear that publication of secret U.S. documents—even old ones—would raise doubts among such countries about the ability of the U.S. government to assure secrecy in its negotiations, thereby damaging sensitive relationships and threatening the success of the talks. Publication of classified documents might more directly undermine national security by revealing government secrets, sources, and strategies. Complacency in the face of such a massive leak of government documents might precipitate still more leaks. Publication of the "Pentagon Papers" might also fuel the growing antiwar movement, put more pressure on the U.S. government to unilaterally withdraw from Vietnam, and thereby undermine the president's efforts to achieve a negotiated peace settlement. Indeed, when the *New York Times* had sought legal counsel from the law firm Lord, Day, and Lord before publishing their first installment of the "Pentagon Papers," their advice was clear: do not publish. Herbert Brownell, the *Times*'s lawyer at the firm (who had previously served as attorney general under President Dwight Eisenhower), was particularly blunt. He said publication was prohibited by section 793 of the Espionage Act (Salisbury, 1980, p. 171). The *Times* proceeded with publication anyway.

Immediately after speaking with Nixon on Monday, Mitchell sent a telegram to *Times* publisher Arthur Ochs Sulzberger. Mitchell wrote that the excerpts from the "Pentagon Papers" the *Times* had published on June 13 and 14 contained information relating to the national defense and had a "top secret" classification. "As such, publication of this information is directly prohibited by the provisions of the Espionage Law, Title 18, United States Code, Section 793." He said that further publication of such excerpts "will cause irreparable injury to the defense interests of the United States. Accordingly, I respectfully request that you publish no further information of this character and advise me that you have made arrangements for the return of these documents to the Department of Defense" (quoted in Salisbury, 1980, p. 240).

Still, even after Mitchell had gone to court to obtain an injunction, Nixon remained eager to see portions of the "Pentagon Papers" relating to the Kennedy administration published. In an Oval Office meeting with Haldeman and Kissinger on Tuesday, Nixon asked: "The injunction was only to the *Times,* Bob. Right?" He goes on to say: "Stuff on Kennedy I'm gonna leak. We'll just leak it out. . . . Now that it's being leaked, we'll leak out the parts we want" (quoted in Ellsberg, 2002, p. 424).

In addition to sending the telegram, Mitchell called Brownell. The two were old friends who had last seen each other at Tricia Nixon's wedding on Saturday. Mitchell reminded Brownell that, as Eisenhower's attorney general, Brownell had written an executive order that created the classification system Mitchell would rely on if the government decided to sue the *Times*. Mitchell said he would call Brownell as a government witness if the case went to trial. Thus, when the *Times*'s general counsel, James C. Goodale, called Brownell for legal advice after receiving the Mitchell telegram on Monday evening, Brownell said that his firm could not represent the paper. Brownell also expressed "shock" that the *Times* might defy the telegram. But defy it they did. By 9:00 P.M., the *Times* had crafted a response to Mitchell's telegram: "The *Times* must respectfully decline the request of the Attorney General . . ." The managing editor of the *Times*, Abe Rosenthal, had already told the printers to go ahead with the next day's edition, which contained the next installment in the series. When Rosenthal entered the City Room to relay the news, 150 employees were waiting anxiously to hear what would happen next. "Go ahead!" Rosenthal said. The crowd let out a cheer, and the presses began rolling (Salisbury, 1980, pp. 242–246).

By noon the next day, the two sides were in federal court. The *Times* had retained new outside counsel: Yale law professor Alexander Bickel. Michael D. Hess, head of the civil division of the U.S. Attorney's office for the Southern District of New York, represented the government. At the instruction of the Justice Department, Hess was seeking to enjoin further publication of the "Pentagon Papers." Judge Murray Gurfein presided over the case. It was only his second day on the job. Just appointed by President Nixon, he had been sworn in the previous Thursday and started his new job the day before. Nixon and Mitchell were pleased. "We got a good judge on [the case], Murray Gurfein," Mitchell told Nixon that afternoon.

NIXON: Oh yeah! . . . I know him well—smart as hell.
MITCHELL: Yeah, and he's new, and he's appreciative, so—
NIXON: [laughing] Good!
MITCHELL: —we ought to work it out (June 15, 1971, 6:35 P.M.).

Bickel and Hess presented oral arguments in front of Gurfein that afternoon. The task was a daunting one for all sides. Both Bickel and Hess had learned only hours earlier that they would be arguing the case, and Gurfein had to make an immediate decision about whether to stop the next day's installment in the *Times*. None of them could possibly read all 7,000 pages of the "Pentagon Papers" to determine if they really posed a threat to national security, nor did they necessarily have the expertise to make that determination.

Bickel's legal argument for the *Times* was an interesting one. Instead of arguing against the injunction on First Amendment grounds, he relied on a separation of powers argument: the executive branch did not have the power to sue the *New York Times*, because Congress had never authorized such power. Thus, instead of relying on *Near v. Minnesota* and the law on prior restraint, he concentrated on *Youngstown Sheet & Tube Co. v. Sawyer* (343 U.S. 579 [1952]), and the scope of presidential inherent power. In *Youngstown*, a 6–3 majority of the Supreme Court struck down President Harry Truman's seizure of striking steel mills during the Korean War on the grounds that he had exceeded his power. Two of the justices, Hugo Black and William O. Douglas (both whom were still on the Supreme Court in 1971) had argued that presidents have no inherent power. In other words, presidential power is limited to those powers enumerated (or implied by enumerated powers) in the Constitution, and to powers granted to the president by Congress under its constitutional authority. The power to seize the steel mills was authorized neither by the Constitution nor by Congress. The other four members of the majority (none of whom was still on the Court in 1971), were unwilling to say that presidents never have inherent power. Still, all four believed that President Truman had gone against the will of Congress by seizing the steel mills, and had thus exceeded his authority.

Bickel assumed the "Pentagon Papers" case would get to the Supreme Court, and his decision to rely on the separation of powers argument was a strategic one. He did not worry about getting the votes of Black and Douglas—he was confident they would side with the *Times,* but he did worry about how to get the votes of the centrist justices on the Supreme Court. He believed that they would be more responsive to a narrow separation of powers argument than to a broad First Amendment argument. Thus, he pointed out that neither the Constitution nor Congress had explicitly given the executive branch the authority to sue for the injunctive relief it sought. Absent such authorization, the executive branch could not proceed without usurping the power of Congress and violating separation of powers (Rudenstine, 1996, pp. 104–106; see also Gora, 1998).

Judge Gurfein issued a temporary restraining order to bar the *Times* from publishing any more installments in the "Pentagon Papers" for four days and scheduled further arguments for Friday, June 18. Instead of Wednesday morning's installment of the "Pentagon Papers," the *Times* ran a story about Gurfein's ruling. For the first time since the ratification of the Constitution, a federal judge had stopped the presses. As a protest, the *Times* had considered—but rejected—the idea of publishing the Wednesday edition with blank pages where the "Pentagon Papers" would have been. Daniel Ellsberg, who had leaked the papers, was frustrated. He was also angry that Neil Sheehan had published his first installment in the *Times* without warning him, and that since publication Sheehan had not returned his phone calls. Therefore, on Wednesday, Ellsberg called the *Washington Post.* Would they publish the "Pentagon Papers" if he handed them over? The *Post* agreed (Ellsberg, 2002, pp. 384–394). Friday morning—the same day that Gurfein had scheduled his hearing—the *Post* published its first installment of the "Pentagon Papers." The *Times* had spent three months reviewing the papers before deciding to publish. The *Post* had spent one day.

While Gurfein held his hearing in New York, Assistant Attorney General Rehnquist telephoned *Washington Post* executive editor Benjamin Bradlee. Rehnquist requested that the *Post* refrain from further publication and turn its set of the "Pentagon Papers" over to the government. Bradlee refused, and by 5:00 P.M. the administration was in federal court in Washington, D.C., seeking an injunction against the *Post* from Judge Gerhard Gesell, who had been appointed by President Johnson in 1967. Thus, two courtroom dramas were playing themselves out simultaneously in two different cities. While Judge Gurfein in New York was thought to be sympathetic to the government position, Judge Gesell in Washington was not.

In New York, Gurfein held three hearings on Friday: one open to the public in the morning, a closed session that began at 4:30 in the afternoon and lasted for more than four hours, and a final public session that began at 9:50 P.M. Despite the normal presumption of open judicial proceedings, an in camera hearing allowed the government to discuss its national security claims without fear of harmful public revelations. Still, the government was secretive. In part, it was impossible for even the government lawyers to digest fully the contents of the "Pentagon Papers." They had only received a copy two days earlier. But government officials did not help. As U.S. attorney Seymour wrote in his memoirs: "Impossible as it may be to believe, the Defense and State Department representatives simply would not explain to the government lawyers which of the documents in the forty-seven volumes of the Pentagon Papers presented specific risks to national security, although they were absolutely positive that such documents existed" (Seymour, 1975, p. 199).

The Justice Department wanted Seymour to argue that the court should rule in favor of the government simply because the documents the *Times* wanted to publish were properly classified "top secret." Haldeman reiterated this point in his June 15 diary entry: "The real problem is to try to establish clearly that the Administration's interest here in the violation of Top Secret classifications rather than in the release of particular material" (Haldeman, 1994, p. 364). Even government witnesses who testified at the closed hearing were told by the Justice Department not to offer specific references to documents in the study that posed a particular threat to national security (Rudenstine, 1996, p. 154).

While Judge Gurfein presided over the closed hearing in New York, Judge Gesell denied the government's request for a temporary restraining order. Nonetheless, he cautioned that the *Washington Post* stood "in serious jeopardy of criminal prosecution" for printing classified government documents (quoted in Rudenstine, 1996, p. 188). The government immediately appealed

Gesell's decision. In less than two hours, a three-judge appeals panel in Washington was hearing the appeal. At 1:20 A.M. on Saturday, June 19, the panel—by 2–1 vote—reversed Judge Gesell and issued a temporary restraining order. For the second time in less than four days, a federal court had stopped the presses.

The next day, Judge Gurfein in New York issued his ruling: he denied the government's request for an injunction. He rejected the idea that the executive branch lacked inherent power to seek injunctive relief, but he said the government had not met the evidentiary burden during the in camera proceeding. In short, the government had not demonstrated that publication posed a significant enough threat to national security to impose a prior restraint. Although he had been initially sympathetic to the government, its unwillingness to identify specific national security threats within the papers seemed to backfire. Nixon's newly appointed judge had ruled against the administration. It was a significant blow. The government immediately appealed to the U.S. Court of Appeals for the Second Circuit. Appeals court judge Irving Kaufman issued another temporary restraining order until an appeals panel could hear the case.

The government now had to prepare for appeals in both the Second Circuit and the D.C. Circuit. In stark contrast to normal appeals, the cases proceeded with tremendous speed. Both courts heard the appeal during the week of June 21. By then, the leak of the "Pentagon Papers" had extended beyond the *New York Times* and the *Washington Post*. The *Boston Globe* and the *Chicago Sun-Times* published excerpts on Monday, June 21; the *Los Angeles Times* and eleven newspapers in the Knight chain published excerpts on Tuesday; and the *St. Louis Post-Dispatch,* the *Christian Science Monitor,* and *Newsday* all followed suit over the next week. Daniel Ellsberg also arranged for Sen. Mike Gravel (D-AK) to receive a set of the "Pentagon Papers." On June 29 Gravel called a meeting of a Senate subcommittee he chaired and began reading the papers into the record in front of television cameras. He also distributed copies to the Associated Press and to other members of the news media.

In preparing their appeals, lawyers for the *Post* and the *Times* emphasized different legal arguments. The *Times* continued to emphasize the separation of powers argument, while the *Post* rested its argument squarely on the First Amendment. Stunned by Gurfein's decision to deny the government's request for an injunction, government lawyers also prepared a secret brief, known as the "Special Appendix," which it submitted to the Second Circuit Court of Appeals on June 21. It identified seventeen specific secrets contained in the "Pentagon Papers," which the government argued would irreparably harm national security if publicly divulged. David Rudenstine first gained access to the "Special Appendix" when writing his 1996 book on the "Pentagon Papers." (See Rudinstine, 1996, chapter 16.) The entire brief is available online at The National Security Archive (http://www.gwu.edu/~nsarchiv), along with commentary on each of the seventeen items identified in it. Use of the "Special Appendix" was controversial, because the factual record developed at trial usually cannot be supplemented on appeal.

Given the importance of the case, both the Second Circuit and the D.C. Circuit appeals courts met en banc rather than in the typical three-judge panels. On Wednesday, June 22, the Second Circuit remanded the case to Judge Gurfein by a 5–3 vote. Although it identified no reversible error, the appeals court instructed Gurfein to hold further in camera proceedings focusing on the items contained in the "Special Appendix" (Rudenstine, 1996, pp. 236–237). Late that same afternoon, the D.C. Circuit Court rejected the government's appeal and upheld Judge Gesell's ruling by a 7–2 vote. By Thursday the government had filed for immediate Supreme Court review. The next day, eight of the nine justices convened for the last scheduled conference of the term. (Justice William O. Douglas, who had already left for vacation, communicated by phone.) Although the "Rule of 4" usually applies when granting certiorari, five votes are needed in expedited appeals, such as this one, which bypass the intermediate appeals court. (No final ruling had yet come out of the Second Circuit Court.) Four justices (Black, William Brennan, Douglas, and Thurgood Marshall) were prepared to accept the expedited appeal. Indeed, they were prepared to offer summary judgment for the *Times* and *Post.* Four others (Warren Burger, Harry Blackmun, John Marshall Harlan, and Byron White) wanted to wait until the October term to hear the case and argued that a temporary restraining order should remain in effect until then. Potter Stewart, appointed by President Eisenhower in 1958, thus became the decisive vote. He voted to accept the expedited review. They set oral argument for the very next day, with Douglas flying back to participate (Woodward & Armstrong, 1979, pp. 141–142). This meant that lawyers for both sides had less than twenty-four hours to write their briefs for the Court and to prepare for the oral argument.

Although the justices rejected the government's request for an in camera hearing, the Court—by a 5–4 vote (with Black, Brennan, Douglas, and Marshall dissenting)—granted its motion to submit a sealed brief. This included the "Special Appendix" that had been submitted to the Second Circuit Court, as well as a separate brief written by Solicitor General Erwin Griswold, who argued the government's case before the Supreme Court. Griswold's short, thirteen-page brief focused on eleven points (it is also available online at http://www.gwu.edu/~nsarchiv). Each referred to specific information in the "Pentagon Papers," not already published, that the government claimed would pose an immediate threat to national security if divulged. Griswold reportedly felt stymied. He had only hours to prepare the brief, yet he calculated that it would take him ten weeks to read all of the "Pentagon Papers." Thus, he had to rely on government officials to help him identify specific portions of the papers to highlight in his brief. He is even reported to have called Attorney General Mitchell and complained that the government should never have sought an injunction in the first place, because it could not win (Woodward & Armstrong, 1979, p. 142).

Oral arguments before the Supreme Court can be listened to in their entirety online at Northwestern University's Oyez Project (http://www.oyez .org). Griswold argued for the government, Alexander Bickel argued for the *New York Times,* and William R. Glendon argued for the *Washington Post.* In his continuing strategy to win over centrist justices on the Court, Bickel conceded that the First Amendment is not an absolute bar against prior restraint and proceeded with his separation of powers argument. Glendon, as he had before the D.C. Circuit, rested his argument on First Amendment grounds, although he, too, conceded that it was not absolute—thus raising the ire of Justice Black.

Oral arguments ended at noon and the justices reconvened that afternoon to vote. Several justices read portions of the "Pentagon Papers" in the interim, although Justice Black—the literalist—saw no need. To him, the First Amendment always barred prior restraint. Justice Douglas's notes from the conference (printed in their entirety in Dickson, 2001, pp. 369–372) show that seven of the nine justices had clearly made up their mind. Three (Burger, Harlan, and Blackmun) voted for the government. Four (Black, Douglas, Brennan, and Marshall) voted, for various reasons, against the government. White and Stewart remained undecided. White said that he would "probably vote against the United States in this case," but he left open the possibility that he would change his mind—presumably if a closer reading of the "Pentagon Papers" convinced him of a clear threat to national security. Stewart said he was not yet ready to vote, although he, too, seemed inclined to vote against the government. By Monday, June 28, both White and Stewart had decided to vote against the government, but the majority remained fractured on its reasoning.

In the end, the 6–3 majority issued a brief per curiam decision—an unsigned opinion used either when the conclusion reached by the Court is so straightforward that no extended discussion is needed, or (as in this case) when the Court is so fragmented that it can only reach agreement on the narrow result announced. Each of the nine justices on the Court wrote a separate concurring or dissenting opinion, with no coalition gaining more than three votes. The per curiam ruling held that the government had not met the heavy burden necessary to impose a prior restraint. Black and Douglas argued that government could never impose a prior restraint. The remaining four justices in the majority all recognized that prior restraints might be possible under some circumstances, but not in this case. Only Justice Marshall explicitly based his opinion on Bickel's separation of powers argument. The three dissenters all criticized what Harlan called the "almost irresponsibly feverish" pace with which the courts were forced to decide the case, and called for judicial restraint in the face of the frenzy: the Court should defer to the executive on matters of national security.

Publication of the "Pentagon Papers" in the *Times* and *Post* resumed immediately after the Supreme Court ruling. The *Times* also published a 677-page Bantam Book edition of the papers, and other book-length versions followed. The government did not attempt to prosecute the newspapers after publication, although nothing in *New York Times v. U.S.* (403 U.S. 713 [1971]) would have prevented that. Clearly, the "Pentagon Papers" led to a landmark ruling by the Supreme Court, but their release also set in motion the undoing of the Nixon administration. President Nixon had been convinced that the injunction sought by his Justice Department would help the Democrats by preventing the publication of material damaging to Presidents Kennedy and Johnson. For Democrats to become the most vocal critics of the injunction infuriated him. It intensified his anger against the newspapers for publishing the papers, exacerbated his paranoia about political "enemies," and set in motion a series of covert operations that eventually led to the Watergate break-in. The Supreme Court defeat further embarrassed the administration, as did the FBI's initial inability to locate Ellsberg (while the FBI hunted, Walter Cronkite interviewed Ellsberg on national television from an undisclosed location on June 23). Ellsberg surrendered to authorities on Monday, June 28, and a federal grand jury indicted him on June 30.

Convinced that Ellsberg should be convicted both in the court of law and the court of public opinion, Nixon created the so-called "Plumber's Unit" to control leaks from the administration: stop those that the administration did not want, and aid those that it did. On June 30, the day the Supreme Court issued its ruling, Nixon vented about Ellsberg in an Oval Office meeting with Mitchell and Kissinger: "Just get everything out. Try him in the press. Try him in the press. Everything, John, that there is on the investigation get it out, leak it out. We want to destroy him in the press. . . . Is that clear?" (Kutler, 1997, p. 6).

As early as June 17, Nixon had suggested breaking into the Brookings

Institution to gather damaging information about President Johnson that could then be leaked to the press (Kutler, 1997, p. 3). After the Supreme Court ruling, he was even more vehement. In an Oval Office meeting that afternoon, Nixon reminded Haldeman that Brookings had a lot of material. "I want Brookings, I want them just to break in and take it out. Do you understand?"

HALDEMAN: Yeah. But you have to have somebody do it.

NIXON: That's what I'm talking about. Don't discuss it here. You talk to [E. Howard] Hunt. I want the break-in. Hell, they do that. You're to break into the place, rifle the files, and bring them in.

HALDEMAN: I don't have any problem with breaking in. It's a Defense Department approved security—

NIXON: Just go in and take it. Go in around 8:00 or 9:00 o'clock (Kutler, 1997, p. 6).

Hunt and G. Gordon Liddy became part of the Plumber's Unit. On the night of September 3, 1971, they led a group that broke into the Los Angeles office of Ellsberg's psychiatrist in an attempt to gather information that could be leaked to the press as part of an effort to discredit Ellsberg. When they accidentally damaged a filing cabinet trying to open it, they ransacked the office to make it look like a burglary by addicts in search of drugs. On September 8, Ehrlichman (who oversaw the Plumber's Unit) alluded to the break-in during an Oval Office meeting with Nixon. "We had one little operation," Ehrlichman said. "It's been aborted out in Los Angeles which, I think, is better that you don't know about. But we've got some dirty tricks underway. It may pay off. We've planted a bunch of stuff with columnists . . ." (Kutler, 1997, p. 28). Later, Hunt and Liddy participated in the ill-fated Watergate break-in that led to the resignation of Nixon and resulted in criminal trials of many of his top aides—including Mitchell, Mardian, Haldeman, and Ehrlichman.

Ironically, revelations of the break-in at Ellsberg's psychiatrist's office led to a mistrial in Ellsberg's case, and the government eventually dropped its charges against him. In his memoir, Nixon wrote: "Today the break-in at Ellsberg's psychiatrist's office seems wrong and excessive. But I do not accept that it was as wrong or excessive as what Daniel Ellsberg did, and I still believe that it is a tragedy that . . . John Ehrlichman went to jail and Daniel Ellsberg went free" (Nixon, 1978, p. 514). It is that ongoing debate over the balance between the public's right to know and the extent to which government can curb civil liberties to protect national security that assures the continued relevance of this case.

NOTE

1. This and tapes of other conversations relating to the "Pentagon Papers" can be listened to on line at http://www.gwu.edu/~nsarchiv. The site also has transcripts of the conversations.

REFERENCES

Dickson, D., ed. (2001). *The Supreme Court in conference (1940–1985): The private discussions behind nearly 300 Supreme Court decisions.* New York: Oxford University Press.

Ellsberg, D. (2002). *Secrets: A memoir of Vietnam and the Pentagon Papers.* New York: Viking.

Gora, J. M. (1998). The Pentagon Papers case and the path not taken: A personal memoir on the First Amendment and separation of powers. *Cardozo Law Review, 19,* p. 1311.

Haldeman, H. R. (1994). *The Haldeman diaries: Inside the Nixon White House.* New York: G. P. Putnam's Sons.

Kutler, S. I. (1997). *Abuse of power: The new Nixon tapes.* New York: Free Press.

Levy, L. W. (1988). *Original intent and the Framers' constitution.* New York: Macmillan.

Nixon, R. (1978). *The memoirs of Richard Nixon.* New York: Grosset & Dunlap.

Rudenstine, D. (1996). *The day the presses stopped: A history of the Pentagon Papers case.* Berkeley, CA: University of California Press.

Salisbury, H. E. (1980). *Without fear or favor: An uncompromising look at the* New York Times. New York: Times Books.

Seymour, W. N., Jr. (1975). *United States attorney: An inside view of justice in America under the Nixon administration.* New York: William Morrow.

Woodward, B., & Armstrong, S. (1979). *The Brethren: Inside the Supreme Court.* New York: Simon and Schuster.

TAPES OF PRESIDENTIAL CONVERSATIONS

(audio and transcripts available online at The National Security Archive, http://www.gwu.edu/~nsarchiv)

1971, June 13. 12:18 P.M. Telephone conversation between Richard Nixon and Alexander Haig.

1971, June 13. 3:09 P.M. Telephone conversation between Richard Nixon and Henry Kissinger.

1971, June 14. 7:13 P.M. Telephone conversation between Richard Nixon and John Ehrlichman.

1971, June 14. 7:19 P.M. Telephone conversation between Richard Nixon and John Mitchell.

1971, June 15. 6:35 P.M. Telephone conversation between Richard Nixon and John Mitchell.

Search and Seizure

Mapp to Legal Change and Policy Retreat

United States v. Leon (1984)

RICHARD L. PACELLE, JR.

In *Mapp v. Ohio* (367 U.S. 643 [1961]), the Supreme Court upheld the exclusionary rule—the requirement that illegally obtained evidence against a criminal defendant not be introduced in a trial. The rationale was that, to enforce the Fourth Amendment's prohibition against unreasonable searches and seizures, the exclusionary rule would serve as a deterrent to the potential excesses of the police. But, what if the police—through no fault of their own—happened to engage in an illegal search? In *U.S. v. Leon* (455 U.S. 433 [1976]), the Court confronted the question of whether the exclusionary rule applied, even when law enforcement behaved conscientiously?

"A person's home is his castle." In England, this meant that even common citizens would enjoy the same rights as kings or queens. The colonists felt that the British did not respect this tradition in dealing with them. When they achieved their freedom and had to construct their own government, this lesson was not forgotten. The Fourth Amendment to the Constitution reflected those concerns.

The Fourth Amendment guaranteed the right of people to be secure in their persons, homes, papers, and effects against unreasonable search and seizure and required probable cause to issue warrants for such searches. But as John Domino (2003, p. 172) notes, "while the words of the Fourth Amendment are undeniably eloquent, they are but a statement of constitutional theory." It was left to the courts to determine their meaning in specific circumstances. As a result, the amendment has been the subject of dynamic policy change over time.

One of the most important practical questions for the courts was how would the amendment be enforced if the government conducted an illegal search. Under British common law, a judge was not required to exclude evidence that was tainted as a result of an illegal search. In its decision in *Weeks v. United States* (232 U.S. 383 [1914]), the U.S. Supreme Court departed from this tradition. The Court created the so-called "exclusionary rule" to deal with the effects of an illegal search. Under this rule, the fruits of any search that violated the Fourth Amendment could not be used in court against the accused. The idea behind the rule was that if the police knew that they could not use illegally obtained evidence, it would deter them from questionable searches.

The exclusionary rule has been controversial. First, it was judge-made law, not mentioned in the Constitution or passed by the elected branches. Second, while the Fourth Amendment and the exclusionary rule eliminated many abuses, evidence gathered when police officers made honest mistakes or searches that had small technical flaws might also be excluded. New York judge Benjamin Cardozo, who would later become a Supreme Court justice, criticized the exclusionary rule when he wrote "The criminal is to go free because the constable has blundered" (*People v. Dafoe* [242 N.Y. 13 (1926)]). Supporters of the rule countered that the effectiveness of a right depends on the method of enforcement. Many saw the exclusionary rule as the only effective means of enforcing the Fourth Amendment. As Justice Tom Clark wrote, "Nothing can destroy a government more quickly than its failure to observe its own laws, or worse, its disregard of the charter of its own existence" (*Mapp*, at 653).

The impact of the exclusionary rule had been minimized, because, like the Bill of Rights, it pertained only to the federal government. Thus, states did not have to abide by the Fourth Amendment or the exclusionary rule.[1] This created some curious results, most notably the "silver platter doctrine." Under this doctrine, state or local police could conduct a search, free of the strictures of the exclusionary rule, and present the evidence on the proverbial silver platter, to federal agents.

In 1949 the Supreme Court incorporated the Fourth Amendment to the states through the Fourteenth Amendment.[2] But the exclusionary rule was not incorporated at the time. Thus there was no mandated enforcement for state violations of the amendment. A decade later, the Court incorporated the exclusionary rule to the states in *Mapp v. Ohio*.[3] The impact of *Mapp* was significant, because most criminal statutes are state laws and most criminal cases occur in the state courts.

The Warren Court, which issued the *Mapp* decision, officially began when Chief Justice Earl Warren was appointed to the Supreme Court. President Dwight Eisenhower believed that he was selecting a moderate conservative to head the Court. But Warren turned out to be very liberal and marshaled a unanimous Court to desegregate the schools in *Brown v. Board of Education* (1954). With the addition of a few like-minded justices, most notably Justice William Brennan, the Warren Court ultimately presided over a virtual constitutional revolution that broadened support for civil rights and expanded freedom of expression, religion, and the press, as well as the rights of the accused. The Warren Court nationalized the law, incorporating many provisions of the Bill of Rights to the states and supporting the expansion of federal control over traditional state functions like education and voting.

Mapp was only the beginning of an avalanche of criminal procedure decisions like *Miranda v. Arizona* (384 U.S. 436 [1966]; see Haynie, 2004). The Warren Court articulated a constitutional philosophy that protected individual liberties and civil rights (Justice, 1997, p. 305). The Court was willing to use the Constitution when it supported the justices' conception of good law. When the Constitution did not provide the authority, the Court would interpret the document more broadly to create the power (Pacelle, 2002, p. 43). The creation of the exclusionary rule and its subsequent extension to the states were examples of constitutional change.

While the Warren Court's civil rights decisions rankled the South, the decisions that protected the rights of the accused angered the entire nation. Police and prosecutors adapted to *Miranda* and *Gideon v. Wainwright* (372 U.S. 335 [1963]), which required the appointment of attorneys for the poor, but they resented *Mapp*. The public perception was that these decisions were handcuffing law enforcement officers and letting the guilty go free on legal technicalities. The Fourth Amendment might have been designed to protect innocent citizens in their homes, but over time critics of the exclusionary rule have been effective in arguing that it merely protected the guilty. Not everyone shares the view that the costs of the exclusionary rule have outweighed the benefits. Analysts and practitioners in the criminal justice system have argued that the exclusionary rule has had positive effects, improving police practices and enhancing the professionalization of law enforcement (Skolnick, 1994, p. 279; Uchida & Bynum, 1991; Walker, 2001, p. 87–95).

The Warren Court increasingly became a whipping boy for politicians and a campaign issue (Powe, 2000, p. 262). Richard Nixon campaigned on a law and order platform, promising to reshape the Court. President Nixon made good on that promise, replacing Chief Justice Earl Warren with Warren Burger. Over the next few years, he appointed three more justices, moving the Court to the right. For Nixon, law and order was the litmus test his appointees had to pass. Soon after Ronald Reagan was elected, he had the opportunity to continue the work that Nixon had begun.

The Warren and Burger courts were dominated by competing philosophies. When the Warren Court balanced civil liberties with the government's authority to keep order, it was done with a heavy thumb on the scales in favor of the individual. This was referred to as the "preferred position doctrine." The rights of individuals and insular minorities would be held in a preferred position over the authority of government (Pacelle, 1991). The Burger Court balanced these competing interests on a more equal level. But despite the fact that it was significantly more conservative than its predecessor, the Burger Court did not initiate a full-blown retreat or "counterrevolution" (Baum, 1989). In civil rights, for instance, many Burger Court decisions were logical extensions of the Warren Court. The Burger Court was the first to address gender discrimination, recognize reproductive rights, and create broad remedies like affirmative action and busing. Conversely, the Burger Court issued less-expansive First Amendment decisions and retreated from the Warren Court doctrine in criminal procedure (Pacelle, 2002, p. 45).

Chief Justice Burger and the other Nixon appointees were not fans of the exclusionary rule. Indeed, some have claimed that the Burger Court appeared to be "stalking the exclusionary rule" and undermining the foundation of *Miranda* (Urofsky, 1991, p. 167). In a few instances, they had begun to create exceptions to the rule and to the *Miranda* warnings that police must recite when questioning a suspect or taking someone into custody. In *United States v. Calandra* (414 U.S. 338 [1974]), the Burger Court ruled that illegally seized evidence did not have to be excluded from grand jury proceedings, which are used to indict individuals before they are brought to trial. In *United States v. Janis* (428 U.S. 433 [1976]), the Court ruled that the exclusionary rule did not apply to civil trials. In *Stone v. Powell* (428 U.S. 465 [1976]), the Court continued its assault by ruling that state prisoners could no longer petition for a writ of habeas corpus to review their convictions on Fourth Amendment grounds. The Court created another exception to the exclusionary rule, when it allowed prosecutors to use illegally seized evidence (and ill-gotten confessions) to impeach the testimony of the defendant. In *Nix v. Williams* (467 U.S. 431 [1984]), the Court created the "inevitable discovery" exception. Thus, if the Court felt that the evidence would have ultimately been discovered, the tainted evidence did not have to be excluded.

There were two ways to reduce the effect of the exclusionary rule: either the Court could shrink the scope of the Fourth Amendment or it could restrict the circumstances under which evidence was excluded. The Burger Court did both (Kamisar, 1987, p. 157). It became an annual ritual for legal scholars to predict the ultimate demise of the exclusionary rule. But while the multiple exceptions were important, they tended to involve peripheral issues (Schwartz, 1990, p. 360). That would not be the case for *United States v. Leon* and *Massachusetts v. Sheppard* (468 U.S. 981 [1984]).

The Facts of the Case

On the basis of a tip from a confidential informant of questionable reliability, Burbank police began an investigation that ultimately led them to Alberto Leon, a known drug dealer. Officer Cyril Rombach, a narcotics investigator, prepared an application for a warrant to search Leon's home. A state judge issued the warrant. The resulting search produced large quantities of drugs. Leon and his codefendants filed motions to suppress the evidence. The district court concluded that the officer acted in good faith, but that the evidence had to be suppressed because there was no probable cause to issue the warrant. A divided panel of the court of appeals affirmed the district court's decision.[4] The court of appeals, relying on a two-prong test created by the Supreme Court, ruled that the information in the affidavit was "stale" and did not establish the credibility of the informant. As a result, the court of appeals did not feel compelled to consider the Fourth Amendment question (*Leon*, pp. 900–904).

Leon was accompanied by a grisly murder case from Boston. Osborne Sheppard allegedly killed his girlfriend and burned her lifeless body. Police officers searched his car and found blood and hair samples that matched the victim. On the basis of that evidence, Detective Peter O'Malley drafted an affidavit for a search warrant for Sheppard's residence. Because it was Sunday, the local court was closed and O'Malley could not find the appropriate form for a murder warrant. He could only find an affidavit for a search warrant for drugs. With his typewriter, O'Malley deleted the words "controlled substance." The judge was willing to accept the doctored form because he did not have the correct forms either. As a result of the search, police discovered incriminating evidence and, Sheppard was charged with first-degree murder.

At a pretrial suppression hearing, the trial judge concluded that the warrant did not conform to the requirements of the Fourth Amendment. But the judge ruled that O'Malley acted in good faith in executing what had been represented as a valid warrant. As a consequence, Sheppard was convicted. The superior court affirmed the decision, but the Supreme Judicial Court of Massachusetts reversed the conviction. The state appealed the decision to the U.S. Supreme Court (*Sheppard,* pp. 983–988).

The U.S. government filed a petition for a writ of certiorari in the *Leon* case, asking the Court to review the court of appeals decision. In the brief for the government, Solicitor General Rex Lee asked the Court to decide whether there should be a good-faith exception to the exclusionary rule.

There were a number of factors that called attention to these cases. First, the Office of the Solicitor General, filing for the government, is well regarded by the Court. No litigant files more briefs and is more successful having its cases accepted, a function of the excellence of its petitions and its ability to litigate strategically (Pacelle, 2003, pp. 20–27). Second, virtually all decisions of three-judge courts of appeals are unanimous. When there is lower-court dissent, the Supreme Court takes notice, improving the chances that the case will be accepted. Finally, perhaps the most important reason to accept a case is because the justices wish to further their policy preferences. Most cases are accepted because the justices want to overturn lower-court decisions they disagree with (Perry, 1991). A majority of the Burger Court justices were inclined to support the government in criminal procedure cases and many had expressed antipathy for the exclusionary rule. The Court granted the writ of certiorari and agreed to consider the exclusionary rule issue, rather than whether the informant was credible.

The written briefs, oral arguments, and amici (or "friends of the court") briefs that are filed in cases are important sources of information for the justices. Because the briefs are directed toward the specific issues at hand, they enable the justices to make more precise calculations (Epstein & Knight, 1998, p. 146).

Amici briefs are filed by groups that are not parties to the case, but will be affected by the decision. The briefs fulfill a number of different roles. First, they expand the issue in the case beyond the parties. Second, they offer general and specific expertise to help the justices make their decision. Finally, they provide the Court with an informal tally of public opinion (Pacelle, 1991, p. 32).

Criminal procedure cases like *Leon* and *Sheppard* have an unmistakable individual component to them. The cases are fact driven and involve the alleged misbehavior of an individual defendant. At the same time, the decisions of the Supreme Court create precedent for similar future cases. The individual defendants in these cases seldom care about the long-term implications of the decision and how it will affect those in similar situations. Rather, they are interested in their particular case and getting the least punishment possible. A number of groups, some favoring the rights of the accused, others supporting law enforcement and the victims of crime, have joined the fray to remind the Court of the broader consequences of its decisions. The American Civil Liberties Union (ACLU) was active in trying to protect the rights of the accused. The ACLU considered its support of the rights of defendants as its greatest contribution to the civil rights movement. Though few of the major criminal procedure landmarks involved race, the ACLU felt that decisions protecting the rights of the accused would protect African Americans in the South (Walker, 1990).

For many years, the ACLU and those interested in protecting the rights of the accused faced little group opposition to their position. The Warren Court was sympathetic to the rights of the accused, and the ACLU and, on occasion, the National Association for the Advancement of Colored People (NAACP) entered cases as amici to seek favorable precedents. The solicitor general was typically the lone voice favoring the state. Beginning with *Terry v. Ohio* (1968), nonprofit groups supportive of law enforcement such as the Americans for Effective Law Enforcement and the Criminal Justice Legal Foundation, as well as groups dedicated to the rights of victims, began to proliferate. Such groups felt the states were doing an inadequate job defending their position, so they lent their expertise and increasing numbers (Epstein, 1985).

Changes in the ideological balance of the Supreme Court altered the environment for these groups. During the Warren Court, the ACLU was aggressive in trying to stretch the provisions of the Bill of Rights by expanding favorable precedents. As the Court got more conservative, the ACLU was pushed into a defensive posture, trying to protect the precedents it had helped establish.

For decades, the Burger and Rehnquist Courts have been narrowing the rights of defendants, encouraging states and the groups representing victims and law enforcement to become more aggressive. State attorneys general increasingly coordinate their efforts and have expanded their involvement in the appellate courts (Waltenburg & Swinford, 1998; 1999). Favorable decisions have encouraged these groups to ask the justices to create additional exceptions to *Mapp* and *Miranda* and even seek to overturn those precedents (Epstein, 1985). Criminal procedure, most notably search and seizure, self-incrimination, and capital punishment, continues to be a battleground between different philosophies and the groups that support those perspectives.[5]

In *Leon*, the government's brief argued that the Court had never articulated a rationale for excluding evidence pursuant to a warrant. Solicitor General Lee put his toe in the water in case the Court was ready to jettison the exclusionary rule in its entirety, arguing that the rule was merely judge-made law. If the Court was not going to overturn the exclusionary rule, then the solicitor general would advocate a good-faith exception and ask the Court to create such an exception. Lee argued that deterrence was now the primary rationale for the rule, although he claimed it did not work. If it was a deterrent, he reasoned that nothing would be achieved by punishing the police when they acted in good faith. In *Leon* and *Sheppard*, the mistake was made by the magistrates, not the police. Thus, the only consequence of applying the rule in such circumstances was to keep evidence from the jury. Lee argued that there was "no rational justification for applying the exclusionary rule to these situations, which bear not the slightest relationship to the egregious police misconduct for which the rule was first devised."

Lee argued that the presumed benefits of the exclusionary rule must be weighed against its costs. First, the rule excludes the evidence that is most relevant. Second, when the rule is applied in circumstances in which the deterrence of future misconduct is unlikely, it benefits only those who would have been found guilty. Third, the application of the rule diminishes public respect for the judicial system by enhancing the perception that guilty defendants are freed on "technicalities." Fourth, the rule lacked proportionality when applied to marginal violations. Behavior that a well-trained officer could not be expected to know violates the Fourth Amendment was subjected to the same draconian "remedy" as the most flagrant abuses of police power. Finally, the application of the rule clogged the system because it encouraged the filing of suppression motions, regardless of whether misconduct had occurred, consuming finite judicial resources (Brief for United States, no. 82-1771).

Attorneys for the defendants asked the Court to return to the original issue involving probable cause. They urged the Court to avoid the good-faith issue, because it had not properly been raised in the lower courts. Because the solicitor general and amici briefs had raised the issue of overturning the exclusionary rule, attorneys for Leon and Sheppard had to defend the rule. They argued that the good-faith exception would, in effect, "obliterate" the rule. The defense attorneys and amici in support of them argued that excluding evidence would deter police from hurried warrants or from shopping for the judges most likely to issue warrants (Brief for Respondents, no. 82-1771).

Because the two decisions would have a profound effect on criminal justice systems across the nation, fifteen associations representing district attorneys and defense lawyers, as well as attorneys general from thirty-five states and the NAACP, filed amici briefs to explain how the decision would affect them. Several states filed briefs asking the justices to eradicate the exclusionary rule altogether. One amicus brief argued that several justices had expressed the belief that the exclusionary rule was not constitutionally mandated, and that view was shared by President Ronald Reagan and many members of Congress (Epstein & Knight, 1998, p. 146).

The Supreme Court's Decision

The central question for the Court was whether the exclusionary rule should be modified to create a good-faith exception when the police rely on a detached and neutral magistrate for a warrant that turns out to be unsupported by probable cause. All four of the Nixon appointees and Sandra O'Connor, the first Reagan appointee, were on record as opposed to the exclusionary rule or as interested in seeing it narrowed considerably (Schwartz, 1990, p. 359). When the Court accepted the case, there was little doubt that Burger would support the creation of the good-faith exception. Many thought he would adopt the position that some of the briefs urged: eliminate the rule altogether.

In conference, Burger supported the good-faith exception, arguing that it would be disastrous to wipe out the exclusionary rule. Strategically, Burger felt he could not get the Court to accept a wholesale rejection of the rule. Had Burger attempted to overturn the exclusionary rule, he might not be able to build a majority for the good-faith exception. By narrowing an issue that could have splintered the Court, "Burger paved the way for a fundamental change in search and seizure law" (Epstein & Knight, 1998, pp. 90–93).

Five justices agreed with the chief justice that the good-faith exception should be adopted, though Justice Harry Blackmun underscored the unavoidably provisional nature of the exception. He argued that if weakening the exception would harm compliance with the exclusionary rule, it would be necessary to rethink the exception (Wasby, 1991, p. 90).

Justice William Brennan, a supporter of the exclusionary rule, knew he did not have votes to prevail, so he urged the Court to avoid the good-faith question. He argued that the Court should vacate the judgment in light of the recent *Illinois v. Gates* decision, which made it easier to show probable cause for issuing a warrant. Like Brennan, Justice John Paul Stevens feared that when the police lacked probable cause, they would have nothing to lose by gambling that a magistrate would issue a warrant on an insufficient affidavit. This would reduce the likelihood that the rule would deter illegal searches (Canon, 1991, p. 367). Justice Thurgood Marshall, who joined the dissent, claimed that the exception would "put a premium on police ignorance of the law" and encourage governmental officials to seek expedient solutions to combat crime (Daniels, 1991, p. 223).

In its decision, the Court created the most significant exception to the exclusionary rule. After hinting for a decade, the Court adopted a good-faith, or more precisely, a reasonable-mistake exception (Kamisar, 1987, p. 145). Burger assigned the opinion in the 6–3 decision to Justice Byron White, who held that the exclusionary rule should not be applied to circumstances when the officers act in a reasonable fashion and when it is not designed to deter such behavior. The Court ruled that the problem was caused by the magistrate's error and the police had acted in good faith. White maintained that the exclusionary rule was not designed to safeguard the rights of the accused, but rather to serve as a deterrent to illegal police behavior. White followed the evolving standards that increasingly used balancing tests in a variety of areas to determine the costs and benefits of the rule. He echoed the solicitor general's brief in reciting the costs of overenforcement of the rule.

The Court dismissed as "speculative" the arguments that excluding evidence would deter police from hurriedly constructing flawed applications for warrants. The Court held that "the marginal or nonexistent benefits produced by suppressing evidence obtained in an objectively reasonable reliance on a subsequently invalidated search warrant cannot justify the substantial costs of exclusion." Suppression of evidence was only justified if police misled the magistrate. Justice White accepted the argument that the exclusionary rule could be modified without jeopardizing its intended functions.

White doubted that this exception would make a big difference. He argued that this should not be construed as a signal the Court would not enforce the Fourth Amendment (*Leon*, pp. 906–926). Justice Brennan, however, felt that, taken in conjunction with the other exceptions to *Mapp* and *Miranda*, it was hard to draw any other conclusion. Brennan warned that a majority was increasingly positioning itself to abandon the exclusionary rule altogether. Brennan claimed the Court's slow strangulation of the exclusionary rule was now complete.

Brennan argued that the protection of civil liberties and civil rights was important in and of itself and based on important constitutional principles that could not be balanced in a cost-benefit analysis. He argued that the majority had exaggerated the costs, while denigrating the benefits. The dissenters maintained that the Fourth Amendment did not pertain to a particular actor, but to government as a whole. They argued that the gathering and admission of evidence represented a single governmental action. Police were not responsible for the errors of judges and magistrates, but the tainted evidence would eventually be argued in their courts (*Leon,* pp. 928–960).

Putting the Decision in Context

The decision was an important symbol of the Burger Court's jurisprudence. As opposed to the Warren Court, this approach meant the Court might forgive individual transgressions if, after considering all factors in the case, the defendant had not been unduly prejudiced. Cost-benefit analysis would become the dominant standard for Bill of Rights decisions. In effect, this changed the exclusionary rule from a focus on rights and remedies to a balancing test. Prior to these cases, the question was whether a procedural right or due process had been violated. This standard had been based on a principled notion that it was a constitutional right and police should be held to a high standard (Urofsky, 1991, p. 161). After *Leon,* the Court asked a different question: did the benefits of the violation outweigh the costs? (Schwartz, 1990, p. 364). The Burger Court preferred a test balancing the alleged violation of the right with the severity of the sanction, rather than a rigid application of the exclusionary rule. The Court felt the latter placed an unreasonable burden on police. The balancing standard, however, gave police and prosecutors more leeway than the rules created by the Warren Court did. The Burger Court found the deterrent effects questionable but concluded they could be achieved without a rigid rule (Urofsky, 1991, pp. 175–180).

Critics argued that there were no objective standards for this balancing. Rather, it would be based on each justice's attachment of values for the costs and the benefits. The former were relatively easy to quantify compared to benefits. Critics claimed the costs were typically exaggerated, while the benefits were trivialized or "made to disappear with a mere wave of the hand" (Schwartz, 1990, p. 364). How much is freedom from an illegal search worth? More specifically, how does one balance liberty and privacy versus police efficiency or law and order (Kamisar, 1987, pp. 162–163)?

The Court adopted the position that the Fourth Amendment, unlike some provisions of the Bill of Rights, was not vital to the trustworthiness of the fact-finding process (Landynski, 1991, p. 282). Just a year earlier, the Court diluted the probable cause standard in *Illinois v. Gates* and now it established the reasonable mistake or good-faith exception prompting Yale

Kamisar (1987, p. 164) to remark that the Court "killed one bird with two stones."

If the exclusionary rule is considered solely as a deterrent, then the *Leon* and *Sheppard* decisions make sense. Police had checked with the magistrates before proceeding. So, the costs in terms of law enforcement morale would be high, with no significant benefits, because it would not modify police tactics. However, if the integrity of the legal system is considered the most important criterion, then *Leon* was problematic. It matters little to the victim whether the police or the magistrate is the one who blundered; in either case, the accused loses some of his rights (Urofsky, 1991, p. 183). The justices were satisfied to live with a "pruned" exclusionary rule and a "workable" Fourth Amendment. Their opponents referred to it as a "battered" exclusionary rule and a "shrunken" Fourth Amendment (Kamisar, 1987, p. 167).

How much did public opinion influence the Court's retreat and legal change? Certainly, it had at least an indirect effect. The public was never supportive of rulings that protected the rights of defendants. Public officials characterized the decisions as hindering the peace forces and helping criminals. The Court appeared to move in the direction of public opinion because Republican presidents were able to appoint justices who were less supportive of individual liberties. Even the Clinton appointees, when Democrats took back the White House, were more likely to support the government than the individual in criminal procedure cases.

Did *Leon* and *Sheppard* lay down a general exception to undermine the exclusionary rule, or are they limited to specific factors? The conference discussion suggested the justices intended to confine the good-faith exception to warrants, but read in conjunction with other criminal procedure decisions, it suggested a growing hostility to the rule. Indeed, the Rehnquist Court continued to extend the good-faith exception, though most have been peripheral extensions (O'Brien, 2000, p. 358). Has the door been opened for the ultimate reversal of the exclusionary rule? Now that the viability of the rule is based on empirical evidence and cost-benefit analysis rather than principled theory, it appeared vulnerable. But while the Court created exceptions, it did not overturn the exclusionary rule. The Court established a similar set of exceptions to the *Miranda* requirements but stopped at the brink, refusing to overturn *Miranda* in 2000 (Haynie, 2004).

The Burger Court applied the brakes to the expansion of some rights and began retreats that have accelerated during the Rehnquist Court, but it directly overturned few precedents and so the exclusionary rule remains, if somewhat weakened (Pacelle, 2002, p. 45). Paradoxically, by narrowing the exclusionary rule, the Court may have spared it. Because fewer searches are invalidated, there has been less pressure to get rid of it (Kramer, 1991, p. 422). Legislation to legitimate the good-faith rule was introduced in Congress in 1986, but it has not been adopted. The Court continues to examine searches on an ad hoc basis and the justices remain divided. Because it is a judge-made rule, it can be judge-altered (Abraham & Perry, 1994, p. 142).

In many ways, the *Leon* precedent has not had the dramatic impact many predicted. The bottom line as a result of *Leon* is that evidence will rarely be suppressed when a judge issues a warrant (Fleissner, Mabery, & Wiggins, 2001, p. 1331). But some state supreme courts have found a legitimate means to extend procedural rights by declaring that rights denied by the Supreme Court under the U.S. Constitution are protected independently under state constitutions. At least nine state supreme courts have held that there is no good-faith exception to the rules of search and seizure in their constitutions (Baum, 2001, p. 231; Friedman, 2000).

If police and prosecutors thought that such decisions were a symbol of a significant retreat and further change, they have been mistaken. The Rehnquist Court has issued a number of recent decisions that suggest law enforcement officials occasionally go too far. In cases like *Kyllo v. United States* (use of thermal imaging as a form of search), *Bond v. United States* (searches of luggage on buses), *Indianapolis v. Edmond* (broad discretion for police checkpoints), and *Knowles v. Iowa* (searches of automobiles stopped for speeding), the Rehnquist Court placed limits on the ability of law enforcement officers to conduct searches.

When the Supreme Court decides to expand or contract constitutional provisions, it can, in essence, change the very nature of the Constitution. In practical terms, it only takes five of the nine justices to "rewrite" the charter of our government. As a consequence, the Constitution adapts over time, combining changes in society with the enduring principles grounded in the document (Fisher, 1988, pp. 13–14).

The legal change that yielded exceptions to the exclusionary rule resulted from changes in the composition of the Court, which elevated a different legal philosophy to prominence. The changes were also a function of issue evolution (Segal, 1984). Cases like *Mapp* that involved police searches without a warrant were clearly illegal. *Leon* and *Sheppard* involved less heavy-handed tactics and raised more difficult questions. Fourth Amendment doctrine will continue to change, because new justices will bring new philosophies to the bench, new technology will bring new situations to the police, and new social mores will bring new perspectives to the public.

NOTES

1. Of course, states have their own constitutions, many of which have prohibitions against illegal searches. In addition, some states had their own exclusionary rules.

2. Incorporation means that the Fourth Amendment was enforceable to the states.

3. *Mapp*, one of the classic cases in American history, started as an obscenity case, but an amicus curiae brief by the American Civil Liberties Union argued that this was a search and seizure issue. The Court agreed.

4. The dissenting judge was Anthony Kennedy, who would later be a Reagan appointee to the Supreme Court.

5. I am indebted to Kent Scheidegger, legal director of the Criminal Justice Legal Foundation (CJLF), for providing information about his group's activities.

REFERENCES

Abraham, H., & Perry, B. (1994). *Freedom and the Court.* New York: Oxford University Press.

Baum, L. (1989). Comparing the policy positions of Supreme Court justices from different periods. *Western Political Quarterly, 42,* pp. 509–522.

Baum, L. (2001). *The Supreme Court,* 7th ed. Washington DC: CQ Press.

Canon, B. (1991). Justice John Paul Stevens: The Lone Ranger in a black robe. In Charles Lamb and Stephen Halpern (Eds.). *The Burger Court: Political and judicial profiles.* Champaign, IL: University of Illinois Press.

Daniels, W. (1991). Justice Thurgood Marshall: The race for equal justice. In Charles Lamb and Stephen Halpern (Eds.). *The Burger Court: Political and judicial profiles.* Champaign, IL: University of Illinois Press.

Domino, J. (2003). *Civil rights & liberties in the 21st century,* (2nd ed.). New York: Longman.

Epstein, L. (1985). *Conservatives in court.* Knoxville, TN: University of Tennessee Press.

Epstein, L., & Knight, J. (1998). *The choices justices make.* Washington, DC: CQ Press.

Fisher, L. (1988). *Constitutional dialogues: Interpretation as political process.* Princeton, NJ: Princeton University Press.

Fleissner, J., Mabery, S., & Wiggins, J. (2001). Constitutional criminal procedure. *Mercer Law Review, 52,* pp. 1305–1366.

Friedman, L. (2000). The constitutional value of dialogue and the new judicial federalism. *Hastings Constitutional Law Quarterly, 28,* pp. 93–144.

Haynie, S. (2004). The Court's protection against self-incrimination: *Miranda v. Arizona.* In G. Ivers & K. T. McGuire (Eds.), *Creating Constitutional Change.* Charlottesville, VA: University of Virginia Press.

Justice, W. W. (1997). The two faces of judicial activism. In D. O'Brien (Ed.) *Judges on judging: Views from the bench* (pp. 302–314). Chatham, NJ: Chatham House.

Kamisar, Y. (1987). The "police practices phase" of the criminal process and the three phases of the Burger Court. In Herman Schwartz, (Ed.). *The Burger years: Rights and wrongs in the Supreme Court 1969–1986* (pp. 143–168). New York: Penguin Books.

Kramer, D. (1991). Justice Byron R. White: Good friend to polity and solon. In Charles Lamb and Stephen Halpern (Ed.). *The Burger Court: Political and judicial profiles.* Champaign, IL: University of Illinois Press.

Landynski, J. (1991). Justice Lewis F. Powell, Jr.: Balance wheel of the Court. In Charles Lamb and Stephen Halpern (Eds.). *The Burger Court: Political and judicial profiles.* Champaign, IL: University of Illinois Press.

O'Brien, D. (2000). *Storm center: The Supreme Court in American politics* (5th ed.). New York: Norton.

Pacelle, R. (2003). *Between law and politics: The solicitor general and the structuring of race, gender, and reproductive rights policy.* College Station, TX: Texas A&M University Press.

Pacelle, R. (2002). *The role of the Supreme Court in American politics: The least dangerous branch?* Boulder, CO: Westview Press.

Pacelle, R. (1991). *The transformation of the Supreme Court's agenda: From the New Deal to the Reagan administration.* Boulder, CO: Westview Press.

Perry, H. W. (1991). *Deciding to decide: Agenda setting in the United States Supreme Court.* Cambridge, MA: Harvard University Press.

Powe, L. (2000). *The Warren Court and American politics.* Cambridge, MA: Harvard University Press.

Schwartz, B. (1990). *The ascent of pragmatism: The Burger Court in action.* Reading, MA: Addison-Wesley Publishing.

Segal, J. (1984). Predicting Supreme Court cases probabilistically: The search and seizure cases, 1962–1981. *American Political Science Review, 78,* pp. 891–900.

Skolnick, J. (1994). *Justice without trial: Law enforcement in democratic society* (3rd ed.). New York: Macmillan.

Uchida, C. & Bynum, T. S. (1991). Search warrants, motions to suppress, and "lost cases": The effects of the exclusionary rule in seven jurisdictions. *Journal of Criminal Law & Criminology, 81,* pp. 1034–1066.

Urofsky, M. (1991). *The continuity of change: The Supreme Court and individual liberties 1953–1986.* Belmont, CA: Wadsworth.

Walker, S. (1990). *In defense of American liberties: A history of the ACLU.* New York: Oxford University Press.

Walker, S. (2001). *Sense and nonsense about crime* (5th ed.). Belmont, CA: Wadsworth.

Waltenburg, E., & Swinford, B. (1998). *Litigating federalism: The states before the Supreme Court.* Westport, CT: Greenwood Press.

Waltenburg, E., & Swinford, B. (1999). The Supreme Court as a policy arena: The strategies and tactics of state attorneys general. *Policy Studies Journal, 27,* pp. 242–259.

Wasby, S. (1991). Justice Harry A. Blackmun: Transformation from "Minnesota Twin" to independent voice. In Charles Lamb and Stephen Halpern (Eds.). *The Burger Court: Political and judicial profiles.* Champaign, IL: University of Illinois Press.

Evidence

The Court's Protection against Self-Incrimination

Miranda v. Arizona (1966)

STACIA HAYNIE

> Under Chief Justice Earl Warren, the Supreme Court overhauled the law of crim-
> inal procedure. It established the right to legal counsel, allowed defendants to con-
> sult with attorneys during police questioning, and imposed the exclusionary rule
> for illegally obtained evidence. Probably the most controversial of these policies,
> however, was a decision requiring criminal suspects to be informed of their rights
> when taken into custody. To some, the decision represents an important safeguard
> against self-incrimination. To others, it has frustrated effective law enforcement
> and permitted the guilty to go free.

In March of 1963 John F. Kennedy had successfully avoided a nuclear crisis
with the Soviet Union over missiles in Cuba but was struggling with U.S.
policy in Vietnam. While George Wallace's segregationist platform had
proved successful in Alabama, Martin Luther King was preparing to deliver
a speech entitled "I Have a Dream" in Washington, D.C., that August. The
Supreme Court under the leadership of Earl Warren had ruled state-

sponsored prayer in public schools unconstitutional. Stamps were a nickel, gasoline was thirty cents a gallon, and a movie ticket was seventy-five cents at the Paramount Theatre in Phoenix, Arizona, where eighteen year-old Patricia Wise[1] worked as an attendant at the concession stand. John Wayne and Robert Mitchum had finished their final battle scenes in the evening showing of *The Longest Day,* and Patricia left the popcorn machines, the candy, and the uniform behind as she headed to her bus stop to await the 11:45 bus home.

Shortly after midnight Patricia got off the bus and started the short walk to her apartment, which she shared with her mother, sister, and brother-in-law. She was almost struck by a car pulling out of a parking lot, driven by a young Hispanic man who parked the car just ahead of her, got out, and headed toward Patricia. She would later learn his name—Ernesto Miranda, known as Ernest, a twenty-three-year-old truck driver. Miranda grabbed her arm, covered her mouth, and told Patricia not to scream; he wouldn't hurt her if she didn't scream. He forced her to lay face down in the back seat of the car. He tied her ankles and hands with a thick rope; a sharp object scraped against her throat accompanied by a second warning not to scream. While Patricia cried quietly in the back seat, terrified of moving or speaking, Miranda drove to the mountains some twenty minutes away.

After parking the car, Miranda waited for nearly thirty minutes before moving to the back seat, seemingly unsure of how he would proceed. He eventually directed Patricia to remove her clothes. Pleading through her tears, "Please don't," Patricia begged Miranda to let her go. Miranda then proceeded to remove her clothes himself, Patricia too fearful to resist. An awkward first attempt to penetrate Patricia proved unsuccessful, and only after a repeated effort did Miranda succeed in raping her. He returned to the front seat, drove Patricia to within three blocks of her home, and let her go. After reaching her home, Patricia collapsed, crying hysterically. It would take almost fifteen minutes for her sister to calm Patricia sufficiently to unravel the horrid tale. Her sister then called the police to the apartment.

By the time Patricia Wise accused him of raping her, Ernest Miranda had already put together a lengthy rap sheet. He was first placed on probation at fourteen for stealing a car, followed shortly afterward by an attempted rape and assault charge. While walking past a residence, Miranda peeked through a window and noticed a woman sleeping naked on her bed. Careful not to wake the unsuspecting victim from her slumber, Miranda entered an unlocked door and crawled into the bed. His presence was discovered only when the husband arrived home shortly after and quickly called police. Miranda later dropped out of school in the middle of his first year of high school. By age seventeen he had been picked up as a Peeping Tom and placed on probation. He was arrested twice in 1957 for suspected involvement in two armed robberies, though he was never convicted. He joined the army in 1958 but spent six of his eighteen-months' service in the stockade for pursuing his Peeping Tom proclivities while AWOL. He was given a dishonorable discharge. In 1959 Miranda served a year in the federal penitentiary for transporting stolen automobiles across state lines. After being released from jail, Miranda settled in Phoenix with his common-law wife and their daughter, who was seven months old at the time Patricia Wise accused him of rape. Miranda had come to the attention of the police after Patricia's brother-in-law, now walking her home from the bus stop, took down the license plate of an old Packard automobile he noticed cruising the neighborhood, one that Patricia also thought looked very familiar. The car was traced eventually to Miranda.

On March 13, 1963, Miranda was brought to the police station for identification. After the lineup, he was taken to Interrogation Room Number 2 by a couple of police officers at 11:30 A.M. There was no indication Miranda was physically threatened, abused, or coerced into responding to the questions, but by 1:30 P.M. Miranda had signed a confession to the rape of Patricia Wise. Miranda's confession was important for the prosecution's case. Ms. Wise provided a somewhat confusing account that surfaced as contradictory testimony at trial. At one point she testified that Miranda had penetrated her only with a finger. Later, she had said it was a penis, and finally, under cross-examination, she conceded she didn't know. By her own admission, Patricia Wise was a sexual novice. She was young, frightened, and naive, and according to her brother-in-law, Patricia was the intellectual equivalent of a twelve or thirteen year old. Thus Miranda's written statement that he "Could not get penis into vagina got about 1/2 (half) inch in" was seen as an important element for the prosecution. As in most defense strategies, the struggle to suppress the confession began in earnest, and the efforts to protect its inclusion were equally fierce, ultimately leading to a twenty-to-thirty year sentence—and docket number 759.

Rewriting the Law of Confessions: The Court Sets the Agenda

Docket number 759 was one of 2,774 petitions the U. S. Supreme Court received for the 1965 term. It was one of only 167 cases that would be granted full review by the Court that term, and it would lead to the Court's landmark decision defining the meaning of an individual's guarantee to remain silent, embedded in the Fifth Amendment, as well as the right to an attorney, provided in the Sixth Amendment.

Miranda v. Arizona was argued before the U.S. Supreme Court on February 28, 1966. Chief Justice Earl Warren presided over the oral arguments and, from 1953 to 1969, presided over a Court that would transform constitutional doctrine in a number of areas, including the rights of the accused. *Miranda* concerned not merely the protection against coerced statements and the ancillary right to a lawyer, but also the right to be informed of these protections. The Court had previously ruled in *Gideon v. Wainright* (372 U.S. 335 [1963]) that the due process clause of the Fourteenth Amendment included the Sixth Amendment's counsel provision: indigents accused of crimes must be provided an attorney at state expense. Further, the Court ruled in *Escobedo v. Illinois* (378 U.S. 478 [1965]) that once the investigation begins to focus on a particular individual, the denial of counsel for an individual not warned of his or her constitutional right to remain silent violated due process, and statements made under those circumstances could not be used by the state at the trial. The Court was not unanimous in its understanding of the phrase "due process"—nor whether the Fifth and Sixth Amendment's protections were essential to achieve it. The fate of Ernesto Miranda was not at all clear as the oral arguments before the Supreme Court began.

John Flynn, a well-known and well-respected criminal lawyer, was enlisted by the American Civil Liberties Union (ACLU) to argue the case on behalf of Miranda. Flynn argued that individuals, particularly individuals with little education or financial resources, must be informed of their right to remain silent and to counsel; otherwise the rights existed only for those intelligent enough or wealthy enough to obtain counsel, or those with sufficient stamina to resist often lengthy and exhausting police interrogations. If we as citizens are unaware of our rights, there is clearly little substance to them, Mr. Flynn argued. He also noted that the courts of appeals as well as the state supreme courts were split on how to approach the issues of protection against self-incrimination and right to counsel. He argued that the Supreme Court should establish a right to be informed of your constitutional protections at the moment the adversary process begins.

Gary Nelson argued for the state of Arizona and suggested that Miranda had been informed of his right to an attorney and to remain silent, though he admitted the precise point at which those warnings were given was unclear. It could have been as early as the beginning of the two-hour interrogation or at its end, immediately before he signed the confession used against him at the trial. Regardless, Nelson argued that state legislatures should determine the appropriate way to secure due process in criminal procedures.

Duane Nedrud, executive director of the National Association of District Attorneys, argued as amicus curiae on behalf of the prosecution. (Amicus curiae is Latin for "friend of the court.") The Court, particularly since the 1940s, has allowed the submission of amicus briefs by third parties that wish to advance a point of view important to a particular group not represented by the principal parties in the case. Nedrud argued that the Court should not provide a blanket ruling that would create some sort of protection for the accused. While he conceded that a lawyer was essential in an accusatory system of law, Nedrud countered that the right to an attorney only began at trial. During oral argument Justice William Douglas noted that "[v]ery important rights can be lost many days, many weeks prior to the trial." Justice Douglas suggested that the individual surely is entitled to a lawyer at some point before the trial. Nedrud refused to concede, asserting that if the Court were to insist that counsel be provided at the point at which the individual becomes a focus of the investigation, "you will have fewer convictions. If this is what is wanted, this is what will occur."

Miranda presented an issue before the court that involved the relationship of counsel to the voluntariness of statements. Statements that are coerced invariably cannot be trusted even if the statements represent the truth. If an individual is tortured and confesses to the crime, does the confession represent a truthful recognition of wrongdoing or merely an attempt to stop the abuse? Since statements that are not made voluntarily are inherently suspect, how can we determine if the confession was made without any coercion—physical, mental, or otherwise? Obviously, the presence of an attorney, or the mere fact that an individual has secured representation, would limit abuse. After all, the attorney immediately would inform her client that she has an absolute right to remain silent and that nothing can be inferred from exercising that right. Silence for the defense attorney is golden indeed.

The Right to Counsel: What did the Framers Intend?

The right to remain silent was held precious by the Framers, who were familiar with the use of compulsion in English history, the most egregious involving the infamous Court of the Star Chamber. The Chamber's legal heritage dated to medieval times, and its progeny would become the definition of abuse of power. Its arbitrary and secretive proceedings were used to extract various concessions from those in opposition to the king and proved particularly effective in religious persecutions. Exactly what the Framers intended by the right to remain silent, as with most of the Constitution, is debatable, and inevitably that debate is resolved by the decisions of the United States Supreme Court, the final arbiter for all things constitutional.

While the language of the Sixth Amendment has not changed since its adoption in 1791, the Court's understanding of that language certainly has.

As the composition of the Court changes, a factor that represents shifting social and political climates, the force and effect of phrases like "assistance of counsel" and "compelled . . . to be a witness" will often shift as well. Even more amorphous is the guarantee that every state must afford its citizens "due process of law" found in the Fourteenth Amendment. Since the adoption of the Fourteenth Amendment in 1868, the Supreme Court has spilt much ink determining what is or is not included in the concept of due process. While the federal government was required to follow the dictates of the Bill of Rights in its actions, the restrictions on state government action was less clear. The Supreme Court would spend a century harmonizing the protections an individual has against federal government action with the protections an individual has against state governments.

Justice Hugo Black argued that the due process clause of the Fourteenth Amendment included or incorporated all of the protections found in the Bill of Rights, making them applicable to the states. For Justice Black the rights and liberties afforded citizens should not differ between the federal and state governments (see, for example, Justice Black's dissent in *Duncan v. Louisiana,* 391 U.S. 145 [1968]). The Court itself has never adopted such an interpretation. The Court evaluated on a case-by-case basis what protections against state action should or should not be included in the phrase "due process." For example, the Court ruled in *Gitlow v. New York* (268 U.S. 652 [1925]) that a state law punishing an individual for speech considered "dangerous" or "subversive" violated the due process clause of the Fourteenth Amendment as well as the guarantee to freedom of speech protected by the First Amendment. But *Gitlow* spoke only to state laws dealing with freedom of speech. Continuing a pattern that extended back to the post-Reconstruction period, the Court refused to conclude that the due process clause of the Fourteenth Amendment extended any other provisions of the Bill of Rights to the states.

That changed in 1932 when the Court, in the *Scottsboro Boys Case,* ruled that death sentences imposed by the states without counsel violated the meaning of due process. Nine uneducated and indigent black youths, ranging in ages from twelve to nine, had been summarily convicted of the rape of two white women by the state of Alabama. The accused were nominally appointed counsel, who met with them for a few brief minutes before their trial began. There were serious questions surrounding their guilt, and, in fact, all were later exonerated. No doubt this played some role in the Court's decision, but the Court put the nation on notice that states would be required to provide counsel, at least in capital cases where the poor and illiterate were concerned. Four years later the Court would overturn the convictions of three illiterate black men based on confessions derived by Mississippi police officers, confessions not easily obtained. In fact, two of the three had been beaten with a leather strap, a buckle at its end, while naked. The third had been hung to the limb of a tree and whipped until his confession was obtained. Whatever due process meant, the Court determined it surely was not this. Such tactics were commonplace in many parts of the country. Indeed, the 1931 National Commission on Law Observance and Enforcement revealed that police brutality and the use of violence was widespread. In subsequent cases where state officials had not engaged in the types of physical abuse embraced by Mississippi, the Court, nonetheless, concluded that admissions made via mental torture or coercion were intolerable.

How a Florida Drifter Changed the Law

Clarence Gideon, prisoner No. 003826 of the Florida State Penitentiary, had requested that the Supreme Court reverse his misdemeanor conviction for petty larceny.[2] He had written the petition to the Court himself on official prison stationary. Gideon had filed the petition in forma pauperis, or in the form of a pauper, for which he surely qualified. As such, the filing fees and other requirements were waived. Gideon argued that Florida's refusal to furnish him a lawyer had made a fair trial impossible. Florida had complied with previous Supreme Court precedents. There was no capital crime involved, and considering the "totality of the circumstances"—the Court's requirement for those cases like Gideon's—the judge had required Gideon to represent himself. He was evidently a better appellate attorney than a trial lawyer.

Clarence Earl Gideon had been accused of breaking into a pool hall and absconding with a small amount of change, some beer, and some wine. He had requested a lawyer but had been denied one. The trial was short and based primarily on the testimony of a single eyewitness. Though Gideon knew the evidence against him to be weak, he had no experience with cross-examinations, closing arguments, and other trial tactics. A jury of six men convicted him in short order. While his luck seemed to have run out in the state of Florida, he was fortunate indeed to have been submitting his petition for review to the U.S. Supreme Court of 1962. Gideon's case would lead the Warren Court's revolution in expanding the rights of the accused, a revolution that would reach its apex with the establishment of the so-called Miranda warnings.

While Florida had not furnished Gideon a lawyer, the U.S. Supreme Court—as they do for all indigents—provided him an exceptional one to argue his case. Indeed, his lawyer, Abe Fortas, would go on to serve on the nation's highest bench himself. The Court unanimously established in

Gideon v. Wainwright (372 U.S. 335 [1963]) that appointment of counsel is a fundamental right that is essential to a fair trial. If an individual like Clarence Gideon could not afford an attorney, one must be provided at state expense. The noble ideal of the Constitution—that every defendant stands "equal before the law"—was meaningless if that equality depended on the ability to hire a lawyer. Lawyers, the Court indicated, were "necessities," not "luxuries," in a system based on the rule of law.[3]

What the Court did not indicate, however, was exactly *when* that right emerged. Was it at arrest? At arraignment? At trial? *Gideon* left many questions unanswered, and law enforcement officials were anxious about the answers. If lawyers had to be provided at arrest, or more perilously at the point an individual is detained, all manner of chaos was sure to ensue. Many police officials believed they would be hamstrung in their investigations if lawyers could intervene on behalf of a suspect before they could begin their questioning.

Expanding the Right to Counsel: The Case of Danny Escobedo

A twenty-two-year-old Chicago laborer, Escobedo had been arrested in connection with the murder of his brother-in-law. He had retained a lawyer the previous week in relationship to a personal injury claim against the Chicago Transit Authority. Though the police questioned Escobedo for fourteen hours, he made no statement. He was released only after his lawyer obtained a state court order demanding it. He was arrested again and immediately repeated the advice given to him by his attorney after his release ten days earlier, "I am sorry, but I would like to have advice from my lawyer." He was ignored. After learning of his arrest, his attorney tried repeatedly to see his client, something he was allowed to do by Illinois statute, but was repeatedly refused by Chicago police. Eventually, Escobedo signed a statement that would be used to convict him of the murder.

While the Court had been unanimous in its decision to require states to provide indigents with counsel, they were much less united in assessing when that right began. In a 5–4 decision (*Escobedo v. Illinois,* 378 U.S. 478 [1964]), Justice Arthur Goldberg, joined by Justices Black, William Brennan, William Douglas, and Earl Warren, determined that counsel was essential when, as in Escobedo's case:

> the investigation is no longer a general inquiry into an unsolved crime but has begun to focus on a particular suspect, the suspect has been taken into police custody, the policy carry out a process of interrogations that lends itself to eliciting incriminating statements, the suspect has requested and been

denied an opportunity to consult with his lawyer, and the police have not effectively warned him of his absolute constitutional right to remain silent, the accused has been denied the "Assistance of Counsel" in violation of the Sixth Amendment to the Constitution as "made obligatory upon the States by the Fourteenth Amendment" [due process clause], and that no statement elicited by the police during the interrogation may be used against him at a criminal trial.

The Court recognized the concerns of law enforcement that the number of confessions would decline significantly if individuals were given access to attorneys during custody, when the vast majority of interrogations occur. But the Court also recognized that the right to an attorney would "indeed be hollow" if it were provided after the advice was most needed. The Court stressed that convictions based on confessions alone, obtained under the intrinsically coercive atmosphere of police custody, "will, in the long run, be less reliable and more subject to abuses than a system which depends on extrinsic evidence independently secured through skillful investigation." Most important for Ernest Miranda, the Court set the stage for his appeal when it chided its critics noting that:

> no system of justice can, or should, survive if it comes to depend for its continued effectiveness on the citizens' abdication through *unawareness* [emphasis added] of their constitutional rights. No system worth preserving should have to fear that if an accused is permitted to consult with a lawyer, he will become aware of, and exercise, these rights.

Justice John Marshall Harlan castigated the decision as "most ill-conceived," arguing that it "seriously and unjustifiably fetters perfectly legitimate methods of criminal law enforcement." Justice Potter Stewart's dissent denounced the Court's ruling as "supported by no stronger authority than its own rhetoric." For the dissenters, the accusatory process began with the formal indictment, and it was at this stage that counsel must be provided. Routine police investigation processes, practiced day in, day out across the country, did not engender a sufficient due process threat to necessitate the provision of counsel. Justice Byron White set the stage for Ernset Miranda's appeal with his dissent, which was joined by Justices Tom Clark and Stewart, wherein he argued that "it was incongruous to assume that the provision for counsel in the Sixth Amendment was meant to amend or supersede the self-incrimination provision of the Fifth Amendment." The tenor of the majority's opinion hinted at precisely this—it would be only in conjunction with each other that either would mean much.[4]

Escobedo v. Illinois suggested that the exercising of constitutional rights should not pose a threat to a constitutional democracy. But it too left several questions unanswered. What if an individual did not request a lawyer, as Escobedo had? What if an individual did not assert a right to remain silent? What if an individual was completely ignorant of the ability under our Constitution to do either?

"You Have the Right to Remain Silent": Bridging the Fifth and Sixth Amendments

After oral arguments in Miranda's case, the justices met to decide his fate. The chief justice, who, if he is voting with the majority, retains the privilege of assigning the justice to write the opinion, decided to assign the writing of one of the most controversial decisions of the Court to himself. On May 18 of 1966, the chief justice circulated his first draft; two more would follow on June 6 and June 11. On Monday, June 13, Ernest Miranda, incarcerated in the state penitentiary in Florence, Arizona, learned his fate from the local news.

Warren's decision in *Miranda v. Arizona* (384 U.S. 436 [1966]), decided with the identical voting coalitions of *Escobedo,* evaluated the history of determining the voluntary nature of the confession. Appellate courts across the nation had invested large sums of resources over the appeals of contested confessions. The Court itself had attempted repeatedly to assess the requisites of voluntariness. While the Court was correct in *Escobedo* when it recognized that "any lawyer worth his salt will tell the suspect in no uncertain terms to make no statement to police under any circumstances," it was also true that any lawyer worth his salt would also challenge inculpatory statements at trial and on appeal. To be truly voluntary, the Court asserted in *Miranda,* such statements must be made "knowingly and competently." But that verbiage was no better definition of "voluntariness" than the word itself. How and when would a judge or magistrate be confident that the statements were made absent coercion and with "full opportunity to exercise the privilege against self-incrimination"?

For the Court, the test should be a bright line, which ultimately would benefit police, because the ability to challenge such statements would be essentially impossible. It would benefit society at large, because the Constitution would not be applicable to a privileged few. Those without the intellectual capacity to comprehend constitutional protections (or to hire someone who does) are most in its need; those without the human will to resist coercive police interrogation would be protected. In sum, the Court required, in those now familiar words, that an individual must be warned prior to any questioning that he has the right to remain silent, that anything he says can and will be used against him in a court of law, that he has the right to the presence of an attorney, and that if he cannot afford an attorney one will be appointed for him prior to any questioning if he so desires.

Absent these warnings, or their functional equivalent, nothing derived from those conversations, neither the statements themselves nor any evidence that flowed from them, could be used against the accused at trial. The Court, though mindful of the burden that would be placed on law-enforcement officials with its decision, pointed to the Federal Bureau of Investigation's techniques, which had already incorporated the Miranda precepts without any evident reduction in effectiveness. Surely the "practice of the FBI can readily be emulated by state and local enforcement agencies." After all, the California Supreme Court had required the essential warnings in a 1965 decision, and police officers and judges were busy implementing the ruling by the time Ernest Miranda's conviction was being overturned by five justices of the U.S. Supreme Court. The Court was sensitive to its critics, but as Warren concluded, "As courts have been presented with the need to enforce constitutional rights, they have found means of doing so."

In three separate opinions, the dissenters did not mince words in their criticism of the Court's decision. Justice Clark argued that, "[s]uch a strict constitutional specific inserted at the nerve center of crime detection may well kill the patient." Justice Clark argued that nothing in the Court's previous decisions paved the way for such a monumental shift in precedent that would require an affirmative waiver of the Fifth and Sixth Amendment's protections; would shift the burden to the prosecution if confessions were challenged; would require counsel at the accusatory stage and that the counsel be paid for if necessary; and equated admissions, even exculpatory statements, with confessions. All these were being consumed in a single "gulp" that should cause the Court to "choke" over the many precedents overturned by the majority's ruling.

Justice Harlan's dissent, joined by Stewart and White, thought the Court had gone far afield of the intention of the Fifth Amendment to establish "voluntariness with a vengeance." The Court had surpassed its boundaries as a judicial institution, which, by its very nature, should require resolution on a case-by-case basis and had instead created a public policy that was "so dubious that there can be no due compensation for its weakness in constitutional law."

Justice White's dissent, joined by Justices Harlan and Stewart, evaluated the historical context of the protection against self-incrimination and the right to counsel. He argued these were protections derived from two very different and distinct trajectories of legal history and that they had never been dependent on one another, as the majority asserted. The Court had fashioned a "new law and new public policy," which would prove to be a "constitutional straitjacket" and was designed as a "deliberate calculus to prevent interrogations, to reduce the incidence of confessions and pleas of guilty and increase the number of trials." For Justice White the Court should be more concerned with the community costs when the inevitable occurs, and those who would have been convicted absent *Miranda's* strictures are allowed to return to the streets "to repeat his crime whenever it pleases him."

While "Impeach Earl Warren" bumper stickers had littered the landscape before *Miranda*, a firestorm of criticism followed directly in its wake. Law-enforcement officials warned that 75 to 80 percent of criminal convictions depended on confessions and that *Miranda* had destroyed a very effective method of solving crime. Congress responded by adding section 3501 to the U.S. Criminal Code. This new addition gave the judge in a federal trial the ability to determine the "voluntariness" of a confession, and it specifically did not require Miranda warnings for the confession to be admitted.[5] The law-and-order plank figured prominently in the 1968 Republican presidential campaign. The party's nominee, Richard Nixon, attributed the rising crime rate to Supreme Court decisions, *Miranda* in particular, which protected criminals and bridled police. He promised to appoint individuals opposed to decisions of the Warren Court and placed a special emphasis on those decisions that had expanded the rights of the accused. True to his campaign promise, his first appointee, Warren Burger as chief justice, was a noted critic of the Court's Fourth and Fifth Amendment jurisprudence. Ultimately, Nixon would appoint three additional members to the Court: Harry Blackmun, Lewis Powell, and William Rehnquist. The latter would prove time and again to be in opposition to the Warren Court's precedents.

Despite these additions, the Court has never overruled the central holding of *Miranda*. It has, however, added a variety of exceptions. Adverse statements obtained without the requisite warnings can be admitted when they are used to impeach the credibility of the defendant (*Harris v. New York*, 401 U.S. 22 [1971]), when the statements are made during a noncustodial interview (*Beckwith v. United States*, 422 U.S. 341 [1975]; *Oregon v. Mathiason*, 429 U.S. 492 [1977]), when made to a grand jury or a parole officer (*United States v. Madujano*, 425 U.S. 564 [1976]; *Minnesota v. Murphy*, 465 U.S. 420 [1984]), when there is a danger to the public safety (*New York v. Quarles,* 467 U.S. 649 [1984]), or when statements are given to an undercover police agent (*Illinois v. Perkins,* 496 U.S. 292 [1990]). The Court has also ruled that if the judge believes the accused would have been convicted with evidence obtained independent of the confession, a coerced confession can be deemed a "harmless error" (*Arizona v. Fulminante,* 499 U.S. 279 [1991]).

In the post-Miranda years, social scientists have attempted to assess the effect of the *Miranda* decision on police investigations. Early studies immediately following the Court's decision found little effect on either the police or the suspects. Police were not consistently giving the warnings, and suspects were not consistently remaining silent or requesting counsel, though some research indicated a drop in confessions generally (Medalie, Zeitz, & Alexander, 1968; Seeburger & Wettick, 1967; Wald, Ayres, Hess, Schantz, & Whitebread, 1967). More recent studies have focused on the overall cost of *Miranda* on actual convictions. One study of nine medium-sized counties in the 1970s found that fewer than 1 percent of convictions were lost as a result of excluded confessions (Narduli, 1983). Similar results held true for studies of convictions in Chicago, Jacksonville, and San Diego (Narduli, 1987). Several scholars found that individuals who had previous felony convictions were more likely to invoke their *Miranda* protections, and those who did not were more likely to plea bargain (Neubauer, 1974). Studies of appellate decisions also found little substantive effect on reversals of convictions (Davies, 1982).

In 1996 there was a renewed effort to assess the effects of *Miranda.*[6] Paul Cassell's work suggested that *Miranda* had a significant effect on the prosecutor's ability to convict. Cassell compared the reduction in the confession rates reported in previous studies to the estimates of the importance of confessions to solving crimes. He determined that almost 4 percent of crimes are lost to *Miranda*'s effects. He calculated 4 percent of federal arrests to be some 28,000 lost cases (Cassell, 1996). Cassell's work has been highly criticized for the inferential leaps made with his data. After all, previous studies found that while confession rates dropped, conviction rates did not. Cassell's work argues precisely this. Lost confessions are presumed to result in lost cases (Cassell 1996; Cassell & Hayman, 1996).

Critics of Cassell's work have argued that the studies on which Cassell relied were poorly designed and that while these studies were informative, they were not sufficiently rigorous to provide the reliable and valid data Cassell's assertions would require (Leo 1996; Thomas, 1996). Second, studies noted that law enforcement officials have adapted to *Miranda*'s effects over the three decades since its pronouncement (Leo, 1996). Indeed, many police officers have found that challenges to confessions are nearly impossible if the cursory guarantees of *Miranda* are delivered in a perfunctory fashion. Cassell's research relies on data that are some thirty years old, and thus ignores the "rebound" effect of the post-*Miranda* years (Schulhofer, 1996). Today's police officers have known no approach other than that required by *Miranda*. A variety of effective strategies have been developed to counteract the potential of *Miranda*'s warnings. Some now view *Miranda* as little more than a formality that protects the officers on appeal.

One incontrovertible effect of the Court's decision is that Ernest Miranda's name has become a household phrase to convey protections for the accused. While most will not know the story of Ernest Miranda, or even the exact Fifth and Sixth Amendment verbiage, for over thirty years the scripts from *Columbo* to *Miami Vice* to *Law and Order* and *NYPD Blue* have made the phrasing of the Court's opinion common knowledge.

Miranda, however, did little to help Ernest. Miranda was retried in 1967. Based on statements he had made while in prison to his common-law wife and the testimony of Patricia Wise, who had married and moved from Phoenix, he was again convicted. After serving one-third of his sentence, Miranda was paroled in December of 1972. A routine traffic stop in July of 1974 led to a drug charge against him. However, based on Warren Court precedent, the judge threw out the search as unconstitutional. Nonetheless, the drug possession led to Miranda's parole revocation. He was now thirty-three and back in prison. Rehabilitation proved illusive. Following his second release from prison, Miranda found work as an appliance store deliveryman in Phoenix. He was suspected of drug dealing but had successfully escaped the ever-watchful eyes of police officers. He was also suspected of cheating at cards, which had led to a bloody bar-room brawl with two Mexican immigrants in a seedy section of downtown Phoenix. While Miranda left to wash the blood from his hands in the restroom, one of the two opponents awaited his return with a knife. Miranda was stabbed once in the stomach and once in the upper chest. He was pronounced dead on arrival at the hospital.

Though Miranda's killer escaped down an alley, his partner in the crime would be caught. After the arrest, a small card was pulled from the officer's pocket, and he proceeded to read first in English and then in Spanish:

You have the right to remain silent.
Anything you say can be used against you in a court of law.
You have the right to the presence of an attorney to assist you prior to questioning and to be with you during questioning if you so desire.

If you cannot afford an attorney you have the right to have an attorney appointed for you prior to questioning.

Do you understand these rights?

Will you voluntarily answer my questions?

NOTES

1. This is not her real name. This discussion of the *Miranda* case flows primarily from Baker (1985) and Leo and Thomas (1998), as well as from the petitioner and respondent briefs for the case, the oral arguments before the case, and, of course, the Court's opinion itself.

2. This discussion of *Gideon* relies heavily on Anthony Lewis's classic work *Gideon's Trumpet* (1964) as well as on the briefs, arguments, and opinion of the case.

3. Clarence Gideon was eventually acquitted of the charges following a retrial in 1963. Baker (1985) notes that his only other encounter with the law was for vagrancy, a misdemeanor. The judge offered to hold him long enough to appeal the right to counsel for misdemeanors, which the Court eventually did address, though not this time for Gideon. He pled guilty and was released. In 1972, still a gambler and drifter, he died penniless. He was sixty-one years old.

4. Danny Escobedo was released following the Supreme Court's decision. He was convicted in 1967 on drug charges and spent seven years in the federal penitentiary. In 1984 he was convicted of molesting his thirteen-year-old stepdaughter and was sentenced to twelve years. He appealed the sentence, and while out on bond, he shot a man in a bar. He was convicted for murder and sentenced to eleven years in prison. Ironically, his sister, whose husband's murder began the *Escobedo* ordeal, remarried. Spouse number two was also murdered; the perpetrator was never apprehended.

5. The addition of this section was largely symbolic and was ignored by the Justice Department for three decades. Indeed, the Justice Department refused to defend it before the Supreme Court in *Dickerson v. United States* (530 U.S. 428 [2000]) after it was upheld by the Fourth Circuit. The Supreme Court appointed Paul Cassell, a law professor whose research (cited below) has been critical of the *Miranda* decision, to represent the United States. The Supreme Court's decision, surprisingly authored by Chief Justice Rehnquist, stressed the importance of adhering to precedent as well as noting that *Miranda* was a "constitutional rule" that could not be negated by simple statute.

6. For an extensive discussion of the debate, see Leo and Thomas (1996).

REFERENCES

Baker, I. (1985). *Miranda: Crime, law and politics.* New York: Atheneum.

Cassell, P. G. (1996). *Miranda's* social costs: An empirical reassessment. *Northwestern University Law Review, 90,* pp. 387–499.

Cassell, P. G., & Hayman, B. S. (1996). Police interrogation in the 1990s: An empirical study of the effects of *Miranda. University of California Law Review, 43,* pp. 839–932.

Davies, T. Y. (1982). Affirmed: A study of criminal appeals and decision-making norms in a California court of appeal. *American Bar Foundation Research Journal,* pp. 543–648.

Leo, R. A. (1996). The impact of *Miranda* revisited. *Journal of Criminal Law and Criminology, 86,* pp. 621–692.

Leo, R. A., & Thomas, G. C., III (Eds.) (1998). *The Miranda debate: Law, justice, and policing.* Boston: Northeastern University Press.

Lewis, A. (1964). *Gideon's Trumpet.* New York: Random House.

Medalie, R. J., Zeitz, L., & Alexander, P. (1968). Custodial police interrogation in our nation's capital: The attempt to implement *Miranda. Michigan Law Review, 66,* pp. 1347–1422.

Nardulli, P. F. (1983). The societal costs of the exclusionary rule: An empirical assessment. *American Bar Foundation Research Journal,* pp. 585–609.

Nardulli, P. F. (1987). The societal costs of the exclusionary rule revisited. *University of Illinois Law Review, 1,* pp. 223–229

Neubauer, D. W. (1974). *Criminal justice in middle America.* Morristown, NJ: General Learning Press.

Seeburger, R. H., & Wettick, R. S., Jr. (1967). *Miranda* in Pittsburgh—A statistical study. *University of Pittsburgh Law Review, 29,* pp. 1–26.

Schulhofer, S. J. (1996). *Miranda*'s practical effect: Substantial benefits and vanishingly small social costs. *Northwestern University Law Review, 90,* pp. 500–563.

Thomas, G. C. (1996). Plain talk about the *Miranda* empirical debate: A "steady-state" theory of confessions. *University of California Law Review, 43,* pp. 933–959.

Wald, M. S., Ayres, R., Hess, D. W., Schantz, M., Whitebread, C. H., II. (1967) Interrogations in New Haven: The impact of *Miranda. Yale Law Journal,, 76,* pp. 1521–1648.

Cruel and Unusual Punishment

Capital Punishment and the Mentally Retarded

Atkins v. Virginia (2002)

THOMAS G. WALKER

> *Penry v. Lynaugh,* the Supreme Court's decision permitting the execution of the
> mentally retarded, proved to be enormously unpopular. After the decision was is-
> sued, many states reevaluated this practice, enacting laws prohibiting the death
> penalty for retarded offenders. This movement evidently convinced the Court that
> society had determined that such executions were cruel and unusual punishment.
> So, roughly a decade after it first upheld this practice, the Supreme Court reversed
> the *Penry* decision and declared that it violated the Eighth Amendment.

It was in *Penry v. Lynaugh* (492 U.S. 302 [1989])that the U.S. Supreme Court
first considered the issue of capital punishment and mental retardation. The
case focused on Johnny Penry, sentenced to death by a Texas jury. His crime
was heinous. Penry, a twenty-two-year-old rape parolee, forcibly entered the
residence of Pamela Carpenter, a young East Texas homemaker. He brutally
raped and beat her, finally killing her with a pair of scissors. There was little
doubt that Penry's actions qualified him for the death penalty under Texas

law. But there was much more to Johnny Penry than the rape and killing of Pamela Carpenter.

As a child Penry was habitually beaten by his mother, locked indoors for long periods of time, and made to drink his own urine (Orecklin, 2000). He was removed from public school during the first grade and was later committed to a state school for the mentally retarded. Intelligence tests revealed an IQ of between 53 and 60, clearly falling within the standard definition of mental retardation (an IQ score below 70). He had never learned to read or write. While in prison, he spent his time looking at comic books and drawing with crayons. In some interviews he expressed a belief in Santa Claus.

Lawyers for Penry petitioned the Supreme Court to rule that executing the mentally retarded violates the Eighth Amendment's ban on cruel and unusual punishment. Although the justices found fault with Penry's sentence on more narrow grounds, they rejected, by a 5–4 vote, the invitation to exclude the retarded, as a class, from death penalty eligibility.

The *Penry* decision was a crushing blow to death penalty opponents, who had hoped that the Court would bar the execution of all mentally retarded individuals. But thirteen years later, the case of *Atkins v. Virginia* (536 U.S. 304 [2002]) would once again bring the plight of mentally retarded convicts to the Court's doorstep.

The Supreme Court, the Death Penalty, and Mental Retardation

The *Penry* decision was consistent with the Supreme Court's developing death penalty jurisprudence (Banner, 2002). In *Furman v. Georgia* (408 U.S. 238 [1972]) the Court found that the death penalty was too often applied in an arbitrary manner, frequently at the expense of racial minorities (see Baldus, Woodworth, & Pulaski, 1989). At the heart of the Court's objections was the unguided discretion given to juries when deciding on an appropriate sentence in capital cases. Typically jurors were asked only to deliberate and agree on a recommended penalty. They were provided no legally relevant criteria on which to evaluate the competing options of prison or death. Under such standardless conditions, racial prejudices too easily entered the decision-making process—consciously or unconsciously. The *Furman* decision effectively imposed a moratorium on executions. In response, pro-death penalty states developed new capital punishment statutes designed to remove the constitutional problems identified by the Court.

Georgia was one of the first to do so. Under its new death penalty procedures, cases were heard in bifurcated (two-stage) trials. The first stage determined whether the defendant had committed a capital offense. Upon a guilty verdict, the trial entered the sentencing phase. Here the prosecutor could seek the death penalty by proving the presence of one or more statutorily defined aggravating circumstances. Aggravating circumstances are factors that make a particular murder, for example, more serious than a typical killing. The Georgia statute identified ten such aggravating circumstances. Among them were: (1) murders that are outrageously or wantonly vile, horrible, or inhumane; (2) the murder of a judicial or prosecutorial official during the exercise of his or her duties; (3) murder committed during the commission of rape, kidnapping, armed robbery, burglary, or arson.

To counter these allegations, the defense had the opportunity to prove the presence of mitigating circumstances, factors that made the crime less serious or the defendant worthy of a more lenient sentence. The Georgia statute did not define or limit such mitigating circumstances, but defense attorneys commonly cited such factors as the defendant's background, family responsibilities, psychiatric condition, or chances for rehabilitation.

The jury was required to find the presence of at least one aggravating circumstance before it could sentence a defendant to death. By making the jury focus on factors relevant to the rational imposition of the death penalty on an individualized basis, Georgia hoped to remove the excessive discretion that the Court found so constitutionally objectionable in *Furman*. The Georgia statute also provided for all death sentences to receive an automatic appeal to the state supreme court.

Troy Gregg, sentenced to death for the killing of two individuals from whom he had hitched a ride, challenged Georgia's revised procedures. By this time thirty-five states and the federal government had enacted revised death penalty statutes, and almost 500 defendants had been sentenced to death. In *Gregg v. Georgia* (428 U.S. 153 [1976]), seven justices agreed that the new Georgia aggravating/mitigating circumstances law met constitutional standards, thereby giving permission to states with similarly crafted statutes to resume executions. Only Justices Thurgood Marshall and William Brennan, who believed that all executions violated the Eighth Amendment, dissented.

The *Gregg* ruling jarred death penalty opponents, many of whom had believed that *Furman* truly signaled the inevitable end of capital punishment in the United States (Epstein & Kobylka, 1992; Meltsner, 1973). Many concluded that legal attempts to ban capital punishment outright were not likely to succeed. A more effective strategy would be to challenge specific applications of the death penalty, with the goal of reducing executions incrementally. The Court had set certain standards governing sentencing under the cruel and unusual punishment clause, which provided potential grounds for attacking various death penalty applications. Among them were: (1) a penalty must be graduated and proportionate to the crime (*Weems v. United States,*

217 U.S. 349 [1910]); (2) a sentence must be rationally related to deterrence, retribution, or other legitimate criminal justice goal (*Enmund v. Florida,* 458 U.S. 782 [1982]); (3) a sentence cannot be imposed in an arbitrary or capricious manner (*Furman v. Georgia*); and (4) a criminal penalty must be consistent with evolving standards of decency (*Trop v. Dulles,* 356 U.S. 86 [1958]).

For the most part, the Supreme Court responded negatively to such challenges, generally giving states considerable latitude in administering the death penalty (for example, *McCleskey v. Kemp,* 481 U.S. 279 [1987]; *Payne v. Tennessee,* 501 U.S. 808 [1991]). Capital punishment foes, however, achieved some victories. For example, the Court held that execution was a grossly disproportionate penalty for the crime of rape (*Coker v. Georgia,* 433 U.S. 584 [1977]), that the state cannot place unreasonable limitations on the range of mitigating circumstances considered by the jury (*Lockett v. Ohio,* 438 U.S. 586 [1978]; *Eddings v. Oklahoma,* 455 U.S. 104 [1982]), and that the death penalty is a constitutionally inappropriate sentence for defendants under the age of sixteen years (*Thompson v. Oklahoma,* 487 U.S. 815 [1988]).

Against this backdrop, attorneys for Johnny Penry hoped the Court would remove the mentally retarded, as a class, from being sentenced to death. The four more liberal members of the Court, Brennan, Marshall, John Paul Stevens, and Harry Blackmun, supported Penry's position that the Constitution forbids the execution of the mentally retarded; but William Rehnquist, Antonin Scalia, Byron White, and Anthony Kennedy, the more conservative justices, favored affirming Penry's death sentence. Taking a middle position, and holding the balance of power in the case, was Justice Sandra Day O'Connor, who was given the task of writing the Court's opinion.

O'Connor voted with the conservatives on the central constitutional issue, holding that the Eighth Amendment does not prohibit the imposition of the death sentence on the mentally retarded. She noted that mental retardation should not be confused with insanity. Unlike the legally insane, retarded individuals in many cases possess the ability to distinguish right from wrong and to comport their behavior to the dictates of the law. Furthermore, O'Connor and the conservatives were unconvinced that a national consensus had developed against the execution of the mentally retarded. Only two states (Georgia and Maryland) had passed laws prohibiting capital punishment for such persons. If there were a growing national consensus that such executions were wrong, more states would have done so. Thus, O'Connor wrote that mental retardation should continue to be a mitigating circumstance that juries should consider on an individual basis rather than treating low intelligence levels as a factor automatically sparing a convict from execution.

The Court's decision in *Penry* renewed the national debate over the death penalty. A second capital punishment ruling handed down the same day exacerbated the perception that the Court had taken an excessively harsh position. In *Stanford v. Kentucky* (492 U.S. 361 [1989]), the justices held, by the same 5–4 vote, that the execution of individuals who were as young as sixteen years at the time they committed murder did not violate the cruel and unusual punishment clause of the Eighth Amendment.

Subsequent legislative deliberations resulted in many states changing their laws with respect to the mentally retarded. Between 1990 and 2001, sixteen death penalty states (Arizona, Arkansas, Colorado, Connecticut, Florida, Indiana, Kansas, Kentucky, Missouri, Nebraska, New Mexico, New York, North Carolina, South Dakota, Tennessee, and Washington) and the federal government joined Georgia and Maryland in excluding the retarded from capital punishment eligibility. Public opinion polls reflected sharp opposition to such executions. Even President George W. Bush, a supporter of capital punishment generally, declared in June 2001 that "We should never execute anybody who is mentally retarded." International sentiment overwhelming disfavored the practice (Hood, 1996). Between 1995 and 2002, only Japan and Kyrgyzstan, along with the United States, executed any mentally retarded prisoners.

These developments prompted death penalty foes to believe that a new consensus had developed. Imposing capital punishment on mentally retarded convicts could now be viewed as a violation of contemporary standards of decency. It was time to ask the Court to reconsider the *Penry* decision. The task of doing so was left to the legal team representing convicted murderer Daryl Atkins.

Daryl Atkins and the Murder of Eric Nesbitt

August 16, 1996, found eighteen-year-old Daryl Reynard Atkins in the Hampton, Virginia, apartment he shared with his father. Just before noon, Atkins was joined by William A. Jones. Atkins and his twenty-six-year-old friend spent the rest of the day drinking, smoking marijuana, and watching television. Periodically others dropped by and joined them.

Around 11:30 that night, Jones and Atkins walked to a nearby convenience store to replenish their beer supply. When they arrived at the 7-Eleven, Atkins realized that he did not have enough money to buy the beer. At about that time, Eric Nesbitt, a twenty-one-year-old airman first class from Langley Air Force Base, drove up to the store in his small Nissan pickup truck. As Nesbitt left the store, Atkins confronted him with a semiautomatic handgun a friend had given him. Atkins and Jones forced Nesbitt to relinquish control of the truck.

With Jones at the wheel, the three sped off, sideswiping another car as they left. Atkins removed $60.00 from Nesbitt's wallet. While doing so, he noticed an automated bank teller card. Atkins instructed Jones to drive to a local branch of the bank and ordered Nesbitt to withdraw $200 from the cash machine. A surveillance camera at the bank filmed the transaction. The videotape clearly showed Nesbitt sitting in the front seat of his truck, flanked by two African American men—Jones in the driver's seat and Atkins on the passenger side. All the while, Atkins had the gun pointed at Nesbitt.

Atkins instructed Jones to drive to a remote wooded spot about eighteen miles from Hampton. When they arrived, Atkins exited the truck and ordered Nesbitt to do the same. Although Nesbitt pleaded with his abductors not to hurt him, he took no more than two steps before Atkins opened fire. Jones attempted to stop Atkins, and during their struggle Atkins was shot in the ankle. Later, Atkins sought treatment at a local emergency room, where doctors removed the bullet.

A passerby found Nesbitt's body at about 4:00 A.M. on August 17 and called the police. An autopsy later revealed that Nesbitt had been shot a total of eight times, with bullets piercing his chest, thorax, abdomen, arms, and legs. Three of the wounds were lethal, although Nesbitt lived for several minutes before blood loss ultimately caused his death.

At the scene a sheriff's department investigator found Nesbitt's bank card. A check of bank records revealed the transaction that had taken place the previous night. Television stations broadcasted photographs from the videotaped ATM withdrawal and urged local residents to help find the suspects. Viewer response was swift. Jones was quickly identified and linked to Atkins. Police arrested Atkins at his home. Jones, who had cut his hair and was moving from motel to motel to avoid being identified and caught, was apprehended not long thereafter.

Evidence against the two suspects was overwhelming. The bank videotape indisputably showed Jones and Atkins with a gun trained on Nesbitt. Although the murder weapon was never located, six shell casings found at the scene of the crime, three bullets taken from Nesbitt's body, one bullet recovered from the Nissan truck, and the bullet removed from Atkins's ankle were all linked to the same gun. Blood samples taken from the truck were consistent with the blood types of Atkins and Nesbitt and were not likely to have come from any other source. Atkins admitted to police that he had been involved in the crime but claimed that Jones had orchestrated the event and was the actual triggerman. Atkins, however, contradicted this story in statements he made to a cell mate while awaiting trial.

The state initially charged both Jones and Atkins with capital murder. The prosecutor ultimately became convinced that Atkins was the actual killer and offered Jones protection from the death penalty in return for his testimony against Atkins. Jones agreed to the arrangement and was later sentenced to life plus three years in prison.

The state considered Atkins's crime to be particularly vile. Although only eighteen years old, Atkins was no stranger to the criminal justice system. He had multiple prior felony convictions, including robbery, attempted robbery, breaking and entering, abduction, grand larceny, maiming, and several counts of using a firearm during the commission of a felony. In the state's judgment, Atkins was a serious danger to society, and he should pay for the murder of Eric Nesbitt by forfeiting his own life.

In February of 1998, Daryl Atkins stood trial before York County Circuit Court judge N. Prentis Smiley, Jr., for the capital murder of Eric Nesbitt and related offenses. Local criminal defense attorneys George M. Rogers III and Bryan L. Sanders served as his court-appointed lawyers. The state's case, presented by Commonwealth Attorney Eileen Addison, rested on the testimony of Jones, supported by the ballistic evidence, blood samples, and Atkins's contradictory stories. Atkins testified on his own behalf, claiming that Jones, in fact, committed the actual murder. The jury found Atkins's version lacking in credibility, declared him guilty, and recommended execution.

The Virginia Supreme Court affirmed the conviction, but sent the case back to the trial level for resentencing because of a defect in the original jury verdict form (*Atkins v. Commonwealth of Virginia*, 257 Va. 160 S.E. 2nd 445 [1999]). Judge Smiley again presided at the second sentencing hearing held in August 1999, but an entirely different jury heard the evidence.

The prosecutor argued that two aggravating circumstances recognized under Virginia law were present: (1) that the crime was outrageously or wantonly vile, horrible, or inhuman and (2) that Atkins was a serious and continuing threat to society. To prove the vile nature of the crime, the prosecution presented Nesbitt's autopsy results and demonstrated that the victim had been brutally shot many more times than necessary to accomplish the act of murder. As for the issue of societal danger, the state provided evidence of Atkins's multiple criminal transgressions and presented testimony from some of his previous victims, including a woman who had been shot in the stomach without provocation while she tended her lawn.

The defense countered by claiming that Atkins should be spared the death penalty because of his diminished mental capacity. Key testimony came from Dr. Evan Nelson, a clinical and forensic psychologist. Nelson had given Atkins a standard intelligence test. The results demonstrated an IQ of 59. This placed Atkins in the lowest 1 percentile nationally and classified him as having mild mental retardation with the cognitive ability of a normal child between nine and twelve years of age. This finding was consistent with Atkins's academic record. Although never declared retarded by the Hampton public schools, Atkins's performance was uniformly poor. He scored below the 20th percentile on every standardized test he took, failed the second and tenth grades, and was socially promoted from the fourth to the fifth grade. He received intensive remedial instruction in high school and attended classes for slow learners. He had a grade-point average of 1.26 (on a 4.0 scale) and did not earn sufficient credits to graduate. He had never lived on his own or successfully held a job, indicating a low capacity for adaptive behavior. Nelson also diagnosed him as having an antisocial personality disorder. He judged Atkins to have an impaired, but not destroyed, ability to appreciate the criminal nature of his actions.

The state countered Nelson's testimony with that of Dr. Stanton Samenow, a clinical psychologist. Based on two interviews and responses to selected questions from intelligence tests, he concluded that Atkins was at least of average mental ability. Samenow found that Atkins possessed a reasonably sophisticated vocabulary, had little difficulty with memory exercises, was aware of major current events, and was able to understand cause and effect relationships. Samenow believed that Atkins's poor performance in school could be explained by his lack of motivation, low levels of concentration, and poor study habits—factors that were repeatedly mentioned in the reports of his teachers. Samenow concluded that in spite of having an antisocial personality disorder, Atkins was able to appreciate the criminality of his actions and was capable of conforming his behavior to the requirements of the law.

The jurors deliberated on these conflicting evaluations for less than two hours before concluding that the state had established the necessary aggravating circumstances. The jury was unconvinced that Atkins's mental condition provided significant mitigation and recommended that he be put to death. The Virginia Supreme Court, with two justices dissenting, relied on the *Penry* precedent and affirmed the death sentence (*Atkins v. Commonwealth of Virginia*, 260 Va. 375 2000).

Daryl Atkins and the U.S. Supreme Court

With the help of attorney Robert E. Lee and the Virginia Capital Representation Resource Center, Daryl Atkins petitioned the U.S. Supreme Court to review his sentence. His petition for certiorari reached the justices after they had already declared their interest in reconsidering the *Penry* precedent. In March, 2001, the Court accepted the petition of Ernest Paul McCarver, a mentally retarded North Carolinian who had been convicted of stabbing a coworker to death in 1987. Before the justices could hear the case, however, the North Carolina legislature passed a law baring the execution of the mentally retarded. In response, the Court dismissed McCarver's appeal and granted review to Daryl Atkins. The justices instructed the attorneys in *Atkins* to confine their arguments to the issue of whether evolving standards of decency had made the execution of mentally retarded convicts cruel and unusual punishment in violation of the Eighth and Fourteenth Amendments.

Only five justices who had participated in the *Penry* decision remained on the Court in 2002. Four of those justices (Rehnquist, O'Connor, Kennedy, and Scalia) had rejected the argument that the mentally retarded should be constitutionally exempt from the death penalty, and only one (Stevens) had favored banning such executions.

The more recently appointed justices, however, provided a ray of hope for capital punishment opponents. Ruth Bader Ginsburg, Stephen Breyer, and David Souter appeared likely to favor a death penalty exemption. Clinton appointees Ginsburg and Breyer, both moderate Democrats, had voting records in criminal cases much more liberal than the Court as a whole. Souter, a moderate Republican, also often found himself at odds with the Court's conservative decisions in criminal rights cases. In addition, Souter, a former New Hampshire attorney general, came from a state that had not conducted an execution since before the *Furman* decision. Conversely, Clarence Thomas was viewed as an almost certain vote for the state of Virginia. Thomas had become one of the Court's most conservative justices on criminal matters, supporting the claims of criminal defendants in only about 20 percent of cases presenting such issues.

At the outset, therefore, it appeared likely that the justices would split 5 to 4 in favor of maintaining the status quo. To overrule *Penry,* lawyers for Atkins knew they would have to convince at least one of the more conservative justices to change positions. O'Connor and Kennedy were the most likely candidates.

The justices allowed amicus curiae briefs already filed in the *McCarver* case to be used in *Atkins*. Briefs supporting Atkins were submitted by the American Bar Association, the American Civil Liberties Union, the United Catholic Conference, and a coalition of groups concerned with the rights of the mentally retarded, led by the American Association on Mental Retardation. Additionally, the European Union submitted a brief stressing the anti–death penalty position of the international community, and a group of American diplomats argued that permitting the execution of the mentally retarded jeopardized America's foreign affairs interests. Five states (Alabama, Mississippi, Nevada, South Carolina, and Utah) and the Criminal Justice Legal Foundation, a pro-law-enforcement organization, supported Virginia.

At oral argument James Ellis, a law professor at the University of New Mexico and a mental health specialist, represented Atkins. Virginia Assistant Attorney General Pamela Rumpz presented the views of the state. From their questions and comments, Justices Breyer, Souter, and Ginsburg seemed unconvinced by the state's arguments in defense of its law; Chief Justice Rehnquist and Justice Scalia appeared similarly unmoved by the positions taken by the death penalty opponents ("Oral Argument," 2002). Little could be discerned from the behavior of the other four justices.

On June 20, 2002, four months after oral arguments, Justice Stevens, who had authored a dissenting opinion in *Penry,* delivered the opinion of the Court. A six-justice majority ruled that societal standards had evolved to the point that the execution of the mentally retarded now constituted cruel and unusual punishment. In so holding, the Court effectively negated *Penry v. Lynaugh.* Four liberal/moderate justices (Stevens, Ginsburg, Souter, and Breyer) voted to impose a constitutional ban on such sentences. They were joined by O'Connor and Kennedy, who, apparently convinced that a new national standard of decency had emerged, abandoned their *Penry* positions. The changing views of O'Connor and Kennedy, then, were primarily responsible for the switch in Court policy. The more hard-line conservatives (Rehnquist, Scalia, and Thomas) held to the position that *Penry* was correctly decided and that its precedent should be followed.

Steven's majority opinion began by noting two principles that have guided Eighth Amendment interpretation. The first is that "punishment for crime should be graduated and proportioned to the offense" (*Weems,* 1910; *Harmelin v. Michigan,* 501 U.S. 957 [1991]; *Robinson v. California,* 370 U.S. 660 [1962]), and the second is that "The Amendment must draw its meaning from the evolving standards of decency that mark the progress of a maturing society" (*Trop,* 1958). With these guiding principles in mind, Stevens offered the following reasons for the Court's conclusions:

First, the nation's evolving standards have reached the point that execution of the mentally retarded is no longer constitutionally acceptable. Following the principle that laws passed by the state legislatures are the most objective indicators of national standards, Stevens reviewed how eighteen capital punishment states had outlawed the execution of the mentally retarded since 1986. In fact, every state that had altered its laws did so in the direction of barring such executions. Added to these were the twelve states that prohibit capital punishment altogether and those that rarely impose death sentences (e.g., New Hampshire, New Jersey). According to Stevens, only five states (Alabama, Louisiana, South Carolina, Texas, and Virginia) had executed a mentally retarded person since the Court handed down *Penry.* In support of the Court's conclusion that standards had changed, Stevens also cited the results of public opinion polls as well as amicus curiae briefs filed by a diverse set of religious and professional groups in opposition to the death penalty. Even the position of the international community, as reflected in an amicus submitted by the European Union, was offered as evidence of changing world attitudes on the execution of the mentally retarded.

Second, the traditional justifications for capital punishment, retribution and deterrence, do not easily apply to the mentally retarded. Those with low levels of intelligence may have difficulty reasoning, communicating, and controlling their impulses, thus reducing their moral culpability. These factors lessen the appropriateness of execution as retribution. Furthermore, the retarded have a lower capacity to reason and learn, making it unlikely that the threat of potential execution will deter them from criminal acts.

Third, while Stevens acknowledged that the mentally retarded may still know the difference between right and wrong and be competent to stand trial, he said that their diminished ability to process and understand information makes them more vulnerable to receiving capital punishment. The retarded may unwittingly make incriminating statements, may be unable to assist effectively in the preparation of a legal defense, and may be more prone to exhibit courtroom behavior that conveys an unwarranted impression of a lack of remorse.

The Court left to the states the responsibility of defining mental retardation. As for Daryl Atkins, he was not yet out of jeopardy. The Court remanded his case to the state courts to determine whether his mental condition exempted him from capital punishment. The state of Virginia, of course, had held all along that Atkins was not retarded.

Two dissenting opinions were filed. Chief Justice Rehnquist rejected as irrelevant the majority's use of statements by professional and religious organizations as well as the opinions of other countries, and he claimed that because of potential methodological problems, public opinion polls could not be trusted. Instead, Rehnquist argued that legislative enactments and jury decisions were the two best objective measures of evolving national standards. Thus, for Rehnquist (and Thomas and Scalia, who agreed with him), the majority had used inappropriate sources to arrive at its conclusions and had ignored totally one of the best indicators of national decency standards (jury decisions).

Justice Scalia's dissent also focused the way the majority arrived at its national consensus conclusions. Scalia's words were caustic. At the very outset he proclaimed that "Seldom has an opinion of this Court rested so obviously upon nothing but the personal views of its members." And later he charged the majority with an "assumption of power that takes one's breath away."

Scalia, whose opinion was endorsed by Rehnquist and Thomas, challenged the majority by arguing that of the thirty-eight states that permit capital punishment, only eighteen (47 percent) had passed legislation prohibiting the execution of the mentally retarded. For Scalia, these numbers fell short of constituting a national consensus. Furthermore, the states that had barred such executions had done so very recently, and there was no assurance that these changes were anything more than an experiment the states might later reverse. Scalia condemned the majority's use of interest group opinions; and he argued that the views of the world community, "whose notions of justice are (thankfully) not always those of our people," were immaterial to the question of a national consensus in the United States. Scalia also rejected the majority's conclusions concerning the disadvantages faced by the mentally retarded when charged with capital crimes. These were but assertions, he argued, not backed by any reliable empirical evidence. Rather than treat all retarded defendants the same, Scalia thought the individualized determination of culpability as incorporated into the *Gregg* and *Penry* decisions was the proper way to handle the problem. He predicted that the Court's decision would turn capital trials into a game in which defendants would fake retardation to escape execution.

The Impact of *Atkins v. Virginia*

Using the well-established "evolving standards of decency" test of the Eighth Amendment, the Court concluded that, although the mentally retarded may be convicted and punished for criminal activity, Americans no longer see their execution as constitutionally acceptable. But will this legal change have a significant impact on the application of the death penalty? At the time *Atkins* was decided, 2,455 persons were on death row in the twenty states that allowed such executions, but there is no way to know how many of those inmates were mentally retarded.

The impact of *Atkins* will be determined in large measure by the way the affected states satisfy their obligation to implement the ruling. If they follow the lead of the eighteen states that previously barred such executions, a three-part test to determine mental retardation will be used:

1. An IQ of less than 70;
2. Significant deficiencies in adaptive functioning (i.e. living independently, academic performance, effective communication skills, and so forth); and
3. The recognition of retardation characteristics prior to adulthood.

Critics of the *Atkins* decision, including the dissenters, have argued that convicts will now feign retardation to avoid the death chamber. Eileen Addison, the Atkins case prosecutor, for example, said "You bet I could score a 59 (on an IQ test) if my life depended on it" (Frank, 2002). The second and third prongs of the consensus test of retardation, however, reduce the odds that such last-minute attempts to qualify as retarded will be successful. It is not simply a matter of failing an intelligence test. Evidence of retardation must come from periods in the defendant's life that predate the capital crime committed. Thus, convicted murders such as Johnny Penry (still on death row twenty-three years after his crime) have a better chance of avoiding the death penalty than Daryl Atkins. Penry was diagnosed as retarded during childhood; whereas, Atkins was never formally classified as retarded before he murdered Eric Nesbitt.

Although the *Atkins* decision favored the interests of the mentally retarded with respect to the death penalty, it can be seen as potentially detrimental in other areas. Many mental retardation advocates argue that the retarded should be evaluated on an individual basis when being considered for employment and other opportunities. The *Atkins* approach of treating all mentally retarded as members of a class not fully responsible for their actions may not be so benign in the long run if it should spread beyond the criminal context.

A final question is whether the *Atkins* ruling signals a change in the Court's capital punishment jurisprudence. The answer is unclear. The justices handed down other decisions in 2002 that buoyed the hopes of death penalty opponents. For example, the Court held that death sentence questions must be decided by juries and not judges (*Ring v. Arizona*, 536 U.S. 584 [2002]). Death penalty foes, however, suffered a serious setback when the justices refused to reconsider their 1989 ruling that murderers as young as sixteen at the time of the crime could be executed (*Foster v. Florida*, 537 U.S. 990 [2002]; *In Re Stanford*, 537 U.S. 968 [2002]). The Court split 5–4 on this question, with the votes of O'Connor and Kennedy swinging back to the pro–death penalty position.

If evolving standards of decency spur the justices to revise their interpretations of the Eighth Amendment, then additional change may be in the offing. According to Justice Department statistics for 2001, the number of inmates on death row (3,581) declined for the first time in twenty-five years; the number of death sentences imposed by juries (155) was the lowest total since 1973 and represented a third straight year of declines; and of the thirty-eight states that have the death penalty, only fifteen carried out executions. The declining use of the death penalty has been attributed to the availability of more severe prison options (e.g., life in prison without the possibility of parole), new DNA evidence techniques, a growing awareness of cases in which defendants have been wrongly convicted, and the imposition of death penalty moratoriums in some states. If such patterns continue over a number of years, the Supreme Court may again find itself faced with the question of evolving societal standards. Only this time the issue may not focus on specific applications of the death penalty, but on capital punishment itself.

REFERENCES

Baldus, D. C., Woodworth, G., & Pulaski, C. A. (1989). *Equal justice and the death penalty: A legal and empirical analysis.* Boston, MA: Northeastern University Press.

Banner, S. (2002). *The death penalty: An American history.* Cambridge, MA: Harvard University Press.

Epstein, L., & Kobylka, J. F. (1992). *The Supreme Court and legal change: Abortion and the death penalty.* Chapel Hill, NC: University of North Carolina Press.

Frank, J. (2002, June 22). Critics fear inmates on death row will fake IQ. *The Virginian-Pilot.*

Hood, R. G. (1996). *The death penalty: A world wide perspective.* New York: Oxford University Press.

Meltsner, M. (1973). *Cruel and unusual: The Supreme Court and capital punishment.* New York: Random House.

Oral argument: Court weighs execution of mentally retarded prisoners. (2002, March 5). *United States Law Week, 70,* pp. 3543–3545.

Orecklin, M. (2000). Should John Penry die? Retrieved on http://www.CNN.com website on December 20, 2002.

Racial Discrimination

Brown Moves North

Swann v. Charlotte-Mecklenburg Board of Education (1969)

STEVEN TAYLOR

Swann v. Charlotte Mecklenburg Board of Education is often viewed as the complementary bookend to *Brown v. Board of Education* (1954), the decision outlawing racially segregated public schools. In *Swann,* the justices went beyond the abstract ruling in *Brown* and authorized the federal courts to compel the dismantling of racially segregated schools through judicially designed remedies. Many believed this ruling would antagonize the South and harden opposition to desegregation rather than promote integration of the public schools. The decision is an excellent illustration of how the Supreme Court monitors the implementation and effectiveness of its legal mandates.

The U.S. Supreme Court's 1971 decision in the *Swann v. Charlotte-Mecklenburg* (402 U.S. 1 [1971]) case opened the door for school desegregation cases to be filed in jurisdictions throughout the United States. This decision followed a series of unanimous Supreme Court decisions on school desegregation, dating back to the 1954 *Brown v. Board of Education of Topeka, Kansas* (349 U.S. 294) decision outlawing segregation in public education.

These decisions—from 1954 to 1969—span all the years of Earl Warren's tenure as chief justice, and they reflected the Warren Court's general support for desegregation of public educational facilities, hence the unanimity.

The Warren Court's last major school desegregation case was the 1968 case of *Green v. County School Board* (391 U.S. 430), which originated in Kent County, Virginia. In this case the Court held that school districts that had previously mandated segregation (most of which were in southern and border states) must eliminate all vestiges of segregation and "convert to a unitary system in which racial discrimination would be eliminated root and branch" (*Green*, p. 438).

Chief Justice Warren retired in 1969 and was replaced by the much more conservative Warren Burger, who was appointed by President Richard Nixon. Nixon came to office after having reached out to southerners, many of whom were opposed to further court intervention in public schools. The appointment of Warren Burger appeared to reflect Nixon's efforts to mollify conservatives in the South and throughout the nation. Immediately upon assuming the role of chief justice, Burger was faced with a school desegregation case, that of *Alexander v. Holmes County Board of Education* (396 U.S. 19 [1969]). In this case the state of Mississippi was challenging a decision by the Fifth Circuit Court of Appeals that ordered the state to submit plans for the desegregation of thirty-three of that state's school districts. The Nixon Administration sided with the state of Mississippi, but Chief Justice Burger and the eight associate justices reimposed the Fifth Circuit's order and mandated that every school district "terminate dual school systems at once and . . . operate now and hereafter only unitary schools" (*Alexander*, 20). Chief Justice Burger extended the Supreme Court's tradition of unanimity in school desegregation cases.

The *Swann* Case Progresses through the Federal Courts

One year after the *Alexander* case was decided, the Supreme Court was presented with the case of *Swann v. Charlotte-Mecklenburg Board of Education*. Though this case originated in a southern state (North Carolina) with a history of state-mandated segregation, the implications reached beyond the South. The *Swann* case dealt with court-ordered remedies of de jure segregation, or segregation that was the result of actions by public officials such as school board members. What was at issue in *Swann* was a U.S. district court's decision imposing mandatory busing as a means to bring about racial balance in the Charlotte-Mecklenburg Public School District. The case began when the district decided to comply with the *Brown* decision by simply closing down several all-black schools. The plan was coupled with new attendance zones for most of the district's schools, and a "freedom of choice" plan that would allow students to transfer to schools outside of their zones, provided that they provided their own transportation and that the school had empty seats. The plaintiffs objected to this plan, as it would place the burden of desegregation on black students. Moreover, the school district's plan did very little in the way of desegregating schools. Only 490 of the system's 20,000 black schoolchildren went to schools with white students, and there remained a number of black students in Charlotte who were denied admission to the school nearest them (Schwartz, 1986, p. 10).

One such student was six-year-old James Swann, the son of a Theology professor at Charlotte's Johnson C. Smith University, a predominantly black nonpublic university. Young James Swann was chosen by the petitioners to be the first-named plaintiff in the case (Schwartz, 1986, pp. 10–11). The attorney who argued the case on behalf of Swann and the other plaintiffs was Julius LeVonne Chambers, who was affiliated with the National Association for the Advancement of Colored People Legal Defense Fund. Chambers played the same role that future Supreme Court Justice Thurgood Marshall played in the 1954 *Brown* case, when Marshall, working for the same organization, argued the case on behalf of public school student Linda Brown and the other plaintiffs. In the Charlotte case, Chambers picked James Swann to be named as the plaintiff because Swann's father had a secure position at a private black university and, presumably, would not have to worry about reprisals at his place of employment (Schwartz, 1986, p. 11). Chambers, however, was subjected to reprisals. Early in the case his car and house were dynamited, and two months before the Supreme Court decision was rendered, his law office was firebombed by an arsonist (Schwartz, 1986, p. 21).

Chambers first brought the case before the federal district court in 1965. The plaintiffs challenged the school board's desegregation plan and demanded that the attendance zones be adjusted to allow more integration. This demand was rejected outright by the judge, J. Braxton Craven, who ruled on behalf of the school board (*Swann v. Charlotte-Mecklenburg Board of Education*, 243 Supp. Western District of NC 667–670 [1965]). One year later Judge Craven's decision was affirmed by the Court of Appeals for the Fourth Circuit (*Swann v. Charlotte-Mecklenburg Board of Education*, 369 F. 2nd [Fourth Circuit] 29 [1966]).

At this point the plaintiffs chose not to pursue the case to the U.S. Supreme Court. However, in 1968 the Supreme Court's *Green* decision cast doubt on the constitutionality of the Charlotte-Mecklenburg School District's student assignment plan. In September of that year, the plaintiffs returned to the district court and argued that, although there was no longer any statute requiring that black and white students attend separate schools, the school board's student assignment plan perpetuated the segregated patterns that had historically existed in the school system. This, the plaintiffs argued, was in violation of the Fourteenth Amendment as interpreted by the U.S. Supreme Court in the *Brown* decision. Three years after Judge Craven accepted the District's plan, nearly 60 percent of Charlotte-Mecklenburg's black students were concentrated in 21 schools (out of a total of 107) that were at least 99 percent black (*Swann*, 1971, 1).

The judge in this case, James B. McMillan, issued his opinion on April 23, 1969. He noted the above statistics and ruled that the Charlotte-Mecklenburg school system was still illegally segregated. McMillan gave the school board less than three weeks to submit a plan to desegregate the faculty and students of the school system. The school board did submit a plan, but McMillan held that it was unsatisfactory, and therefore appointed an expert, Dr. John Finger, to develop a desegregation plan for the system. Finger's plan, submitted in February 1970, divided the school systems into districts that paired black and white neighborhoods. Black students from inner-city sections of the district would be transported (by bus) to outlying white suburban neighborhoods within the respective districts. McMillan ordered the adoption of the Finger plan, but the school board immediately filed an appeal.

The case went to the Fourth Circuit Court of Appeals, where the judges provided a split decision: they ordered the implementation of the Finger Plan for secondary school students, but stayed its implementation for primary school students. The plaintiffs were not satisfied, and therefore filed a petition for a writ of certiorari, asking the Supreme Court to overturn the decision of the appeals court. Certiorari was granted.

Crafting a Unanimous Decision

The Supreme Court was now confronted with a case that differed greatly from other school desegregation cases. The plaintiffs were challenging neighborhood-based student assignment plans, which, they held, were maintaining school segregation even though there no longer was any statute mandating segregation. Moreover, the plaintiffs were requesting that the Supreme Court reimpose a district court's remedial plan that would require cross-district busing. Like many urban areas throughout the United States, Charlotte's housing patterns were segregated. Therefore, any effective desegregation plan would necessitate the imposition of busing, such as that ordered by Judge McMillan. Should McMillan's order be reinstated, the implications would extend beyond southern states with a history of state-mandated segregation. Urban school districts throughout the United States were as segregated as those in Charlotte, and in many municipalities the segregation was the result of school boards taking advantage of segregated housing patterns to create racially homogenous attendance zones. This was particularly true in the Northeastern and North-central states, where housing patterns were the most segregated. While the previous school desegregation cases before the Supreme Court concerned practices that were primarily confined to the South, the plaintiffs in the *Swann* case challenged practices that were common in urban school districts throughout the United States. More significant, the remedy they were proposing—cross-district busing— is one that would be upheld in many nonsouthern urban districts, should the Supreme Court rule in favor of the plaintiffs. This case presented challenges that would make it very difficult for the Supreme Court to maintain its tradition of unanimity in school desegregation cases.

Chief Justice Warren Burger spent much of the winter of 1970–71 crafting the decision that would be rendered in the *Swann* case. Simultaneously, the Supreme Court was in the midst of a transformation. In 1970 the chief justice was joined on the Court by his childhood friend, Harry Blackmun, who also had a reputation as a conservative. The appointments of Burger and Blackmun threatened to change the pro-desegregation direction the Court had moved in throughout the fifteen years Warren was chief justice.

Burger's career in the federal government had begun in the 1950s during Dwight Eisenhower's administration, where he served as an assistant attorney general. In 1956 President Eisenhower appointed the Minnesotan to the U.S. Court of Appeals for the District of Columbia. There Burger developed a reputation as a judicial conservative in criminal cases. Though Burger sided with the plaintiffs in the *Alexander v. Holmes* decision, he expressed reservations about Judge McMillan's order that the Charlotte-Mecklenburg schools begin cross-district busing (Schwartz, 1986, pp. 30, 101, 112).

It also appeared that Burger's close friend and fellow Minnesotan Harry Blackmun would oppose McMillan's action. Blackmun had attended grade school with Burger and remained his friend into adulthood. When Burger was married, Blackmun served as his best man. After a distinguished career with a Minneapolis Law Firm, Blackmun was appointed by President Eisenhower to serve as a justice on the Eighth Circuit Court of Appeals. In 1970 President Nixon elevated Blackmun to the U.S. Supreme Court. Known as a conservative, Blackmun had expressed support for "neighborhood schools" (Schwartz, 1986, pp. 42, 104), which was an indication he shared his friend Burger's reluctance to uphold Judge McMillan's decision. Meanwhile, President Nixon, who had appointed both Burger and Blackmun, issued a condemnation of busing. Referring to it as "forced busing," the president also affirmed his support for "neighborhood schools" (Sample, 1970, p. 1). Nixon's solicitor general, Erwin Griswold, argued before the U.S. Supreme Court that Judge McMillan's order should be overturned.

Another Supreme Court justice who expressed opposition to McMillan's decision was Hugo Black, an appointee of Franklin Roosevelt. Black, the senior justice on the Supreme Court, was from the state of Alabama, where he had served as a judge and a district attorney and from where he was elected to the U.S. Senate. When President Roosevelt nominated Senator Black to the Supreme Court, the greatest controversy surrounding the senator was his past membership in the Ku Klux Klan. Despite this, Black was confirmed and became known as a prominent civil libertarian, particularly with First Amendment issues. Black was not quite as liberal in his interpretation of the equal protection clause of the Fourteenth Amendment. Though somewhat supportive of civil rights, in 1964 Black voted to uphold the convictions of certain "sit-in" demonstrators whom he believed were infringing on the "property rights" of business owners to make their own determinations as to whom they should serve (*Bell v. Maryland,* 378 U.S. 226 [1964]). In this case Justice Black parted with the liberals on the Warren Court. One year later, when the Warren Court recognized a right to privacy, Black, a self-styled constitutional literalist, again split with the liberals. Black's view was that no such right was mentioned in the U.S. Constitution (*Griswold v. Connecticut,* 381 U.S. 479 [1965]). Black held similar views about busing; he did not believe that the Constitution supported busing children away from their neighborhood schools (Woodward & Armstrong, 1979, p. 97).

On the other side of the ideological divide, Justices William O. Douglas, John Marshall Harlan, William Brennan, and Thurgood Marshall (the only black justice) were strongly in support of Judge McMillan's order, while Justices Potter Stewart and Byron White were more mildly supportive of McMillan. The *Swann* case threatened to disrupt the tradition of unanimity in school desegregation cases. Now Chief Justice Burger was faced with two alternatives: (1) join Justice Black in a dissent, while Marshall, Douglas, Brennan, or Harlan would write a majority opinion allowing expansive use of busing to achieve racial balance, or (2) assign the opinion to himself and build a unanimous opinion upholding McMillan's order, while allowing some restrictions on busing that Black and the chief justice himself would favor. Burger chose the latter option.

Much in the same way that Chief Justice Warren crafted a unanimous decision in the *Brown* case, Burger set about to do likewise in the *Swann* case. The fundamental difference was that Warren was an unquestioned liberal on the issue of school desegregation, and he was strongly in support of ruling in favor of the black plaintiffs in the *Brown* case. In the *Brown* case Warren knew that there were enough votes to support a ruling in favor of the plaintiffs, but he also knew that a unanimous decision (with no separate concurring opinions) was necessary in order for the public to accord legitimacy to a decision that would upset generations of tradition. Warren assigned the opinion to himself and decided to write it in such a way as to mollify those justices who were not inclined to accept the opinion. This potential minority included Justices Black, Tom Clark, Robert Jackson, and Stanley Reed. Warren met with these potential dissenters and wrote an opinion that included the concessions necessary to convince them to support a unanimous decision. These concessions included omitting a discussion of a timetable for the elimination of school segregation and refusal to specify remedial action to be used against school districts that refuse to abide by the *Brown* decision (Schwartz, 1983, p. 93).

The issue of remedies was largely left to Chief Justice Burger. Though supportive of the *Brown* decision, Burger harbored objections to the use of busing as a remedial device in school desegregation cases. This viewpoint, however, was not shared by the majority of justices who sat on the court at that time. Justices Douglas, Harlan, Brennan, Marshall, White, and Stewart were likely to affirm McMillan's order, while only Black and Burger were strongly opposed to McMillan. Blackmun's past reservations about busing were no longer apparent when Chief Justice Burger conferred with the associate justice about the *Swann* case. Blackmun now expressed qualified support for McMillan's use of busing to remedy racial imbalance in the Charlotte-Mecklenburg school system (Schwartz, 1986, pp. 104–105).

After assigning the opinion to himself, the chief justice circulated a series of drafts to the associate justices, with the hope that he would eventually develop the type of opinion he sought. The first draft reflected his misgivings about the use of busing to remedy de jure segregation. Here Burger stressed that the U.S. Constitution required only the elimination of state-enforced segregation, not a fostering of integration. This is the point of view many northern conservatives of the 1970s were taking. The draft supported courts using remedial power in districts found guilty of having practiced de jure segregation, but remedies (such as busing) could be imposed only for the purpose of bringing about "a system functioning on the same basis as school systems in which no discrimination had ever been enforced" (Schwartz, 1986, p. 115). This was unacceptable to the Court's supporters of Judge McMillan, who felt that Burger's draft reflected an overly restrictive interpretation of the language of the landmark 1964 Civil Rights Act.

A second draft contained much of the same language as the first and elicited the same reaction among the Court's liberals. Burger also incorporated an argument used by Charlotte-Mecklenburg, which was that the Civil Rights Act of 1964 limited the remedies that could be imposed on school districts, and that it proscribed the use of transportation to ensure racial balance (CQ Publications, 1964, p. 340). McMillan's supporters on the Supreme Court outright rejected this restrictive interpretation of the Civil Rights Act.

In a third draft, Burger left out earlier language stating that the *Brown* decision prohibits segregation but does not require integration. However, the third draft included a statement that "it is beyond judicial authority [to] establish in each school a fixed ratio of Negro to white students equal to that for the district as a whole" (Schwartz, 1986, p. 146).

One important concession the chief justice made in the third draft was an express affirmation of Judge McMillan's order, something the liberals demanded in the opinion. This affirmation, which came at the end of the draft, was not enough to persuade the liberals to join with Burger. Justice Douglas objected to his refusal to acknowledge that racially segregated public housing developments and restrictive covenants, which resulted in racially homogenous schools, constituted de jure school segregation. Instead of recognizing public housing segregation and restrictive covenants as methods by which the state contributes to school segregation, Burger's third draft said that "racial prejudice in residential patterns, employment practices, location of public housing, or other factors [are] beyond the jurisdiction of school authorities, even when those patterns contribute to disproportionate racial concentrations in some schools" (Schwartz, 1986, p. 149).

In the fourth draft Burger began to accept the role of the federal courts in promoting racial balance to remedy segregation. This draft stated that if local school districts refuse to remedy their own violations, "a district court has broad power to fashion a remedy that will assure a unitary system." The fourth draft also proscribed school construction or closings as a means to perpetuate a dual system (Schwartz, 1986, pp. 159–160).

There were still key points of disagreement that prevented the liberals from signing on. These were more closely addressed in the fifth draft. In that draft Burger omitted earlier language affirming the supremacy of local school boards and substituted it with a statement that "Judicial powers may be exercised only on the basis of a constitutional violation." On Brennan's suggestion, Burger omitted the statement that "There is no constitutional requirement that any racial balance or ratio be permanently maintained." This was replaced with a statement that "the limited use of mathematical ratios is within the equitable remedial discretion of the District Court" (Schwartz, 1986, pp. 167–169).

After the fifth draft was circulated, Justice Black sent a letter to the chief justice threatening to dissent. Black believed that court-ordered busing was an unconstitutional expansion of judicial power. He also objected to the following statements that were included in the fifth draft:

a. A statement that school siting is used to promote segregation. Black said that this implies that neighborhood schools are unconstitutional.
b. A statement that school boards found guilty of de jure segregation have the burden of demonstrating that the presence of one-race schools (exclusively or heavily) is not the result of discrimination.
c. A statement that the 1964 Civil Rights Act was enacted "to expand and define the role of the Federal Government in the implementation of the *Brown I* decision." Black also objected to a sentence that stated "It is clear that Title IV of the Civil Rights Act of 1964 was not intended to limit the permissible remedies for a violation of the Fourteenth Amendment in school desegregation cases" (Schwartz, 1986, pp. 177–178).

Burger did not agree to Black's request to remove the burden from school districts that maintained one-race schools, but he did concede on other points. In reference to the 1964 Civil Rights Act, the words "expand and" were eliminated, as was the sentence stating that the act does not limit the permissible remedies. The chief justice also removed the references to school siting.

The final decision provided some satisfaction to both factions of the court. The liberal holdovers from the Warren Court were able to maintain the former chief justice's tradition of unanimity in school desegregation cases. Unanimity was especially important in the *Swann* decision, as it would be at least as controversial as the *Brown* decision. The American public would now see an undivided Supreme Court supporting busing to achieve racial balance. Burger and Black could be satisfied in that the decision was not as far-reaching as it would have been had Marshall, Douglas, Brennan, or Harlan written the opinion, supported by White, Stewart, and Blackmun.

On April 20, 1971, the chief justice announced the unanimous decision upholding Judge McMillan's order that the Charlotte-Mecklenburg Schools implement Dr. Finger's plan for cross-district busing. The media and much of the public saw it as a landmark decision that would pave the way for the implementation of busing orders throughout the United States, not just in those southern states with histories of state-mandated segregation. Burger, however, did not view the *Swann* decision this way. According to Bob Woodward and Scott Armstrong, the chief justice did not see the decision as being one to encourage busing, and he felt that some district judges were misinterpreting the decision when they ordered massive busing to achieve racial balance. Burger believed that they were ignoring *Swann*'s limitations on the use of busing. Brennan and the liberals disagreed and felt that the district judges who ordered busing were correctly interpreting *Swann* (Woodward & Armstrong, 1979, p. 154). They placed less emphasis on the limitations secured by Burger and Black.

The limitations on busing enshrined in the *Swann* decision would be reiterated three years later in the *Milliken v. Bradley* (418 U.S. 717 [1974]) decision, in which the Burger Court enjoined federal courts from ordering interdistrict busing. While the *Swann* decision affirmed that school districts have the discretionary power to implement a policy that ensures racial balance in each school, it also made clear that if there is no finding of a constitutional violation, a federal court does not have the authority to implement such a policy (*Swann*, 1971, p. 17). The Court also refused to address those cases where segregated schools were the result of actions by state entities other than school boards. In some of the school desegregation cases, plaintiffs argued that the housing discrimination that led to segregated schools was practiced by governmental agencies, thus rendering the localities guilty of de jure segregation. Most frequently, as in the desegregation cases involving the cities of Boston and Buffalo, discriminatory housing patterns were the result of actions by public housing agencies of the city (Taylor, 1998, pp. 50–51, 61–62.). The remedies allowed by the *Swann* decision, however, were restricted to localities where racial segregation was practiced by the school district. The decision states that "We do not reach in this case a question whether a showing that school segregation is a consequence of other types of state action, without any discriminatory action by the school authorities, is a constitutional violation requiring remedial action by a school desegregation decree. This case does not present that question and we therefore do not decide it" (*Swann*, 1971, p. 23).

The justices were also ambiguous on the topic of one-race schools. In cases where school districts were found to have operated a dual system, they had the burden of demonstrating that one-race schools were not the result of past or present discrimination on the part of school officials. However, the justices also stated that "the existence of some small number of one-race, or virtually one-race, schools within a district is not in and of itself the mark of a system that still practices segregation by law" (*Swann*, 1971, p. 26). The decision also proscribed the use of racial quotas in situations where no constitutional violation was found (*Swann,* 1971, p. 16), and Chief Justice Burger left in the decision a statement that in an illegally segregated dual school district the Constitution does not mandate that each individual school must reflect the racial composition of the entire school system (*Swann,* 1971, p. 24).

Despite the limitations on busing, the decision was indeed momentous in that it allowed Judge McMillan's decision to stand and allowed other federal judges to order cross-district busing to ensure racial balance of previously dual school systems. The affirmation of McMillan's order (which pleased the liberals), paired with the restrictions on busing (which satisfied Justice Black), are what led to another unanimous school desegregation decision.

School Desegregation Cases in the Aftermath of *Swann*

The tradition of unanimity was soon to come to an end with the appointment of more conservative justices to the Court. In 1972, upon the retirement of Justices Black and Harlan, President Nixon appointed two conservatives to the Supreme Court. The new justices, Lewis Powell and William Rehnquist, were strongly opposed to court-ordered busing. In 1954 Rehnquist had gone so far as to oppose overturning the doctrine of "separate but equal" in public education (Martz, McDaniel, & Malone, 1986, pp. 20–21).

Powell and Rehnquist's accession to the Supreme Court came one year too late for them to rule against Judge McMillan's decision in the *Swann* case. However, they were on the Supreme Court when that body was presented with a major nonsouthern school desegregation case that involved court-ordered busing. This 1974 case, which was called *Milliken v. Bradley,* originated in Detroit, Michigan, and its suburbs. Here the Detroit Board of Education had been found guilty of having illegally segregated the city's public schools. The U.S. district court ordered that the remedy include a metropolitan-wide desegregation plan that involved Detroit and fifty-three outlying school districts, and the U.S. Court of Appeals for the Sixth Circuit affirmed the district court's decision. In response, some of the affected suburban school districts appealed the case to the U.S. Supreme Court, which granted certiorari. The plaintiffs argued that Michigan law granted limited autonomy to local school districts, hence the districts were all state entities and could be subjected to a common desegregation plan.

The case was argued before the Supreme Court on February 27, 1974. Five months later, on July 25, a divided Supreme Court rejected the argument that the school districts had limited autonomy and ruled that any remedy had to be confined to the city of Detroit, as it was Detroit, not any of the outlying districts, that was found guilty of illegally segregating its schools. In the ruling the Court relied on principles established in the *Swann* case three years earlier. The *Swann* decision specifically stated that busing is a remedy a federal court can impose only if a district has been found guilty of a constitutional violation. Since the fifty-three outlying school districts were not found guilty, the majority opined that the federal district court had overstepped its bounds by requiring those districts to participate in the program desegregating Detroit's schools. Some could argue that the housing discrimination that was tolerated and sometimes encouraged by the outlying municipalities led to a situation where their public schools were all white, and thus illegally segregated. The *Swann* decision rejects this argument, as it does not allow the implementation of busing in situations where discrimination has been practiced by public entities other than the school systems.

The *Milliken v. Bradley* decision utilized the restrictions on busing imposed by the *Swann* decision and enjoined district courts from imposing interdistrict busing plans. While proponents of school desegregation had hoped the *Swann* decision would open the door for effective desegregation plans, the majority in *Milliken* placed severe limitations on the ability of federal courts to bring about racial balance in many metropolitan areas. The five-person majority in the *Milliken* case included Chief Justice Burger (who wrote the decision), along with the other three Nixon appointees: Blackmun, Rehnquist, and Powell. They were joined by Justice Stewart. The dissenters were Justices Douglas, White, Marshall, and Brennan. This reflected a partisan split, with all justices who were appointed by Democratic presidents dissenting, while all Republican appointees, save for Brennan, joined the chief justice's majority. Thurgood Marshall, in his dissent, said that the majority's holding was "More a reflection of a perceived public mood that we have gone far enough in enforcing the Constitution's guarantee of equal justice, than it is the product of neutral principles of law" (*Milliken*, 1974, p. 815).

Swann's Impact on Presidential Politics

The "public mood" Marshall was referring to was one in which busing was one of the most contentious political issues of the day. After the *Swann* decision upheld the use of busing as a remedy for both southern- and northern-style school segregation, busing quickly rose in importance as a cutting-edge issue in U.S. politics. It was the most highly discussed domestic political issue in the early 1970s. The *Swann* decision was handed down at a time when Americans were preparing for a presidential election campaign season, one in which busing would be a prominent topic. As the campaigns got under way in early 1972, Nixon asked for a one-year moratorium on busing and requested that Congress pass his bill, which he named the "Student Transportation Moratorium Act" ("Nixon's Plan on Busing," 1972, p. 26).

The president's opposition to busing was shared by two leading Democratic senators, Hubert Humphrey (of Minnesota) and Henry "Scoop" Jackson (of Washington), each of whom hoped to become the nominee to oppose Nixon in the November election. The two were forced to reveal their feelings about busing in February 1972, as they were campaigning for the Florida primary election, one in which a busing referendum was also on the ballot. Hubert Humphrey, the former vice president, and a senator who was regarded as one of the staunchest supporters of civil rights, stated his opposition to busing. Humphrey told reporters, "I'd be less than frank . . . if I didn't add that I don't think busing is the answer." Humphrey also stated that he was against "forced busing," because "It hasn't solved racial problems. It has been divisive. It has used funds needed for education. It has become an emotional issue, not an educational asset" ("Campaign '72," 1972, pp. 24, 28). Senator Jackson took his opposition a step further than Humphrey by proposing a constitutional amendment to guarantee students the right to enroll in their "neighborhood schools" ("Can Congress Solve?" 1972, pp. 20–32).

Despite Humphrey and Jackson's opposition to busing, the Democratic candidate who captured the hearts of the most steadfast opponents of busing was Alabama governor George Wallace, who had risen to prominence as a vocal defender of segregation. In the 1960s, when he vowed to support "segregation forever," Governor Wallace was viewed as a fringe candidate, and he had little support outside of the South and a few small working-class ethnic enclaves in the Northeastern and North-central states. This situation changed after the U.S. Supreme Court handed down the *Swann* decision. Now many nonsouthern communities could be forced to desegregate their schools through the use of busing. This gave rise to sentiment that would assist George Wallace, whose candidacy revolved around the busing issue. Wallace won primary victories in the southern states of North Carolina, Florida, and Tennessee, and in the nonsouthern states of Michigan and Maryland (Pearson, 1998, p. A1). But in Maryland his campaigning was cut short when he was paralyzed by a gunman who attempted to assassinate him.

Four years later the busing issue had somewhat faded, but it still remained a topic in presidential politics. Republican president Gerald R. Ford, a vocal opponent of busing, proposed a bill to restrict busing. This bill, the "School Desegregation Standard and Assistance Act of 1976," would limit the scope and duration of court-ordered busing and would encourage local initiatives in desegregation planning. Ford boasted that his plan "would prohibit a court from ordering busing throughout an entire school system simply for the purpose of achieving racial balance" ("Ford's Plan," 1976, p. 18). The bill would have virtually eliminated the effect of the *Swann* decision, but President Ford was unable to get it passed by the Congress. Had he done so, the new law would have been subjected to legal challenges that may have given the increasingly conservative Supreme Court an opportunity to overturn the *Swann* Decision. Meanwhile, Ford's solicitor general, Robert Bork, appeared before the Supreme Court asking that the justices hear appeals on busing cases in Boston, Massachusetts, and Louisville, Kentucky. The Supreme Court rebuffed the Ford administration and denied certiorari in those cases, something the justices would have been far less likely to do had Ford's bill been passed in Congress and subjected to judicial review.

Swann's Impact on the U.S. Congress

Though Ford did not get his antibusing bill through Congress, there had been strong antibusing sentiment in Congress since the early 1970s. This sentiment emanated from both sides of the political aisle. After the *Swann* decision, the House of Representatives granted Nixon's request that none of the $1.5 billion in desegregation assistance be used for busing. Both houses of Congress also moved to pass bills that would prohibit most busing for racial balance. Though none of these bills ever became law, they did have a great deal of support in the House and Senate, and presumably among white voters, whose opposition to busing increased exponentially after the *Swann* decision. In August 1972 the House of Representatives passed a busing moratorium by nearly a 2–1 margin that included the support of many liberal Democrats. The bill would forbid federal judges from ordering desegregation beyond neighborhood schools or the next closest school and would require that existing desegregation plans conform to new orders. The bill died in the Senate when pro–civil rights members maintained a filibuster to prevent passage (Matthews, 1972, pp. 420–421).

During this period of time there was also a move for a constitutional amendment to ban busing. In the Senate the amendment's principal supporters were Scoop Jackson and Michigan Republican Robert Griffin, who was running for reelection. Griffin, who had previously been supportive of civil rights, was sponsoring stringent antibusing legislation, but also chose to pursue the amendment route. The fact that some antibusing senators were trying to achieve their aims by amending the Constitution demonstrates that they were skeptical about the ability of their legislation to survive court challenges. Griffin himself conceded that his legislation (stripping federal courts of the power to order busing) was of dubious constitutionality ("The Tortured Politics," 1972, p. 30). An amendment, however, would settle all questions about the constitutionality of antibusing legislation. Nevertheless, there was not enough support in Congress to amend the Constitution around the busing issue.

Despite this activity by the Congress, the preeminence of busing as a national political issue did not last very long. The 1973 *Roe v. Wade* (410 U.S. 113 [1973]) decision caused abortion to displace busing as the most polarizing domestic issue. In the 1976 campaign, busing was still discussed in the presidential campaigns, but it did not generate the emotions that it had in 1972.

The Rehnquist Court and School Desegregation

The years of 1981–92 saw Republicans in the White House, which led to a more conservative federal judiciary and a greatly decreased likelihood that district court judges would order school districts to bus students to achieve racial balance. Presidents Ronald Reagan and George H. W. Bush appointed five justices to the Supreme Court, while the most conservative justice, Rehnquist, was promoted to chief justice. The Rehnquist Court's position on the issue of school busing was made clear in 1991 in the case of *Board of Education of Oklahoma City v. Dowell.* This case again pitted attorney Julius LeVonne Chambers against a Republican solicitor general, but this time the solicitor general was Kenneth Starr, who argued the Bush administration's position on the case.

The plaintiff—the Oklahoma City School District—was challenging a U.S. Court of Appeals ruling that prevented the school district from abandoning a "Finger Plan" remedy and implementing a neighborhood-based student assignment plan. The school district claimed that years of compliance had made theirs a unitary district. A federal district court agreed with the school district, but Chambers appealed the case to the U.S. Court of Appeals for the Tenth Circuit, which reversed the district court's decision. The school district then appealed the case to the U.S. Supreme Court, which, by a 5–3 vote, reversed the judgment of the court of appeals and remanded it to the district court. Writing for the majority, Chief Justice Rehnquist stated that, "A school district which has been released from an injunction imposing a desegregation plan no longer requires court authorization for the promulgation of policies and rules regulating matters such as assignment of students and the like. . ." (*Board of Education of Oklahoma City v. Dowell*, 498 U.S. 250 [1991]).

Rehnquist also delivered the opinion in the most recent major school desegregation case, the 1995 case of *Missouri v. Jenkins.* This case began in 1972 in Kansas City, Missouri, when that city's public schools were found guilty of practicing de jure segregation. Though the schools were declared "unitary" in 1977, the U.S. District Court maintained some oversight. Among the remedies imposed by the court were the transformation of many of the Kansas City schools into "magnet schools" with specialized curricula. The hope was that such schools would attract suburban students and soften the impact of "white flight," which had resulted in the school system becoming over two-thirds black (*Missouri v. Jenkins,* 515 U.S. 74 [1995]. Among the methods used to make the city schools more attractive were capital improvements and salary increases for system employees. Since the city of Kansas City was unable to afford the ordered remedies, the district court ordered that the state impose an additional tax to fund the improvements of Kansas City's schools.

The state challenged the tax increases, contending that the constitutional violation was confined to Kansas City, hence the remedy should be limited to that municipality, as the Court had ruled in the *Milliken v. Bradley* decision. The state argued that the tax was an *interdistrict* remedy to correct an *intradistrict* violation (*Missouri,* p. 79).

The U.S. Court of Appeals for the Eighth Circuit rejected the state's argument and affirmed the decision of the district court. The state of Missouri appealed the decision to the U.S. Supreme Court, which granted certiorari. In a 5–4 decision, the Supreme Court ruled that, since the remedial plan of the district court was for the purpose of encouraging interdistrict transfers, the district court had exceeded its authority, as the *Milliken* ruling states that remedies should be confined to the district(s) where the violation occurred (*Missouri,* pp. 91–92). The ruling of the court of appeals was reversed.

The dissenting opinion was written by Justice David Souter, who argued that constitutional violations by the state of Missouri and the Kansas City School District helped perpetuate the existence of segregated schools, which led to white flight to suburban districts. The dissenters also noted that nothing in *Milliken* indicates that a remedy that takes into account conditions outside of the district in violation is an "interdistrict remedy" (*Missouri,* pp. 156, 166). Souter wrote that the majority decision limits *Milliken* by misreading that 1974 decision.

Joining Rehnquist in the majority were Justices Sandra Day O'Connor, Antonin Scalia, Anthony Kennedy, and Clarence Thomas, while the minority included Justices Souter, John Paul Stevens, Ruth Bader Ginsburg, and Stephen Breyer. Seven years later, these are the same nine justices on the Supreme Court, and the division in the *Missouri v. Jenkins* case reveals the ideological fault line of the Court. The five justices in the majority were all appointed by Republican presidents, while the only two justices appointed by a Democrat are in the court's liberal minority. Justices Stevens (appointed by Ford) and Souter (appointed by Bush, Sr.) are the only two of the nine whose current ideological stances do not coincide with their partisanship. Nevertheless, the Republican majority on the current Supreme Court is a reflection of the federal judiciary at large, which has been shaped by presidents Reagan and Bush, who together enjoyed three consecutive terms in office.

The original decisions in the Oklahoma City and Kansas City desegregation cases came in 1972, one year after the *Swann* decision. Because of the latitude given by the *Swann* decision, U.S. district courts were able to order remedies that included busing. Thirty years later, such plans are very infrequently imposed on school districts. This is because twelve years of judicial appointments by Reagan and Bush have brought about a federal judiciary that is vastly different from the judiciary during the days when Judge McMillan ruled in favor of the plaintiffs in the Charlotte-Mecklenburg School District. Though the 1971 *Swann* decision has not yet been overturned, the remedies that it allows are decreasingly likely to be ordered by the current members of the federal judiciary.

REFERENCES

Campaign '72: the busing issue. (1972, February 7). *Newsweek,* p. 24.

Can Congress ever solve the busing issue? (1972, March 13). *U.S. News and World Report,* pp. 30–32.

CQ Publications. (1964). *1964 Congressional Quarterly Almanac.*

Ford's plan to limit court-ordered busing. (1976, July 5). *U.S. News and World Report,* p. 18.

Martz, L., McDaniel, A., & Malone, M. (1986, June 30). A pair for the court. *Newsweek,* pp. 20–21.

Matthews, J. (1972, November 6). Postscript to a filibuster. *Nation,* pp. 420–421.

Pearson, R. (1998, September 14). Former Alabama governor George C. Wallace dies. *Washington Post,* p. A1.

Schwartz, B. (1983). *Super chief: Earl Warren and his Supreme Court—A judicial biography.* New York: New York University Press.

Schwartz, B. (1986). *Swann's way: the school busing case and the Supreme Court.* New York: Oxford University Press.

Semple, R. B. (1970, March 25). President vows to end de jure systems, but not de facto. *New York Times,* p. 1.

Taylor, S. J. L. (1998). *Desegregation in Boston and Buffalo: The influence of local leaders.* Albany, NY: State University of New York Press.

The tortured politics of school busing. (1972, March 6). *Newsweek,* p. 30.

What Nixon's plan on busing means. (1972, March 27). *U.S. News and World Report.*

What the candidates say about forced busing. (1972, February 28). *U.S. News and World Report,* p. 28.

Woodward, B., & Armstrong, S. (1979). *The brethren: Inside the Supreme Court.* New York: Simon and Schuster.

Affirmative Action in Higher Education

Gratz v. Bollinger and Grutter v. Bollinger (2003)

BARBARA A. PERRY

> In 1978 Justice Lewis Powell wrote an opinion in the case of *Regents of the University of California v. Bakke* suggesting that, because a diverse student body was a matter of pressing public necessity for public universities, those schools could take race into account in making admission decisions. Over the next twenty-five years, scholars, judges, policymakers, school administrators, and interest groups debated both the wisdom and the legitimacy of Powell's lone opinion. The justices decided to revisit this issue in two cases that challenged race-conscious admission policies at the University of Michigan. Formally endorsing Justice Powell's view, the Court concluded that making race a factor in college admissions did not violate the constitutional guarantee of equal protection of the laws.

The clock had just struck midnight. It was April 1, 2003. In the darkness surrounding the U.S. Supreme Court building, a few voices whooped and shouted. Could it be revelers engaging in some sort of April Fools' prank? Hardly. Three thousand demonstrators from across the country were amassing around the high court. They encircled the edifice and began marching around it. "Jim Crow, hell no!" "Two, four, six, eight, we don't want to segregate!" "What do we want? Affirmative action! When do we want it? Now!"[1]

What had possessed these young black, white, Asian, and Latino protesters to congregate at the witching hour for a parade around the Supreme Court? They knew that in exactly ten hours the nation's highest court would hear oral arguments in two landmark affirmative action cases from the University of Michigan. The nine justices' decisions would determine the fate of admissions policies promoting racial and ethnic diversity throughout American universities. Undoubtedly, the members of the Supreme Court were home by that late hour, but lights burned brightly in their court chambers. Law clerks, working long into the night, could not escape the display of public opinion at their doorstep.

Nor could the justices when they arrived for work that morning. After dispersing for a few hours' rest, the demonstrators were back at the Court by daybreak. Despite the April date, spectators waiting to enter the building shivered in the unseasonably cool temperatures. The cold did not deter the protesters. An elderly black woman, bundled in her winter coat and hat, held a handwritten placard directed at one justice in particular. Her sign read, "Clarence Thomas—How did you get into law school?"[2] Luke Massie, of the Coalition to Defend Affirmative Action and Integration and Fight for Equality by Any Means Necessary, which organized the rally, remarked to a reporter, "This is the first march of the new civil rights movement" (Wilgoren & Fernandez, 2003, p. B1). The throng of several thousand completed their protest at the Supreme Court and then marched along the Mall to the Lincoln Memorial, site of Martin Luther King's "I Have a Dream" speech nearly forty years before. The 2003 event climaxed with an emotional rendition of the spiritual, "Lift Ev'ry Voice and Sing," recognized by many as an African American anthem.

The Background

Opponents of affirmative action are as steadfast in their views as the policy's proponents are. With the Center for Individual Rights (CIR), a conservative public-interest law firm, taking the lead, those who believe that race-based admissions programs are illegal planned litigation strategy and tactics to challenge such programs around the nation. In 1996 the CIR earned a significant victory when the Fifth U.S. Circuit Court of Appeals invalidated the University of Texas Law School's use of affirmative action (*Hopwood v. Texas,* 78 F. 3rd 932 [1996]). The U.S. Supreme Court denied Texas's appeal, leaving the Fifth Circuit's ruling intact for all state universities in Texas, Louisiana, and Mississippi (the three states constituting the circuit's jurisdiction). In 2001 the Eleventh Circuit struck down the University of Georgia's admissions program that used racial preferences. Affirmative action opponents in California relied on the ballot, rather than courts, to accomplish their goal. They successfully passed Proposition 209, a referendum initiative to ban race-based admissions policies in state universities (Abraham & Perry, 2003, pp. 504–505).

The Center for Individual Rights, with the help of conservative members of the Michigan state legislature, gathered names of potential plaintiffs to challenge the University of Michigan's preferential treatment of racial and ethnic minorities in admissions. One of the individuals included on the CIR's list was Jennifer Gratz. A white Michigan resident, she had scored a 25 (out of 36) on the ACT, placing her in the 82nd percentile of applicants to the University of Michigan's undergraduate program in 1995. She had accumulated a GPA of 3.8 and had been an active participant in the student council, National Honor Society, science club, spirit club, and cheerleading. Her high school did not offer advanced placement courses, but she took three honors classes. Jennifer grew up in a working-class suburb of Detroit, about forty-five minutes from U of M's Ann Arbor campus. Neither of her parents had finished college, but they were enthusiastic supporters of Michigan football. Their daughter's dream was to attend the University of Michigan, and she believed her high school record would make her a competitive admissions candidate.

In fact, Jennifer was so certain that Michigan would accept her that she applied to no other schools. Her first disappointment came when U of M wait-listed her. In April of her senior year, she received the devastating word of her rejection. Tearful, she reportedly asked her father, "Dad, can we sue [the university]?" She submitted a late application to Notre Dame, which also denied her admission. The University of Michigan at Dearborn, however, accepted her into its honors program. She reluctantly attended the school, where she majored in math and earned her degree in 1999. Jennifer later said of her experience at Dearborn's commuter campus, "It wasn't college" (Hull, 2003, pp. A16, A17).

At least Gratz could take comfort in the fact that the CIR had chosen her, after an interview with the Center's attorneys, as a plaintiff in the 1997 suit challenging the University of Michigan's affirmative action program in its undergraduate school. From 1995 through 1997 the university's admissions officers used tables or grids that reflected a combination of the applicant's adjusted high school GPA and ACT or SAT score. To promote racial and ethnic diversity, the university used different grids and admissions criteria for applicants who were members of preferred minority groups. Michigan also set aside a prescribed number of seats in the entering class for minorities to meet its ethnic diversity target. The university conceded that Gratz would have been accepted had she been a minority candidate.

With Gratz's lawsuit under way, Michigan dropped its admissions grid system in 1998 and replaced it with a 150-point "selection index." Admissions officers assigned applicants points based on various factors, including test scores, "legacy" status, geographic origin, athletic ability, socioeconomic level, and race/ethnicity. The more points an applicant accumulated, the higher the chance of admission. Applicants from racial and ethnic groups considered "underrepresented" at Michigan (African Americans, Latinos, and Native Americans) were assigned a twenty-point bonus. Scholarship athletes and students who were economically disadvantaged also received an automatic twenty-point bonus. (Applicants could only receive *one* twenty-point bonus award, however, even if they qualified in two or three categories.)

Desired geographic origin earned six points extra, the child of an alumnus four points, and an "outstanding" admissions essay three points.

Battles in the Lower Courts

In 2000 the U.S. District Court for the Eastern District of Michigan ruled that the University of Michigan's grid-based admission procedure in place before 1999, which maintained a set-aside for minorities, violated the Fourteenth Amendment's equal protection clause. Yet the district court upheld the "selection index," reasoning that it did not use quotas and used race only as a "plus" (*Gratz v. Bollinger,* 122 F. Supp 2nd [E.D. Mich] 811 [2000]).

Both parties in the case (Gratz and the university, whose president at the time, Lee Bollinger, was named in the title) appealed to the Sixth U.S. Circuit Court. It heard oral argument in the case, but, when an opinion was not forthcoming, Gratz's lawyers successfully petitioned the Supreme Court to take the unusual step of granting an appeal without a circuit opinion. The Sixth Circuit, which includes Michigan, Ohio, Kentucky, and Tennessee, is among the more ideologically contentious of the U.S. courts of appeals. Nominations to the circuit have been especially conflictual, because it is closely divided between liberals and conservatives. Disputes among its judges have gone beyond dissenting opinions to include off-bench denunciations. Sixth Circuit Judge Alice M. Batchelder, a George H. W. Bush appointee, publicly accused the circuit's chief judge, Boyce F. Martin, Jr., a Jimmy Carter nominee, of manipulating the University of Michigan Law School affirmative action case, *Grutter v. Bollinger,* as it made its way through the circuit. Batchelder claimed that Martin had appointed himself (instead of using the traditional random-selection procedure) to a three-judge panel that was to hear the *Grutter* case. When Barbara Grutter, an unsuccessful white applicant to Michigan's Law School, requested a hearing by the full complement of circuit judges, Batchelder argued that Martin delayed action on the request until two conservative judges had taken senior status and were no longer eligible to decide on the appeal.

Whether Batchelder's accusations were true, the Sixth Circuit voted 5–4 to uphold the law school's affirmative action plan, which since 1992 had given special consideration to applicants (particularly, but not solely, African Americans, Latinos, and Native Americans). The same U.S. district court that had upheld the "selection index" for U of M's undergraduate admissions system had declared the law school policy unconstitutional for its heavy reliance on race and its attempts to produce a 10- to 17-percent level of minority students in the entering class (*Grutter v. Bollinger,* 137 F. Supp. 2nd [E.D.

Mich] 821 [2001]). Reversing that ruling, the Sixth Circuit argued, per Judge Martin's majority opinion, that the law school did *not* use quotas or set-asides, had a compelling interest in achieving a diverse student body, and had narrowly tailored the program to meet its goals (*Grutter v. Bollinger,* 288 F. 3rd [6th Cir.] 732 [2002]).

In an unusual on-the-record interview just a few weeks before the Supreme Court handed down its opinion in the affirmative action cases, Judge Martin accused Judge Batchelder of trying to discredit his decision in the law school case to boost the chances that the high court would overturn it. "They [his dissenting colleagues on the circuit] [ha]ve chosen to embarrass me to influence the Supreme Court" (Lane, 2003). Batchelder had no public comment on Martin's unusual accusation in response to her criticism of him.

The Legal Context

The constitutional question the Supreme Court focused on in both the *Gratz* and *Grutter* cases asked whether the University of Michigan affirmative action policies violated the equal protection clause of the Fourteenth Amendment to the Constitution. The Michigan cases also raised a statutory question: Whether the U of M admissions programs violated Title VI of the 1964 Civil Rights Act, prohibiting discrimination on the basis of race, color, religion, and national origin by any institution receiving federal funding, or Section 1981 of the U.S. Code (Volume 42), which proscribes the use of race in contracting, including educational contracts (Kmiec, 2003, p. 350). Sometimes the Supreme Court, in an effort to restrain itself, will confine its rulings to the more narrow purview of *statutory* interpretation (Abraham, 1998, pp. 403–405). In the affirmative action cases, however, it could not dodge the fundamental *constitutional* dispute.

The portion of the Fourteenth Amendment pertinent to the U of M cases is deceptively simple: "No state shall . . . deny to any person within its jurisdiction the equal protection of the laws." Yet, in applying the equal protection clause to various governmental classifications that treat people differently, the Supreme Court has developed several tiers of analysis. In the upper level, if a challenged law or policy uses "suspect classifications" (race, ethnicity, or alienage), the courts apply "strict scrutiny." The law or policy will pass constitutional muster only if it exists to further a "compelling state interest" and is "narrowly tailored" to achieve that interest. In the middle level, if classifications are based on gender or illegitimacy, the courts apply "intermediate scrutiny," which requires an "important state interest" and a "close fit" between it and the classifications. At the lowest level of equal protection analysis, which the courts use for classifications based on indigency, age, education, or welfare status, the courts merely ask whether a "rational relation" exists between the classifications and the state's interest.

Until the University of Michigan cases appeared on its docket, the U.S. Supreme Court had not decided an affirmative action case in higher education in a quarter century, since its initial decision in 1978's *Regents of the University of California v. Bakke*. Before 1978 the University of California at Davis Medical School operated two separate admissions programs. One used only applicants' GPAs and test scores. The other, for "disadvantaged" students (in practice, minorities), gave special consideration to applicants' race and ethnicity. Of the 100 seats available in each entering medical school class, 16 were set aside for students admitted under the special program. Allan Bakke was twice rejected for admission, while minority students with much lower scores were accepted through the affirmative action policy.

Justice Lewis Powell's judgment for the court (he was the swing vote between two four-justice factions) invalidated Davis's rigid quota as creating an unconstitutional broadly tailored, two-track admissions process on the basis of race and ethnicity. He emphasized the mathematical inequality of allowing white applicants to compete for only 84 seats, while minority students could vie for all 100. Nevertheless, he argued that "the interest of diversity is *compelling* [emphasis added] in the context of a university's admission program [at the undergraduate, graduate, and professional levels]" (*Regents of the University of California v. Bakke,* 438 U.S. 265, 314 [1978]). Moreover, a narrowly tailored plan for admitting minorities could survive strict judicial scrutiny. Powell offered Harvard's admissions model as a constitutional example, in which the university used race and ethnicity as a "plus" (along with other personal attributes like "geographic origin or a life spent on a farm") but did not segregate a minority applicant from comparison with other applicants or use quotas for admitting minorities (*Bakke,* p. 316).

Supreme Court Dynamics

In 2003 only two justices (William Rehnquist and John Paul Stevens) remained from the Supreme Court that had decided *Bakke*. Rehnquist, an associate justice in 1978, had been promoted to chief justice in 1986 by President Ronald Reagan. Chief Justice Rehnquist has been a consistent opponent of affirmative action since *Bakke*. Conversely, Justice Stevens has a mixed record on racial preferences. In *Bakke* he opposed such preferences, but he altered course a decade later (Abraham & Perry, 2003, pp. 488–506). Most recently, he voted to uphold affirmative action for federal government contracts in the 1995 case of *Adarand v. Peña* (515 U.S. 200). Justices Antonin Scalia and Clarence Thomas are on the record as unequivocally opposed to affirmative action, convinced that race-based policies per se violate the equal protection clause. Although Justice Anthony Kennedy is a swing voter in some decisions, his votes in race cases are usually with the conservatives. He was expected to side with Grutter and Gratz in their arguments against the University of Michigan. Conversely, Justices David Souter, Ruth Bader Ginsburg, and Stephen Breyer are considered safe votes for racial diversity policies. Thus, the justices seemed as evenly divided as they were in *Bakke,* with four justices supporting affirmative action and four opposing it. Many observers thought the fate of racial preferences in higher education was in the hands of the court's other swing voter, Justice Sandra Day O'Connor. She, along with Ginsburg and Thomas, are the members of the Court most likely to have experienced gender or racial discrimination. Ginsburg and Thomas have ended up on opposite sides of the affirmative action debate (Perry, 2001, chapters 1–9). With which side would O'Connor cast her lot?

The justices had a wide variety of arguments to consider. In addition to the briefs from each side in the case, at least a hundred friend-of-the-court briefs arrived at the Court's doorstep. One that garnered considerable publicity, in light of the ongoing war in Iraq, was submitted by high-ranking retired military officers, led by General Norman Schwarzkopf. The brief asserted that to lead a modern, multiethnic military, it is necessary to produce a diverse officer corps, trained at the U.S. service academies, which employ affirmative action admission procedures. After debate in the Bush administration over how to approach affirmative action in higher education, the president announced that he was opposed to race-based admissions policies because they are "divisive, unfair and impossible to square with the Constitution" (Goldstein & Milbank, 2003, p. A1). Solicitor General Ted Olson, a long-time opponent of affirmative action, filed a brief on behalf of the U.S. government that strongly criticized the Michigan programs for their use of quotas, declared unconstitutional in *Bakke.*

The undergraduate and law school cases each received the standard one hour for oral argument, and Olson was allotted time to plead the government's position before the justices. With thousands of protestors assembled outside, and the courtroom packed with over three hundred spectators, including Gratz and Grutter, the oral argument took on the palpable excitement so characteristic of landmark cases.

All eyes were on the potential swing voter in the case, Justice O'Connor. As always, she was an active questioner of counsel. She revealed her skepticism that admissions policies should be completely colorblind and noted that the court had allowed race-based decisions in various settings. Yet O'Connor also articulated her concern over how long affirmative action programs would have to remain in effect. Kirk Kolbo, an attorney from a Minneapolis law firm, argued for both Gratz and Grutter. He attempted to bolster the foundation of his position, namely, that racial and ethnic diversity in higher education does not constitute a compelling state interest. Even if it did, the university's goal of creating a more diverse student body by admitting a "critical mass" of minority students (both in the undergraduate and law schools) was equivalent to a quota, unconstitutionally invalid since *Bakke*. Awarding bonus points to certain minorities, as the undergraduate admissions office did, was blatantly in violation of the equal protection clause. Olson added that the University of Michigan should attempt to increase minority enrollment by constitutional race-neutral alternatives, including recruitment and outreach. Other suggested alternatives encompassed "percentage plans" (whereby the top portion of students in a state's high schools are automatically admitted to public undergraduate universities), socioeconomic criteria, and "experiential diversity" (based on life experiences).

Counsel for the University of Michigan Law School, Maureen Mahoney, of the prestigious Washington law firm, Latham and Watkins, had an added advantage (McGuire, 1993, pp. 161–164). She had clerked for Rehnquist and was a familiar face at the court. The chief justice even called her by her first name once during the argument—an unusual occurrence in the formal atmosphere of the nation's highest tribunal. Her premise asserted that diversity in law education was a compelling state interest, because it combats racial/ethnic stereotypes, fosters racial/ethnic understanding, creates a range of ideas and viewpoints, and produces lawyers and leaders for a pluralistic society.

Counsel rarely have a chance to include all such details from their written briefs in their presentations at oral argument, where they are subject to the questions justices pose. In the April 1, 2003, oral argument, Justices Ginsburg, Souter, and Stevens focused on the military leaders' brief supporting affirmative action at the U.S. service academies. Considerable time elapsed for Kolbo and Olson as they attempted to address the concerns raised by the trio over how to produce a diverse officer corps *without* affirmative action.

Mahoney and John Peyton, who argued for the U of M undergraduate school, received a barrage of questions from Rehnquist, Scalia, and Kennedy on whether racial/ethnic diversity in education is a compelling state interest, the meaning of a "critical mass" of minorities, and the precedential weight of Powell's judgment in *Bakke,* particularly his reference to the Harvard plan.

The only African American on the current Supreme Court, Clarence Thomas, is typically silent during oral argument. Off the bench, he has explained, "My grandmother told me, 'You can't talk and listen at the same time.' If I wanted to talk a lot, I'd be on the other side of the bench" (Perry,

2001, p. 108). Yet in the Michigan cases he spoke up at the very end of the two-hour session. He asked Peyton, who is also African American, "Do you think that your admissions standards overall at least provide some head wind to the efforts that you're talking about?" Misunderstanding the metaphor, "head wind," which blows *against* the direction desired, Peyton replied, "Yes, I do." After attempting to clarify his question, Thomas eventually posed the final query of the session. "Would the same arguments with respect to diversity apply to [historically black colleges]?" With time running out, Peyton concluded, "I believe most every single one of them do have diverse student bodies" (Lane, 2003, p. A12).

The Decision

Monday, June 23, 2003, was the penultimate scheduled "Opinion Day" of the Supreme Court for its 2002–2003 term. The much-anticipated decisions in the Michigan cases were likely to come down on this hot summer morning in Washington. At the ready were national news correspondents, packed into the press box in the courtroom, and the broadcast satellite dishes and spotlights, erected on the sidewalks around the court building. The journalists and spectators were not disappointed. After decisions from two other cases were announced from the bench, Justice O'Connor intoned to a hushed audience, "I have the opinion of the court to announce in *Grutter v. Bollinger.*"[3]

The outcome was immediately clear from the start of her summary. O'Connor's opinion, joined by Stevens, Souter, Ginsburg, and Breyer, ruled that the University of Michigan Law School's use of race "as a plus" in admissions was narrowly tailored to achieve diversity, which she deemed a compelling state interest, as Justice Powell had determined in *Bakke*. From the bench, O'Connor cited studies suggesting the salutary effects of racial/ethnic diversity on citizenship, military leaders, and the law profession. The "critical mass" of minorities sought by the law school did *not* constitute a quota, nor was the admissions procedure a two-track system that treated minority and nonminority applicants separately. Moreover, race-neutral measures were unsuccessful for achieving diversity at the law school, and nonminorities were not unduly harmed by the plan. Repeating her worry from oral argument about the longevity of affirmative action, she noted that twenty-five years had elapsed since *Bakke;* she hoped that another quarter century would eliminate the need for racial preferences to achieve diversity.

In dissent, Chief Justice Rehnquist argued that Michigan Law School's "critical mass" goal was, in reality, "a naked effort to achieve racial balancing," which was not narrowly tailored to meet its compelling interest. Scalia and

Thomas each wrote pointed dissents reflecting their consistent opposition to affirmative action. Scalia labeled as "anticonstitutional" racial preferences in state educational institutions, while Thomas, after quoting the nineteenth-century black abolitionist Frederick Douglass, wrote, "Like Douglass, I believe blacks can achieve in every avenue of American life without the meddling of university administrators" (*Grutter v. Bollinger,* 156 L.Ed. 2d 304 [2003], p. 346).

When Rehnquist announced that he had the opinion of the court in *Gratz v. Bollinger,* affirmative action supporters knew that their narrow 5–4 victory in *Grutter* would not be repeated in the undergraduate case. Indeed, O'Connor joined the chief justice, Scalia, Kennedy, and Thomas in the ruling to invalidate Michigan's undergraduate admissions plan. Breyer concurred in part and dissented in part, making the vote 5.5–3.5. In full dissent were Stevens, Souter, and Ginsburg. Rehnquist's opinion for the court maintained that the twenty-point bonus in the selection index was not narrowly tailored to meet the compelling state interest of diversity. The *arbitrary* assignment of the bonus based on race/ethnicity violated the *individualized* model of admissions consideration that Justice Powell had established in *Bakke.* Powell argued that no single characteristic should determine admission, but race in the Michigan undergraduate admissions procedure was decisive (*Gratz v. Bollinger,* 156 L.Ed. 2d 257 [2003]).

Ramifications and Reactions

Although the results in the Michigan cases produced a split decision on affirmative action, O'Connor's victory in the law school ruling was broader than a first glance might indicate. She garnered a majority (albeit a narrow one that could be overturned if she retires and is replaced by a more conservative justice) for the proposition that racial/ethnic diversity in education constitutes a compelling state interest. Even Rehnquist accepted that premise. The proposition on diversity had been Justice Powell's solo judgment in *Bakke,* and questions remained about its precedential value. Liberal justices in the *Bakke* decision, led by Justice William Brennan, had noted that affirmative action could be constitutionally employed to remedy past discrimination against minorities. Powell's approbatory reference in *Bakke* to Harvard's use of race as a "plus" was considered *dictum,* that is, not part of the central holding in the case. O'Connor has now enshrined that element in settled law, though how long it will remain settled is unknowable. Her statement that the court expected no need for affirmative action in twenty-five years added another unusual twist to the opinion. The fact that she had upheld and strengthened Powell's *Bakke* judgment must have given her special satisfaction. The courtly Powell befriended and mentored O'Connor when she arrived at the high tribunal as its first female member in 1981. They were fond of saying that they were the first two justices ever to dance together! O'Connor placed a flower on Powell's coffin at his burial service in 1998.

To the extent that the Michigan cases produced divided decisions, they reflect the paradox in public opinion. A 2003 Pew Research Center survey discovered that Americans approved 2 to 1 "programs designed to increase the number of black and minority students." Yet the same survey reported that Americans disapproved 3 to 1 "giving [minorities] preferential treatment" (Von Drehle, 2003, p. A1).

According to Constantine Curris, president of the American Association of State Colleges and Universities, the court's rulings were "essentially an affirmation of policies that most institutions have followed" (Fletcher, 2003, p. A9). Mary Sue Coleman, the University of Michigan's current president, who was present in the courtroom when the cases came down, observed that the law school ruling gave a "green light" to universities to pursue diversity (Lane, 2003, p. A9). Taken together, the *Gratz* and *Grutter* cases, might be said to add a "yellow light." Universities must take caution not to give arbitrary, formulaic preferences to minority applicants, but individualized consideration of race/ethnicity, among other characteristics, is constitutional. The challenge for large institutions, with thousands of applicants, will be how to provide individualized assessment.

Now married and working as a software trainer for a vending machine company in California, Jennifer Gratz at least has the satisfaction of knowing that her law suit might spare other university applicants the nightmare she suffered from unconstitutional and illegal treatment by her "dream school."

NOTES

1. I witnessed the boisterous rally that night and the one that followed in the morning before oral argument, as I waited to attend the Supreme Court session. Protesters are a common sight at the Court, particularly on oral argument days. Yet the affirmative action rally was among the largest ever staged, and it was unusual for starting the night before the scheduled argument.

2. Photograph citation. (2003, April 2). *Washington Post,* p. A12.

3. Once more, I was fortunate to have a seat in the courtroom the day the affirmative action cases came down.

REFERENCES

Abraham, H. J. (1998). *The Judicial process: An introductory analysis of the courts of the United States, England, and France* (7th ed.). New York: Oxford University Press.

Abraham, H. J., & Perry, B. A. (2003). *Freedom and the Court: Civil rights and liberties in the United States* (8th ed.). Lawrence, KS: University Press of Kansas.

Fletcher, M. A. (2003, June 24). Decision means most colleges will stay course. *Washington Post*, p. A9.

Goldstein, A., & Milbank, D. (2003, January 16). Bush joins admissions case fight. *Washington Post*, p. A1.

Hull, A. (2003, February 23). A dream denied leads woman to center of suit. *Washington Post*, p. A16.

Kmiec, D. W. (2003). Does the Constitution allow universities to consider their applicants' race? *Preview, 6*, pp. 350–362.

Lane, C. (2003, June 24). Affirmative action for diversity is upheld. *Washington Post*, p. A1.

Lane, C. (2003, June 7). Judges spar over affirmative action. *Washington Post*, p. A4.

Lane, C. (2003, April 2). O'Connor questions foes of U-Michigan policy. *Washington Post*, p. A1.

McGuire, K. T. (1993). *The Supreme Court bar: Legal elites in the Washington community.* Charlottesville, VA: University Press of Virginia.

Perry, B. A. (2001). *"The Supremes": Essays on the current justices of the Supreme Court of the United States.* New York: Peter Lang.

Von Drehle, D. (2003, June 24). Court mirrors public opinion. *Washington Post*, p. A1.

Wilgoren, D. & Fernandez, M. (2003, April 2). A defense team of thousands. *Washington Post*, p. A12.

Gender Discrimination

Public Education for Men Only

United States v. Virginia (1996)

JENNIFER SEGAL DIASCRO

Since its inception in 1839, the state-funded Virginia Military Institute admitted only men. As a military college, it operated on the assumption that its rigorous physical and psychological training regimen was ill-suited for women and that having women present would compromise the effectiveness of that training. Nonetheless, by 1990, several hundred women had inquired about joining the Corps of Cadets, but they were turned away. Believing that VMI's men-only policy violated the Equal Protection Clause of the Fourteenth Amendment, the federal government intervened on their behalf. For women would-be cadets, this policy denied them an opportunity readily available to men. For VMI, admitting women would destroy the very distinctive character on which its reputation was built.

It was in May of 1864 that the United States and the Virginia Military Institute (VMI) first confronted each other. That was a life-and-death engagement that occurred on the battlefield at New Market, Virginia. The combatants have again confronted each other, but this time the venue is in this court. Nonetheless, VMI claims the struggle is nothing short of a life-and-death confrontation—albeit figurative.

—U.S. v. Virginia *766 F. Supp. 1407, 1408 (1991)*

So Judge Kiser began his ruling in the case *United States of America versus the Commonwealth of Virginia* on June 14, 1991, summarizing the essential nature of this conflict over VMI's male-only admission policy. Like many legal disputes, this one was not only about the law, but also about culture, values, and tradition. Neither side of the dispute was plainly right or wrong. Instead, they viewed the disagreement from decidedly different perspectives. The significance of this divergence is evidenced by the framing of the issues, the cyclical trip through the lower courts, the positions taken by interest groups, and ultimately the U.S. Supreme Court decision. As was true for the Battle of New Market, VMI and its cadets would emerge victorious at this initial stage of litigation in Kiser's court. As was also true in 1864, the United States ultimately won this legal war. But just like the Civil War, the effects of which have not been fully resolved, the legal, political, and social implications of *U.S. v. Virginia* are not fully understood or realized.

What Was the Problem?

Fundamentally, *U.S. v. Virginia* was a conflict over the validity of a long-standing tradition at VMI, the adversative process, which was designed to transform immature, disruptive boys into mature, disciplined men. Both the United States and Virginia agreed that this process made VMI unique among institutions of higher education, but they disagreed about the contemporary relevance of the distinctiveness. A complete understanding of their disagreement, particularly of VMI's reluctance to admit women, requires a brief history of the institute and the formation of traditions that had survived for over 150 years.

Despite its name, the Virginia Military Institute was not created to train career soldiers, but rather by the desire of many who lived in Lexington to remove from the community the rambunctious young militiamen charged with guarding the local arms depot (Brodie, 2000, p. 13; Strum, 2002, pp. 9–12). The idea was to establish a school near the Lexington Arsenal where young men would be trained as citizen-soldiers; the primary goal was to educate them, but also to train them to protect the depot and take up arms for Virginia should the need arise (which it did at the Battle of New Market). Virginia adopted the proposal and established VMI in 1839.

The first students to attend VMI were generally of the same caliber as the disruptive militiamen. Consequently, the first administrators were committed to establishing discipline and used military strategies to achieve this goal. They adopted the adversative process, the hallmark of the VMI experience (Strum, 2002, p. 40). Their purpose was to break individualistic, willful traits; to rebuild psyches to include self-confidence and responsibility; and to create a fiercely strong sense of camaraderie. Through rigorous training, respectful and competent young men would emerge as assets to their community. The most intensive part of this training came (and still does) during the first year at VMI.

Freshman cadets, or Rats, undergo a rite of passage for seven months, during which they are subjected to the adversative process, or rat line. Among the many rigorous elements of the rat line are the extensive verbal abuse by upperclassmen; the rigid forms of walking, sitting, and standing at all times of day; spontaneous recitation from the student handbook (*The Bullet,* aka *The Rat Bible*); regularly interrupted sleep and study; and severe physical tests of strength and endurance. More generally, for all cadets there is essentially no privacy; cadets use communal toilets and showers without stalls or curtains. They live in bare barracks, wear uniforms, and have the same closely shorn hair cuts. They have rigorous study procedures, early-morning drills, and physical fitness tests. The training as a whole, and the freshman experience particularly, are designed to forge a lifelong brotherhood.

And it has. VMI's alumni association, one of the most powerful and resourceful in the country, includes many renowned graduates and is considered the primary measure of the effectiveness, necessity, and success of the adversative process. Perhaps, then, it is not surprising that some young women expressed interest in VMI's unique method of training. In 1989 the Department of Justice's (DOJ) Civil Rights Division received a complaint from a woman whose application to VMI had been refused. Upon investigating, the DOJ saw no valid reason for VMI to deny the admission and filed suit in federal district court.

He Said, She Said: The Issues

CONSTITUTIONAL ISSUES: EQUAL PROTECTION AND FEDERALISM

The Government's case was based on the equal protection clause of the Fourteenth Amendment. The DOJ expressed concern that women who would like to take advantage of VMI's unique education and training were denied that opportunity solely because of their gender. Because VMI was established by the state and received public funds, the DOJ argued it was bound by laws prohibiting discrimination based on gender. From the government's perspective, Virginia had not provided the necessary justification for maintaining VMI's male-only admission policy. The intentional and systematic exclusion of women interested in the VMI experience denied women the same opportunity as men, a violation of equal protection.

Underlying Virginia's response to the equal protection argument was its belief that the government's position violated another important constitutional principle, federalism. The government's involvement in VMI's admission policies, it appeared, was illegitimate interference in state policymaking and one more example in a long struggle by southern states to ward off the overwhelming power of the federal government (Brodie, 2000, chapter 1; Strum, 2002, p. 51; also, Hohler, 1997). As a prominent alumnus lamented, ". . . it is unfortunate that the Justice Department is conducting its assault . . . at the very time that our society is demanding less federal government intrusion and the return of the balance of power to the 50 states" (Warner, 1996). It was Virginia's prerogative to provide an educational experience to its sons and not to its daughters. If the people of Virginia desired a change in this policy, they could achieve it through the legislative process.

OTHER ISSUES: DIVERSITY AND PEDAGOGY

In response to the equal protection argument made by the DOJ, Virginia argued that VMI's male-only admissions policy was justified by the state's interest in achieving educational diversity. Both coeducational and all-female universities existed in Virginia from which women could choose; VMI provided young men an important choice in their college experience.

Perhaps, the government responded, but if women were interested in a VMI-style training, they had no choice at all. Furthermore, as a Supreme Court justice remarked during oral argument, young men who wanted to attend an all-male college without military training had no choice either (U.S. Supreme Court Oral Arguments, 1996, pp. 26–27). Thus, Virginia's goal of educational diversity appeared to be disingenuous, and therefore did not justify VMI's admissions policy.

A critical part of the diversity debate was the value of single-sex education. While both the United States and Virginia saw the adversative process as the essence of VMI's program, they differed in their understanding of how the admission of women would affect it. VMI argued that the adversative process was not suitable to coeducation. Despite the lack of systematic analysis, VMI claimed that admitting women to its ranks would disrupt fundamentally this training. Not only would women be unlikely to accept the aggressive nature of the rat line (not to mention the lack of privacy), but male cadets also would have great difficulty doling out abuse to women. Additionally, there was concern about whether such abuse would constitute sexual harassment. Ultimately, VMI would cease to be VMI. Without this process, there would be no reason for students, male or female, to choose VMI over any of the other military academies in the country.

Moreover, Virginia suspected that few women would be interested in VMI. This would be problematic in terms of the expense required to make the necessary infrastructure changes (like erecting stalls in bathrooms and additional outdoor lighting) to accommodate so few female cadets. Also, too few women would make the acclimation and achievement of these cadets very difficult. Even those at VMI who supported the admission of women, and there were some, expressed this concern (Allison, 1996). Thus, the enrollment of women would not only deny all cadets the unique VMI experience but, more broadly, the end of single-sex education at VMI would also mark the end of single-sex education across the country.

Not surprisingly, the government saw the value of VMI's single-sex education differently. Fundamentally, it did not see the admission of women as the death knell of the adversative process. Rather, the DOJ argued, there was reason to believe that women interested in VMI were aware of, attracted to, and prepared to meet the challenges of the process. Additionally, there was no systematic evidence that a successful adversative process required a male-only admissions policy. While VMI might prefer to maintain a male-only policy, the DOJ saw no constitutionally valid reason for Virginia to support it.

Beyond VMI, though, the issue of single-sex education was more difficult for the DOJ because the government *was* supportive of *some* single-sex education, particularly in the context of private women's colleges (Strum, 2002, p. 252). As a result, it was difficult to decide how closely discriminatory policies should be examined and how carefully it should be justified. On the one hand, the DOJ was interested in promoting a very high standard for governments to meet in justifying gender classifications. The Supreme Court had adopted its highest of three standards of review, "strict scrutiny," for policies that discriminated by race; considered inherently suspect, race classifications were to be *closely* related to a *compelling* governmental interest. On the other hand, the DOJ was concerned that such a high level of review would make it *too* difficult to justify *any* single-sex policies. Second to strict scrutiny was the Court's "intermediate scrutiny," which it applied in previous gender discrimination cases to require the classification to be *substantially* related to an *important* governmental interest. This standard might serve the dual purpose of defeating VMI's policy and preserving the same-sex policies of other educational institutions. In the end, though, the government's petition to the

Court requested that the Court raise the standard for gender discrimination to strict scrutiny when evaluating VMI's admissions policy.

En Route to the Supreme Court

LOWER COURT PROCEEDINGS

The path of *U.S. v. Virginia* to the Supreme Court was not linear. Instead, it included two trips each to the federal trial court in Roanoke, Virginia, and the Court of Appeals for the Fourth Circuit, whose rulings highlight these vast disagreements between the parties.

The case began in the United States District Court for the Western District of Virginia. After a six-day bench trial, Judge Kiser ruled in support of VMI's male-only admission policy. From his interpretation of the Supreme Court's affirmative action ruling in *Regents of the University of California v. Bakke* (438 U.S. 265 [1978]), Kiser argued that universities had the prerogative to promote diversity within and among educational institutions (*U.S. v. Virginia*, 766 F. Supp. 1407, 1409 [1991]). Adopting intermediate scrutiny from *Mississippi University for Women v. Hogan* (458 U.S. 718 [1982]), he determined that Virginia's goal of educational diversity was an "important governmental objective" and VMI's single-sex education policy was "substantially related to the achievement of [that objective]." (*Hogan*, p. 730, in *Virginia*, 766 F. Supp., p. 1410).

Insofar as the effects of coeducation on VMI, Kiser understood the expert testimony to mean that, ". . . even though some women are capable of all of the individual activities required of VMI cadets, a college where women are present would be significantly different from one where only men are present." Additionally, "even if the female could physically and psychologically undergo the rigors of the life of a male cadet, her introduction into the process would change it. Thus, the very experience she sought would no longer be available" (*Virginia*, 766 F. Supp., p. 1414).

The United States appealed to the Court of Appeals for the Fourth Circuit. While the three-judge panel agreed that VMI should remain all male to preserve its unique training process, it ruled unanimously that Virginia could not justify the process on the basis of diversity while denying women access to a program like it. "While VMI's institutional mission justifies a single-sex program, the Commonwealth of Virginia has not revealed a policy that explains why it offers the unique benefit of VMI's type of education and training to men and not to women." The Fourth Circuit gave Virginia three possible remedies to this constitutional problem: admit women to VMI, eliminate pubic funding of VMI, or create a "parallel" institution for women (*United States v. Virginia,* 976 F.2d 890, 898, 900 [1992]).

Neither party was satisfied with the Fourth Circuit's ruling. The United States filed a petition for a rehearing, but it was denied (*United States v. Virginia,* 1992 U.S. App. LEXIS 30490 [1992]). Virginia filed a petition for a hearing before the Supreme Court (a writ of certiorari), but it was also denied. According to Justice Antonin Scalia, who in an uncommon move wrote a concurrence to the denial, the Court preferred to grant certiorari after the litigation completed its journey through the lower courts. Nevertheless, he provided an early indication of his views on the dispute. "Whether it is constitutional for a State to have a men-only military school is an issue that should receive the attention of this Court before, rather than after, a national institution as venerable as the Virginia Military Institute is compelled to transform itself" (*VMI v. United States,* 508 U.S. 946 [1993]).

In the meantime, Virginia chose to design the Virginia Women's Institue for Leadership (VWIL) at the already all-female Mary Baldwin College in Staunton, Virginia, to produce graduates comparable to those from VMI. The United States was not satisfied with this effort; it interpreted the circuit's ruling to require a "mirror image" of VMI's program, particularly in light of VMI's unique training program. The government saw VWIL as falling far short of VMI in many ways, not least because it emphasized cooperative rather than adversarial training (*United States v. Virginia,* 852 F. Supp. 471, 473 [1994]).

When presented with the VWIL plan, Kiser approved it as a constitutional remedy for VMI's all-male status. While acknowledging the differences between the proposed programs, Kiser relied on expert testimony that concluded, "VWIL is a good design for producing female citizen-soldiers and will be unique in the country" and "that the VWIL approach towards educating and preparing women leaders was preferable to the VMI approach." Ultimately, Kiser argued, "If VMI marches to the beat of a drum, then Mary Baldwin marches to the melody of a fife and when the march is over, both will have arrived at the same destination" (*United States v. Virginia,* 852 F. Supp. 478, 480, 484 [1994]).

The government appealed once again to the Fourth Circuit, arguing that women ". . . want to go to VMI precisely because it is such a demanding and challenging school. The remedial plan approved by the district court does nothing for them," and therefore fails to fulfill equal protection requirements. The original three-judge panel again supported Virginia, but not unanimously. The dissenting opinion argued that VWIL did not meet con-

stitutional requirements because it was merely a plan without the actual implementation necessary to accurately evaluate its remedial potential. Additionally, it reasoned, the question remained whether VWIL ever could be
seen as constitutional under "separate but equal" jurisprudence (*United States
v. Virginia,* 44 F.3d. 1229, 1235, 1243, 1246 [1995]). From this view, Virginia
could fulfill its constitutional obligation *only* by admitting women to VMI
or abandoning its funding of the institute.

This dissent reflected broader disagreement among other Fourth Circuit
judges, which manifested itself in an attempt to have the case reheard en
banc. After that failed, and a strong dissent was registered (*United States v.
Virginia,* 52 F.3d. 90 [1995]), the United States appealed to the Supreme
Court. This time, the Court granted certiorari.

AMICUS CURIAE

Before the Court ruled in the case, a number of interested individuals and
groups registered their support for the parties through briefs of amicus curiae, or friends of the court. The most notable characteristic of the amici was
the division of opinion among women. A number of women's organizations,
including the National Organization for Women Legal Defense and Education Fund; Federally Employed Women, Inc.; and the National Women's
Political Caucus, supported the United States and expressed opposition to
VWIL as a remedy to VMI's admissions policy.

Female (and male) academics, scholars, and academic programs, as well
as active and retired military women (and men) also championed the government's cause. One brief included Carol Gilligan, a well-known psychologist, whose research examined learning differences among boys and girls;
Cynthia Fuchs Epstein, a prominent and prolific sociologist; the American
Association of University Professors; the Center for Women Policy Studies;
and the Program on Gender, Science, and Law. These amici focused largely
on the scientific issues raised in the litigation, claiming that, ". . . the lower
courts relied on tenuous theories about alleged sex-based differences and the
purported benefits of single-sex education for men" (Brief of American Association of University Professors et al., 1996; see also Epstein, 1997). Additionally, WANDA's Fund, an advocacy group for women in the military, and
other military personnel submitted a brief opposing the gender stereotypes
they saw used to justify the exclusion of women from VMI and the creation
of VWIL.

Virginia was also supported by women's organizations, including the
Eagle Forum and Concerned Women for America, concerned largely with
the implications that strict scrutiny would have for military choices and

family law. Well-known women such as Lynne Cheney, author, doctor of English, and wife of the current vice president, Dick Cheney; Linda Chavez, author, political commentator, and President George Bush's original nominee for secretary of labor; and, Christina Hoff Sommers, an associate professor of philosophy, supported single-sex education and states' rights in determining the distribution of education resources.

Women's colleges were not in agreement about single-sex education either. Many supported the position taken by the United States, among them Brenau Women's College (Georgia), Hartford College for Women (Connecticut), Midway College (Kentucky), Trinity College (Washington, D.C.), and the College of St. Catherine (Minnesota). While supporting choice for women interested in *private* women's colleges, these schools opposed VMI as a *public* institution with an admissions policy based on traditional gender stereotypes.

Those colleges supporting Virginia included Mary Baldwin College (Virginia), which supported the creation of VWIL; and several military colleges, including South Carolina Institute of Leadership for Women, the Citadel, and the Military College of South Carolina, all with an interest in supporting *public* female leadership institutions. Another brief from Women's Schools Together, Inc.; Boys' Schools: An International Coalition; and several individual academics, expressed concern about the implications of the case for single-sex education as a legitimate pedagogical approach.

Finally, states across the union were divided also. Among those in support of the United States were Maryland, Hawaii, Massachusetts, and Oregon, which invoked *Brown v. Board of Education* as the basis for states' obligation to provide equal opportunity in education. Among the states registering their support for Virginia were Pennsylvania and Wyoming, which argued for diversity and creative solutions in promoting equality in education.

If the justices gleaned nothing else from the amicus briefs, they surely were aware of the cross-cutting nature of gender discrimination in higher education. Women, military personnel, single-sex universities, scholars, and states were all divided in their support for the parties to this case. And the Court's ruling reflected this complexity.

The Supreme Court Speaks

After a vigorous oral argument at which Ted Olson, the current solicitor general of the United States, argued for Virginia, Justice Ruth Bader Ginsburg wrote the majority opinion, to which Chief Justice William Rehnquist concurred. The choice of Ginsburg was not surprising; her illustrious career as an advocate for women's rights, and her interest and familiarity with the issues, made her a logical choice for expressing the views of the majority. Justice Scalia wrote an impassioned dissenting opinion, to which Justice Clarence Thomas surely would have joined had he not recused himself from the case because his son was a student at VMI. The three opinions clearly illustrate the issues and concerns of both sides in their battle over law and tradition.

THE MAJORITY

Announced on June 26, 1996, the Court's decision was a significant defeat for Virginia and VMI, as it judged VMI's male-only admission policy a violation of the equal protection clause and the establishment of VWIL an inadequate remedy. This decision, however, was not a complete victory for the United States insofar as the Court did not adopt the strict scrutiny standard of review that the government had requested. As a result, the Court left open the question of the constitutionality of gender discrimination.

In developing her argument, Ginsburg looked to the Court's previous rulings in cases like *Reed v. Reed* (404 U.S. 71 [1971]), *Frontiero v. Richardson* (411 U.S. 677 [1973]), *Califano v. Goldfarb* (430 U.S. 199 [1977]), and *Mississippi University for Women v. Hogan* (1982), from which she drew several conclusions about the appropriate approach to the gender discrimination in *U.S. v. Virginia*. Perhaps the most significant was that gender-based classifications should not be treated with the same level of suspicion as race classifications. Instead, there may be circumstances in which gender classifications are reasonable and therefore constitutional. Not only are "[p]hysical differences between men and women . . . enduring," but gender distinctions may serve legitimately to make up for women's past economic inequities and promote their future development (*United States v. Virginia*, 518 U.S. 515, 533 [1996]). Such distinctions should not be used, however, "to create or perpetuate the legal, social, and economic inferiority of women" (*Virginia*, 1996, p. 534). To underline these points, Ginsburg referenced several amici, particularly the private women's colleges, when she explained that "We do not question the State's prerogative evenhandedly to support diverse educational opportunities. We address specifically and only an educational opportunity recognized . . . as 'unique'. . ." (*Virginia*, 1996, note 7), so as not to deny qualified men or women.

The implication of this rationale was to deny the application of strict scrutiny to gender discrimination. Instead, the intermediate scrutiny standard (or skeptical scrutiny, as Ginsburg referenced it) requiring an "exceedingly persuasive justification" was more appropriate (*Virginia*, 1996, p. 531).

While prohibiting governments from establishing discriminatory policies based on stereotypical gender classifications, this standard allows for the possibility of *some* gender discriminatory policies.

Two conclusions emerged from the application of this standard to Virginia's defense of VMI. First, Virginia had demonstrated neither that diversity in higher educational choices was a state goal (indeed, as Ginsburg's reasoning suggests, the conversion to coeducation of most of Virginia's single-sex institutions, including the University of Virginia, seemed to demonstrate the opposite goal) nor that VMI was established with this goal in mind. In the Court's view, the diversity claim seemed a pretext for excluding women from participating in VMI's program (*Virginia*, 1996, p. 539) and was therefore an equal protection violation.

Second, the argument that women would fundamentally alter the unique VMI experience was constitutionally flawed. While acknowledging the likelihood of some changes, Ginsburg held, "The notion that admission of women would downgrade VMI's stature, destroy the adversative system and, with it, even the school, is a judgment hardly proved . . ." and one based on gender stereotypes that do not meet the "exceedingly persuasive justification" standard (*Virginia*, 1996, pp. 542, 545).

As a result, the Court held that VWIL was an inadequate remedy of VMI's unconstitutional admissions policy. Not only was the pedagogy of the woman's institute based on gender stereotypes, it argued, but, "In myriad respects other than military training, VWIL does not qualify as VMI's equal. VWIL's student body, faculty, course offerings, and facilities hardly match VMI's. Nor can the VWIL graduate anticipate the benefits associated with VMI's 157-year history, the school's prestige, and its influential alumni network" (*Virginia*, 1996, p. 551). With this language, the Court invoked separate but equal arguments levied in race desegregation cases and concluded that the appropriate remedy was to open VMI to women.

REHNQUIST'S CAVEATS

While he agreed with the majority's final decisions to admit women to VMI, the chief justice had concerns about the manner by which the Court reached its conclusion. Among them, two were particularly noteworthy. First, Rehnquist was uncomfortable with Ginsburg's use of the phrase "exceedingly persuasive justification," which he thought confused the meaning of the intermediate standard of review. "That phrase is best confined, as it was first used, as an observation on the difficulty of meeting the applicable test, not as a formulation of the test itself" (*Virginia*, 1996, p. 559). In other words, the two should be distinct, and intermediate scrutiny's requirement of a "substantial" relationship between discrimination and the government's "important" objective should be emphasized over an "exceedingly persuasive justification."

Additionally, Rehnquist disagreed with the judgment that admitting women to VMI was the only constitutional remedy to the violation of equal protection. Virginia may have failed to create a satisfactory women's institute in VWIL insofar as the plan was ". . . distinctly inferior to the existing men's institution and will continue to be for the foreseeable future. VWIL simply is not, in any sense, the institution that VMI is." However, in his view, a separate but more equal institution for women was conceivable and could be constitutional (*Virginia,* 1996, pp. 566, 563, 565).

SCALIA'S LAMENT

The theme of Justice Scalia's dissent was one common to his decisions, based on a judicial restraint approach to constitutional interpretation: the power to change laws lies with citizens through their elected officials, not with the Court, whose role is, "to prevent backsliding from the degree of restriction the Constitution imposed upon democratic government, not to prescribe, on our own authority, progressively higher degrees" (*Virginia,* 1996, p. 568). He could not have been clearer than when he decried,

> The virtue of a democratic system with a First Amendment is that it readily enables the people, over time, to be persuaded that what they took for granted is not so, and to change their laws accordingly. That system is destroyed if the smug assurances of each age are removed from the democratic process and written into the Constitution. So to counterbalance the Court's criticism of our ancestors, let me say a word in their praise: they left us free to change. The same cannot be said of this most illiberal Court, which has embarked on a course of inscribing one after another of the current preferences of the society . . . into our Basic Law. (*Virginia,* 1996, p. 567)

Scalia saw the majority opinion as a glaring example of this unwarranted exercise of power. In his view, VMI's admissions policy, and single-sex education more generally, were long-standing traditions in American society, the future of which should be decided by the people, not the Court.

Moreover, Scalia was troubled by the Court's seemingly disingenuous application of intermediate scrutiny. In his view, the majority had actually adopted a *strict* scrutiny standard to evaluate VMI's admissions policy. Not only was the Court "irresponsible" in suggesting that an "exceedingly persuasive justification" was equivalent to intermediate scrutiny, which was a "calculated" effort to "destabilize current law" and "muddy the waters," but also the requirement that VMI accommodate even just *one* woman who might be interested in its program was evidence of a strict scrutiny analysis. "There is simply no support in our cases for the notion that a sex based classification is invalid unless it relates to characteristics that hold true in every instance" (*Virginia,* 1996, pp. 571, 574).

In the end, the Court's ruling "ensures that single-sex public education is functionally dead." And, Scalia suggested unhappily, the only way that single-sex private education could survive the ruling would be for the Court to disregard in future cases the standard applied in this case—just as it had neglected in this ruling the standard applied in previous cases (*Virginia,* 1996, pp. 596, 600).

The Silent Death Knell: The Resiliency of VMI and Single-Sex Education

The impact of *U.S. v. Virginia* on VMI was powerful and swift. (See Brodie, 2000, for a detailed account.) After rejecting the idea of going private (Intress & Allison, 1996), VMI opened its doors to female cadets in 1997. From the ninety-one women applicants ("VMI Admissions Applications Break 1,400," 2001), thirty female cadets entered as freshmen, twenty-four continued on to their second year (Taylor, 1998), and fourteen graduated in VMI's first coed class in 2001 (DiBiase, 2001); an additional two were transfer students and graduated with the Class of 1999 ("First Women to Graduate," 1999). Seven women graduated in the Class of 2002 ("245 Receive Degrees," 2002). In 2001 the number of female applicants rose to 100 ("VMI Admissions Applications Break 1,400," 2001) and, significantly, that was the second highest number of total applicants since 1965. Overall, 61 of the 1,280 cadets enrolled in 2001 were women ("VMI Cadet Pregnant," 2001).

This attraction of both men and women to VMI came with relatively few changes in the VMI experience. Among the modifications were increases in safety measures and privacy, new dating rules and procedures for dealing with pregnancy, which have come under attack recently (see, e.g., the ACLU press release, "VMI Pregnancy Policy Discriminates," 2001; Drummond, 2001), sexual harassment classes and policies, the addition of women's sports, and the hiring of women in senior positions (Hohler, 1997). But most of the rat line went unchanged, to the apparent satisfaction of the new female cadets (Abrams, 1998). Despite complaints by the ACLU, the National Organization of Women, and others as to the treatment of women, particularly as appearance, physical standards, and harassment were concerned ("NOW, ACLU Blast Plans," 1996; McPherson, 1996), women (like men) were expected to have very short hair cuts, wear no makeup, wear uniforms, meet rigorous physical requirements, and endure verbal abuse (Brodie, 2000, chapter 11; Cain, 1997) Overall, officials and cadets indicated the changes "have neither affected nor altered the essence of a VMI experience." According to one senior, "Anyone who feels that door shades or separate bathroom stalls are a big deal is concentrating on the wrong things" (Abrams, 1998).

It is too soon to know if integration has been successful; indeed, it is unclear how success should be defined. The VMI administration has continued to be concerned about the relatively low number of women enrolled ("VMI Board of Visitors Meeting," 2002), yet it is apparent that women are interested in VMI and that they successfully complete the program. And, significantly, the admission of women has not diminished interest of male applicants. Thus, while there has been dissent (in fact, several VMI alumni have worked to develop a private, Christian, all-male military institute in Alabama to carry on the VMI tradition; see http://www.south-mil-inst.org), many reactions have been positive. As one male cadet observed about the first female rats, "They've pretty much blended in. . . . The girls really impressed me. They work really hard and have gotten really strong. . . . They're just as proud of the institution as we are. They're like sister rats" (Taylor, 1998; see also Abrams, 1998; Brodie, 2000).

If the impact of the Court's ruling on VMI was immediate and obvious, the broader implications of the ruling have been slow and ambiguous. As Rehnquist and Scalia predicted (or perhaps because of their predictions), there was and is confusion about the appropriate standard of review for gender discrimination and single-sex educational institutions. Some VMI supporters understood the Court's ruling to mean that *any* single-sex education would have to meet the very high standard of strict scrutiny that required absolute equality among programs. In contrast, the DOJ argued that the Court rejected only the obviously "substandard" quality of the women's alternative and suggested that the ruling would have no impact on private institutions and perhaps little on many public institutions (Innerst, 1996). And experts of various legal and political perspectives disagree on the meaning of Ginsburg's argument and the merits of Rehnquist's and Scalia's concerns (e.g., Brake, 1997; Cowan, 1997; Douglas, 1997; Hurd, 1997; Smiler, 1998).

Meanwhile, single-sex education appears to have survived as a means of managing gender classifications in private and public schools. While disagreement continue among scientists and educators about the utility and necessity of single-sex education, and groups like the ACLU and NOW continue to vehemently oppose segregating males and females in classrooms, the last several years have seen students, parents, and politicians continue to promote these programs (Weiss, 2002). Not only was VWIL ultimately established, but it remains a viable, public women's military institute (Chittum, 1997). Most notable, however, have been President George W. Bush's efforts to increase the number of public single-sex schools across the country. With Bush's No Child Left Behind Act, Congress condones the use of federal funds to create single-sex schools and programs; to accomplish this, the Department of Education's Office for Civil Rights has begun the process of revising federal regulations to allow for such programs (Salomone, 2002).

It appears, then, that *U.S. v. Virginia* did not lead to the end of single-sex education. Rather, in the wake of VMI's transition to coeducation, there has been an effort to *expand* single-sex educational opportunities. For better or worse, this development is likely to continue until the Court agrees once again to sort through the complexity of gender and education.

The author wishes to acknowledge the invaluable research provided for this chapter by Kate Hudson.

REFERENCES

Abrams, A. (1998, May 11). Changed, yes. Different, no. Virginia Military Institute has survived its first year with women—Who, says a dean, would feel themselves demeaned by a relaxation of the standards. *Newsday,* p. B06.

Allison, W. (1996, May 12). No stranger to battle, VMI fights feeling of frustration. *Richmond Times Dispatch,* p. A1.

Brake, D. L. (1997). Reflections on the VMI decision. *American University Journal of Gender & the Law, 6,* p. 35.

Brief of American Association of University Professors, et al. Amicus Curiae. *U.S. v. Virginia.* 518 U.S. 515. (1996). 1994 U.S. Briefs 1941 (Lexis Nexis).

Brodie, L. F. (2002). *Breaking out: VMI and the coming of women.* New York: Pantheon Books.

Cain, A. (1997, August 13). VMI, women prepare for new life as comrades: One female "rat" relishes the challenge. *Washington Times,* p. A1.

Chittum, M. (1997, November 30). VWIL determined to carry on marching for merit of its own. *Roanoke Times & World News,* p. A1.

Cowan, J. R. (1997). Distinguishing private women's colleges from the VMI decision. *Columbia Journal of Law and Social Problems, 30,* p. 137.

DiBiase, B. L. (2001, May 23). VMI sense of family prevails as first VMI coed class graduates. *News-Gazette.*

Douglas, E. A. (1997). *United States v. Virginia:* Gender scrutiny under an "exceedingly persuasive justification" standard. *Capital University Law Review, 26,* p. 173.

Drummond, D. F. (2001, July 14). Pregnancy policy may cost VMI federal aid; Justice says plan violates Title IX. *Washington Times,* p. A1.

Epstein, C. F. (1997). The myths and justifications of sex segregation in higher education: VMI and the Citadel. *Duke Journal of Gender Law & Policy, 4,* p. 101.

First women to graduate from VMI. (1999). *VMI News.* Retrieved on December 8, 2002,

from the Virginia Military Institute website at www.vmi.edu/news/ir/may99/women
.html.

Hohler, B. (1997, August 18). First women to learn drill as VMI "rats." *The Boston Globe*,
p. A1.

Hurd, W. H. (1997). Gone with the wind? VMI's loss and the future of single-sex public
education. *Duke Journal of Gender Law & Policy, 4*, p. 27.

Innerst, C. (1996, June 27). Same-sex military schools doomed? The Citadel, women's
program in peril. *Washington Times*, p. A6.

Intress, R. S., & Allison, W. (1996, June 27). Going private would be costly; Institute officials caution brethren. *Richmond Times Dispatch*, p. A1.

McPherson, P. J. (1996, October 12). Don't demean women by coddling them at VMI.
Roanoke Times & World News. Editorial, p. A9.

NOW, ACLU blast VMI co-ed plans. (1996). ACLU News Wire. Retrieved on September 17, 2002, from the ACLU website at www.aclu.org/news/w092396b.html.

Salomone, R. (2002, July 22). Single-sex schools: Federal standards met? *National Law
Journal*, p. A25.

Smiler, S. M. (1998). Justice Ruth Bader Ginsburg and the Virginia Military Institute: A
culmination of strategic success. *Cardozo Women's Law Journal*, p. 541.

Strum, P. (2002). *Women in the barracks: The VMI case and equal rights*. Lawrence, KS:
University Press of Kansas.

Taylor, A. (1998, January 28). Changing times at VMI; Fletcher grad: School has adjusted
to female cadets. *Florida Times-Union*, p. 1.

245 receive degrees at VMI. (2002). *VMI News*. Retrieved on December 8, 2002, from
Virginia Military Institute website at www.vmi.edu/news/commencement02.asp.

United States Supreme Court Oral Arguments. *U.S. v. Virginia*. 518 U.S. 515. (1996). 1996
U.S. Trans Lexis 9. January 17. pp.1–53.

Virginia Military Institute pregnancy policy discriminates against women, ACLU warns.
(2001). ACLU press release retrieved on September 17, 2002, from ACLU website at
www.aclu.org/news/2001/n120701a.html.

VMI admissions applications break 1,400. (2001). *VMI News,* Retrieved on December 8,
2002 on the Virginia Military Institute website at www.vmi.edu/news/adm_numbers
.html.

VMI Board of Visitors meeting, August 31–September 1. (2002). Issuance of the VMI administration, retrieved on December 8, 2002, on the Virginia Military Institute website at http://admin.vmi.edu/Aug02.doc.

VMI cadet pregnant, plans to stay at school. (2001, February 17). *San Diego Union-
Tribune* (Reuters report), p. A-12.

Warner, H. H. (1996, January 7). VMI's critics rely on myths to build a case. *Richmond
Times Dispatch*, p. F1.

Weiss, S. (2002, July 21). Sex and scholarship. *Washington Post Magazine*, pp. 18–23.

Contributors

ERIN ACKERMAN is a PhD candidate in political science at Johns Hopkins University. She received her BA in government at The American University in Washington, D.C.

STEVE BROWN is an Assistant Professor of Political Science at Auburn University. He is the author of *Trumping Religion: The New Christian Right, the Free Speech Clause, and the Courts* (University of Alabama Press, 2002). His current research focuses on the diversity of policies governing religious expression in the public schools.

JENNIFER SEGAL DIASCRO is an Assistant Professor of Political Science in the Department of Government in the School of Public Affairs at American University. She earned her PhD in political Science in 1995 from Ohio State University and spent seven years on the faculty of the Department of Political Science at the University of Kentucky. She was selected by the Supreme Court Fellows Commission to serve as the 2000–2001 Judicial Fellow at the U.S. Sentencing Commission in Washington D.C. She is coauthor of *Television and the Supreme Court: All the News That's Fit to Air* (with Elliot Slotnick, Cambridge University Press, 1998) and has published in *Political Research Quarterly, Judicature, American Review of Politics,* and the *Federal Sentencing Reporter.*

HOWARD GILLMAN is Professor of Political Science and Law and the University of Southern California. His most recent book is *The Votes That Counted: How the Court Decided the 2000 Presidential Election* (University of Chicago Press, 2001). His first book, *The Constitution Besieged: The Rise and Demise of Lochner Era Police Powers Jurisprudence* (Duke University Press, 1993), received the C. Herman Pritchett Award for best book from the Law and Courts Section of the American Political Science Association. He has edited (with Cornell Clayton) two other books on the Supreme Court and has published numerous articles on judicial politics and constitutional history in leading journals of political science and legal studies.

JOEL B. GROSSMAN is Professor of Political Science at the Johns Hopkins University. Before that, for many years, he was Professor of Political Science and Law at the University of Wisconsin-Madison. He is the author of many books and articles on constitutional law and related subjects, and he is a section editor of the *Oxford Companion to American Law* (Oxford University Press, 2002) and the *Oxford Companion to the Supreme Court* (2nd edition, in progress).

KATY J. HARRIGER is Professor in the Department of Political Science at Wake Forest University, where she teachers courses on American constitutional law, law and politics, and women and politics. She is the author of *The Special Prosecutor in American Politics,* second edition. (University Press of Kansas, 2000). Her research has appeared in law reviews and professional journals of political science. In addition, she is editor of Congressional Quarterly's forthcoming *Separation of Powers: Commentary and Documents.*

STACIA HAYNIE teaches at Louisiana State University, where she is Professor of Political Science and a recipient of the Alumni Association Faculty Excellence Award. Her teaching interests include constitutional law and the judicial process. She has written extensively on the decision making of appellate courts in the United States and abroad, and her scholarship on American and comparative judicial politics has been featured in various journals of political science, including the *Journal of Politics, Political Research Quarterly, American Politics Quarterly,* and *Law & Society Review.*

GREGG IVERS is Professor in the Department of Government in the School of Public Affairs at American University. His teaching and research focus on American politics, constitutional law, and religion and politics. His books include *American Constitutional Law* (Houghton-Mifflin, 2002) and *To Build a Wall: American Jews and the Separation of Church and State* (University Press of Virginia, 1995). He has also authored many scholarly articles and book chapters. Currently he is coediting, with Jennifer Segal Diascro, *Inside Judicial Politics* (Houghton-Mifflin, Forthcoming).

JOSEPH F. KOBYLKA is Associate Professor of Political Science at Southern Methodist University, where he has won numerous awards for outstanding teaching and research. He has written notable books on the role of interest groups in judicial policymaking, including *The Politics of Obscenity* (Greenwood Press, 1990) and *The Supreme Court and Legal Change: Abortion and the Death Penalty* (University of North Carolina Press, 1992), and he is currently writing a book on Justice Harry A. Blackmun. His articles on the Supreme Court, constitutional law, and American political thought have appeared in several different scholarly journals and law reviews.

JOHN ANTHONY MALTESE is Associate Professor of Political Science at the University of Georgia. His books include *The Selling of Supreme Court Nominees* (Johns Hopkins, 1995; winner for the "C. Herman Pritchett Award" from the Law and Courts section of the American Political Science Association) and *Spin Control: The White House Office of Communications and the Management of Presidential News* (University of North Carolina Press, 1992). In addition to his work in political science, he has written extensively about classical music and received a Grammy Award from the National Academy of Recording Arts and Sciences in 1996.

MAEVA MARCUS is the Research Director of the Supreme Court Historical Society. In addition to serving as editor of several volumes of *The Documentary History of the Supreme Court of the United States* (Columbia University Press), she is also the author of *Truman and the Steel Seizure Case: The Limits of Presidential Power* (Columbia University Press, 1977) and editor of *Origins of the Federal Judiciary: Essays on the Judiciary Act of 1789* (Oxford University Press, 1992).

NANCY MAVEETY is Associate Professor and Chair of the Department of Political Science at Tulane University. She received her PhD in political science from Johns Hopkins University. Recent publications include the edited volume *Pioneers of Judicial Behavior* (University of Michigan Press, 2002) and the chapter on Justice Sandra Day O'Connor in the forthcoming *Rehnquist Justice* (University of Kansas Press, Earl Maltz, ed.). Current research includes work on judicial decision making in the consolidating democracies of Eastern Europe.

KEVIN T. MCGUIRE is Associate Professor of Political Science at the University of North Carolina at Chapel Hill. He is the author of *Understanding the*

U.S. Supreme Court (McGraw-Hill, 2002) and *The Supreme Court Bar: Legal Elites in the Washington Community* (University Press of Virginia, 1993). His articles on decision making in the Supreme Court have been published in the *American Political Science Review,* the *American Journal of Political Science,* and the *Journal of Politics,* among others. He is also a former Fulbright Scholar.

AMY MCKAY is a PhD candidate in the Political Science Department at Duke University. Before coming to Duke, Ms. McKay worked for three years as a correspondent for Vice President Al Gore. Her research interests center on the relationship between the federal executive branch and the public, including interest groups. She graduated with a BA in political science and policy studies from Rice University in 1997.

MICHAEL MUNGER is Professor and Chair of Political Science at Duke University. He received his PhD in political economy at Washington University in St. Louis in 1984. He has taught at Dartmouth College, the University of Texas at Austin, and the University of North Carolina at Chapel Hill. His research interests include the study of ideology, legislative and judicial institutions, elections, and public policy. His most recent book is *Analyzing Policy: Choices, Conflicts, and Practices* (W. W. Norton, 2000).

JULIE NOVKOV is currently an Associate Professor at the University of Oregon, teaching courses on law, feminism, race, and political theory in the United States. Her book, *Constituting Workers, Protecting Women: Gender, Law and Labor in the Progressive Era and New Deal Years,* was published by the University of Michigan Press in 2001. Among her articles are pieces on miscegenation in Alabama and the battle over child labor legislation. She is currently working on a book addressing the process of racial formation in the context of the legal regulation of miscegenation in Alabama.

KAREN O'CONNOR is Professor in the Department of Government in the School of Public Affairs at American University, where she also serves as Director of the Women and Politics Institute. She has written extensively on a wide variety of topics, including the Supreme Court, abortion, interest groups, and women and politics. Her books include *No Neutral Ground?: Abortion Politics in an Age of Absolutes* (Westview Press, 1996), *American Government: Continuity and Change,* seventh edition (Pearson Longman, 2003), written with Larry Sabato, and *Women, Politics, and American Society,* third edition (Pearson Longman, 2001), written with Nancy E. McGlen, Laura van Assendelft, and Wendy Gunther-Canada. She has also contributed a great many articles to scholarly journals and law reviews.

RICHARD L. PACELLE JR. is Professor and Chair of Political Science at Georgia Southern University. His most recent book is *Between Law and Politics: The Solicitor General and the Structuring of Race, Gender, and Reproductive Rights Litigation* (Texas A&M University Press, 2003). His other scholarship on the Court includes *The Supreme Court in American Politics: The Least Dangerous Branch* (Westview Press, 2001) and *The Transformation of the Supreme Court's Agenda: From the New Deal to the Reagan Administration* (Westview Press, 1991). He is also the recipient of several awards for distinguished teaching.

BARBARA A. PERRY is the Carter Glass Professor and Chair of Government and Foreign Affairs at Sweet Briar College. Among her numerous books and articles on the Supreme Court are *The Priestly Tribe: The Supreme Court's Image in the American Mind* (Praeger Publishers, 1999) and *Freedom and the Court: Civil Rights and Liberties in the United States,* eighth edition (University Press of Kansas, 2003), coauthored with Henry J. Abraham. A former Judicial Fellow in the Office of the Administrative Assistant to the Chief Justice at the U.S. Supreme Court, she teaches courses on constitutional law and servers as Director of the Center for Civic Renewal.

REGINALD S. SHEEHAN is Associate Professor of Political Science at Michigan State University, where he teaches constitutional law and judicial process. Together with Donald Songer and Susan Haire, he is coeditor of *Continuity and Change on the United States Courts of Appeals* (University of Michigan Press, 2000), a volume that reflects his more general research interest in the Courts of Appeals. His published work, which appears in such journals as the *American Political Science Review* and the *American Journal of Political Science,* also includes articles on the impact of public opinion and organized interests on the U.S. Supreme Court.

STEVEN TAYLOR is an Assistant Professor of Government at American University, in Washington, D.C. He is the author of *Desegregation in Boston and Buffalo: The Influence of Local Leaders* (State University of New York Press, 1998). His articles on race and urban public education have appeared in the *Negro Educational Review* and in *Urban Education.* Taylor received his MA and PhD in political science from the University of Minnesota and a Master of Education from Florida A&M University.

THOMAS G. WALKER received his PhD in political science from the University of Kentucky and is currently Professor of Political Science at Emory University, where he teaches courses in constitutional law, judicial process, and judicial behavior. Among his published works are: *Constitutional Law for a*

Changing America (with Lee Epstein; Congressional Quarterly, 2003), *The Supreme Court Compendium* (with Lee Epstein, Jeffrey Segal, and Harold Spaeth; Congressional Quarterly, 2003), and *A Court Divided* (with Deborah Barrow; Yale University Press, 1988), which won the prestigious V. O. Key book award. Professor Walker twice has won his university's highest teaching award.

KEITH E. WHITTINGTON is Associate Professor of Politics at Princeton University. He is the author of *Constitutional Construction: Divided Powers and Constitutional Meaning* (Harvard University Press, 1999), *Constitutional Interpretation: Textual Meaning, Original Intent, and Judicial Review* (University Press of Kansas, 1999), and articles on U.S. constitutional theory and development, federalism, the judiciary, and the presidency. He is currently completing *To Say What the Law Is: Judicial Authority in a Political Context.*

DAVID YALOF teaches and conducts research on constitutional law, judicial politics, and the presidency at the University of Connecticut, where he is Associate Professor in the Department of Political Science. He is the author of *Pursuit of Justices: Presidential Politics and the Selection of Supreme Court Nominees* (University of Chicago Press, 1999), which won the 2000 Richard E. Neustadt Award for the best book on the American presidency. He recently published *The First Amendment and the Media in the Court of Public Opinion* (Cambridge University Press, 2002), coauthored with Kenneth Dautrich.

Index

Page numbers in bold indicate the main essay on a topic

Constitutionalism and Democracy

Kevin T. McGuire
The Supreme Court Bar: Legal Elites in the Washington Community

Mark Tushnet, ed.
The Warren Court in Historical and Political Perspective

David N. Mayer
The Constitutional Thought of Thomas Jefferson

F. Thornton Miller
Juries and Judges versus the Law: Virginia's Provincial Legal Perspective, 1783–1828

Martin Edelman
Courts, Politics, and Culture in Israel

Tony Freyer
Producers versus Capitalists: Constitutional Conflict in Antebellum America

Amitai Etzioni, ed.
New Communitarian Thinking: Persons, Virtues, Institutions, and Communities

Gregg Ivers
To Build a Wall: American Jews and the Separation of Church and State

Eric W. Rise
The Martinsville Seven: Race, Rape, and Capital Punishment

Stephen L. Wasby
Race Relations Litigation in an Age of Complexity

Peter H. Russell and David M. O'Brien, eds.
Judicial Independence in the Age of Democracy: Critical Perspectives from around the World

Gregg Ivers and Kevin T. McGuire, eds.
Creating Constitutional Change: Clashes over Power and Liberty in the Supreme Court